To ALEXA,

Best wishes for a courageous and fulfilling future!

Arion Spitzer

[signature]

GRAND *Theft* AUTO

Alan Spitzer
Alison Spitzer

How Citizens *Fought* for the American Dream

GRAND THEFT AUTO

by Alan Spitzer
with Alison Spitzer

© 2011 by New Year Publishing, LLC
144 Diablo Ranch Ct.
Danville, CA 94506 USA
http://www.newyearpublishing.com

ISBN 978-1-935547-31-0 (Trade Edition)
ISBN 978-1-935547-27-3 (Academic Edition)
Library of Congress Control Number: 2011924803

All rights reserved. No part of this book may be reproduced or transmitted in any form or by any means, electronic or mechanical, including photocopying, recording or by any information storage and retrieval system, without written permission from the publisher, except for the inclusion of brief quotations in a review.

Nothing in the world can take the place of Persistence. Talent will not; nothing is more common than unsuccessful men with talent. Genius will not; unrewarded genius is almost a proverb. Education will not; the world is full of educated derelicts. Persistence and determination alone are omnipotent. The slogan 'Press On' has solved and always will solve the problems of the human race.

Calvin Coolidge

From Alan:

To my loving wife Pat whose support means everything to me and to my six children Alison, Ashley, Alana, Andrew, AJ and Amelia (The A-Team). You're what it's all about!

"One doesn't discover new lands without consenting to lose sight of the shore...!"

From Alison:

My dad made it possible for me to participate in this unlikely battle instigated by the every day hard working American entrepreneur. For that first hand exposure I am eternally appreciative as I am well aware that he could have chosen almost any of his close peers to support him on this journey and probably had a superior, more experienced sidekick. Thank you for the opportunity.

This book is dedicated to my husband, Jeremy, and my daughter, Vera, for allowing me the time away, both physically and mentally, to help dealers across the nation fight for their rights and save their businesses.

Without their patience, understanding and support I can admit confidently that I would not have had the courage to stomach the immensity of the task at hand and press forward. Their unconditional love continues to fuel my efforts to succeed in the professional arena. Thank you and I love you.

FOREWORD

This book tells the story of how Alan Spitzer and his daughter Alison, along with co-leaders Jack Fitzgerald and Tammy Darvish, gave voice to the concerns of auto dealers about their treatment by their manufacturers and the federal government during the financial crisis of 2009, and how they effectively lobbied the decision makers in Washington and Detroit to treat auto dealers fairly during a very trying time. Their memoir should inspire everyone to believe that individual businesses and entrepreneurs can, when the right issues come along, exert a positive influence on policy decisions that end up benefitting millions of consumers in hundreds of local communities all across America. This is a story that needed to be told and I believe it will be a case study in highly effective grass roots business lobbying that will provide a learning guide for many years to come.

Chip Perry, CEO, AutoTrader.com

CONTENTS

Preface. ix
Acknowledgments xii

CHAPTER 1 "I've Got Horrible News" 1

CHAPTER 2 2008: The Perfect Storm 10
Tempest in the Motor City 14
Big 3 vs. Foreign Transplants: Fantasy vs. Reality. . . 15

CHAPTER 3 The Other Shoe Drops 31
What Were the Closing Criteria? 33

CHAPTER 4 Fewer Stores Mean Fewer Sales 38
Never Waste a Crisis 44

CHAPTER 5 Steny Comes to Ohio 48
"A Letter Comes—A Life's Work Is Shattered" 49

CHAPTER 6 "Good Morning, Tammy" 63
Fiasco in the Big Apple 69

CHAPTER 7 "I'm Not Senator Jack" 77

CHAPTER 8 "Zero, zero … ZERO!" 85
The $2 Billion Lie 92
"60 Votes? There's No Way!" 99
All Hands on Deck 101
"We're In the Game!" 103

CHAPTER 9 "How Do You Sleep at Night?" 107
Next Stop: Rules Committee 112
Our Momentum Stalls in the August Recess 118

CHAPTER 10 The Schism—Trying to Negotiate a Solution . 121
September 3: Our Détente 123

CHAPTER 11	Let the Negotiations Begin	**131**
	The Next Insult	142
CHAPTER 12	Black Thursday	**150**
	Twenty Minutes Later, GM Follows Suit	154
CHAPTER 13	Short Response, Long Weekend	**158**
CHAPTER 14	The Fray in the Senate	**165**
CHAPTER 15	Epilogue	**177**
	Afterword	185
	Bibliography	189
APPENDICES		**191**
"Detroit 3" Histories by Gary Witzenburg		191
APPENDIX 1	History of General Motors	192
APPENDIX 2	History of Chrysler	202
APPENDIX 3	History of Ford Motor Company	213
APPENDIX 4	GM Restructuring Plan	223
APPENDIX 5	Chrysler Restructuring Plan	232
APPENDIX 6	GM Viability Determination	252
APPENDIX 7	Chrysler Viability Determination	258
APPENDIX 8	GM Network Analysis	264
APPENDIX 9	Congressional Record (Legislative History)	275
APPENDIX 10	SIGTARP – I	294
APPENDIX 11	SIGTARP – II	340
APPENDIX 12	American Arbitration Association	351
APPENDIX 13	2011 Automobile Dealer Census	377
	Index	381

PREFACE

These are the times that try men's souls.

This well-known passage was penned by author and pamphleteer Thomas Paine in 1776 as he contemplated America's struggle for independence. The words formed the opening sentence in the first of a series of pamphlets Paine published entitled "The American Crisis."

In the 21st century, these words are certainly befitting the events of 2007-2009 when America faced a crisis of a different nature: a financial crisis that wreaked havoc on the economy of the United States and sent shock waves around the globe. A crisis that began on Wall Street had repercussions on Main Street that threatened the financial well-being of virtually every American.

A cataclysmic confluence of events set in motion an unprecedented economic freefall that, in some respects, eclipsed even the Great Depression. These were extremely difficult and dangerous times that called for drastic measures.

The domestic automobile industry had been central to the industrialization of America since shortly after its inception in the latter part of the 19th century. Nevertheless, the precipitous drop in consumer spending that began in the fourth quarter of

2007 soon put General Motors and Chrysler on the brink—and Ford would never survive as the lone U.S. automaker. The prospective fallout on our economy of the demise of the companies once known as "The Big Three" was unfathomable.

While the pages that follow describe the steps taken by the Bush and Obama administrations to save these once vibrant companies from liquidation, the primary focus of this book is to examine the misguided decision to eliminate—actually steal—GM and Chrysler franchises from thousands of small business owners across the country. Twenty-five percent of GM and Chrysler's dealer network—what amounted to 10 percent of the nation's entire automobile dealer population—were "lambs led to the slaughter" in the interest of "shared sacrifice" for the "greater good." These decisions caused further declines in employment when every available job was precious. Lives were being destroyed needlessly as a result of actions by faceless bureaucrats.

Our goal in writing this book is to tell the story of the heroic efforts of thousands of American citizens to challenge and attempt to rescind the decisions by the White House Auto Team, General Motors, and Chrysler to deprive so many of these independently owned businesses of their livelihoods and, in many cases, destroy their lives' work.

The relationship between auto manufacturers and their dealers has always been contentious to varying degrees. It is our hope that the car companies will view lessons learned from the recent past as an opportunity to forge stronger, more transparent relationships. We look forward to an era of improved mutual trust and cooperation where the nation's auto dealers, so integral to the fabric of the American way of life, are treated by the car companies like true collaborative partners in addressing the issues we jointly face.

Preface

Our family has had a long and proud history with both General Motors and Chrysler. We are committed to putting forth our best effort to help both companies succeed for generations to come.

Although the story is presented in a first-person singular narrative, we were both present at almost every turn and the observations on these pages reflect our views through our collective prism.

Alan Spitzer
Alison Spitzer

ACKNOWLEDGMENTS

To properly acknowledge all who were involved in this quintessential grassroots effort would require a volume all its own. Our supporters in Congress and their staffs, the hundreds of dealers who were members of the Committee to Restore Dealer Rights (CRDR), their employees and all their family members, the professionals on our team, the Automotive Trade Association Executives (ATAE), the National Automobile Dealers Association (NADA) and the National Association of Minority Automobile Dealers (NAMAD)—all were vital to this initiative.

Co-leaders Jack Fitzgerald and Tammy Darvish became our soul mates during this process. We were (and still are) truly kindred spirits. Rob Smith was there with Jack every step of the way handling detail after detail with incredible efficiency. Harold Redden and Jack's sister, Dottie, did remarkable work behind the scenes. Blanca Farias and Tammy King were also important members of "Team Fitzgerald." Jack's lawyer, Greg Steinbarth, was a terrific resource. Tammy's assistant, Courtney Wallin, always came through when Tammy needed her (which was all the time).

The Committee to Restore Dealer Rights has more than 400 individual dealer members, not including support from family members and employees who swelled our volunteer army well into the thousands. We are grateful for all their efforts. Some of the dealers with whom we interacted the most included Rachel Bachrodt, Yale King, Patrick Painter, John Rogin, Mark Sims, Colleen and Dave McDonald, Craig and Emilie Wierda, Carlos Planos, Nick Abraham, Carter Myers III, Jim and Kim Tarbox, Phil Axelrod, Jeff Tamaroff, Donna Golden, Karen Carlson, George McGuire, Sandy Taylor, Ed Larkin, John Zimmer, Bud Robke, John Scotford, Jr., Jeannine Roesch, Mark Calisi, Jim Golick, Bill Wallace, Russ Darrow, Jr., Jeff Duvall, Alan Starling, Frank Blankenbeckler III, Mike Callaremi and his daughter Lelica Palecco, and Fred Beans and his daughter Beth Beans Gilbert.

We appreciated the steadfast and intrepid leadership of Ohio Automobile Dealers Association president and ATAE chairman Tim Doran along with his counterparts from Texas and New Jersey, Bill Wolters (ATAE vice chairman), and Jim Appleton, who participated in our negotiations with GM and Chrysler. Yeoman's work was done across the country by an army of all 103 trade association executives. Tim Jackson from Colorado and Minnesota's Scott Lambert worked closely with us. Illinois president Pete Sander convened a critical meeting with Sen. Richard Durbin (D-IL). Pete Kitzmiller (Maryland), Gerry Murphy (Washington, D.C.) and Don Hall (Virginia) couldn't have been more supportive during our negotiations with the manufacturers. Tim Doran also received critical support from Terry Burns (Michigan) and Bob Israel (Louisiana). West Virginia exec. Ruth Lemon had the ear of Sen. Jay Rockefeller (D-WV) whose support was so vital to our effort.

NADA's presence on Capitol Hill was invaluable led by chairman John McEleney, chairman-elect Ed Tonkin, vice president David Regan, and president Phil Brady. They were ably supported by Ivette Rivera, general counsel Andy Koblenz, and Bailey Wood. NADA economist Paul Taylor supplied important data to our committee.

NAMAD was solidly behind our efforts, led by president Damon Lester and chairman Desmond Roberts. They became another voice that spoke volumes to Congress. They were ably supported by Greg Baranco from Georgia during our negotiations with the auto companies. General counsel Todd Bullard was a passionate advocate on behalf of all minority dealers. The Congressional Black Caucus was unanimous in its support of our efforts thanks, in large part, to the efforts of NAMAD.

Of course, we would have been nowhere without our allies in the United States Congress and their hard working staffs. We appreciate the leadership of the following members of the House: Majority Leader Steny Hoyer (D-MD) and Rep. Chris Van Hollen (D-MD) and original sponsors Dan Maffei (D-NY), our lead sponsor, and Frank Kratovil (D-MD). Rep. Betty Sutton (D-OH) opened a lot of doors and her support never wavered. And Rep. Steve LaTourette (R-OH) performed magic in the House of Representatives.

During more than two months of negotiations with GM and Chrysler, we got to see firsthand the incredibly hard work done by key members of Congressional staffs including John Hughes and Michele Stockwell (Hoyer); David Weaver (Van Hollen), Nichole Francis Reynolds (Sutton); Kate Ostrander (LaTourette), Ben Abrams (Kratovil), and Hasan Sarsour (Maffei). Hours meant nothing to these folks.

On the Senate side, we were fortunate to have the support of the No. 2 ranking senator, Richard Durbin (D-IL). His liaison to our group was Albert Sanders who worked hard to broker a compromise with GM and Chrysler. His role was critical. We are grateful to our lead Senate sponsor, Chuck Grassley (R-IA). Our primary contact with his office was Kathy Nuebel Kovarik, who couldn't have been more helpful and responsive. Sen. Sherrod Brown (D-OH) set up an important early meeting with Senate Majority Leader Harry Reid (D-NV).

In the end, we had the co-sponsorship of nearly 300 members of the House and 50 senators. Our thanks go out to each and every member who put his or her name on the line for our cause.

The law firm of Arent Fox LLP skillfully guided us in legal and lobbying matters. We very much appreciate the guidance of Dan Renberg, Mary Jo Dowd, and their team. They were ably assisted by the firm of Quinn Gillespie & Associates. In the trenches on our behalf were David Hoppe and Mike Hussey.

We also had an enormous amount of help editing and wordsmithing this manuscript from Michael Dowding. He was the professor and we were the students. He got us across the finish line with this memoir. Ours was a true collaboration. We'd like to extend a special thanks to Jane Swartz (who happens to be Alison's mother-in-law and a revered high school English teacher) for her numerous thoughtful suggestions and edits.

We would be remiss if we didn't recognize the many members of the Spitzer organization whose capable efforts allowed us to spend virtually full time away from the business for more than a year, including Jim Vella, who provided exceptional leadership for our company during this challenging period for the automotive industry, Debbie Noska, Cathy Schuster, Larry Ward, Ed Grasso, Lyndsey Wlodarsky, and Judi King. Our general managers from our Rejected dealerships have persevered: Jeff Hunt, Rick Masa, Bill Burke, and Mark Arnold. Special thanks go to Corky Covert and Matt Studer for stepping up to the plate when called upon. Tony Giardini has been our company's general counsel for more than a quarter of a century. He was on the front lines with us from day one. Tony also served as secretary and general counsel to CRDR. His law partner Chris Cook capably looked after our company's day to day needs when Tony was occupied with the work of the Committee.

The Gospel of Matthew says that "many who are first will be last." Needless to say, our family has provided unparalleled strength and support along with countless hours of "volunteering" their services: Ashley, Alana, Andrew, AJ and Amelia (Alison's siblings), and our spouses Pat (Alan's wife) and Jeremy Swartz (Alison's husband) as well as Alison and Jeremy's daughter, Vera, who was a true source of inspiration. Special thanks to Kevin (Alan's brother) and his oldest son, Sean. We love you all!

Alan Spitzer
Alison Spitzer

Chapter 1

"I'VE GOT HORRIBLE NEWS"

Adversity has ever been the state in which a man most easily becomes acquainted with himself.

Samuel Johnson

It was a spectacular spring morning on May 14, 2009—the kind of day that those of us from cold-weather states yearn for during the dark cold of winter. But the beautiful sky was a false promise. It was going to be one of the worst days of my career.

It was 8:15 a.m. and I'd just pulled up to the front entrance of Lake Ridge Academy, my daughter Amelia's school, to drop her off when my BlackBerry buzzed. "This is Jack Gannon," the voice said. Jack was the second-highest-ranking executive in the Great Lakes Business Center for Chrysler ("business center" is Chrysler's term for a sales territory in the U.S.). I first met Jack more than 20 years ago when he was a district manager (or area representative) for some of our Chrysler dealerships and he had worked his way up the Chrysler org chart. Over the years, my conversations with Jack became increasingly crucial to our company's relationship with Chrysler. Most recently, we were collaborating on several projects that would help Chrysler navigate through this difficult economy. But that's not why Jack was calling. Not today. "I've got horrible news," he said. "Every one of your stores in the business center was Rejected except Mansfield."

"Jesus, Jack," I replied. And then I could offer nothing but silence ... "Six of our stores? I've heard that negotiations are possible for some of these decisions. We want to cooperate as much as possible."

"I have not heard that negotiations are on the table," said Jack.

"Well, that's the word on the street," I said. "Please let me know if we can discuss it further." And with that, I signed off.

I was stunned. The decades of long days and nights I had spent pouring my heart and soul into the company my grandfather started and my father built now raced through my mind. I slowed the car to a stop, wondering what I was going to do.

"Okay. Bye, Dad ..." I kissed Amelia goodbye, and watched her throw a backpack over her shoulder and walk away. Off she went, greeting a few friends before running in as the bell rang in a new day, much like the day before. As I drove toward the school exit, I tried to comprehend the gravity of the phone call I had just received. More specifically, I wondered how my business, based in Elyria, Ohio, fit into a master plan that was being devised by perfect strangers at the White House.

It was no secret that the domestic car industry was in trouble and stakeholders, we were told, needed to participate in a "shared sacrifice". The media created a circus around the industry's financial turmoil during the winter of 2008/2009. In center ring was the government bailout of GM and Chrysler. One of the main side shows was the discussion regarding projected dealer cuts. Reporters and experts from various walks of life, inside and outside the industry, discussed the topic *ad nauseam*. There was a general assumption that dealer cuts were a necessary evil. However, unlike other so-called stakeholders—vendors, shareholders, employees, and bondholders, among others—cutting back the distribution network by unilaterally eliminating dealers wouldn't save the car companies any money. Dealers are completely independent businesspeople, not owned by the auto manufacturers as many believe. Dealers are the manufacturers' only customers. They are the faces of their brands. Without them, there would be no sales. The inclusion of dealers in the creditor category showed how little the American public—journalists, pundits, and politicians alike—truly knew about this vital industry.

But, like any other sensationalized news story, victims needed to be identified and heads needed to roll. And the pressure was on for swift action. It was common knowledge that President Barack Obama's Automotive Task Force was requiring both Chrysler and General Motors to pare back their dealer networks as a condition for securing the federal funding they needed to stay afloat. Somehow, in the early stages of bankruptcy proceedings, the closure of hundreds of dealerships was deemed necessary. Dealership closures were expected, and, in the back of my mind, I had braced for some bad news, but this was beyond bad. This was shocking. Through one cursory phone call, I was learning that about one-fourth of our business—a business built over multiple generations—was being unilaterally shut down. No negotiation. No meaningful explanation. No appeal process. Just a courtesy call before UPS delivered the termination letters to six Spitzer dealerships informing us that we would have to close down in **26 *days*.**

Let me put that in perspective. Our family owned seven automobile dealerships that were franchised to sell Chrysler products in Ohio. Those seven dealerships had been in our family for a combined 355 years. In just seconds, I learned that six of those seven franchise agreements were being terminated. This meant that hundreds of our loyal employees would be involuntarily divested of their livelihood in a matter of a few short weeks. It was surreal. In plain English, these businesses and the businesses of hundreds of other dealers throughout the United States were literally being stolen under the auspices of, in fact at the direction of, our federal government with no due process of law.

We had read for several weeks in trade publications that the manufacturers' original lists of "Rejected Dealers" (Chrysler's rather ugly term for the dealership terminations) would not be the final lists. An *Automotive News* article by Bradford Wernle crossed the wire at 10:04 a.m. that fateful morning. It included excerpts from a Chrysler memorandum to a group of dealers: "Dealers are learning of their fate via UPS letters to be delivered this morning, the memo says. Dealers will get 23 business days for a 'court review' of their cases, according to the memo, from a sales manager to district dealers. ***All of this information is subject to change.***"[1] Additionally, in the widely read *Ward's Dealer Business,* appearing the day before the termination notices arrived, there was a breaking news article that read, "Chrysler's Valued-Dealer List to be Preliminary Filing; The list will not be a final cut, which means dealers likely will move on and off the list."[2]

In essence, I knew, with a number of GM and Chrysler franchises in our company, we would possibly be directly affected in

---

[1] Wernle, Bradford, *Automotive News.* May 14, 2009.
[2] Banks, Cliff, "Chrysler's Valued Dealer List," *Ward's Dealer Business.* May 13, 2009

some way by the iron-fisted mandates of the Auto Task Force to cut dealers. In the weeks leading up to mid-May of 2009, I had already begun contemplating the best course of action, to somehow mitigate any damage caused by the anticipated actions of Chrysler and GM.

I suppose we envisioned that this would be just like many of the millions of car sales that have taken place in our country in the past century: There'd be some give and take, some haggling, and negotiations—and we'd hammer out a fair deal. As an eternal optimist, I remained firmly convinced that we could salvage most, if not all, of our franchises. My family had been in business for 105 years and had weathered countless storms. This was just another bump in the road—or so I thought.

Just 15 minutes later, I was at our corporate headquarters in Elyria, Ohio, and immediately swung into action. I called Tony Giardini, our general counsel, and Jim Vella, our COO, to break the shocking news. They were every bit as stunned as I was. These closures happened despite the fact that, in many cases, they were performing as well as or better than nearby Chrysler dealerships that were kept. This ugly pattern would repeat itself often throughout the country.

Since the list of Rejected Dealers was being made public, it wouldn't be long before the news reached all of the general managers at our Chrysler dealerships. We wanted them to hear it from us firsthand, so we convened an emergency conference call to tell them what was about to unfold and "rally the troops."

Several of these men had been with our company for more than 20 years. Their careers were successful, and so were the stores under their leadership. In our company, a general manager is our business partner. Our organization was built on the belief that, although product popularity, location, and other factors are important, the success of a store is directly dependent upon the effectiveness of the store's leader. It was for this reason we all needed to make sure our thinking was completely aligned during this unprecedented moment in our history.

"Gentlemen," I said, "you may have already heard the news that we will be receiving UPS letters today terminating some of our Chrysler franchises. We need you, now more than ever, to set the tone for the store and stay focused on productivity. We will be fighting tooth and nail to reverse these decisions, and we will keep you updated as we receive information. Nothing can help us more at this time than you selling more cars. We suggest you gather your teams and share the news with them—as well as our plan of action to stay the course as soon as you hang up this phone."

Many of our general managers mentioned that they had already spoken to their teams. One had even gathered his people to walk outside where he pointed up to the "Spitzer" sign on the fascia of the building. "Ladies and gentlemen," he said, "we work for Spitzer, not Chrysler … Now let's get back to work."

This was no time to be hanging our heads or walking around our showroom floors in a daze. Although they were certainly devastated by the developments, their responses were uniformly professional in every way.

After the difficult call in which we answered as many questions as we could, I returned to my desk and saw an e-mail waiting for me from Matt Studer, the general manager of our Dodge store in Mansfield, Ohio, our only Chrysler store that was not Rejected. I opened his attachment and got my first look at the complete list of Chrysler's 789 Rejected Dealers that had just been posted on a website. I still had not heard anything about our Homestead, FL, Chrysler, Dodge, Jeep store. The

Homestead store was our only Chrysler store not in the Great Lakes Business Center, and our rep had not called that morning to deliver any warning, so I remained optimistic as I swept through the list.

Several years earlier we had adopted Chrysler's latest strategy at that store, code-named "Project Genesis," to create a single dealership that offers all Chrysler brands (Dodge, Chrysler, and Jeep) under one roof. In the industry it is referred to as a "three pack." Chrysler had urged us to embrace this new strategy—at considerable cost to our company. In 2004 we completed an investment of approximately $1 million to expand our facility to accommodate the acquisition of the Chrysler and Jeep brands. That was in addition to the $1.5 million we had paid the neighboring Chrysler-Jeep dealer for those franchises. For all of these reasons, I was hopeful that our Homestead store would survive the purge. But our investments didn't make one bit of difference. It was wishful thinking. Homestead was on the list, too.

I slowly looked up and down the list in utter disbelief, soon realizing that our company was tied with another company, Auto Nation, for the most rejections in the country. Many other dealer names were very familiar to me and my co-workers. While automobile dealers are certainly a competitive lot, there's also a very strong sense of fraternity in our industry. Competition in our business is largely an intensely localized phenomenon. At dealer meetings, conventions, and trade shows, we are a very collegial bunch, eager to share ideas and successes and forge strong networks. So it was painful to see so many familiar names on the chopping block—people I'd known in some cases for decades.

One name in particular caught my attention: Jack Fitzgerald from Maryland—and it appeared numerous times. I first met Jack in the 1970s. He had been a great friend to my late father, John, and my uncle, Del. Both of our organizations had been part of the same "20 group" (a group of 20 or so dealers representing the same brand from different parts of the country who convene two or three times a year to share information and discuss best practices). I'd also spent time with him over the years at various Chrysler regional and national meetings and functions. Jack had an outstanding and well-deserved reputation. He was a respected dealer who took care of his customers and employees. Yet here he was, facing multiple rejections, too.

The immediate question that occurred to me was "Why?" How could so many reputable, longstanding dealers suddenly be thrown to the wolves? What was the reasoning? The common theme was that there didn't seem to be any theme. There was no rhyme or reason. Chrysler's process for disclosing these rejections was a textbook example of a public relations and communications debacle. No regard was shown to hundreds of loyal dealers who'd invested decades of their lives supporting this once-proud brand.

I would soon hear stories from some dealers who—once the list was public—learned of their terminations from neighbors, competitors, and media phone calls before their UPS letters had even arrived. It was an appalling way for Chrysler to treat what amounted to 25 percent of its dealer network—loyal partners for years.

Despite all of these terminations, and the certain knowledge that more would ensue when GM disclosed its plans the next day, there was no reason for actual panic at Spitzer. Our ongoing viability wasn't in question or at risk because we held franchises from numerous other brands. Unfortunately, that wasn't the case with many of my colleagues who only (or primarily) flew the Chrysler flag. The UPS letters poured in around the country and as the envelopes were opened, venerable family businesses were being handed their death sentences.

For most dealers, the business is much more than a job. It is their life. A car dealer typically eats, sleeps, and breathes the business 24 hours a day, seven days a week, 365 days a year. It defines him or her in every way and he or she often sacrifices family and social life for the love and sake of the business. The brand in the community is their flesh and blood for all practical purposes. Basically, these independent businessmen—and women—were losing not just money, bricks, and mortar. They were losing their way of life.

Before I tell you how we set about to right this gross injustice, I think it might be helpful to give you some background about our company and the auto industry in general.

Chapter 2

2008: THE PERFECT STORM

*History is the story of events,
with praise or blame.*

Cotton Mather

I'm proud to say that automotive retailing has been in my family for about 100 years, since the earliest days of the industry. My grandfather, George G. Spitzer, a successful hardware merchant in Grafton, Ohio, since 1904, obtained a Ford dealership in 1912. These were the humble beginnings of an organization that today represents multiple brands in multiple states. And the success we enjoy today certainly would not have been possible without the farsighted vision of his son, John—my father.

Fresh out of The Ohio State University in 1939, John was charged by my grandfather with shutting down an unprofitable DeSoto dealership in Grafton so that the family could devote more capital and attention to the hardware business. The problem was, my father saw things slightly differently than Grandpa and, in just 90 days, under my father's watchful guidance, the dealership added cars, parts, and employees and reached a breakeven point. Chagrined, my grandfather gave my father an

Spitzer Hardware & Supply Co., the beginning (circa 1904)

Our first service department

Spitzer Hardware adds Ford franchise (circa 1912)

additional 90 days to see what would happen—and that's when the business took off. After a stint in the armed services in World War II, John opened a Dodge store in the Cleveland suburb and Lorain County seat of Elyria, Ohio, and soon assembled a family of 14 dealerships spanning four states by the mid-1950s.

My father was one of the first multiple dealer operators or "megadealers" as they would later be dubbed by the media (a term I dislike). His younger brother Del joined him in 1951 after he graduated from college. Their working relationship proved to be very fruitful. My father worked behind the scenes to plan our company's growth while Del became a well-known local public figure as the passionate spokesperson in our advertising campaigns.

Soon, John and Del's success caught the attention of Ford Motor Company, which offered them the chance to open a dealership in Cleveland—what they would call "The Spitzer Ford Supermarket." Thanks to their innovative "10 Step Sales Procedure," as well as a great sales organization, aggressive marketing, and a strong management team, sales of Ford vehicles soared. Ford management in Dearborn, Mich., thought it all seemed too good to be true. No one could sell that many cars without cutting corners or engaging in shady tricks—could they? To find out, Ford sent over a few "mystery shoppers" to "buy" cars, only to learn that our success was driven by good promotions, competitive pricing, and ethical sales processes. In fact, one of those anonymous shoppers actually purchased a vehicle for his personal use. Ford asked my dad and uncle to share their sales secrets on film. They were soon on a plane to Chicago en route to Wilding Studios where they made a training film that Ford used for several years to instruct dealership salespeople nationwide and it became the basis of industry-wide sales-training initiatives. Because of this film, many of our people were "recruited out." In hindsight, John might like to take that one back.

John (right) and Del Spitzer produce training film for Ford Motor Company (1958)

Over the next decade, our company experienced measured growth riding out two economic recessions. Dealers are no strangers to constant change, challenges, and movement in this volatile industry. In 1969, after graduating from Baldwin-Wallace College in Berea, Ohio, and a year in the Case Western Reserve University MBA program in Cleveland, I went to Columbus to manage our Dodge dealership there. About 18 months later, we took over a Chrysler-Plymouth dealership in Akron, which became my first opportunity as a dealer principal. This dealership had been wholly owned by Chrysler Corp. and had been hemorrhaging cash under Chrysler's management. It soon became one of the top stores in the country for Chrysler—without any fleet sales (which quite often inflate a dealer's sales volume without adding much to the bottom line). In 1981, my brother Kevin joined the organization full time after graduating from Ashland (Ohio) University. My brother soon became a major contributor to our company's success along with many long-term managers. Coincidentally, the age difference between Kevin and me is almost exactly the same as my father and his younger brother, Del.

There were many key elements to our success, but our innovative approach to marketing was at the core. In the early 1960s, we were one of the first auto retailers to embrace television advertising, making the Spitzer brand a household name across the Midwest. Even today, people can still recite our famous tag line, read on screen by Del's son, and my cousin, Donn: "My dad wants to sell you a car now!" In later years, we branched out with imports such as Acura, Kia, Mazda, Mitsubishi, Nissan, Toyota, and Volkswagen. When 2009 rolled around, we had 23 dealerships representing 31 franchises in Ohio, Pennsylvania, and Florida.

TEMPEST IN THE MOTOR CITY

By the time these termination notices arrived, Detroit had been on its heels for nearly 30 years, the victim of a toxic mixture of unforeseeable external events, unforgivable internal misjudgments, and unthinkable corporate hubris. Most observers agree that a culture of union entitlements coupled with a sense of invincibility within top management eventually saddled the manufacturers with unsustainable legacy labor costs. The following sales graph and opinion piece from the December 1, 2008, issue of *The Wall Street Journal* illustrates the disparity in labor costs between Detroit carmakers and Asian transplants in the U.S.:[3]

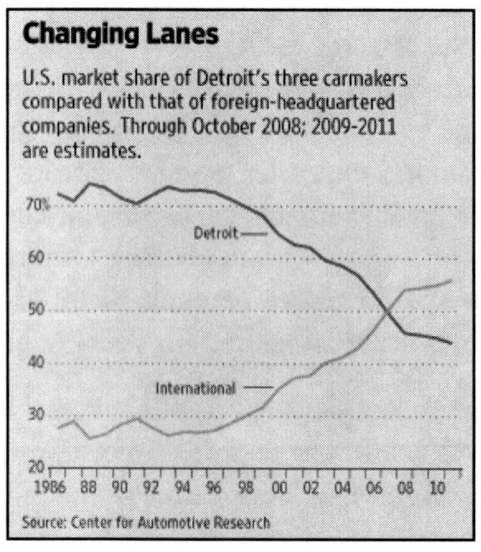

---

[3] Perry, Mark, "Big 3 vs. Foreign Transplants," *The Wall Street Journal*. December 1, 2008

Big 3 vs. Foreign Transplants: Fantasy vs. Reality

The men from Detroit will jet into Washington tomorrow—presumably going commercial this time—to make another pitch for a taxpayer rescue. Meanwhile, in the other American auto industry you rarely read about, car makers are gaining market share and adjusting amid the sales slump, without seeking a cent from the government.

These are the 12 "foreign," or so-called transplant, producers making cars across America's South and Midwest. Toyota, BMW, Kia and others now make 54% of the cars Americans buy (see chart above). The internationals also employ some 113,000 Americans, compared with 239,000 at U.S.-owned carmakers, and several times that number indirectly.

The international car makers aren't cheering for Detroit's collapse. Their own production would be hit if such large suppliers as the automotive interior maker Lear were to go down with a GM or Chrysler. They fear, as well, a protectionist backlash. But by the same token, a government lifeline for Detroit punishes these other companies and their American employees for making better business decisions.

The root of this other industry's success is no secret. In fact, Detroit has already adopted some of its efficiency and employment strategies, though not yet enough. To put it concisely, the transplants operate under conditions imposed by the free market. Detroit lives on Fantasy Island.

Consider labor costs. Take-home wages at the U.S. car makers average $28.42 an hour, according to the Center for Automotive Research. That's on par with $26 at Toyota, $24 at Honda and $21 at Hyundai. But include benefits, and the picture changes. Hourly labor costs are $44.20 on average for the non-Detroit producers, in line with most manufacturing jobs, but are $73.21 for Detroit (see chart that follows).

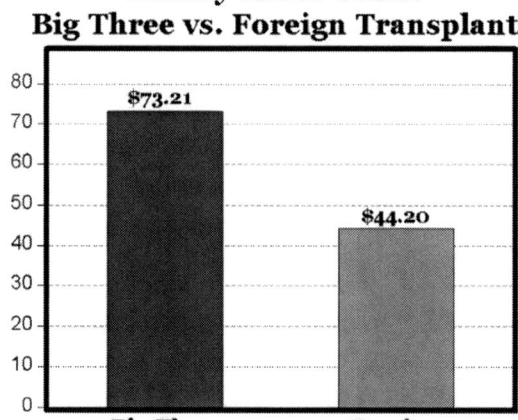

This $29 cost gap reflects the way Big Three management and unions have conspired to make themselves uncompetitive—increasingly so as their market share has collapsed (see the top chart above). Over the decades the United Auto Workers won pension and healthcare benefits far more generous than in almost any other American industry. As a result, for every UAW member working at a U.S. car maker today, three retirees collect benefits; at GM, the ratio is 4.6 to one (see chart below).

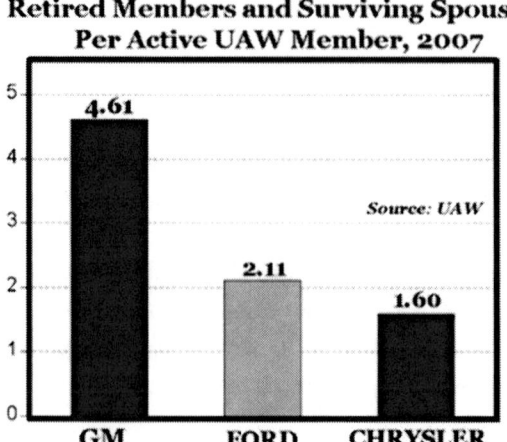

> The international producers' relatively recent arrival has spared them these legacy burdens. But they also made sure not to get saddled with them in the first place. One way was to locate in investment-friendly states. The South proved especially attractive, offering tax breaks and a low-cost, nonunion labor pool. Mississippi, Alabama, Tennessee, and South Carolina—which accounted for a quarter of U.S. car production last year—are "right-to-work" states where employees can't be forced to join a union.
>
> The absence of the UAW also gives car producers the flexibility to deploy employees as needed. Work rules vary across company and plant, but foreign rules are generally less restrictive. At Detroit's plants, electricians or mechanics tend to perform certain narrow tasks and often sit idle. That rarely happens outside Michigan. In the nonunionized plants, temporary workers can also be hired, and let go, as market conditions dictate.

A colossal miscalculation of the impact of foreign competitors caught domestic car-makers flat-footed in the '70s and '80s. They naïvely believed that these upstart newcomers couldn't compete with the so-called "Big Three."

After all, they had dominated the industry since Henry Ford implemented his "mass production" model in 1913 after introducing the ubiquitous Model T in 1908. In the decades that followed, titans such as Alfred P. Sloan, Jr., GM's legendary leader, and Walter P. Chrysler had placed an indelible stamp on the automotive industry. Certainly, fledgling car companies like Toyota and Honda weren't a real threat. They might become a minor irritant—a temporary nuisance maybe—but not a long-term problem.

Before Henry Ford came along, contributions to the industry's evolution came from all over the globe. Leonardo DaVinci and Sir Isaac Newton created the first known theoretical drawings of a motor vehicle, or horseless carriage, in the 16th and 17th centuries respectively. In 1672, Belgian missionary Ferdinand Verbiest actually built the first self-propelled vehicle, powered by steam, when he was living in China.[4] Frenchman Nicolas-Joseph Cugnot built the first road vehicle, also powered by steam, which sped along at 2.5 miles per hour.[5] The first electric car was built by Robert Anderson of Scotland in the 1830s.[6]

German engineers Karl Benz and Gottlieb Daimler, working independently, each without knowledge of the other's work, were the first to develop the internal combustion engine that powered the vehicles that were the forerunners of today's cars.[7] Benz was granted the first automobile patent for his *"automobile fueled by gas" Motorwagen* in 1886[8]. In 1926, long after Daimler's death in 1900, DMG, the company he founded, merged with Karl Benz's Benz & Cie., to become Daimler-Benz AG. The company then began producing vehicles named Mercedes-Benz, after Mercedes Jellinek, the 10-year-old daughter of a Daimler board member.

The first American automobile factory was actually started by bicycle makers Frank and Charles Duryea when they founded the Duryea Motor Wagon Company in 1896 in Springfield, Mass. The brothers hand assembled a total of 13 identical vehicles in their first year in business.[9]

---

[4] *1679-1681-R.P. Verbiest's Steam Chariot, History of the Automobile: Origin to 1900.*

[5] Manwaring, L.A., *The Observer's Book of Automobiles* (12th ed.) 1966.

[6] http://www.gm.ca/inm/gmcanada/english/about/OverviewHist/hist_auto.html

[7] *Mercedes-Benz History.* Edmunds.com.

[8] DRP's patent No. 37435 (PDF, 561 kB, German) was filed Jan. 29, 1886 and granted Nov. 2, 1886, thus taking effect Jan. 29.

[9] Georgano, G. N., *Cars: Early and Vintage, 1886-1930.* (London: Grange-Universal, 1985)

From its introduction in the USA in the late 19th century until 1908 "the automobile was then widely regarded ... as a sport. It was priced out of the mass market, it was mechanically unreliable, and good roads were scarce."[10] That year "the industry produced only 65,000 'machines' in the United States."[11] Two events occurred in 1908 that made an indelible mark on the industry, catapulting it into becoming one of the most important components of the dawning industrial age in America. In the same year that Henry Ford began production of the Model T that dominated the auto industry for the next nineteen years, William C. "Billy" Durant, a Flint, MI carriage maker, acquired a few struggling auto companies and formed the General Motors Company on September 16, 1908.

All the foregoing innovations notwithstanding, it was Henry Ford who made the automobile affordable to the masses and for the next seven decades the oligopoly that became known as the Big Three more or less owned the auto market in the United States. Foreign competition was not on their radar ... yet!

Ultimately, the car business is a product business. In the final analysis, if a manufacturer doesn't build well-designed, well-made, competitively priced vehicles, that company's market share will continue to erode. Other important pieces of the puzzle such as dealership networks, aggressive captive finance companies, advertising, rebates, and incentives will never overcome products that are poorly accepted by consumers. Due in large part to the monopoly they enjoyed, "The Big Three" took their eye off the ball. Instead of building smaller, better-quality, fuel-efficient cars, as their Japanese competitors were doing, Detroit largely ignored trends in consumer preferences and kept churning out sub-standard vehicles plagued with design flaws and manufacturing failures.

---

[10] Sloan, Alfred P., Jr. *My Years With General Motors,* Doubleday, 1963
[11] Ibid

When W. Edwards Deming, a revered mathematics professor from New York University, went to Detroit after World War II to share his innovative theories about quality, he was quietly and quickly ushered off the premises. Attention to detail and quality took a back seat in Detroit while management determined that, in many cases, it was cheaper to pay warranty claims than go back to the beginning of the assembly line and fund proper design and engineering. In 1965, consumer activist Ralph Nader tried in vain to warn Detroit about their shoddy quality and disregard for safer vehicles in his book, *Unsafe at Any Speed—The Designed-In Dangers of the American Automobile*. Nader's criticisms were trivialized and eventually dismissed by the Big Three. GM even tried to "shoot the messenger" through a smear campaign to discredit him. They hired private investigators to pry into his personal life and even hired women to attempt to lure him into compromising situations. In 1970, after years of a very public feud, GM paid Nader $425,000 ($2.4 million adjusted for inflation) in an out-of-court settlement. [12]

Unfortunately, too many ill-conceived designs and boneheaded decisions created massive opportunities for import-car makers, especially those from Japan, who were only too happy to embrace Deming's theories and put them into practice—with devastating effect. In 1950, Dr. Deming actually went to Japan to conduct a series of lectures on quality improvement. Since 1951, the Deming Prize has been awarded for innovations in quality control by the Union of Japanese Scientists and Engineers (JUSE). It is one of the country's most prestigious awards.[13] Ironically, for many years earlier, the words "Made in Japan" had been a joke denoting inferior quality.

---

[12] "GM Settles Out of Court; to Award Nader $425,000." *The Harvard Crimson*. Aug. 14, 1970.

[13] http://www.juse.or.jp/e/deming/

Much of Detroit's focus eventually shifted from sedans to higher-margin sport utility vehicles (SUVs), minivans, and light trucks that became Chrysler and GM's bread and butter. In fact, the American sedan has been a rapidly fading category for the Detroit 3 which, until very recently, largely conceded the segment to Toyota and Honda.

The quality of domestic vehicles has improved significantly in recent years. Several models from Ford and GM have made their way onto the recommended lists from the highly regarded *Consumer Reports*. In the eyes of consumers, they are going toe-to-toe with their Japanese and German rivals in many categories—in some cases even besting them. Inevitably, this should lead to increased market share for both companies. While there has been marked improvement at Chrysler, the company still lags the competition when it comes to quality. Fiat CEO Sergio Marchionne has made quality his top priority since taking over the management of Chrysler.

To be sure, Detroit has raked in billions over the past two decades from the sales of those trucks and SUVs. In fact, the profits were so good that many critics have noted the missed opportunity to regain lost market share through more aggressive pricing. With favorable exchange rates and the healthy demand for these vehicles, domestic manufacturers raised prices and used the profits to make acquisitions in other businesses, many of which were unprofitable.

For example, Chrysler bought Gulfstream Aerospace. GM acquired Electronic Data Systems from future presidential candidate H. Ross Perot and later added Hughes Aircraft. Not only did the car companies often overpay for these and other acquisitions, they distracted top management from their core business of building cars and trucks. Clearly, in hindsight, a much better option would have been to reinvest the profits in developing more competitive, better-quality products to reestablish the dominance they once enjoyed when they really were the "Big Three."

When GM bought EDS from Perot in 1984 for $2.5 billion (more than $5 billion in today's dollars), he was partially paid in GM stock, immediately becoming GM's largest shareholder and securing a seat on the GM board of directors. Perot became a vocal critic of GM quality and other management policies in board meetings, much to the displeasure of GM chairman Roger Smith. The two frequently quarreled. Soon, Smith was being vilified by the press who enjoyed covering the irascible Perot. The following quote from Perot about the GM bureaucracy characterizes his tumultuous relationship with GM and Smith: "An EDS employee who sees a snake kills it. At GM, they form a committee on snakes, hire a consultant who knows about snakes and then talk about it for a year."[14] In the end, as had been the case with Nader, GM decided the problem was not the quality of their vehicles but the upstart Perot. GM put a muzzle on him by buying out his remaining GM shares for $700 million and accepting his resignation from the board.[15]

GM also became an unwitting accomplice to its own eroding market share as a direct result of its misguided and outdated "chain dealer" policy. One store per dealer, period! Their philosophy was: "If you're a GM dealer, don't even think about submitting an application for another one."

Automotive retailing is a risky and capital intensive business. The pool of people who have the talent, access to capital ... and the guts to become a car dealer is relatively small. In the decades after World War II, as the economy expanded, many successful

---

[14] Moore, T., "The GM System is Like a Blanket of Fog," *Fortune*. Feb. 15, 1988.

[15] http://www.famoustexans.com/rossperot.htm

GM dealers saw potential beyond a single store. After all, over the years, they had accumulated the necessary capital and developed excellent employees. Often, they were looking to provide opportunities for their middle managers to move up the ladder within their organizations. Naturally, their first choice was to grow with GM. Unfortunately, GM policy precluded that possibility. Eagerly seeking talented people with capital for their distribution networks, Toyota, Honda, and Nissan welcomed these entrepreneurs into their organizations with open arms. In other words, GM was inadvertently sending its most talented retailers to the competition. Today, many of the most successful sellers of Toyotas, Hondas, Nissans, etc. started, and wanted to stay, in the business of selling GM products. Long after the horse was out of the barn in the mid-1980s, GM relaxed its policy and allowed dealers to own and operate multiple GM dealerships.

In the spring of 2008, a gallon of gasoline was approaching an unprecedented $5.00 across the country and Detroit's heavy reliance on low-fuel-economy vehicles was proving disastrous. The only vehicles moving off the lots were fuel-efficient, low-margin cars—the precise vulnerability of American car makers. Hardly flush with cash to begin with and staggering from eroding margins, this spike in fuel prices was the powerful uppercut that put GM and Chrysler on the canvas.

I believe that the surge in fuel prices was also a mostly invisible but deadly contributor to the housing crisis that soon followed. When gas increased from $2.50 a gallon to $4.50 per gallon in a matter of weeks, the impact on people's wallets was direct and significant. Suppose a homeowner drove a vehicle 2,000 miles a month and achieved 20 mpg. That extra $2 per gallon in gas prices translates into $200 per month *after taxes*. If you take $200 per month from a working family that's struggling to pay a large mortgage, there's a portion of the population—the portion that's saddled with an adjustable rate mortgage that got "adjusted" skyward, an interest-only loan, or a 130 percent loan-to-value mortgage—who will get dragged underwater. That housing crisis created even more bad news as the drop in housing cooled off the construction industry—which led to a precipitous drop in demand for pickup trucks, one of the few profitable bright spots for American manufacturers.

In 2008, the auto industry as a whole lost 18 percent of its sales volume from the prior year. Unfortunately, the domestics were faring far worse than the rest of the industry. Sales of foreign cars declined by 12 percent and the Detroit Three were off 24 percent. This steep decline continued unabated throughout 2009. In the two-year period from 2007 to 2009, the domestic automobile industry was off a staggering 45 percent. 2009 saw the lowest number of vehicles sold in the U.S. in nearly three decades with no end in sight to the misery. In fact, in the second half of the year, things grew worse at a catastrophic pace. Exacerbated by the collapse of the venerable investment banking firm Lehman Brothers on September 15th, 2008, the economy was in free fall. The Dow was dropping by hundreds of points almost daily. The collective wealth and, in turn, purchasing power, of our country had been reduced by trillions of dollars virtually overnight.

The Commodity Futures Modernization Act of 2000 created an unregulated instrument for banks and hedge funds to bet on credit defaults. In other words, a lender could buy "insurance" against its losses in case a borrower failed to make the payments on a loan. The escalating economic crisis resulted in an unprecedented number of foreclosures that nearly caused global insurance giant American International Group (AIG) to go broke, which would have been catastrophic. The worldwide financial meltdown that would have followed is unthinkable. The U.S. government loaned AIG $85 billion to avoid this calamity. These "credit default swaps" (or CDSs) were created in the late '90s by a group of employees from J.P. Morgan Chase bank known as the "J.P. Morgan Mafia." The group was led by an English born woman named Blythe Masters. In the days following the Lehman collapse, the UK newspaper *The Guardian* called her *"the woman who built financial weapon(s) of mass destruction."*[16]

In just weeks and with no margin for error or cushion to fall back on, GM and Chrysler were hurtling toward bankruptcy. They needed a serious infusion of cash—at exactly the wrong time. Credit markets in late 2008 were virtually non-existent, particularly for industries facing such steep sales declines.

In November and December 2008, in a series of highly publicized hearings, leaders from Chrysler and General Motors went to Washington, D.C., seeking that crucial capital from the lender of last resort, the federal government. The government had already passed the $700 billion Troubled Asset Relief Program (TARP) and, like the banks, American International Group et al., the car manufacturers were there, hats in hand, seeking capital to stay afloat.

GM CEO Rick Wagoner and Chrysler chief Bob Nardelli appeared before the Senate Finance Committee chaired by Sen. Chris Dodd (D-CT). They were joined by United Auto Workers president Ron Gettelfinger and Ford CEO Alan Mulally. It was Mulally who quickly emerged as the star of the show.

Mulally was recruited as CEO in 2006 by chairman and then-CEO William Clay Ford after his first two choices,

---

[16] Teather, David, "The Woman Who Built Financial 'Weapon of Mass Destruction' | Business." *The Guardian*. September 20, 2008.

Renault-Nissan's Carlos Ghosn (rhymes with own, the s is silent) and Daimler-Chrysler's Dieter Zetsch, turned down the job. Mulally had spent his entire career with Boeing where he rose to the position of executive vice president. Born in Oakland, California, but raised in Lawrence, Kan., the affable Mulally brought a freshness to the hearings that stood in stark contrast to the buttoned-down testimony of Wagoner and Nardelli.

Ford CEO Alan Mulally

Mulally's background was engineering, and on joining Ford, he immediately began to emphasize the need to build high-quality, well-designed cars and trucks. He sold the unprofitable Jaguar and Land Rover brands so the company could focus on its domestic brands. The most prescient decision Mulally made after taking the reins was to raise capital when capital was still available before the credit markets froze. Sensing the dwindling supply of cash in Ford's coffers would likely not be reversed any time soon, Mulally borrowed $23.6 billion by mortgaging virtually all of Ford's assets including the company's blue oval logo.[17] It turned out to be a stroke of genius helping Ford avoid the need for a cash infusion from TARP. Nonetheless, Mulally attended the hearings to support his counterparts at GM and Chrysler. Later, when asked what advice he had for CEOs facing a crisis, he told a large audience in Detroit, "Have a plan before the shit hits!"[18] He clearly did.

Conversely, liquidity had reached crisis proportions at GM and Chrysler. When their CEOs appeared before the Senate Finance

---

[17] Vlasic, B., "Choosing Its Own Path, Ford Stayed Independent." *The New York Times*. April 8, 2009.

[18] LaReau, J., "Mulally says he has work to do before retiring." *Automotive News*. Jan. 18, 2010.

Committee that fateful December, both testified their companies would most likely run out of cash before the end of the year.

Chrysler had been living on the edge for years. For the past four decades, or nearly half its existence, the company had embraced what is known as the "push" production model where vehicles are essentially built independent of consumer demand and "pushed" to the dealer who must "push" them to consumers. This is in contrast to the "pull" model, a method that calls for building cars and trucks that match consumer demand so that consumers will "pull" them from dealers.

Since the late 1960s, Chrysler's antidote for slow car sales was to build inventory—often into the tens of thousands of units for which they had no orders—park them in storage lots near the assembly plants, and browbeat dealers into taking them off their hands. These "sales bank" units, as they were called, were frequently slow-moving models, equipped with options consumers didn't want.

This approach was deemed preferable by Chrysler management to reducing capacity by temporarily or permanently closing plants. The problem was compounded in 1984 when the UAW negotiated with the Big Three to create a "jobs bank" where laid-off workers would still receive 95 percent of their income. In the eyes of top management, it made sense to keep the assembly lines moving if they had to pay their employees anyway, even if they had no buyers for their vehicles.

Over the years, Chrysler made several attempts to get off this dangerous merry-go-round when business was good, but when demand softened, it always reverted back to the old methods. The company's circumstances grew increasingly dire in the summer of 2008. These unordered vehicles were coming off the assembly line in record numbers. The sales bank had grown to more than 100,000 units. Unable to persuade dealers to buy them, even at a deep discount, and in a desperate attempt to raise cash, Chrysler took these new vehicles to dealer auctions and sold them as "used" vehicles at fire sale prices. The cars were dumped on the market at as much as 40 per cent below dealer cost.

Beginning in the winter of 2008, in a series of conference calls with its dealers, each more desperate than the one before, Chrysler sales and marketing president Jim Press, along with executive vice president Steve Landry, took their case directly to the dealers across the country. Many dealers interpreted these requests as thinly veiled threats to order their quota of vehicles, whether they needed them or not. In almost all cases, they did not. The calls continued into 2009, right up to the Chrysler bankruptcy. There was an infamous call on Feb. 5, 2009, when Press said to his dealers, "You have two choices. You can either help us or burn us down." And then shockingly: "Those of you who don't give us the orders, you better hope we fail … because we've got a long memory!"

I remember listening to the conference call with Jim Vella when Press delivered these chilling words. We looked at each other in stunned disbelief. Dealers were aghast at the intimidation tactics. But in the end, most bought their fair share to help save the company, fully realizing it was a terrible business decision for their own operations. But they were "taking one for the team!" A few scant months later, 789 of these loyal dealers were rewarded for their allegiance by having their franchise Rejected in bankruptcy. Most of the unwanted inventory was still unsold on the dealers' lots. It was the Rejected dealers' problem now, not Chrysler's!

The Senate hearings on the auto bailout brought a spotlight onto an important philosophical question: Should Chrysler and GM be allowed to fail? Should Adam Smith's famed "invisible hand" be allowed to finish off these carmakers after decades of mismanagement and bad decisions? As with any debate, there are arguments pro and con. Ultimately, I believe the automakers needed to be saved. While the manufacturers did themselves few favors over the years through their mismanagement, the larger macro economy was clearly also a major factor in this crisis. At that point in time, with companies shedding jobs across industries, the country couldn't afford the financial or psychological impact of a spectacular and chaotic bankruptcy. And, with the country fighting lengthy wars on two fronts, the shuttering of key manufacturing capacity could have been regrettable if military events and conditions shifted significantly.

Suitably convinced that GM and Chrysler needed to be saved, Congress created the Automotive Industry Financing Program (AIFP) on December 19, 2008. Due to the credit-constrained climate, this adjunct to TARP went beyond loans or guarantees and enabled the U.S. Treasury Department to make actual investments in GM and Chrysler that would help the companies restructure their operations and prevent bankruptcies and their potentially disastrous effects on the U.S. economy. These investments would eventually top $80 billion.

Only a fool would believe that those monies didn't have strings attached. The U.S. government was now an owner of these two companies. And it wasted little time in exercising ownership authority. First, President Barack Obama created "The Presidential Task Force on the Auto Industry," commonly called the Auto Task Force, in February 2009. Headed by Treasury Secy. Timothy Geithner and National Economic Council Director Larry Summers, the Task Force would become the government's watchdog overseeing its billions of dollars invested in GM and Chrysler and reviewing the restructuring plans that were a condition of the loans.

The Obama administration also created a separate group—the Treasury Auto Team. This group of 14, was led by Steven Rattner, a private-equity investor, and Ron Bloom, an investment banker and head of collective bargaining for the United Steelworkers. Rattner and Bloom reported to Geithner and Summers. The Treasury Auto Team's mission: to analyze the ongoing viability of GM and Chrysler from a more granular, operational level. Tellingly, not one member of that Auto Team had any experience in the automotive industry. What they did have were extraordinary levels of hubris and arrogance.

It soon became clear to me that those weren't merely strings attached to that loan money. They were ropes—ropes that would be fitted snugly around the necks of thousands of honest, hard-working auto dealers in the coming months.

CHAPTER 3

THE OTHER SHOE DROPS

*Without free enterprise,
there can be no democracy.*

Dwight D. Eisenhower

More bad news for dealers did, indeed, arrive the following day via FedEx when GM sent notifications to 1,124 of its dealers that their franchise agreements, set to expire in October 2010, would not be renewed, a process GM called a "Wind Down." Hundreds of more businesses and thousands of more employees would now join their Chrysler brethren, discarded in the junk yard like a rusted jalopy, all based on a decision-making process in which the dealers had no chance to contribute their two cents.

That morning, I received FedEx envelopes for two of our six General Motors stores. I immediately called Tony, our general counsel, with the news. This meant within 24 hours, we'd been told that nine of our dealerships would lose their franchises. There were several differences in GM's approach, which was somewhat more humane. It didn't carry the whiff of panicked desperation that Chrysler's notifications displayed. GM didn't disclose its list of cuts to the entire world on the Internet.

Additionally, the Chrysler closures were slated to take effect in 26 days on June 9. There was no appeals process and no compensation to dealers who'd spent decades in business. Initially, there wasn't even an offer to repurchase parts or vehicles. (Later, after significant pressure from Congress, Chrysler grudgingly offered to help relocate vehicle inventory and repurchase parts, albeit at 68 cents on the dollar.)

By contrast, GM's Wind Down agreements did include some compensation. However there was no explanation as to how the compensation was determined. We later learned in private meetings with GM officials that it was based on a formula that factored in rent and new vehicle inventory. Most dealers were never informed of the basis for calculating the compensation GM was offering. Don't get me wrong—it was still appallingly insufficient compensation for essentially stealing someone's business—but it was better than what Chrysler offered: nothing. I guess you could say it was the difference between execution by lethal injection vs. a guillotine. One might be more humane than another, but either way, you're still dead.

The compensation in GM's Wind Down agreement wasn't without its own strings, of course. First, GM informed the Wind Down dealers that "[W]e must receive the enclosed agreement on or before June 12, 2009 ... If we do not receive the enclosed agreement GM will ... reject your dealer agreement. If we reject your dealer agreement, we cannot offer any Wind Down or termination assistance in connection with such dealer agreement."

In other words, each dealer had four weeks to, in many cases, forfeit their life's work or they would become ineligible for any compensation from GM. Paradoxically, the agreement also contained a clause declaring that the dealer was not signing the contract under any duress (which, of course, they were—but signing under duress legally invalidates a contract). And, finally, GM dealers would be ineligible to order any 2010 vehicles from GM. So, although the dealership could remain open and operate as a GM-branded store and perform warranty repair work until October 2010, the lack of direct access to 2010 models would be a crippling blow that effectively invalidated the dealer's ability to become much more than a garden-variety seller of used cars.

GM also offered what amounted to what we'd later learn was merely a "show-trial" of an appeals process. Wind Down dealers were permitted to submit written appeals to GM's headquarters by June 1, 2009, to request reevaluations or reconsiderations of their terminations. However, this was clearly a *pro forma* process and it's very hard to believe that the appeals received a fair shake. Some were declined as little as *two hours* after the FedEx courier dropped them off at GM's Renaissance Center headquarters in Detroit to be reviewed by GM officials. It's hard for me to shake the mental image of unopened letters still sitting in the GM mail room when we heard our appeals were denied "after careful consideration." We later learned that GM reversed its decisions on only slightly more than 5 percent of the 1,316 appeals submitted.

What Were the Closing Criteria?

One of the first questions we had on that fateful May morning was a simple one: What were the criteria that the manufacturers used to determine which dealerships would be Rejected? It was a simple question without simple answers.

Rejected/Wind Down Dealers By State

State	Chrysler	GM	Total	State	Chrysler	GM	Total
AK	0	0	0	MT	4	16	20
AL	12	33	45	NC	14	36	50
AR	8	17	25	ND	8	6	14
AZ	5	11	16	NE	8	21	29
CA	32	65	97	NH	6	6	12
CO	12	15	27	NJ	30	33	63
CT	7	11	18	NM	4	10	14
DE	3	2	5	NV	5	3	8
FL	35	35	70	NY	28	60	88
GA	13	24	37	OH	47	79	126
HI	1	2	3	OK	12	17	29
IA	22	46	68	OR	9	21	30
ID	3	8	11	PA	53	90	143
IL	44	66	110	RI	1	3	4
IN	21	48	69	SC	11	24	35
KS	16	29	45	SD	7	16	23
KY	9	23	32	TN	14	30	44
LA	17	10	27	TX	50	55	105
MA	12	29	41	UT	10	6	16
MD	17	21	38	VA	26	26	52
ME	4	14	18	VT	2	8	10
MI	40	58	98	WA	15	18	32
MN	19	39	58	WI	18	50	68
MO	27	38	65	WV	17	25	42
MS	6	14	20	WY	5	6	11
				Total	789	1323*	2111

*GM sent 1124 Wind Down notices on May 15, 2009 and another 199 on June 1, 2009.

The Other Shoe Drops

Actually, in Chrysler's case, the answer was painfully simple: There were no meaningful, objective criteria. It chose its Rejected Dealerships on a case-by-case basis in individual markets based on, among other things:

- Whether, in Chrysler's opinion, the dealership's location was desirable
- Its volume of new-vehicle sales
- Whether it offered all three Chrysler brands
- "Minimum Sales Responsibility" (Chrysler's method for evaluating sales performance)

These were terrible metrics that were followed intermittently and with very many exceptions, making it difficult for many dealers to believe that the closures were not also affected by whether the dealer was in the good graces of Chrysler management. New-vehicle sales volumes vary wildly based on a range of external factors. Suppose there was a successful Jeep dealership that was breaking sales records—but was not franchised to sell Dodges. Should that dealership be Rejected simply because it didn't carry all three brands?

Toledo, Ohio, has three Jeep plants. The people employed at these factories, their families, as well as retirees and their families get special purchase consideration for buying or leasing Chrysler products. Essentially, they pay what the dealer pays. Naturally, as one might suspect, there is a bias toward the purchase of Chrysler products in the Toledo metropolitan market. Would it surprise anyone to learn that of the 160 dealers in Ohio franchised to sell Chrysler products in May, 2009, when the terminations were decided, those dealers located in the Toledo area were among the highest performers in the state in market penetration? Conversely, in the city of Columbus there are no Chrysler factories. Instead, there's state government, The

Ohio State University, and a large white-collar work force. Government employees, college students, faculty and white-collar workers historically purchase foreign cars much more than domestics. Naturally, all dealers who sold Chrysler products in the Columbus area fared poorly on the same list.

Yet Chrysler dealerships in each instance were held to the same performance standard. Any rational observer can quickly grasp the unfairness of this comparison, yet these scenarios persisted. Dealer after dealer throughout the country was held to unreasonable performance requirements.

General Motors employed a different approach, devising a formula it called the "Dealer Performance Summary" (DPS) score based on:

- A "Retail Sales Index" (RSI)—50 percent weighting
- A "Customer Satisfaction Index"(CSI)—30 percent weighting
- Capitalization—10 percent weighting
- Profitability—10 percent weighting

There were many problems with these metrics as well. The RSI compares the dealer's actual sales in his market with a sales quota based on the state average market share—*without* accounting for any mitigating factors such as demographics, economic conditions, local employment factors, and other nuances.

Perhaps the most significant flaw in evaluating dealer sales performance was that both companies used state average market share as par. This was grossly unfair if an individual dealer's market demographics were skewed away from the brand that dealer sells as compared with the rest of the state.

Another key concern was the fact that GM failed to apply this loose set of standards on anything resembling a consistent basis. A subsequent government review showed that GM retained hundreds of dealerships that, on the basis of its own standards, met the criteria for termination. And it terminated dozens of dealerships that did *not* meet its own defined criteria.

Equally troubling was the time frame both companies used to take their performance "snapshots": 2008. All data before 2008 was completely disregarded. In other words, a dealer could have performed extremely well in the years prior to 2008, had a sub-par year in '08, and had his franchise agreement terminated. And remember, 2008 featured arguably the worst economic conditions our nation had seen since the Great Depression.

When I added it all up, the conclusions were inescapable. At best, this was a shoddy process that led to poor decisions. At worst, these closures were grossly affected by favoritism, revenge, rumored side-deals, and subjective measures that gravely damaged one of America's most important industries. For the thousands of dealers across the country—from large to medium-size chains to the smaller "single point" stores scattered across the country—these slapdash closures, opaque processes, and shaky reasoning all amounted to what I'd call "Grand Theft Auto" on a massive scale. But what Detroit and Washington didn't realize was that this wholesale injustice unleashed a wave of righteous anger that would reach the highest offices in the land. I was determined that, as soon as possible, we were going to take aggressive action to right these wrongful actions.

Chapter 4

FEWER STORES MEAN FEWER SALES

A wise and frugal government, which shall leave men free to regulate their own pursuits of industry and improvement, and shall not take from the mouth of labor the bread it has earned – this is the sum of good government.

Thomas Jefferson

As 2008 drew to a close, the domestic automobile industry had the lifeline it sought: commitments for financing drawn from the federal government's TARP coffers. Ostensibly, those monies were to help Chrysler and GM draw up new business plans to reestablish their competitiveness, more aggressively pursue green technologies, preserve jobs up and down the automotive supply chain, protect retiree benefits, and generate demand for new sales. The Automotive Industry Financing Program (AIFP) loans also carried restrictions on executive compensation and other specific requirements. One of those requirements: the submission of detailed restructuring plans to the Treasury's newly created Auto Team that explained how the manufacturers planned to turn things around. The financing they would receive was contingent upon those plans sufficiently demonstrating viability.

On Feb. 17, 2009, GM and Chrysler presented those plans that called for significant changes. GM proposed a reduction of plants from 47 to 32 by 2014 and trimming 20,000 jobs by 2012. The Saturn, Saab, and Hummer brands would be phased out or divested and the 500 dealerships representing those brands would be eliminated by 2014. Pontiac was slated to be reduced to a "niche brand." An additional 1,100 GM dealerships would also shut down through attrition and consolidation of brands and locations also by 2014.

Chrysler presented various scenarios for its future that were at once both vague and stark. It could continue as an independent entity after receiving billions in loans from the government. It could pursue its planned partnership with Fiat to focus on fuel-efficient vehicles in a wider range of markets. Or it could file for bankruptcy, shut down, and be liquidated. Nowhere did Chrysler even *mention* dealership closures in this initial report.

Over the next several weeks, the Auto Team mulled these plans, consulted with advisors such as the Boston Consulting Group and Rothschild North America, and had conveniently off-the-record conversations with "experts" at Bain, UBS, J.P. Morgan, and others—none of whom, of course, had any hands-on experience in running car companies or dealerships. And that led to what can only be charitably described as profoundly naïve analyses by the Auto Team.

This group was led by Steven Rattner, Ron Bloom, and Brian Deese, a 31-year-old Yale Law School student and automotive industry neophyte who, when Chrysler and GM submitted their viability plans, was the only full-time member. Deese told *The*

New York Times. "It was a little scary."[19] The Auto Team soon obsessively focused on what was dubbed "The Toyota Model" that emphasized smaller dealer networks to reduce competition among dealers and increase sales volumes at the remaining dealerships.

The fascination with the Toyota Model was particularly ironic—galling, even—given the difficulties that company was enduring and the fact that it was losing as much as (or even more) than GM at that time. Some experts, from a former Chrysler deputy CEO to a representative from J.D. Power & Assoc. as well as highly respected industry observer David E. Cole warned that the Toyota model wouldn't apply well to Chrysler and GM.

Below is a detailed map that illustrates where the domestics and the imports have most of their customer loyalty.

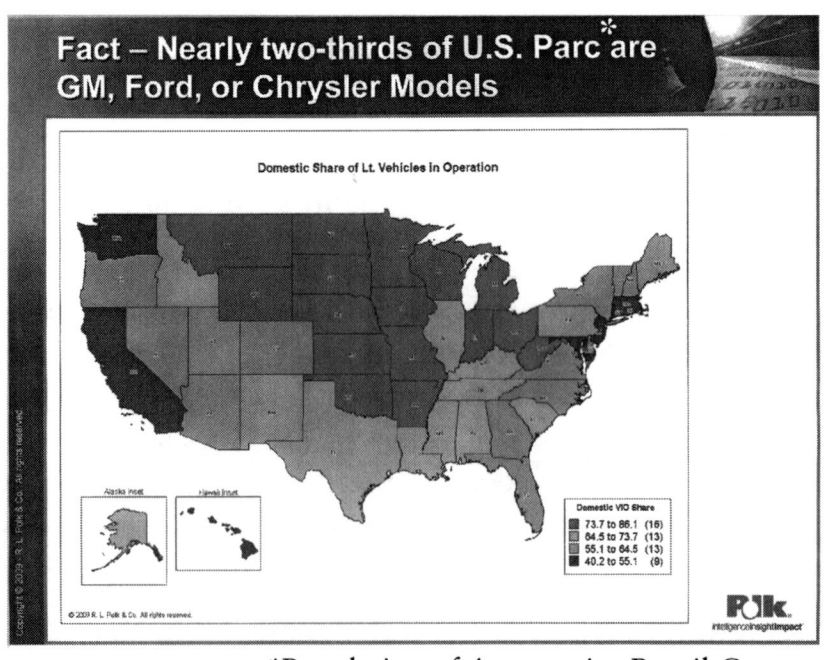

*Population of Automotive Retail Counts

---
[19] Sanger, D., "The 31-Year-Old in Charge of Dismantling G.M." *The New York Times.* May 31, 2009.

And data supplied by R.L. Polk made it inescapably clear why: in vast swaths of the heartland, domestic vehicles—including light trucks and SUVs—dominate the sales picture. Imports simply aren't as popular there. GM and Chrysler's strong presence in rural markets was something that the imports had largely conceded.

But there was something even more disturbing: a lack of basic understanding and common sense about the nature of the automobile distribution network. First and foremost—these dealers simply were not part of Chrysler and GM. Dealers are independent companies that enter into franchise agreements with manufacturers. They invest their own money, hire all their own employees, and own or lease their facilities with no assistance from the car companies. They purchase vehicles and spare parts from the manufacturers, resell them to consumers and, hopefully, retain the profits. Dealers *make money* for the manufacturers. The expenses? In the end, they're all dealer-paid: training, specialty tools, advertising, brochures, signage—it's all paid for by the dealer, not GM or Chrysler. What's more, the manufacturer gets paid—money in the bank—before the vehicle ever arrives at the dealer's lot.

What should matter to GM and Chrysler is how many cars they sell, not how many stores they sell them through. In other words, the manufacturers have no dog in this hunt. If they sell 1 million cars through one dealer or 1 million cars through 10,000 dealers—it's still 1 million cars and their financial picture is largely unchanged. The only potential incremental cost to the manufacturers for additional dealerships would be the relatively insignificant expense of more field personnel to contact the dealerships periodically. That's assuming a dealership is ever contacted by a real person. A high percentage of dealerships, especially smaller ones, conduct all of their business with the manufacturers online. Of course, the dealership is billed monthly for computer access.

It's a unique franchising model that differs from other industries. For instance, Seattle-based coffeehouse chain Starbucks owns more than half of its stores and rightly exercised its prerogative to close unprofitable or underperforming stores that it owns. However, Chrysler and GM have no ownership stake whatsoever in the franchised dealerships that sell their vehicles and therefore should not have the power to unilaterally close a dealership they do not own.

But Deese, a self-confessed automobile neophyte, and the rest of the Auto Team had already locked in on dealership reductions. Often overlooked in the debate over the size of the dealer network is the fact that GM and to a greater extent, Chrysler, used their respective bankruptcies, in many cases, not to *reduce* the dealership population, as had been advertised, but to *eliminate* one dealer in favor of another. Hundreds of franchises were stolen from their rightful owners and re-assigned or "gifted" to other dealers.

On March 30, 2009, the Team delivered its Viability Determinations, rejecting GM and Chrysler's reorganization plans and declaring, among other things, that the proposed pace of store closures was too slow and would be an impediment to their future viability. In essence, the Auto Team determined that the companies needed to be more aggressive in three areas: plant closings, reduction of operating expenses, and a precipitous downsizing of their dealer networks. There were compelling arguments to support the first two; however, cutting dealers was, by their own admission, just a theory. It was a theory that made no sense!

By what logic did the Auto Team expect GM and Chrysler to actually *expand* their businesses by *cutting* their dealership networks? Consumers would have longer waits for service and longer drives to *get* sales and service. Would a car buyer really want to drive 50-75 miles, or more, to purchase a Chrysler? Or would he stick closer to home and purchase a Ford (or a Subaru)?

The Auto Team's plan was intended to promote its rather inane concept of "throughput," which it believed was a key metric to evaluate dealerships: the number of vehicles sold per store—irrespective of profitability and other key measures. The result would almost assuredly be a lower volume of cars coming from Detroit and moving through a thinned-out dealer network. Chrysler Co-President Jim Press himself said to Brad Wernle of *Automotive News* that fewer stores would mean fewer sales[20]. Any financial gain would accrue to the surviving dealers—*not* the carmakers. By extension, we had the appalling situation of a government task force using public money to reconfigure a company to reduce competition and increase prices—blatantly anti-consumer behavior.

Not only was the logic and rationale behind this so badly flawed, this determination and recommendation far exceeded the scope of the AIFP mandate. It might sound simplistic or jingoistic, but—was this really America? We had a central government intervening in a massive private enterprise and effectively telling them how to run their company, conspiring to take businesses away from hard-working small business owners and jack-up prices to penalize consumers.

Was this still the land of the free? The average dealership throughout the country employed dozens of hard-working,

---

[20] Wernle, B., "A Hero Falls, Hard." *Automotive News*. Oct. 26, 2009.

taxpaying American citizens. They delightedly served thousands of customers, helping them acquire a valuable commodity: personal transportation. And their businesses were being stolen from them by some uninformed Wall Streeters who *theorized*, quite incorrectly, that fewer dealers would somehow improve the performance of the manufacturers.

Never Waste a Crisis

Not surprisingly, with billions of dollars in loans hanging in the balance, GM and Chrysler quickly caved into the intense pressure from the Auto Team and hastily rebuilt their reorganization plans with dramatically accelerated timetables for dealership closures. All the while—and far afterward—the carmakers continuously denied that they were responding to any such pressure, a laughable assertion.

However, the big speed bump in all of these plans to commit dealer genocide was the one thing that protected dealers: an intricate set of state franchise laws. Although the particulars vary from state to state, essentially, dealers in each of the 50 states are specifically protected from arbitrary closings except for contractual breaches or just cause. And there are excellent reasons for these laws.

First, the state governments themselves have a very compelling interest in the health and well-being of vehicle dealerships in their states for economic reasons. States earn about 20 percent of their sales tax revenue from auto dealers. Most of this tax revenue comes from new car dealerships that deal directly with the manufacturers. What's more, dealerships comprise as much as 7–8 percent of all retail employment (Canis and Platzer, 2009, p. 5, 12, table 1).

The result is a legal framework that broadly protects dealers from price incompatibilities and other unfair business practices that, unfortunately, characterized the dealer-manufacturer relationship in the first half of the 20th century. The theory behind these legal protections is that the dealer must make substantial investments in property, inventory, equipment, training, advertising, and more. If such protections against exclusivity, arbitrary franchise cancellation, and other questionable practices weren't in place, few dealers would be willing to assume the risks of opening and operating a car dealership.

GM CEO Richard Wagoner

But soon, GM and Chrysler would get their chance in bankruptcy court. It seemed to me and many others that the Obama administration was taking to heart White House Chief of Staff Rahm Emanuel's oft-repeated cynical, Machiavellian quote shortly after taking office: *Never let a crisis go to waste.*

The day before the Viability Determinations were released, the Auto Team had already flexed its newfound muscle by firing, or technically forcing the resignation of, GM CEO Rick Wagoner. Wagoner was a graduate of Duke University and Harvard Business School before joining GM in 1977 as an analyst in the Treasurer's office. In the eight years after he was named chief executive officer, the company had lost an astounding $85 billion.[21] Many of the seeds of GM's demise had been sown by some bad management decisions long before he ever took over the helm, but as Harry Truman said famously, "The buck stops

---

[21] Levin, Doron and Jeff Green, "General Motors Chief Rick Wagoner Said to Step Down." Bloomberg.com. March 29, 2009.

here!" In a solemn meeting in the office of Task Force head Steve Rattner, Wagoner reluctantly resigned.

On April 30, exactly one month after receiving its Viability Determination from Obama's Auto Team, Chrysler filed for bankruptcy under Chapter 11 of the U.S. Bankruptcy Code. GM followed soon after on June 1. Much later, documents would emerge from the Special Inspector General for TARP that laid bare the Auto Team's strategy. Ron Bloom, for instance, flatly declared that GM and Chrysler should use bankruptcy as an opportunity to eliminate dealerships quickly and that it would have been a "waste of taxpayer resources" to leave the dealership configurations undone before emerging from bankruptcy.

"We have a once-in-a-lifetime opportunity to right-size and realign the dealer body," said Jim Press, Chrysler vice chairman and president in a conference call with media the day the terminations were announced.[22] He might have added, "And ruin the lives of untold thousands of Americans in the process."

The goal was to take advantage of bankruptcy to sidestep these state laws that might have otherwise presented insurmountable obstacles to the terminations. Another document declared that the "best chance of success may well require utilizing the bankruptcy code in a quick and surgical way" and reject dealers without incurring significant upfront costs. It was the Treasury's version of shock-and-awe. They wanted to treat our massive investments and franchise agreements as if they were simple executory contracts—as if we were just renting them copying machines they no longer needed.

---

[22] Krebs, M., "Chrysler Cuts 789 Dealer Agreements; GM Slashes Dealerships Friday." *Auto Observer*. May 14, 2009.

We had the answer to the question on most outsiders' minds: "What's the big hurry? Why close so many dealerships so quickly? Why close 789 Chrysler dealerships in less than a month?" The answer: because a small window of opportunity to sidestep inconvenient state laws had emerged. And, again, with billions of dollars at stake, GM and Chrysler were only too happy to go along for the foolish ride.

Chapter 5

STENY COMES TO OHIO

If liberty and equality, as is thought by some are chiefly to be found in democracy, they will be best attained when all persons alike share in the government to the utmost.

Aristotle

In the days after May 14, 2009, as we began to process the impact of these stunning events, a few things emerged. First, there simply was going to be little or no give-and-take with the manufacturers on their Rejection or Wind Down decisions. Under the watchful eyes of their new minders in the U.S. Treasury Department, the manufacturers were in no mood to listen to our cases.

While our company is involved in other businesses, the car business has been my love my entire life. My late father was fond of saying the automobile business was not his vocation but his avocation. I feel the same way. I have always held GM and Chrysler in high regard because, over the years, they've made some great products that have bettered the lives of millions of people. But I didn't, and still don't, have those same sentiments for the Auto Task Force and the Auto Team, a group of uninformed, albeit intelligent, people with questionable intent and pre-conceived agendas. And later investigations would demonstrate that in spades.

The second fact was that there was an unbelievable mixture of shock, pain, and anger out in the dealer community. Some were in glassy-eyed shock, almost numb to the axe falling on their dealerships. Others -grown men with tears in their eyes, told me stories that broke my heart. I talked to Eldon Palmer of Palmer Dodge in Indianapolis. "Al, they terminated me just a couple of weeks before I was set to open a completely remodeled dealership," he said. "I put $4 million into this facility and they are cutting me off!" Eldon had been in business for about 60 years and his family name was a household word in Indianapolis. He was a friend of my late father. I've known of him for as long as I can remember.

"A Letter Comes—A Life's Work Is Shattered"

"Balzekas Motor Sales, Inc. has been selling Chrysler products on the South Side of Chicago since 1933. On May 14, Stanley Balzekas Jr., 85, learned that it all ends after June 9."[23]

These words written by *Automotive News* reporter Bradford Wernle were on page 1 of the May 18, 2009, issue along with a picture of this 85 year-old second-generation dealer reading his Rejection Notice. Chrysler dealer Greg Mauro, also from Chicago, invested $6 million in his new store and had been open only nine months before receiving his termination letter. It was cases precisely like this that had led to the enactment of state

---
[23] Wernle, B., "A Letter Comes—A Life's Work Is Shattered." *Automotive News*. May 18, 2009.

laws protecting franchises from this kind of egregious, arbitrary behavior by carmakers.

I'm an optimist, a can-do kind of person. I guess you have to be that way to survive in the car business. But even I was staggered for a couple of days. After talking to so many of my colleagues from across the country and realizing that Chrysler's list of Rejections was written in stone, not clay, I knew we had to take action and fight back. My wife Pat said to me, "The man I married wouldn't take this lying down." She was right. Something had to be done. This was grand theft auto, and we, the citizens, were going to have to take the law into our own hands. Little did I realize at the time what that would entail and how prescient that sentiment would be.

I called Tony Giardini, our lawyer, and discussed the situation with him. He saw an opportunity in bankruptcy court.

"Al, you know, these franchise agreements might survive the Chapter 11 proceedings," he said. "I think we have a good case to make that bankruptcy doesn't mean GM and Chrysler can just walk away from these franchise agreements."

I was encouraged by Tony's comments, so I made plans to go to the bankruptcy court in New York to testify at the proceedings on June 4. In the meantime, my instinct was telling me that we needed to be doing more. I kept hearing so many gut-wrenching stories from my peers—I knew we couldn't sit passively and hope things would improve. Next, with a lot of help from Tim Doran, president of the Ohio Automobile Dealers Association, we persuaded Richard Cordray, the Ohio attorney general, to file an objection with the bankruptcy court—and our AG managed to get 11 other states to join him in the objection. It was a faint hope, but we thought it might give the judge some useful input into his decision.

I also knew that I couldn't pursue this all alone. There's strength in numbers—and we needed some like-minded, savvy players to press our case. We needed to channel this pain and anger into a far greater force that would command attention at the highest levels of Detroit and Washington. Federal laws trump state laws and, of course, the bankruptcy laws are federal statutes that could potentially eviscerate dealer protections afforded them in their states. Barring a miracle in bankruptcy court, it was increasingly apparent to me that the only avenue for justice would be for Congress to enact another federal law that, presumably, would leapfrog the bankruptcy statutes and overturn the terminations. In my view, these actions represented a threat, not just to the nation's 18,000 car dealers, but to our entire franchise system that is so fundamental to the way business is conducted in America. It was a very dangerous precedent, a road I didn't believe we should travel down.

A couple of nights later, I tuned in to Fox News to watch Greta Van Susteren's "On the Record." And that's when I saw Jack.

Jack Fitzgerald, one of the industry's legendary dealers and owner of the highly respected FitzMall chain of dealerships, was on my TV, eloquently making the case for dealers across the country facing Rejections and Wind Down agreements. Since he was based in Maryland, I knew he was well-acquainted with our nation's capital. (I later learned that he had grown up only a stone's throw from the Capitol building that would soon become a second home). I called him up and spoke to him the next evening.

"Jack," I said, "there are a lot of avenues for us to pursue, starting in bankruptcy court next month. But I'll be honest with you. Sooner or later, I think we've gotta go to Congress to try to get legislation enacted to overturn these terminations."

Jack Fitzgerald

"Al," he replied, "I'm with you. We need to start lining up some top-shelf talent to cover all the bases. In the meantime, I've hired Mary Jo Dowd from Arent Fox to attend the Chrysler trial in New York. She's a bankruptcy lawyer."

It was great to know that someone with Jack's stature and senior status was willing to partner with me. We were two longtime car men joining forces, girding up for what would be perhaps the toughest battle we'd ever face.

Earlier in May, the day after Chrysler filed for bankruptcy, Tony hosted a reception for local Congresswoman Betty Sutton at the Quaker Steak and Lube restaurant in Sheffield Village, Ohio. I made it a point to attend because I was concerned that this bankruptcy, and GM's strongly rumored bankruptcy that was expected to follow, would soon be used as a basis to unfairly close hundreds of dealerships as government regulators had been urging. I wanted to lay the groundwork for a response when that scenario arose.

I had a lengthier conversation on the subject with Nichole Francis Reynolds, Sutton's chief of staff. Near the end of the May 1 event, Nichole told me that Rep. Sutton would be hosting House Majority Leader Steny Hoyer in the Akron area for another event in a few weeks.

Two weeks later, after the terminations were sent out, Nichole's invitation to the event with the second-highest-ranking member of the House took on greater importance. Sensing an opportunity, as the event drew nearer, I asked if we could get an audience with Hoyer prior to the start of that event. Nichole told me she would speak to the Congresswoman and Hoyer's office about it and let me know. A few days before the June 1 event, Nichole reported back to me with great news. Hoyer would meet with us at 5:15, 45 minutes before the reception was scheduled to begin. This meeting may have been the equivalent of the "Hail Mary" pass in football but I was looking for any opportunity to get the attention of someone either with access to the President or someone who had some influence in Congress. Steny Hoyer filled the bill in spades ... in both categories.

From: Reynolds, Nichole Francis
Sent: Wednesday, May 27, 2009 7:06 PM
To: Alan Spitzer
Cc: T. Giardini
Subject: Rep. Sutton—correspondence to CEOs and President

Mr. Spitzer,

I enjoyed talking with you this evening and look forward to working with you. Per our discussion, I have attached the following:

1) Letter from Majority Leader Steny Hoyer, Congresswoman Sutton and other members to the CEO of GM and Chrysler.

2) Letter from Rep. Sutton along with other members to both CEOs

3) Letter from Rep. Carnahan, Rep. Sutton and other members to the President.

I will do the following: (1) Talk with the Congresswoman this evening about possible "dealer protection" legislation and get back to you shortly, and (2) Send the letter you wrote to President Obama to Dan Turton, the Deputy Assistant to President Obama for White House Legislative Affairs.

Also, please send me the objection filed by the Attorneys General concerning "dealer protections".

Take care and I look forward to meeting you soon. I have copied Mr. Giardini on this email.

My direct office line is 202.xxx-xxxx and cell phone is 703.xxx-xxxx. I will be in Lorain tomorrow afternoon until Friday evening. I will be in Akron on Monday June 1st. If you can't reach me on my direct line, call my cell phone.

Best,
Nichole

```
_____
Nichole Francis Reynolds
Chief of Staff
Congresswoman Betty Sutton (D-OH)
1721 Longworth House Office Building
Washington, D.C. 20515
Phone: 202.xxx xxxx
Fax: 202.xxx xxxx
```

We arranged for about a dozen Rejected Dealers to assemble at the Hilton Inn in the Akron suburb of Fairlawn to meet with the Majority Leader. This was a golden opportunity to press our case with one of the most powerful politicians in Congress. I knew that any potential legislation would need the support of House and Senate leadership.

My colleagues and I worked around the clock to ensure we made the most of our precious time with Steny. Pat recalls waking up and looking over at me in the middle of any given night over the next several months only to find my BlackBerry shining down on me as I held it overhead to compose or read an e-mail. There simply weren't enough hours in the day and balancing work with a personal life was, for all intents and purposes, impossible. I particularly remember one lengthy phone call with Nichole as the meeting date drew near. We discussed many of the arrangements before I frantically hurried to my daughter Amelia's performance as Alice in "Alice in Wonderland" at her school. As I sat in the school auditorium while she performed, I found my mind drifting to the Capitol Building in Washington, D.C., or the Federal Courthouse in Southern Manhattan and then it would snap back to the Bettcher Auditorium at Lake Ridge Academy in North Ridgeville, Ohio.

Next, I exchanged e-mails with Lou Vitantonio, vice president of the Greater Cleveland Automobile Dealers Association to enlist his help in recruiting Rejected Dealers for the reception with Steny Hoyer.

From: Alan Spitzer
Sent: Friday, May 29, 2009 2:48 PM
To: Lou Vitantonio
CC: Gary Adams; Jim Vella
Subject: Steny Hoyer Reception

Lou,

We have a private meeting with Congresswoman Sutton and Leader Hoyer (No. 2 in the House to Pelosi) at 5:15. I'm hoping we can move him to try to get to President Obama either directly or through the Speaker. We need a strong showing. I would think it would be good to have everyone there (Fairlawn Hilton) by 4:45 at the latest so we can discuss our approach. Tony Giardini who, as you know, is a heavyweight Democrat, will be there as well to help facilitate the meeting.

Alan Spitzer

From: Lou Vitantonio
Date: Fri, 29 May 2009 15:36:53 -0400
To: Alan Spitzer
Subject: RE: Steny Hoyer Reception

Alan:

We are sending this out to the affected Chrysler dealers.

I will let you know who is able to attend.

Lou

We contacted each of the invited dealers to confirm attendance and ask them to arrive at 4:45 p.m. so we could review the agenda before Hoyer arrived. Tony would lead the discussion and I urged each dealer to speak only when called on by Tony. The last thing we needed was a bunch of upset dealers talking over one another in an attempt to be heard. All of the attendees were Chrysler dealers who were just days away from having their franchises and, in some cases, their life's work snuffed out without any recourse. I was concerned this meeting could potentially veer off into unproductive outbursts. We needed to keep things under control. Our goal was to get Hoyer to ask President Obama to intervene on behalf of the terminated dealers (a long shot), or convince the Majority Leader to champion potential legislation to reverse the terminations.

After a weekend of intense preparation and strategizing, we were ready. On Monday, June 1, we assembled at the Hilton. Many came early and everyone was in place by 4:45. But 5:15 came: no Hoyer. Soon it was 5:30, then 5:45. We all grew very nervous and disappointed. The reception was starting in 15 minutes. I was concerned that, even if we got an audience at all, it would only be for a few minutes and not provide us the opportunity we needed to properly explain the extent of these injustices.

Finally, at 5:50, Rep. Sutton arrived with Hoyer and his entourage. We arranged for a private room away from where the reception was being held. Hoyer is a tall, immaculately groomed, and smartly dressed, silver-haired man who has an incredibly commanding presence when he enters a room. After shaking hands with each of the dealers, Hoyer sat at a conference table directly across from Tony. I sat to Tony's left and the other dealers fanned out on both sides. Tony began to state our case—laying it out clearly and effectively like a courtroom lawyer—as Hoyer listened intently. I looked at the clock. It was a few minutes past 6 and Hoyer's aides were starting to encircle

House Majority Leader Steny Hoyer

Rep. Betty Sutton

him, motioning that the reception was underway. He dismissed them with a wave of his arm and continued listening to Tony.

It's impossible to know with certainty how anyone is internally reacting to a presentation like this, of course. But Hoyer appeared to be quite taken aback by what he was hearing as Tony began to call on dealers one by one to tell their stories. I listened to dealers I'd known for decades pour their hearts out to the Majority Leader. They were good people, solid citizens, successful businessmen brought to tears by the arbitrary actions of some faceless bureaucrats. Hoyer paid rapt attention to the individual dealers' accounts. We had his ear for nearly one hour, making him quite late for the reception. Before he left, he vowed to try to help. "When I get back to Washington," he said, "I'm going to assign this to John Hughes (one of his key aides). From now on, that's the man to contact."

With that, the meeting broke up and we all went upstairs to the reception. Before he left for the evening, I spent a few more minutes with Hoyer to reinforce some of the most important points. I also gave him a copy of a letter I had recently written to President Obama, asking him to reconsider the decision to terminate the dealers *(see sidebar)*. Hoyer gave the letter to an aide with the request to be sure he read it on the plane ride home. (Soon, under the direction of Hoyer, several dozen members of Congress would send a letter to Pres. Obama as well, expressing grave concerns about the dealer terminations *(see sidebar)*.)

As their cars pulled away from the Hilton, we felt a sense of "Mission Accomplished." It was an important first step for our team that was starting to take shape. Just a day later, I received a thorough follow-up from Nichole. We were clearly on their radar and building momentum with the right people. Later in the week in a conversation with Tony, Jack, who had known Hoyer for a long time, said, "You guys sure fired Steny up!"

SPITZER MANAGEMENT, INC

150 East Bridge Street   Elyria, Ohio 44035
Phone (440) 323-4671   Fax (440) 323-3623
www.spitzer.com

May 26, 2009

Dear President Obama,

I am the third generation leader of an automotive retail organization that has been in business since 1904. We operate thirty franchises in three states (Ohio, Pennsylvania and Florida). Over the next few years we will be transitioning to fourth generation members of my family to lead the approximately 1000 associates whose families depend on our company for their livelihood. Unfortunately, seven of our dealerships are Chrysler Corporation stores that are among those targeted to be cancelled by Chrysler. No dealer organization in the country has been more adversely affected. These franchises have been in our family for a combined 320 years. One has been in business for **over sixty years**, three for more than **fifty** and two for nearly **forty years** All of them have a very good customer satisfaction rating with more than adequate facilities and most are in excellent locations. One of them is in the process of relocating, at Chrysler's insistence, to a new location on a parcel of land that we have **already purchased at a cost of $1,600,000** (land cost only)! A few years ago, our Dodge dealership in Homestead, Florida acquired the local Chrysler-Jeep dealer for **two million dollars** plus spent another **one million dollars** on improvements to our facility, all at Chrysler's insistence. Another Dodge store relocated to a location by an interstate and acquired a competing Dodge store in the process for **one million dollars** as part of Chrysler's consolidation. That does not include the roughly **five million dollars** for a new facility.

Again, this was Chrysler's call as well!

Yet another **led the Cleveland, Ohio metro market in Dodge sales just last month** and has been at or near the top for years. Our **Dodge store in Columbus, Ohio sold more Dodges than any other dealer in the Columbus metro market for the full year 2008.** We're not perfect by any means but we're well capitalized and have tried to be team players and work with Chrysler to help them accomplish their goals. On more occasions than I can count we've purchased vehicles from Chrysler that we didn't need because they said they needed the orders.

Over 100 Years of Serving You Better...Saving You More

We are a strong company with a lot of great people and there is no doubt in my mind that we will survive. Our intent is to be in business for another 105 years and beyond. Sadly, hundreds of others are less fortunate. Many of the dealers slated to be terminated have their entire life's work and all their net worth wrapped up in their Chrysler franchise(s), only to have them abruptly terminated with **no** due process and **no** reparation. In many cases, including most of our own Chrysler stores, they are thriving, reasonably well managed **and** profitable.

In fact, in one of the markets in which we operate we are slated to **gain** the franchises of two terminated dealers. I guess that benefits us but there is something inherently wrong in the way it was handled and I certainly don't feel good about it.

I can assure you beyond a shadow of a doubt that these dealership closings will make Chrysler **less viable**, not more, which, after all, was the stated goal. **Dealers are independent businesses who cost Chrysler zero.** (This is completely unlike Starbucks who closed hundreds of unprofitable outlets. In that case they **were** owned by Starbucks and, unlike Chrysler, there was a cost savings.) With these closings Chrysler is guaranteed to **lose** market share!

Most customers are not going to obligingly drive significantly further distances than they have been accustomed to driving just out of loyalty to Chrysler, which has historically been one of the least loyal brands to begin with. In fact, unless you are prepared to pour an almost infinite amount of taxpayer dollars into the company, this move will almost certainly sound the death knell of Chrysler and send them into oblivion (same for GM if they follow the same formula). In the process these actions will not only devastate the lives of families numbering in the tens, maybe hundreds, of thousands in both small towns and large cities across America; they will almost certainly send our already fragile economy further into an abyss from which it may take decades to recover.

I have attached a link to our web site on which there is an open letter from me to our Dodge, Chrysler and Jeep customers. I hope you will read it. On my letter there is another link to an interview by Greta Van Susteren with Jack Fitzgerald who is a dealer from the D.C. area. Our family has known Mr. Fitzgerald for more than forty years. He has an outstanding reputation, is a wise and savvy businessman who takes care of his employees and provides top notch service to his customers. He is an inspirational leader in his community, devoted patriot and dedicated American citizen. He is all these things, yet **all seven** of his Chrysler franchises are slated to be cancelled. Please explain how this decision makes Chrysler more viable. In my opinion it is madness!! It will be worth the twenty minutes or so it takes to watch his interview. He is a street wise veteran who frames the issues very well.

I understand the Automotive Task Force is seeking to replicate the Toyota model of fewer dealers, more sales per dealer, etc. On paper that may make sense, until one realizes that Toyota lost one billion dollars **more** than GM in the first quarter of this year. It looks as though the Toyota model isn't perfect after all! Their CEO very recently resigned. Right now they, like most all car makers, are like a "deer in the headlights!" We also represent the Toyota brand and know firsthand the frustration that they are experiencing. Toyota is a great car company and will certainly "figure it out" and, unlike GM and Chrysler, Toyota is in a much better cash position. Of course, they haven't had to pay the hundreds of billions in legacy costs to retirees that Detroit has. As the saying goes, "Let no good deed go unpunished!"

The larger problem is that when the market goes from 17 million vehicles sold in the U.S. per year to 9 million almost overnight it is virtually impossible for **any** car maker, foreign or domestic, to be profitable in the near term. And to compound the problem, as you are acutely aware, this is not a situation unique to this country. Car makers **and** dealers **and** suppliers are struggling all over the globe. I am not aware of any safe haven anywhere in the world in the auto industry today.

The reality is that the free market has been making the necessary adjustments to the dealer count pretty rapidly through attrition (i.e., voluntary closings, dealer consolidations, etc). Equilibrium will be established in the next three or four years that will be much more palatable, much more humane and wreak far less havoc on our society and our economy than the current plan. **Please put a stop to these terminations** or at least **put them on hold**. There has to be a better way!

Mr. President, I am solidly behind you in your efforts to rebuild our economy in these extremely difficult, arguably unprecedented, times. Furthermore, I pray that you are successful in guiding our country to new heights as the pre-eminent leader of the free world.

I believe I can speak for all of our associates and the vast majority of my colleagues in the automotive industry when I tell you that we really want to be part of the solution. All we want is the opportunity. Thank you for listening.

Most respectfully yours,

Alan Spitzer
Chairman & CEO
Spitzer Management, Inc.

CHRIS VAN HOLLEN
8TH DISTRICT, MARYLAND

COMMITTEE ON
WAYS AND MEANS

COMMITTEE ON OVERSIGHT AND
GOVERNMENT REFORM

Congress of the United States
House of Representatives
Washington, DC 20515

1707 LONGWORTH HOUSE OFFICE BUILDING
WASHINGTON, DC 20515
(202) 225-5341

DISTRICT OFFICES:
51 MONROE STREET, #507
ROCKVILLE, MD 20850
(301) 424-3501

SUITE C-201
8475 NEW HAMPSHIRE AVENUE
HYATTSVILLE, MD 20783
(301) 891-6982

www.vanhollen.house.gov

June 8, 2009

The Honorable Barack Obama
President of the United States
The White House
1600 Pennsylvania Avenue
Washington, D.C. 20500

Dear President Obama:

We are writing to express our concerns about General Motors' and Chrysler's decision to close profitable automobile dealerships across the country, and urge you to ask GM and Chrysler to delay final action on proposed closures pending further review of the decision to consolidate dealerships and the process by which Chrysler and GM selected the dealerships to close.

Closing these dealerships will put over 100,000 jobs at risk at a time when our country is shedding jobs at an alarming rate. We also question the criteria being used to determine which dealerships should be closed and the fundamental fairness involved in this effort. It is our view that the market should make these decisions rather than leaving it up to the manufacturers whose poor leadership contributed to their demise. Furthermore, we believe car dealers will be key players in any effort to revive the American auto industry.

We believe the dealerships are one of the auto industry's key sources of strength and the manufacturers should continue to honor their agreements and contracts. The dealerships, and their more than 1 million employees, form personal relationships with customers that often contribute to brand loyalty and will be key to General Motors' and Chrysler's recovery following this economic downturn. While we understand the desire to reduce the number of unprofitable dealerships, no one has yet sufficiently explained the need to close profitable dealerships.

We recognize that efforts by your Auto Task Force prevented the total liquidation of General Motors and Chrysler, as well as their dealership networks. We commend your efforts to help these businesses survive these challenging economic times. However, we are concerned that manufacturers are closing profitable dealerships to circumvent current contracts which could require expensive buy-outs under normal conditions. We are also concerned about allegations that dealers that have previously stood up for their rights against the manufacturers are being targeted by these closures. We believe that the forced closures of profitable dealerships needs to be scrutinized by the Task Force to prevent additional future financial loses to General Motors and Chrysler and job loses across the United States.

THIS STATIONERY PRINTED ON PAPER MADE OF RECYCLED FIBERS

> We may consider legislative proposals to ensure that dealers and their employees are treated fairly, and we look forward to your timely response.
>
> Sincerely,
>
> Chris Van Hollen Steny H. Hoyer Daniel B. Maffei
>
> Frank Kratovil Artur Davis
>
> Suzanne Kosmas Carol Shea-Porter
>
> Rick Larsen Betty Sutton
>
> Daniel Lipinski Mary Jo Kilroy
>
> Jim Costa Tim Holden
>
> Glenn Nye Michael Arcuri
>
> Harry Teague Leonard Lance
>
> Phil Hare John Salazar
>
> Andre Carson Christopher Carney

* The actual letter contains a total of 116 signatures and has been truncated.

Chapter 6

"GOOD MORNING, TAMMY"

*This is a court of law, young man,
not a court of justice.*

Oliver Wendell Holmes, Jr.

DETROIT (Reuters)—A U.S. Bankruptcy Court judge approved the sale of most of Chrysler LLC's assets to a group led by Italy's Fiat S.p.A. hours before an expected bankruptcy filing by General Motors. Judge Arthur Gonzalez approved the $2 billion sale of the assets to a new company that will be 68 percent controlled by a healthcare trust aligned with the United Auto Workers union. Fiat will control 20 percent, the U.S. and Canadian governments will control the other 12 percent.

That was the story that hit the newspapers across the nation on June 1, 2009. Chrysler had recently been in intense negotiations with Fiat S.p.A. to sell the remaining assets of Chrysler after the bankruptcy. A deal was struck pending the outcome of the bankruptcy. The fate of the terminated dealers was sealed when Judge Gonzalez ruled to approve the sale of Chrysler's assets to Fiat *before* even listening to the objections of the dealers.

One of Chrysler's key witnesses in the Chrysler bankruptcy trial was chairman and CEO Robert Nardelli. After a long career with General Electric that began in 1971, he lost a three-way race to succeed legendary CEO Jack Welch. He left GE in 2000 to become chief executive officer of The Home Depot. He was ousted from The Home Depot by the board in 2007, receiving an astounding and quite controversial $210 million severance package. The 60-year-old Nardelli had been with Chrysler for slightly more than one year when he joined GM CEO Rick Wagoner and Ford CEO Alan Mulally before the Senate Finance Committee. He appeared tense and uncomfortable during the hearings and not readily in command of basic facts. His testimony before Judge Gonzalez in the Chrysler bankruptcy trial six months later was even less reliable, especially with respect to the company's relationship with its dealers. The following is a portion of his testimony before Judge Gonzalez that day:

Chrysler CEO Robert Nardelli

Q. Rejecting these 789 dealers will not save Chrysler any direct expenses, will it?

A. Yes, it will.

Q. And what direct expenses will be saved?

A. Well, every dealership—there are specialty tools that the manufacturer has to supply. There is service training that we provide. There is dealer support in the local markets for advertising. There is incentive payments and spiffs that we run, those brochures. I mean, there's a host of expenses that go into supporting the dealers.

By Ms. Brown:

Q. Mr. Nardelli, has Chrysler made any effort to quantify the cost savings related to specialty tools for rejecting the dealership agreements for the 789 dealers?

A. I don't have that number available, but I'm sure there was some cost associated with that.

Q. My question is has Chrysler made any effort to quantify the cost savings associated with specialty tools in rejecting the 789 dealerships' agreements?

A. I'm not aware that we would look at, going forward, what the cost of new tools would be that we would not have to incur with 789 less dealers.

Q. And how about service training? Are you aware of any efforts to quantify the cost that will be saved in service training by rejecting the dealership agreements of the 789 dealers?

A. Not that I could provide you right now ... I think, again, we'd have to get a hold of Jim (Press) and the team and see if we can find it.

Q. Don't dealers pay for specialty tools?

A. In some cases they pay for tools and in some cases we provide—my understanding is we provide some specialty tools. I ...

Q. And don't dealers pay for training?

A. In some cases they do and in some cases I know that we have a pretty extensive service agreement to provide training to the dealerships.

Q. And don't the dealers reimburse for that service training?

A. Not in total.

Q. What percentage do they reimburse?

A. I don't know. I don't know.

Each of the items about which Mr. Nardelli testified is paid for by the dealer. Brochures, special tools, training, computer access, and brand signage are all charged to the dealer on a monthly basis at prices that often seem exorbitant. Many dealers believe these items are marked up, representing a profit center for the manufacturers. Dealers pay from $40,000 to $70,000 or more annually for these items. Mr. Nardelli's testimony is documentably false. The only remaining question is whether he knew it at the time. Sadly, the testimony was left unchallenged during this phase of the trial. It was testimony like this that gave Judge Gonzalez cover for rejecting the dealer franchise agreements.

Against impossible odds, a handful of dealers, including me, made the trek to New York to be heard by Judge Gonzalez. I knew the prospects of any kind of victory in Federal Bankruptcy Court were very dim, but I wanted to at least go down swinging, so off to New York Tony and I went.

Three weeks earlier, when I had reviewed Chrysler's list of 789 Rejected Dealers, another name had caught my eye along with that of Jack Fitzgerald. It was John Darvish, the dealer principal of the DARCARS organization, a name that appeared on the list multiple times. DARCARS is a large, well-respected organization in the Washington, D.C./Maryland area. They also have operations in Florida. John was also a friend of my father and my uncle.

I had met John many times over the years but was better acquainted with his daughter, Tamara. Tammy and I got to know each other pretty well, having both attended several Toyota functions over the years. I knew her as a dynamic (and colorful) personality. She was a no-nonsense woman with high energy and a "let's get it done" mentality. It occurred to me that she could be a valuable part of the legislative effort we were about to undertake. Like Jack, she had the advantage of living in the D.C. area. To top it off, her father, John, at one time had been a manager for Jack Fitzgerald.

Tamara Darvish

My oldest daughter, Alison, had recently joined our company, working at our Homestead, Fla., store and I had introduced her to Tammy a few months earlier. I encouraged Alison to develop a relationship with her, believing Tammy would be a good role model. Before I left for New York and the Chrysler Bankruptcy trial, I asked Alison to contact Tammy to see if she had interest in joining forces. (Alison had her first child, Vera, on March 22 and was unable to join us for this particular trip to New York.) In another remarkable stroke of good fortune, Tammy had been appointed to the Committee of Unsecured Creditors by the Bankruptcy Trustee. Her role required her to be in New York, too.

> **From:** Alison Spitzer
> **To:** Tammy
> **Sent:** Tue, 02 Jun 2009 10:31:07 -0400
> **Subject:** Chrysler: Spitzer & Darcars
> Good morning, Tammy-
>
> We met at a Toyota meeting a while back, I hope you are well.
> My family's business operates out of Cleveland, Ohio and we were told by Chrysler that 7 of our 8 stores will be terminated. I know that you have had a similar experience.
>
> My father, Alan Spitzer (I think you know him), is heading to New York this afternoon and will be testifying tomorrow. He has been in local

media speaking out against Chrysler. We are trying to fight this in any way possible, and thought that you may want to join forces in this—perhaps we could help each other.

Please let me know how I can best reach you to discuss this in further detail.

Thank you,
Alison Spitzer

From: Tammy Darvish
To: Alison Spitzer
Date: Tue, 2 Jun 2009 13:51:15 -0400
Subject: Re: Chrysler: Spitzer & Darcars

Hi, Alison—

Thanks for the e-mail. I am on my way to NY also. Where are you staying? You can reach me on my cell at 202-xxx-xxxx. I arrive at approx. 5 p.m. I'm at the Ritz in Battery Park cuz you can walk to courthouse from there and they have good rates. Call me and let's get together tonight. I'm going live on CNBC at 8 p.m. but can meet after that if you can? Or maybe before?

Let me know.
Thanks
Tammy

Tony and I arrived in New York on the afternoon of June 3 and Alison arranged for us to have dinner with Tammy that evening. We met Tammy and her assistant, Courtney Wallin, at the Ritz-Carlton in Battery Park, within walking distance of the federal courthouse where the Chrysler bankruptcy case was being heard. We were joined by Tammy's financial advisor Larry Lattig. Dinner that night was enjoyable despite the somber backdrop of the trial.

Tony and I returned to my room to prepare for my testimony before Judge Gonzalez. Jack had originally planned to join us and testify as well—but he changed his mind. He correctly reasoned that it was not the best use of his time. The Senate Committee on Commerce, Science, and Transportation, chaired by Sen. Jay Rockefeller (D-WV), was holding hearings regarding the dealer closures. Jack decided to attend the hearings instead of coming to New York. In another stroke of good fortune, that turned out to be an incredibly important and precisely correct decision.

Fiasco in the Big Apple

At 8 a.m. the next morning, Tony and I made our way over to the Federal Courthouse at 1 Bowling Green St. in lower Manhattan. As we walked along, I looked across New York Harbor and spotted the Statue of Liberty. I was struck by how ironic it was that the proceedings we were about to witness were completely opposed to everything that lady in the harbor represented. This couldn't happen in America. Cuba or China, maybe. But in the U.S.A.? Could a judge, strongly rumored to have been handpicked by a forum-shopping Justice Department, bring down the curtain on 789 small businesses, most of which were profitable?

The building's Gothic style was stark and foreboding and the scene in the courtroom was somber, like something from a Charles Dickens novel. It was 8:30 a.m. as lawyers and paralegals scurried around in preparation for the beginning of the morning session.

The largest contingent was from the Cincinnati law firm of Squires, Sanders & Dempsey, which had three or four attorneys and an equal number of paralegals. They were there on behalf of a group who called themselves the Committee of Chrysler Affected Dealers, easily the largest consortium representing dealers.

After the terminations were announced three weeks earlier, the National Automobile Dealers Association (NADA) had sent a notice to all Rejected Chrysler dealers inviting them to band together in bankruptcy court as a bloc. Each dealer was asked to send $4,000 to Squires, Sanders & Dempsey, the law firm selected by NADA to represent the Rejected Chrysler dealers.

The "Squires" letter from NADA was actually the second letter to the Rejected Dealers. NADA's original firm of choice, Arnold & Porter, had to bow out due to a conflict of interest. Arnold & Porter represents NADA on most other matters. Given that the majority of NADA members did not lose franchises, the firm faced the dilemma of potentially representing dealers on opposite sides of the termination issue. As events unfolded over the next few months, this would not be the last time the national dealer organization would find itself in a very awkward position. Many dealers naïvely saw the offer from NADA as their salvation and gladly sent in the requested retainer. Approximately 350 dealers joined the NADA-sponsored effort yielding a tidy $1.4 million. To my knowledge, Squires never gave a complete accounting of the funds and I don't believe anything was refunded. That was $1.4 million for about two weeks of work.

As Tony and I entered the courtroom, we spotted Tammy in the second row and took seats next to her. She was there in her role as a member of the Unsecured Creditors' Committee. She had been present for all of the previous proceedings including the sale to the Italian firm Fiat S.p.A. Just days earlier in the same courtroom, Chrysler had completed the sale of its assets to Fiat in what is known as a "363 bankruptcy," so named for the section number in the bankruptcy code that allows a buyer (Fiat) to acquire the assets of the bankrupt company or debtor (Chrysler) free and clear of all liens. In other words, the cart had gone before the horse. The deal was done before the dealer objections were even heard!

"All rise," bellowed the bailiff at 9 a.m. on the dot and in strode His Honor Arthur J. Gonzalez. As he took his seat on the bench, he silently and impassively surveyed his surroundings. Seated in the U.S. Bankruptcy Court's Southern District of New York, this judge was no stranger to high-profile bankruptcy cases, having presided over the filings of both Enron and WorldCom. A native New Yorker, Judge Gonzalez earned his undergraduate degree and later his law degree from Fordham University. He worked as a teacher in the New York City public school system until 1982 when he became a lawyer for the Internal Revenue Service. He was appointed bankruptcy judge in 1995.[24]

The judge's opening statement apparently sealed the dealers' fate: "Today and tomorrow we will hear objections from dealers whose franchises have been Rejected by Old Chrysler," he intoned. "It seems to me even if the dealers' objections are sustained it would be a hollow victory. They would have a franchise agreement with a bankrupt company." Our worst fears were confirmed. It seemed we were in "kangaroo court" with a judge who had already made up his mind. Even if we win, we lose! It was like trying to roll 13 with a pair of dice.

After a mid-morning break, the bailiff called my name and I was sworn in. Tony questioned me during direct examination, reviewing with me the history of our long and mutually rewarding relationship with Chrysler and the significant financial commitment we had made on its behalf in recent years. I was cross-examined by Jeff Jones of the venerable Cleveland law firm Jones, Day. Jeff and I knew each other fairly well, since we had previously sparred a few times in Ohio—in state court. We

---

[24] McLaughlin, D., "Chrysler Bankruptcy Judge Handled Enron, World Com." *The Wall Street Journal*. May 1, 2009.

had even been on the same side a couple of times. He obviously was using all the ammunition he could to discredit my direct testimony.

Tony asked a few questions on redirect, mostly to repair any damage Jeff may have done. He then asked me if I had anything else to say. I looked directly at Judge Gonzalez and, with as much conviction as I could muster, said, "Your honor, we are a nation of laws. This is not Communist Russia under Josef Stalin. This is not Red China under Mao-Tse Tung. This is the United States of America and *these terminations should not stand!*"

Unfortunately, those words—and the words of many of my peers who would also testify—fell on deaf ears. Judge Gonzalez listened impassively and would not look me in the eye. There were no more questions.

I returned to my seat and listened as dealer after dealer—about a dozen in all—laid out the horrible, sad details of their unjust, unfair closures.

Bob Taylor from Naples, Fla., whose dealership had met or exceeded sales quotas for several years, testified about subtle pressures from Chrysler's district manager who hinted he was getting too old to operate the dealership. Charles Lee, from Southern California, had dramatic testimony as well. He spoke about coming to America from South Korea and how his father dreamed of owning a dealership. His family invested $6.5 million in a Dodge dealership. He feared not only losing the Dodge franchise, but the facility itself. He would be wiped out.

And Jim Tarbox from Rhode Island indicated that he was targeted for termination because he'd successfully protested, as was his right under state law, Chrysler's attempts to install a competitor in a nearby community. Fighting back tears,

Tarbox recalled the day his termination notice arrived. "This must be a mistake," he remembered thinking. He stood to lose everything—his home and his children's college savings—because of these unjust actions. Jim would soon become a symbol for everything that was wrong about these unconscionable terminations. During document discovery for the bankruptcy trial, intra-company e-mails among Chrysler officials confirmed that he was singled out for rejection because of his protest, despite operating one of the highest-performing Jeep dealerships in the nation. (These e-mail messages were originally under a seal order by Judge Gonzalez who later ordered them unsealed).

Rejected Jeep dealer Jim Tarbox

The e-mail exchange between Jessica Montoya, Dina Ellis-Ruskin, and John Bozzella of Chrysler's Government Affairs Office in Washington, D.C., laid bare the brass-knuckle politics behind some of the closures:

> **From:** Jessica Montoya
> **To:** Dina Ellis-Ruskin, John Bozzella
>
> I spoke with Phil Scroggin [Chrysler's Northeast Business Center manager] just now. This is going to be a tough one. His dealerships are performing fine and he has a good scorecard. [Chrysler's measurement of dealer performance].

> **Reply:**
>
> He is a belligerent, combative dealer who litigates and protests any new Jeep franchises in Prov(idence), RI area so management made [the] decision to cut him. He has not operated in good faith.

Good faith?? The Rhode Island legislature enacted a law giving dealers the right to protest the addition of franchise(s) selling the same brand within their market area. The auto manufacturer can still add the new dealership—but first the company must prove the protesting dealer is not adequately serving the market. The existing dealer gets a "day in court." It's quite a leap to suggest that a high-performing dealer who availed himself of protections afforded to him under law has not operated in good faith.

But for a moment, set the protest issue aside and pretend you're running Chrysler. You've got a young 42-year-old, third-generation dealer whose name is a household word in his market. He has outstanding customer satisfaction, is well-capitalized and sells *four to five times* the sales quota you've established for him. Is this somebody you want to get rid of just because he legally protested a competitor being added to his market selling the same brand? And would it be in your company's best interests to then "gift" that Jeep franchise to a nearby Chrysler-Dodge dealer that consistently performs at a lower level? Sound business judgment or a vendetta?

Iowa dealer Jeff Carr testified about how, in 2008, a flood virtually destroyed his dealership facility. As a result, he was forced to relocate. A short time later, in an effort to help Chrysler accomplish its brand consolidation plan known as "Project Genesis," he agreed to sell his Chrysler franchise to the neighboring Dodge dealer. Due to some apparent chicanery behind the scenes, Chrysler's approval process went slower than normal. The prospective buyer purportedly got "cold feet," only to be gifted the Chrysler franchise when Mr. Carr, its rightful owner, had the franchise Rejected in bankruptcy. Shortly after my testimony before a House subcommittee, I received the following message from him:

From: Jeff Carr
Sent: Monday, June 15, 2009 10:08 AM
To: Al Spitzer
Subject: Chrysler Dealer

Mr. Spitzer, I also testified with you in New York in Judge Gonzalez's courtroom. Not sure if you stayed around to hear me testify because I was the last one to do so. I spoke with your son-in-law Saturday and told him that I will do whatever I can to get the word out about H.R. 2743. I know that everybody has a unique story—naturally I do as well. My store was impacted by a flood last year and we were forced to relocate. My people were able to sell cars two days after the flood and built a temporary service department from the ground up to service our customers 7 days after the flood. For the past 5 years Chrysler has been trying under Project Genesis/Alpha to combine my Chrysler store with the Jeep/Dodge dealer across town. Immediately after the flood they initiated and ultimately helped us reach a deal with that dealer. We had an offer/acceptance that included earnest money and a closing date of September 30th, 2008. The dealer got "cold feet" when sales started to decline and the banking world started to collapse. Because the dealer I was selling to is part of the Dealer Council he asked Chrysler not to approve it in time—which is what happened. Now he is getting my franchise for free.

I have been very vocal here in Iowa—television, radio, newspaper, etc. Without being too egotistical—I am pretty good at getting the message across. If I can help you out in any way, or be by your side in Washington, just let me know. I mean that.

Jeff Carr
McGurk Meyers
Coralville/Iowa City, Iowa

There are numerous stories of this nature. They certainly call into question the objectivity of Judge Gonzalez when he wrote in his opinion: "The Court also finds that no evidence has been presented that the Debtors (Chrysler) made their individual decisions irrationally, such that the rejections demonstrate bad faith or whim or caprice."

As the day wore on, something in me changed and this issue became much, much larger than our organization. I guess you could say that a 60-something-year-old business owner became radicalized. I grew more determined than ever to do something to get justice for all of these hardworking, successful small-business owners whose lives were being devastated through no fault of their own. And I was further convinced these actions were going to hurt, not help, the car companies. These people were being destroyed for no good reason. It was the ultimate lose-lose proposition.

These dealer terminations would certainly not move Chrysler toward viability as the President's Automotive Task Force had naïvely believed. If anything, this drastic reduction in the dealer network would accelerate Chrysler's demise and put the taxpayer investment at greater risk.

Most of the dealers being terminated were **profitable.** I was struck by the irony of it. If you connect the dots, profitable Chrysler (and GM) dealers were paying income taxes to the federal government who would use those tax dollars to keep Chrysler (and GM) afloat allowing them to put these same dealers out of business. It was as appalling as it was sad.

I went to New York partly on behalf of our organization, partly on behalf of dealers throughout the country who had suffered a similar fate. But as we left the courthouse and made our way to the airport, I found that the fate of my own company or our at-risk franchises was far from what became my top priority. I knew I had a solid organization with strong management and lots of great people behind me. We were diversified enough and had ample reserves to withstand the blows we had been dealt. But that just wasn't the case for countless others across the nation. I firmly resolved to press our case as zealously and as passionately as possible. I would devote all my energies toward righting the injustices that had been dealt my fellow dealers.

Chapter 7

"I'M NOT SENATOR JACK"

Freedom is when people can speak; democracy is when the government listens.

Alastair Farrugia

As the Chrysler bankruptcy trial unfolded, my new compatriot, Jack Fitzgerald, was working on the problem in another venue. The Senate Committee on Commerce, Science, and Transportation, commonly known as the Commerce Committee, had scheduled a hearing on the dealer terminations the day before. Jack stayed in D.C. to attend the hearing in person. Instead, he sent Mary Jo Dowd from Arent Fox LLP, a well-respected Washington, D.C. law firm, to represent him in New York and submitted his objections via affidavit rather than live testimony. Jack also gave his law firm another assignment: draft a piece of legislation to get the next phase of our strategy underway.

Judge Gonzalez was completely unsympathetic to the dealers' position. Based on his comments and body language, we knew he was poised to rule that federal bankruptcy law should supersede the state franchise-protection laws. Our long shot in federal bankruptcy court wasn't going to come in. Attempts to contact the White House proved futile. President Obama had relegated matters to the Auto Team and apparently wouldn't be bothered. Legislative relief was increasingly looking like our only option.

As Tony and I rode in a taxi in lower Manhattan an e-mail buzzed on my BlackBerry. It was from Jack.

> **From:** Jack Fitzgerald
> **To:** Alan Spitzer
> **Date:** Wednesday, June 03, 2009 3:39 PM
> **Subject:** Draft Legislation on Auto Dealers
>
> Alan,
>
> I'm having this sent while I'm attending the hearing on Capitol Hill. I believe that only our elected officials can correct our current course. I know I'm not Senator Jack, I'm Jack the dealer. I need your help. If you think you can help save jobs and make this a reality, please call me.
>
> Jack
> 301-xxx-xxxx

The message was generically written so he could forward it to other potential supporters in the next few days. There was an attachment to the message, his proposed first draft of legislation that would start the closure reversals.

> **111th Congress**
>
> 1st Session
>
> H.R. ___ / S. ____
>
> To restore the economic rights of automobile dealers and for other purposes.
>
> **IN THE HOUSE OF REPRESENTATIVES/IN THE SENATE**
>
> June __, 2009
>
> Mr./Ms. _____ introduced the following bill; which was referred to the Committee on _____.

A BILL

To restore the economic rights of automobile dealers and for other purposes.

Be it enacted by the Senate and House of Representatives of the United States of America

Congress assembled,

SECTION 1. SHORT TITLE.

This Act may be cited as the "Automobile Dealer Economic Rights Restoration Act of 2009".

SECTION 2. FINDINGS.

The Congress finds the following:

(1) Automobile dealers are an asset to automobile manufacturers that make it possible to penetrate communities and sell automobiles nationally;

(2) The manufacturers obtain the benefits from having a national dealer network at no material costs to the manufacturers; and (3) Historically, automobile dealers have had franchise agreement protections under state law.

SECTION 3. RESTORATION OF ECONOMIC RIGHTS.

(a) In order to protect assets of the federal government, and better assure the viability of automobile manufacturers in which the Federal Government has an ownership interest, no automobile manufacturer in which the Federal Government has an ownership interest may deprive an automobile dealer of its economic rights as they existed prior to the filing of bankruptcy petitions by the manufacturer, including its rights to recourse under state law.

(b) In order to preserve economic rights pursuant to subsection (a), automobile manufacturers covered under this Act shall restore the franchise agreements with automobile dealers that were in effect prior to the filing of bankruptcy petitions by those manufacturers.

At Jack's direction, Arent Fox had drafted the legislation he and I had contemplated and structured it in the correct format. (The language of the bill couldn't name GM and Chrysler specifically—so it referred to "automobile manufacturers in which the federal government has an ownership interest." Naturally, that only could mean GM and Chrysler.)

I read it and immediately showed it to Tony. It was a simple one-page bill that restored all franchises of terminated General Motors or Chrysler dealers to pre-bankruptcy levels and reaffirmed the protections to which they were entitled under various state laws. "This is it," I said to Tony. "Now, we've got to get to work."

Jack had already accomplished the first job I had on my to-do list upon my return from New York: contact a law firm from Washington. Get something on paper. As would often be the case over the following months, Jack was a step ahead of me.

On June 3, 2009, Sen. Rockefeller's Commerce Committee was holding a hearing in Room 253 of the Russell Senate Office Building entitled *"GM and Chrysler Dealership Closures: Protecting Dealers and Consumers"* as Jack sent the proposed legislation to me. Witnesses called in for grilling included GM CEO Frederick "Fritz" Henderson, (who replaced the recently deposed Wagoner), Chrysler co-president Jim Press, and NADA chairman and Iowa dealer John McEleney. In addition, two terminated dealers, Pete Lopez from West Virginia and Russell Aubrey Whatley III from Texas, had been invited by Rockefeller and ranking Republican member Kay Bailey Hutchison (R-TX).

Rockefeller opened the hearing by proclaiming that all members of the Committee were present and this was the "largest turnout he had seen in his 24 years in the Senate." He went on to declare the dealer closures a "nationwide tragedy."

Jack Fitzgerald attends Senate hearing

Each senator on the committee gave a brief opening statement followed by statements from each witness. All of the senators were extremely critical of both car manufacturers and called into question the processes used to determine which dealers were terminated. Predictably, the statements from Press and Henderson were bland. However, more alarmingly, many dealers believed that some of their statements were either partially or completely untrue. Neither man appeared to be very comfortable. During the question-and-answer period, the committee's criticism grew even more caustic and accusatory. Unfortunately, there were no witnesses representing the real culprit behind these unconscionable actions: the President's Automotive Task Force.

Even as he attended the hearing, Jack was busily enlisting support for our nascent bill. He showed it to NADA representatives, who gave it short shrift and said it wouldn't go anywhere. Luckily, there was a reporter present from *The Washington Post*, Dana Hedgpeth, who caught wind of Jack's bill. She was looking for a story—and she found one. The next day, *The Post* ran a 1,000-word story about "Jack's bill" and our efforts on Capitol Hill: "For Car Dealers, the Hardest Sell Is on the Hill." It was great exposure.

Although we had only been in New York for two days, I was eager to return to Ohio. There was a lot of work to do. We flew back late in the afternoon of Thursday, June 4, just a few hours after I had testified (and listened to so many heart-wrenching stories from my fellow dealers). Over that weekend, Jack and I talked numerous times to fine-tune our strategy. I thought of how many times over the years, when referring to a seemingly impossible task, I'd heard people utter facetiously, "It'll take an Act of Congress!" Now, if there were to be any justice, that's exactly what it would take.

Things were moving at warp speed. Every minute counted. We knew we needed to recruit an army to have any chance of success. They were daunting numbers: 100 senators, 435 representatives in the House, more than 2,000 affected dealers. And three formidable opponents: GM, Chrysler, and the Obama Administration! Nonetheless, Jack and I were unfazed. Like quarterbacks on a football team, all our focus was on the next play. Tammy was not officially in the fold but she'd already told me we could count on her, and I was certain she would soon be an invaluable part of our team.

-----Original Message-----
From: Tammy Darvish
Date: Thu, 4 Jun 2009 21:40:03
To: Alan Spitzer
Subject: Re: Fw: Consumer Affairs, Economy: Dear Colleague: Halt Dealership Closures; Sign-On Letter Circulating

Thanks for everything Mr. Spitzer. Hope you had a pleasant trip home. Let's keep up the fight and you can count on me.

See you soon,
Tammy

-----Original Message-----

From: Alan Spitzer
Date: Fri, 5 Jun 2009 02:25:29
To: Tammy Darvish
Subject: Re: Fw: Consumer Affairs, Economy: Dear Colleague: Halt Dealership Closures; Sign-On Letter Circulating

Great to be with you, Tammy. Tony, Jack and I are having a conf. call about 9 am. Do you want to be on it? If so, what number should we call?

Sent via BlackBerry by AT&T

-----Original Message-----

From: Tammy Darvish
Date: Fri, 5 Jun 2009 10:03:07
To: Alan Spitzer
Subject: Re: Fw: Consumer Affairs, Economy: Dear Colleague: Halt Dealership Closures; Sign-On Letter Circulating

Yes please. 202 xxx-xxxx

Sent via BlackBerry by AT&T

-----Original Message-----

From: Alan Spitzer
Date: Fri, 5 Jun 2009 12:27:02
To: Tammy Darvish
Subject: Re: Fw: Consumer Affairs, Economy: Dear Colleague: Halt Dealership Closures; Sign-On Letter Circulating

It'll probably b around ten

Sent via BlackBerry by AT&T

-----Original Message-----

From: Tammy Darvish
Date: Fri, 5 Jun 2009 12:31:29
To: Alan Spitzer; Tammy Darvish
Subject: Re: Fw: Consumer Affairs, Economy: Dear Colleague: Halt Dealership Closures; Sign-On Letter Circulating

My daughters grad is at 10 ... can we do 11??

Sent via BlackBerry by AT&T

-----Original Message-----

From: Alan Spitzer
Date: Fri, 5 Jun 2009 12:42:40
To: Tammy Darvish
Subject: Re: Fw: Consumer Affairs, Economy: Dear Colleague: Halt Dealership Closures; Sign-On Letter Circulating

R u sur 11 is ok? Will the grad b over?

Sent via BlackBerry by AT&T

-----Original Message-----

From: Tammy Darvish
Sent: Friday, June 05, 2009 8:49 AM
To: Alan Spitzer
Subject: Re: Fw: Consumer Affairs, Economy: Dear Colleague: Halt Dealership Closures; Sign-On Letter Circulating

11 will be great. Small class & her last name begins with F so I'll be fine.

Sent via BlackBerry by AT&T

Chapter 8

"ZERO, ZERO ... ZERO!"

Silence never won rights. They are not handed down from above; they are forced by pressures from below.

Roger Baldwin

The following Monday, Tony and I were right back on the road again. This time, it was Washington, D.C., so we could be present when our proposed legislation was being introduced with fanfare, support, and momentum. It was Dan Maffei, a freshman congressman from New York who was tapped by House leadership to sponsor the bill. Among the many co-sponsors: another freshman Frank Kratovil (D-MD) from Maryland's 1st District; Chris Van Hollen (D-MD) from Maryland's 8th District and one of the senior Democrats in Congress; and Steny Hoyer, the House Majority Leader. Our meeting with Hoyer had returned a big dividend. Of course, it didn't hurt that Jack and Tammy also knew Hoyer and had been in contact with his office as well.

On June 9, the day after the bill, now known as H.R. 2743, was filed—and, in a sad coincidence, the last day in business for

Steny Hoyer speaks at press conference about dealer legislation. On left are Tammy Darvish, Jack Fitzgerald and Alan Spitzer

the 789 Rejected Chrysler dealerships—we held a press conference introducing the legislation on the front lawn of the Capitol building. It was attended by dozens of media representatives across the country. Sponsor Maffei, as well as Steny and several other co-sponsors including Van Hollen, Kratovil and Roscoe Bartlett (R-MD) expressed their support for dealers. When it was his turn at bat, Steny asked the question "Do you know how much dealers cost the manufacturers?" He then made a circle with his thumb and forefinger with his right hand and thrust it in the air, exclaiming "Zero, zero ... ZERO!"

That very public stand was a shot in the arm for Jack, Tammy, and me. We even had representation from the "upper chamber" the U.S. Senate, in the form of Ben Cardin (D-MD).

But a raft of Democrats and a token Republican wasn't going to be enough to get our legislation through Congress. We knew it was crucial to have the strong backing of Republicans as well. On Friday, June 5, we'd learned that Steve LaTourette (R-OH) from Ohio's 14th District was solidly in support of our efforts to restore the closed dealerships. Jack called me and informed me that LaTourette had asked for a copy of the bill. In fact, he actually didn't think "Jack's Bill" was strong enough. He created a version that was even tougher—what would become H.R. 2796. From my office in Elyria, I placed a call to LaTourette's Washington office and conferenced in Jack from his office in Maryland. We were eager to get LaTourette's perspective and see how we could align his support with our efforts. Soon, we were talking to Kate Ostrander, his legislative director. She was a very sharp and savvy pro. We told Kate that, given his support, we'd like to meet with LaTourette. Kate promptly scheduled a meeting with the Congressman immediately after the press conference on June 9.

We would later learn that, without this kind of bipartisan support, our bill would have gone nowhere, especially with opposition from the White House.

> **From:** Ostrander, Kate
> **Sent:** Friday, June 05, 2009 2:42 PM
> **To:** Alan Spitzer; T Giardini
> **Subject:** RE: Consumer Affairs, Economy: Dear Colleague: Halt Dealership Closures; Sign-On Letter Circulating
>
> Also, I talked to Rep. Sutton's office. We all should be able to coordinate together on the legislation and continue to work on getting it ready.

> **From:** Alan Spitzer
> **Sent:** Friday, June 05, 2009 2:58 PM
> **To:** Ostrander, Kate
> **Cc:** T Giardini; Jack; Tammy Darvish
> **Subject:** RE: Consumer Affairs, Economy: Dear Colleague: Halt Dealership Closures; Sign-On Letter Circulating
>
> Thanks for the update. With legal arguments coming Tuesday in Bankruptcy Court on the Chrysler case, anything that can be done to stay the closings would be extremely helpful. If you have any thoughts about how I can help move the legislative process along and/or facilitate getting the attention of the White House, please let me know.

Alan Spitzer
Chairman & CEO
Spitzer Management, Inc.
Phone: (440) xxx-xxxx
Fax: (440) xxx-xxxx

From: Ostrander, Kate
Sent: Friday, June 05, 2009 4:20 PM
To: Alan Spitzer
Subject: RE: Consumer Affairs, Economy: Dear Colleague: Halt Dealership Closures; Sign-On Letter Circulating

Thanks. We have the bill copy ready. Mr. LaTourette will introduce on Monday with likely several sponsors jointly—we continue to work on getting other sponsors, including Rep. Sutton, and will keep you posted. Thanks!

Kate Ostrander
Office of Rep. Steven C. LaTourette

When we met, it was clear that he was very committed to our cause. He listened to us and I think he even picked up on a few of the sound bites we had to offer about the Task Force, the viability plans, and the overly aggressive dealer cuts that the administration was determined to force through. It was an excellent, productive meeting, and we left there feeling very heartened. As we left his office, Tammy, Jack, and I agreed that we had a legitimate shot at one of those rarities: true bipartisan legislation. In the increasingly polarized political environment in Washington, this was no small accomplishment.

But we weren't naïve, either. We knew that if we were going to have any success, the drive for passage would have to come from the terminated dealers throughout the country. We couldn't sit back and assume that Congress would let this legislation sail through. And we certainly understood that the manufacturers—and the Obama Administration's Auto Team—would fight us tooth and nail. A true grass roots effort was essential.

That's when Tammy, Jack, and I came up with the idea to form a legal entity: the Committee to Restore Dealer Rights, LLC (CRDR) with the three of us serving as co-chairs. CRDR would give structure and a bit of "arm's-length" independence from our dealerships and enable us to track the costs and finances of this initiative more cleanly. But its primary purpose was to give dealers a sort of command center or headquarters to identify with and communicate to, a tangible rallying point.

Tammy, Jack, and I convened at the law offices of Arent Fox to further discuss strategy along with Fred Beans and his daughter, Beth. Fred is a successful multi-franchise dealer from the Philadelphia area who was losing some GM franchises. He was a passionate supporter of our cause and one of our first contributors. Also present was Jack's longtime right-hand man, Rob Smith, who proved to be an invaluable part of the team. He had an uncanny ability to anticipate what would be needed and always seemed to have whatever information Jack required at the precise moment he needed it. Although Alison couldn't make this particular trip, she was with me every step of the way for the rest of the journey. Alison and Rob moved more or less in lockstep with Jack, Tammy, and me throughout the entire process.

You could argue that NADA should have taken a more aggressive role in this entire undertaking—and you wouldn't get any disagreement from me about that. But NADA's cozy relationships with manufacturers left it in a very compromised position when this crisis erupted. Also problematic, of course, was the fact that about 75 percent of its Chrysler and GM members did **not** lose franchises, creating a clear conflict. NADA appeared to be somewhat bewildered. Instead, with a mission solely focused on securing justice for thousands of wrongly terminated dealers, CRDR was freed from those constraints and better able to pursue courses of action that were fast and targeted. Nonetheless, we were quite happy to have NADA's endorsement. In addition, Iowa dealer and NADA Chairman John McEleney did provide articulate testimony before both House and Senate panels on behalf of the terminated dealers. The support of NADA leadership would prove invaluable in our subsequent negotiations with GM and Chrysler.

Now that CRDR was born, one of our first moves was to secure some expert lobbying assistance. Based on Jack's recommendation, we turned to Dan Renberg, a partner at Arent Fox, the firm with which Jack had already been working. Dan specializes in government relations and is a savvy insider with a lengthy track record of success. Among his other accomplishments, he successfully lobbied the federal government for a major automotive supplier, healthcare firms, and consumer products makers. We were confident in his ability to help us carefully choose our next steps and craft our communication with necessary partners, be they dealer groups or members of Congress, in the months ahead.

One of our first collaborations with Dan came at the perfect time. The House Subcommittee on Oversight and Investigations of the Committee on Energy and Commerce, chaired by Bart Stupak, a conservative Michigan Democrat, was holding a hearing on June 12. The hearing was entitled *GM and Chrysler Dealership Closures and Restructuring.* Subcommittee member Rep. Betty Sutton, who had arranged the pivotal meeting with Steny Hoyer earlier in the month, invited me to testify before the subcommittee *(see sidebar)*. Tony and I spent the entire prior day in the offices of Arent Fox preparing my testimony. My

> HENRY A. WAXMAN, CALIFORNIA
> CHAIRMAN
>
> JOE BARTON, TEXAS
> RANKING MEMBER
>
> ONE HUNDRED ELEVENTH CONGRESS
>
> ## Congress of the United States
> ### House of Representatives
> COMMITTEE ON ENERGY AND COMMERCE
> 2125 RAYBURN HOUSE OFFICE BUILDING
> WASHINGTON, DC 20515-6115
>
> Majority (202) 225-2927
> Minority (202) 225-3641
>
> June 10, 2009
>
> Mr. Alan Spitzer
> Chairman and Chief Executive Officer
> Spitzer Automotive
> 150 East Bridge Street
> Elyria, OH 44035
>
> Dear Mr. Spitzer:
>
> At the request of Rep. Betty Sutton, a member of the Subcommittee on Oversight and Investigations, I am writing to request your testimony at a hearing before the Subcommittee on Friday, June 12, 2009, at 10:00 a.m. in Room 2322 of the Rayburn House Office Building. The hearing is entitled "GM and Chrysler Dealership Closures and Restructuring." Information for witnesses appearing before the Committee is contained in the enclosed Witness Information Sheet. If you have any questions, please contact Theodore Chuang or Scott Schloegel at (202) 226-2424.
>
> Sincerely,
>
> Bart Stupak
> Chairman
> Subcommittee on Oversight and Investigations
>
> Enclosure
>
> cc: Greg Walden
> Ranking Member
> Subcommittee on Oversight and
> Investigations

daughter, Ashley, who was living in the D.C. area, served as our stenographer and was also very helpful as a sounding board as we parsed sentences and carefully searched for just the right words. Dan is an excellent wordsmith, and he checked in with helpful suggestions. The final draft was transmitted to the subcommittee via e-mail at about 8 p.m. Upon submission, we were confident that every word was properly placed and positioned us to have an attention-grabbing few moments the next morning.

It's hard to explain the intense pressure that followed me during this trying time. It wasn't often that I was able to break free for a moment and smell the proverbial roses. The night before I testified before Congress was one of those nights. The significance of the moment was a little overwhelming if I thought about it for very long. We needed to lighten the mood. With that in mind, Tony, Ashley, and I headed to the Cactus Cantina in upper Georgetown for a nice casual dinner of Mexican cuisine, which was a welcomed respite in between what had been several tense and draining days with more certain to follow.

THE $2 BILLION LIE

The Subcommittee on Oversight and Investigations meets in Room 2322 of the Rayburn House Office Building. All the dealer witnesses assembled at NADA's Washington, D.C., headquarters on First Street SE that morning and walked over to the Capitol. When we arrived at 9:30 a.m. for the 10 a.m. hearing, the room was already crowded. C-SPAN was there with cameras rolling so dealers and other interested parties across the country could watch the proceedings on live TV. There were five other dealers scheduled to testify—Robert Thomas, Daniel Kiekenapp, Frank Blankenbeckler III, Jim Golick, and Duane Paddock. We were joined by NADA chairman John McEleney from Iowa, GM CEO Frederick "Fritz" Henderson, and Chrysler co-president James Press. When Stupak gaveled the meeting to order, it was standing room only. I was accompanied by Tony and Ashley who took seats directly behind me. Each member of the committee delivered an opening statement. Most were extremely critical of the car makers' actions.

"Zero, Zero ... Zero!" 93

Swearing-in for Congressional hearing: (l to r) John McEleney, Fritz Henderson, Jim Press, Dan Kiekenapp, Alan Spitzer

Jim Press (right) and Fritz Henderson testify before House Subcommittee

Alan Spitzer and Fritz Henderson listen to testimony

Then it was time for the opening statements of the witnesses. I listened attentively to more of the painful and agonizing stories of the terminated dealers, good people whose lives were being destroyed—for no good reason.

Especially moving was the testimony of Blankenbeckler, owner of Carlisle Chevrolet in Waxahachie, Texas. He was unable to hold back the tears as this third-generation dealer talked about his longtime employees, his family, and especially his late father. "I wear my father's Bronze Star lapel pin on my coat," he said. "He was truly a member of the greatest generation. I'm glad that he is not alive to witness this terrible injustice. To have risked his life for a country that would do what they're doing would have destroyed him. I love my country and I love my state. I feel great pain in what is happening. It is my hope and my prayer that I will be able to continue my life and not be consumed by bitterness should this situation not be reversed and this country not return to the tenets of the Founding Fathers who created it."

Over the next weeks people all over the country, many of whom were not even in the car business, would describe to me how they felt his pain and cried with him.

Each dealer's account was heart rendering. The exception was Paddock who, at the time, was chairman of GM National Dealer Council and was attending at the behest of GM. Not only was his dealership not terminated, he actually defended the terminations. Each carmaker has a National Dealer Council consisting of a group of dealers geographically spread throughout the country who are elected by their peers to meet with manufacturer officials and make recommendations. These bodies are met with varying degrees of cynicism by their fellow dealers, many of whom believe they're only "yes men" (or women) who get wined and dined by "the factory" and then parrot the company line. Conversely, they can often serve as effective sounding boards for new initiatives and occasionally provide valuable input to factory executives. The reality is they serve in a strictly advisory capacity and have no real power to make changes. Having served on national dealer councils for many years, I can attest that there is more than a grain of truth in both points of view.

It was at Stupak's hearings where America heard some of the most appallingly "creative" testimony in history. The lies and half-truths that began in bankruptcy court were now perpetuated by Henderson and Press before Congress. They told us, for instance, that cutting the number of dealers would somehow lead to greater sales. GM CEO Fritz Henderson claimed GM would save more than $1 million per dealership, testimony supplemented by a detailed breakdown of the purported "savings."

The data he submitted was laughable. Most of the alleged "savings" had nothing to do with the number of dealers and everything to do with the number of vehicles sold. "Customer fill-ups" (the courtesy tanks of gas provided to customers on delivery) and consumer rebates are examples. As I wrote in a subsequent letter to the highly respected trade periodical *Automotive News*, "Based on that logic, just think how much GM could 'save' if they didn't sell anything." Other purported savings such as training and special tools were, in fact, not savings at all because they were all paid by the dealers. It was, in short, what *Automotive News* later would dub the "$2 billion lie."[25] Naturally, it infuriated Tammy, Jack, and me—but it also motivated us to redouble our commitment to getting the situation corrected.

For my part, while I knew I needed to refer to our company's plight, I attempted to focus on the big picture and help the subcommittee see the damage from a broader perspective *(see sidebar)*.

It had been an intense and eventful month of June. From the meeting with Hoyer and my testimony in bankruptcy court, the nationally televised hearings in the Senate and the news conference introducing H.R. 2743 to my testimony before a congressional subcommittee and a national TV audience on C-SPAN, our efforts had certainly garnered lots of attention. Tammy and Jack also were highly visible on a regular basis in television interviews in the D.C. area as well as many national programs. Now the real work was just beginning. On the plane ride back to Ohio, Tony and I knew there was no time to reflect on how far we'd come. The ground war would soon begin in the halls of Congress and we would need an army. Somehow,

---

[25] "It's time for GM to admit, finally, its $2 billion lie." *Automotive News*. Nov. 9, 2009.

Testimony of Alan Spitzer before the House Subcommittee on Oversight and Investigations, Rayburn House Office Building, June 12, 2009:

Chairman Stupak, Ranking Member Walden, distinguished members of this Subcommittee, I want to thank you for the honor of appearing here today. I would especially like to thank Congresswoman Sutton for her role in providing me this opportunity to represent my fellow dealers.

We are losing seven dealerships because Chrysler, the bankruptcy court and the executive branch of our government have acted precipitously to deny us our economic rights. This is a public policy issue worthy of your time and worthy of congressional legislation since without your prompt intervention to restore the rights to franchisees under state law, 2,000 small businesses and approximately 100,000 jobs will be lost. As a nation can we really afford to let this take place? I urge Congress to enact H.R. 2743, the bi-partisan Automobile Dealer Economic Rights Restoration Act next week!

We have a long and proud history with Chrysler and GM. The majority of our stores sell these brands and these brands only. None of our stores are dualed with other brands. We have a combined 374 years of business relations with Chrysler alone. We are passionate about both Chrysler and GM and we want both companies to succeed. We are committed to helping them do so. That is why we are both disappointed and perplexed by their recent actions to terminate us and over 2,000 other dealers.

We're not perfect. During those 374 years of operations we've made mistakes. Like Chrysler's managers, our managers aren't perfect either. Nevertheless, we have stood shoulder to shoulder with Chrysler during good times and bad. In fact, my uncle Del, as the president of the Dodge National Dealer Council, lobbied this very Congress for funds to bail out Chrysler the first time. We never quit on them and they shouldn't quit on us and the hundreds of other dealers who remain committed to Chrysler.

This issue is not about the Spitzer family or our seven dealerships that are being terminated or even the 300-plus employees who work in them. It is about destroying the entire net worth and life's work of hundreds of entrepreneurs and the thousands of people they employ. I fear that these actions by Chrysler and GM will lead to their demise. And all of it is unnecessary.

First, our dealerships do not cost manufacturers one dime. All products and services which Chrysler and GM provide are charged back to the dealership at a profit. Whether it's special tools, training or even those colorful brochures, we pay for all of it. We build our own facilities. We provide our own operating capital. We hire our own people. And if we lose money it comes out of our pocket!

Second, Chrysler has argued that the 789 dealerships terminated were for performance reasons or to put all brands under one roof. As demonstrated by the sworn testimony of myself and dozens of other dealers in the bankruptcy court, many of the terminated dealerships were high performing or Genesis stores or both. Chrysler did not terminate dealers for the stated reasons, but rather to rid themselves of outspoken dealers and will now redistribute to other dealers while skirting around the laws of all 50 states; laws which otherwise prohibit this type of arbitrary and capricious action. Profitable, high performing dealerships will be given to our fellow remaining dealers with no due process and no compensation whatsoever.

It is unconscionable for a failed private business to bankrupt another private business which was succeeding, but when our government uses its power, its influence and our money to aid and abet such action it is downright un-American. At a time when our government is spending billions of dollars to stimulate the economy and create new jobs, this action will destroy 37,000 jobs with Chrysler dealers and quite likely another 60,000 or more at GM dealerships. And millions and millions of local tax dollars will be lost. And all for no good reason!

In fact, this plan may ultimately destroy the new Chrysler and severely damage GM's hope of survival. Dealers are their only customers. We are the face of these once proud car companies in our communities. The fact that we have survived and prospered over the last 100 years even as they often produced vehicles American consumers did not want, proves that independent entrepreneurs find ways to survive and create employment opportunities even in tough times.

If Congress does not step in, dealers will be unwilling to invest in new facilities, purchase millions of dollars in inventory and otherwise risk their capital if state law protections are meaningless and if it can all be taken away in the next downturn. Fewer dealers today means fewer sales of Chrysler and GM products tomorrow leading to a further erosion of market share for both companies.

Allow the marketplace to select who lives and who dies, not some committee in Detroit. As of today, approximately 350 of the 789 rejected dealers have accepted their fate by not objecting to their

> terminations. Thus, the accelerated reduction of dealerships has already occurred for those who believe such a reduction was necessary. There is no need to eliminate those of us who remain committed to Chrysler and GM's success.
>
> Thank you, Mr. Chairman, and I can assure you that I will work tirelessly and will not rest until H.R. 2743 becomes law which already has over 100 co-sponsors: Congressman Maffei, Congresswoman Sutton, Congressmen Hoyer and Van Hollen and others who have supported our bill and we've only been out three days. Thank you for your time and I'll answer any questions.

in the back of my mind, I had believed that if Jack and I got the ball rolling, we could step aside and let some amorphous group carry it the rest of the way. But, it was becoming increasingly apparent that wasn't going to happen. The generals in this army of car dealers would have to be Mr. Jack Fitzgerald, Ms. Tamara Darvish, and me.

There were maybe two or three people on the entire planet who had the power to single handedly quash our legislation. Tony and I were about to come face-to-face with one of them in two days: the grand pooh-bah in the U.S. Senate, Majority Leader Harry Reid from Nevada.

"60 Votes? There's No Way!"

We had another key local ally in Sherrod Brown. His election to the U.S. Senate from Ohio in 2006 was a crucial pickup for Democrats because he beat a popular Republican incumbent, Mike DeWine, and his election helped elevate the Democrats, for the time being, to the magic filibuster-proof 60-40 majority. Arcane rules in the U.S. Senate allow the minority party to block legislation through a filibuster where members continue to talk and talk and talk unless 60 of the 100 senators agree to stop debate—a process known as cloture.

Needless to say, Brown was pretty popular with his fellow Senate Democrats—popular enough to entice the top-ranking senator, Majority Leader Reid, to come to Ohio on his behalf. Prior to his election to the Senate, Brown served seven terms in the U.S. House of Representatives from Ohio's 13th Congressional District. Earlier, he was Ohio's Secretary of State. After graduating from Yale University, his first foray into politics was as a state representative from Mansfield. At the start of his political career, he had the distinction of being one of the youngest state reps in Ohio history at the age of 22. Sen. Brown and I had been friends for about three decades and Tony was also a friend and confidante as well.

A few days after the meeting with Hoyer, Brown's office invited us to a reception with Sen. Reid. As we did with Rep. Sutton before the meeting with Hoyer, we asked for a private audience with Reid, and Brown said he would try to accommodate us. "Get there early," he urged. On Sunday, June 14, at 11 a.m., Tony and I arrived at a private residence in Shaker Heights for a noon reception. Minutes later, Sherrod arrived with Sen. Reid in tow through the kitchen. Sherrod introduced Reid to Tony and me then quietly disappeared, leaving us alone for the next 30 minutes with the most powerful man in the U.S. Senate.

Reid was a little standoffish at first. After we broached the topic of the dealer rights legislation that was introduced a few days earlier, he raised his hands in a mock gesture of surrender, saying, "Sixty votes? There's no way!" But he continued to listen, and before long, his body language changed. He became more animated. Soon, he was fully engaged in the conversation, asking questions and making comments that were increasingly positive. Finally he grabbed his pen, wrote down the name of Mark Wetjen, a key aide, and said, "Here's who you call. Tell him you talked to me."

Now, Reid could have let it be known among his colleagues that any dealer legislation was DOA in the Senate. After all, he was close to President Obama and it was Obama who appointed the Automotive Task Force that hatched the plan to terminate dealers. If we could just move Sen. Reid to neutral, it would be a huge victory.

We'll never know the exact impact of our two serendipitous private meetings with Hoyer and Reid, two of the most powerful politicians in the country. What we do know is that Steny Hoyer soon became one of the most passionate advocates on behalf of the terminated dealers, and Sen. Reid didn't lift a finger to impede our efforts.

All Hands on Deck

Alison recruited her husband, Jeremy, her sisters, Ashley and Alana, her brother, Andrew, my nephew, Sean, Cathy Schuster, our company's Director of Real Estate and Development, and Jackie Vella, the wife of Jim Vella, our COO, and other members of our organization to help get CRDR off the ground. The purpose of CRDR was to lead affected dealers through this unprecedented journey. We needed to get the word out to our fellow businessmen and women that we were out there, fighting for them, and we needed their help in spreading the word to increase our visibility. The first step was to canvass the affected dealers. They pulled together the contact list of the 789 Chrysler dealerships and began calling them to seek their support.

(Jack and Tony had previously sent out separate e-mails to the 350 dealers who comprised the largest group in the Chrysler bankruptcy trial—the Committee of Chrysler Affected Dealers—enlisting their contributions.)

During these calls, we weren't necessarily asking for dollars—though that wouldn't have hurt the cause. At this point, contributions were strictly voluntary, based on the ability to pay. We knew that so many of these dealers had been staggered by the closures and simply might not have the cash to spare.

Two of our early supporters, Chrysler dealer John Zimmer and GM dealer Bud Robke, actually drove from their home in Kentucky—about 10 hours, round trip—to meet me in person. They wanted to tell me face-to-face how grateful they were that someone was making an effort to help them. Both men told me about their businesses, their families, and the devastation that had befallen them. It was a very emotional meeting.

Some dealers, stripped of their Chrysler affiliation, hobbled along selling used cars. But many dealers didn't survive in any form after their Rejection. Did that mean the Rejection was a good business decision? Not at all—it was only a fatal blow to businesses on the edge, at a time when our nation was reeling from the worst economy since the Great Depression.

We developed simple scripts and called each dealer personally to ask them to support our cause and press their legislators to support our bill. A great many of the dealers mentioned that they'd seen my testimony on C-SPAN when I spoke about the legislation and pleaded with Congress to consider it as soon as possible. So many dealers told Alison and her team that they were just so happy that someone was *doing* something to help them. It was not unusual for dealers to weep as they told their stories and expressed their gratitude.

Next, we started the more challenging task of cold-calling people who would be decidedly more skeptical about CRDR: members of the United States Congress. We weren't always successful in breaking through to every congressman, but we nonetheless had remarkable results in just a few weeks. Many of the people we spoke to had already been heavily educated by the dealers or trade association executives in their districts and states. We were reaching them from multiple sides and it was clear that our message was getting through—and resonating. Our lobbying efforts soon evolved into a multi-pronged approach, including individual dealers and their employees, the Automotive Trade Association Executives and Dan Renberg and his associates at Arent Fox.

Meanwhile, however, GM and Chrysler weren't sitting still. They were enlisting their networks of surviving dealers to contact legislators to oppose our bill. They were attempting to pit dealer *vs.* dealer. It was ultimately a very unsuccessful strategy. They just weren't able to generate anywhere near the same level of enthusiasm from the go-forward dealers compared with the terminated dealers who were "hell bent for leather." Both car companies were severely criticized by the trade press for this initiative and it soon fizzled.

"We're In the Game!"

Just after noon on July 7, I got a call and a follow up e-mail from Kate Ostrander from Rep. LaTourette's office to give me a heads-up that LaTourette succeeded in getting our legislation into the "mark-up" phase of the powerful Appropriations Committee where representatives meet to review the text of a bill and offer amendments.

From: Ostrander, Kate
Sent: Tuesday, July 07, 2009 1:41 PM
To: Alan Spitzer
Subject: markup amendments, 7/7—LaTourette

Dear Mr. Spitzer—

Steve wanted me to share with you that he is offering two amendments today at the House Financial Services Approps mark-up. This is happening in the full committee—appropriations. His first amendment proposes to de-fund the auto task force. The other works in language from the Auto Dealer Economic Rts Restoration Act to prohibit the federal government from spending funds to provide for dealership closures.

He wanted to make sure you had info about it. The mark-up begins at 7 PM.

Thanks.

Below is the write-up we are sending around:

Mr. LaTourette will be offering two amendments to the Financial Services approps bill.

- One will de-fund the auto task force. Specifically, none of the funds made available in the Act may be used to pay salaries or expenses related to the Presidential Task Force on the Auto Industry. (This is similar to the amendment that Mr. Gohmert tried to offer to the CJS bill on the House floor.)

- The other prohibits the federal government from spending funds to provide for dealership closures. It takes language from H.R. 2796, the Automobile Dealer Economic Rights Restoration Act. The amendment states that no funds may be made available in this Act (or any other) to obtain a financial interest or ownership interest in an automobile manufacturer that deprives an automobile dealer of its economic rights under a dealer agreement and does not assume (or assign to a successor) each dealer agreement which is valid and in existence (and has not been lawfully terminated under applicable State law) before the date of the commencement of a case under Ch 11 bankruptcy by such automobile manufacturer. Effectively, if Chrysler or GM cancelled a franchise while going into bankruptcy without passing that franchise on to the newly established company, this amendment prohibits any funds for that action. If Chrysler or GM have done so, the amendment requires the new entity created to enter into a new dealer agreement on the exact same terms.

These amendments stem from the Chrysler bankruptcy and the subsequent three bills that were introduced in the House (and one in the Senate) to prevent the dealer closures, H.R. 2743, H.R. 2750, and H.R. 2796. Chrysler and GM are attempting to arbitrarily and unilaterally close more than 2,000 dealerships across the country by stripping away protections afforded those dealers by state franchising laws under bankruptcy funded by the federal government. According to estimates, these dealership closings will result in the immediate loss of more than 100,000 direct jobs. More than 200 Members of the House have cosponsored H.R. 2743, including more than 30 Members of the House Appropriations Committee. NADA has supported efforts to address the situation.

Kate Ostrander
Legislative Director
Congressman Steven C. LaTourette
2371 Rayburn House Office Building
Washington, DC 20515
202-xxx-xxxx

These committee meetings often start with members offering some opening remarks. Then they read the bill aloud and committee members can submit proposed amendments to each section. Committees typically debate these proposed amendments for about five minutes each. Usually, a committee doesn't change the actual text of the bill, but only votes on the proposed amendments that members want to recommend to the House when it considers the bill on the floor. The final result of a mark-up is called "reporting the bill to the House" with the amendments it has approved. Getting into the mark-up phase was another important milestone for us. The overall bill was for appropriations for the Securities and Exchange Commission. Since the SEC was managed by the U.S. Treasury Department and the Auto Task Force also reported in to the Treasury, LaTourette's strategy was to amend the House Financial Services

Appropriations Bill to include our language regarding dealership closures. He knew that if our language was attached to an appropriations (spending) bill, there would be no possibility of a presidential veto.

The evening session was available for viewing on the House website via streaming video. I eagerly turned on my PC when I got home that evening so my wife, Pat, and I could watch it together. I called Dan Renberg, who also planned to catch the broadcast. Unfortunately, I wasn't able to reach Jack or Tammy to inform them of this important development ahead of time.

All 60 members of the House Committee on Appropriations were present—a surprising 100-percent attendance rate—when Chairman Dave Obey (D-WI) banged the gavel and called the meeting to order. Several sponsors introduced amendments and there were several narrow votes, too close to determine by voice vote thus necessitating a roll call from the clerk requiring all 60 members of the committee to say "aye" or "nay." However, since we had 32 co-sponsors for our legislation on the committee—in other words, a majority of the committee's members—we felt as if we'd be in good shape. When our amendment came up, there wasn't a "nay" to be heard in the voice vote.

Dan called me on my cell phone immediately afterward. "We're in the game!" he said excitedly. It was a nice call to get, to say the least.

Chapter 9

"HOW DO YOU SLEEP AT NIGHT?"

Democracy is the only system that persists in asking the powers that be whether they are powers that ought to be.

Sydney Harris

Our lobbying efforts, both professional and grassroots, were beginning to yield impressive results. Dan and his team were making contacts with staffers in Congress with whom they had relationships. The Automotive Trade Association Executives was calling members of Congress daily to urge various representatives to support our bill. And the recently recruited members of CRDR from around the country were working the phones as well. Jack and Rob were now making daily visits to Capitol Hill.

After Alison and her team had finished cold-calling the offices of hundreds of Congressional representatives and senators—and after we had successfully emerged from the Appropriations

Committee's markup—Tammy recommended that CRDR make ourselves heard in another key way: face-to-face meetings.

CRDR orchestrated a massive "fly-in" involving hundreds of terminated Chrysler and GM dealers on July 14—coincidentally, the day the Rules Committee would meet about the appropriations bill. The purpose of the fly-in was to storm the halls of Congress to urge support for our legislation, add more names to our 238 co-sponsors of H.R. 2743 and the 18 co-sponsors of S. 1304, the Senate companion bill to H.R. 2743—and defy the so-called experts who continued to predict our demise.

For about two weeks prior to the event, Alison and Tammy worked feverishly with dealers all over the country coordinating appointments with various members of the House and Senate. Tammy and her team, led by Courtney Wallin, did amazing work pulling the event together—even arranging the numerous buses we'd need to transport our CRDR members around the city. We were ready to make a real impact.

On July 13, we had lunch with LaTourette, one of our key Republican allies who recently performed the miracle in the Appropriations Committee. (Of course, mindful of ethics violations, the congressman paid for his own lunch.) Dan, Tony, Rob, Alison, Tammy, Jack, and I were there with LaTourette. We talked with great excitement and enthusiasm about our recent success. "That's all great," Steve said, "but we still need to get past the Rules Committee tomorrow. There's a very real possibility that some Democrats will try to strip out our language. They'll be facing some strong pressure from the White House on this."

"Now, there's a rule forbidding policy amendments on spending bills—so that might be the argument we face there. It's a technicality, but it's possible. If they do use that as the basis for removing the amendment, I'm going to file a protest and raise holy hell because they (the Democrats) do this kind of thing all the time."

The night of the 13th, a large gathering of our members met at a wine-and-cheese reception at the Renaissance Hotel near Capitol Hill on Ninth Street. Tammy, a NADA director, had quietly and patiently (well, maybe not so patiently) brought NADA into the fold, possibly kicking and screaming. Although NADA never made a direct financial contribution, they did fund our reception that evening. More importantly, they came to recognize that these dealership terminations set a terrible precedent, particularly since Ford or Toyota or any other car company could easily follow suit in the coming months and years.

Tammy and Rob Smith were busy coordinating the many details that needed to be attended to. Tammy served as emcee for the presentations. When she introduced Jack and me, the room of about 200 gave us a standing ovation. The feeling of camaraderie was palpable. I think we both felt a heightened sense of commitment after that evening. On the dais with Jack and me were NADA vice president David Regan, incoming NADA chairman Ed Tonkin and ATAE chairman Tim Doran. Regan reiterated NADA's support of the legislation. Tim then gave a passionate talk in support of our bill. Tonkin was more subdued, hinting that the best outcome the dealers could hope for might be a cash settlement—not a popular sentiment based on the audience's reaction. They wanted their franchises back. (Ed would later become an articulate and passionate advocate for the terminated dealers in negotiations with both car companies.)

Jack was up next. When you first meet Jack, he comes off as mild mannered as Clark Kent. Give him a microphone and he turns into Superman. He gave a rousing firebrand of a speech saying, "This is America and we're not gonna let these companies do

Alan Spitzer and Rep. Steve LaTourette at press conference

this to us." He got another standing ovation. I followed Jack to the podium and learned that it's not advisable to follow Jack. I merely reiterated most of his points and congratulated the group for surpassing the 50 percent threshold for co-sponsors in the House. Dan wrapped up the evening with a brief tutorial for the next day's efforts. You might call it "Lobbying 101."

In the weeks prior, Tammy and Alison's teams secured dozens of appointments with key legislators for the fly-in. Suitably prepped and motivated, hundreds of CRDR members fanned out across Capitol Hill the following morning. We literally swarmed the halls of Congress.

While most dealers were scheduled to meet with legislators from their respective states, Tammy, Jack, and I travelled together, attempting to make contact with Congressional leaders. We were able to get an audience with Steny Hoyer and Chris Van Hollen (No. 6 in the House) together. Then we were off to meet with Mark Wetjen, legislative counsel to Sen. Harry Reid, where Tony again articulately made the case for passage of the legislation. We also met some of the key staffers for Rep. Nancy Pelosi (D-CA), the Speaker of the House. She was very cautious and even in her dealings with our people, making it very difficult to get a read on her.

"How Do You Sleep At Night?"

At midday, the swampy D.C. humidity was hard to ignore as we convened a press conference on the lawn in front of the Capitol building where we shepherded several Congressional leaders from *both* parties in front of the cameras to express their support for our efforts to overturn the unjust closures. Hoyer, Van Hollen, and LaTourette all gave passionate speeches on behalf of the dealers and their employees. Rep. Sheila Jackson-Lee (D-TX) gave a particularly rousing oratory imploring Congress to pass the "dealer *civil* rights" bill. NADA Directors Michelle Primm and Kathleen Sims both spoke on behalf of NADA's women dealers east and west of the Mississippi. Each woman questioned the illogical notion of expecting higher sales from fewer dealerships. Michelle delivered a powerful and provocative line when she exclaimed, "If McDonald's wants to sell *more* hamburgers, they don't do it by closing 3,000 restaurants." Also speaking was Lelica Callaremi, daughter of successful GM dealer Mike Callaremi from NJ, whose family was devastated after receiving a Wind Down notice. She asked an emotional and pointed question: "Mr. Press, Mr. Henderson: How do you sleep at night?"

Another member of Congress who spoke articulately on behalf of dealers that day was Rep. Sutton, who had been with us from the very beginning. Rep. Sutton would soon further burnish her credentials as an advocate of automobile dealers by shepherding the popular "Cash for Clunkers" legislation through the House.

Once again, Tammy served as our emcee. She's very comfortable and confident in the limelight. Her two children, Nadia and Nima, were there getting a real-life civics lesson as was my 16 year old son, AJ, who was spending the week in D.C. attending a National Young Leaders Conference (where, ironically, several hundred teenagers conduct a mock Congress). Another irony and complete coincidence was the day of the event: Bastille Day. On July 14, 1789, hundreds of French citizens stormed the prison known as the Bastille in protest to win back their rights. Today, there were hundreds of car dealers "storming" the Capitol for the same purpose—albeit more peacefully.

Tammy Darvish speaks at press conference during dealer "fly-in"

In all, the event accomplished everything we had hoped for. We created much more media attention; dozens more members of Congress met face-to-face with dealer constituents; and the dealers who attended, virtually all members of CRDR by now, got a shot in the arm. Kudos to Tammy, Rob and their team on the ground for the huge task of organizing the activities.

NEXT STOP: RULES COMMITTEE

Later that same day, the small Rules Committee meeting room was packed. Every seat was taken and, stationed behind Steve LaTourette, at his request, I was a little tense as the proceedings got underway. So much was at stake and our opposition—the White House and two of the world's largest manufacturers—would be more than formidable foes.

There are several steps required to get a piece of legislation enacted into law. After a bill is drafted, it is introduced by its sponsor and assigned to the appropriate committee. (Our legislation, H.R. 2743, was introduced in the House and sponsored by Rep. Dan Maffei (D-NY) on June 8. It was assigned to the

Jack Fitzgerald testified before the House Committee on the Judiciary

House Committee on Financial Services, chaired by Rep. Barney Frank (D-MA)).

That committee holds hearings on the merits of the proposed legislation. Both proponents and opponents may testify at the hearings at the discretion of the committee chair. (Most bills don't even get this far. They die in committee without the first hearing). If the committee votes in favor of the bill, it is sent to the Rules Committee. (The need for a hearing on H.R. 2743 was precluded when Rep. LaTourette was successful in getting similar language attached as an amendment to another bill.)

The primary function of the Rules Committee is to decide when, or if, the proposed legislation ever reaches the floor of the chamber for a full vote of all the members, or as the politicians like to say "see the light of day." The Rules Committee is the domain of the Speaker of the House. The Speaker appoints all the committee's members and, as a general rule, appoints only those members who will agree with the Speaker somewhere between 99 and 100 percent of the time. Many bills get bottled up in Rules for long periods of time, often to die a slow death without ever "seeing the light of day." It pays to be on the right side of the Speaker.

When and if the Rules Committee "votes the bill out," it moves to the floor of the chamber. The bill then goes to the other chamber and the process starts all over. Often, to speed up the process, both House and Senate introduce the same (or companion) legislation simultaneously so the bills can move through the system concurrently. Any differences between the two bills are ironed out by a Joint Conference Committee comprised of members from both chambers. After it passes both Houses of Congress the bill goes to the President for his signature. Of course, the President has the power to veto any bill, which kills it unless two-thirds of the legislature vote to override the President's veto.

When our moment came and the Rules Committee reviewed our proposed amendment to the appropriations bill, LaTourette stood before the room and passionately defended it. Who knew that something as mundane as arcane Congressional rules could be so dramatic? But it was. And when the vote was taken, the amendment passed unanimously. It was another milestone victory for CRDR.

However, we weren't out of the woods—far from it. We, of course, still needed a full passage of the House Financial Services Appropriations Bill in the House by a majority of its 435 members. Several abortion-related amendments had been tacked on in committee that were unacceptable to many Republicans and that was a concern. In many cases their opposition to those amendments trumped their support for our legislation. This would be no smooth sailing. The next day I returned to Ohio with cautious optimism.

Late in the afternoon of Thursday, July 16, from our corporate offices in Elyria, Jim Vella, our COO, and I sat and watched the voting on C-SPAN. It was a close call, but the bill passed a roll-call vote, 219-208. It was on to the Senate.

A few weeks earlier, on June 18, our first sponsor and supporter in the Senate, Chuck Grassley (R-IA) had introduced our bill,

S. 1304), into that chamber. Meanwhile, Jack and Rob continued the painstaking work of actively knocking on the doors of various Senate offices. Jack and Rob's face-to-face meetings solidified our support and yielded even more co-sponsors, including the late Sen. Edward M. (Ted) Kennedy (D-MA). The dealer rights legislation was to be one of the last bills he would co-sponsor.

Thanks to their efforts and our successful fly-in, our impressive list of co-sponsors continued to grow. By the end of July, our roster of co-sponsors had grown to 272 in the House and 34 in the Senate.

The White House continued to voice its opposition, saying it was "strongly opposed" *(see sidebar)*. Notably, their statement of opposition stopped short of threatening a presidential veto, an important distinction in the subtle and nuanced language of Washington.

A potential breakthrough opportunity presented itself in late July. John Hughes, Steny Hoyer's senior policy advisor, arranged for a meeting between Ron Bloom, who was about to succeed Rattner as "car czar," Brian Deese, and retired Chrysler executive, E. T. (Tom) Pappert. Tom began his career with Chrysler as a trainee in 1962 and had risen to the rank of vice president of sales and service when Chrysler was under the leadership of Lee A. Iacocca. Tom was firmly convinced that the dealer reductions were not in Chrysler's best interests and, unlike anyone on the Auto Team, had extensive experience on the subject. Jack, Tammy, and I had known Tom for years and we were excited about the prospect of Bloom and Deese meeting with him. He knew more about automotive retailing than anyone the Auto Team had met with to date. Maybe, just maybe, their minds could be changed and the terminations reversed.

The White House Comes Out Against CRDR

Department of the Treasury

The Administration strongly opposes the language in the bill that attempts to restore prior Chrysler and General Motors (GM) franchise agreements. The auto companies, like many in the country, face difficult economic and fiscal decisions. The Administration shares the Committee's concern for dealers affected by Chrysler and GM bankruptcy agreements, and has taken steps to help support viable dealerships during this transition. For example, on July 1st, the Small Business Administration implemented a new program to provide guaranteed floor plan financing loans. However, the decision by Chrysler and GM to rationalize their dealer networks was a critical part of their overall restructuring to achieve long-term viability in order to save jobs in the long run, and to improve the prospects for the companies' repayment of the substantial taxpayer investments. Without the significant steps these automakers have taken to revamp their operations, the companies would have failed—imperiling every GM and Chrysler dealer in the country. Under the automakers' new structure, the overwhelming majority of GM and Chrysler dealers will continue operating with the new companies. The decision to invest taxpayer dollars into these companies required all stakeholders to make difficult sacrifices, and it would set a dangerous precedent, potentially raising legal concerns, to intervene into a closed Judicial bankruptcy proceeding on behalf of one particular group at this point.

http://www.whitehouse.gov/omb/assets/sap_111/saphr3170h_20090715.pdf

From: Tammy Darvish
To: Haley Stevens
Cc: John Hughes
Subject: Meeting with Mr. Pappert
Sent: Jul 30, 2009 10:59 PM

Dear Ms. Stevens:

At the request of John Hughes, we are confirming that Mr. Pappert will be available to meet with Mr. Bloom and Mr. Deese tomorrow (7/31/09) at 10:30am. He will be accompanied by Mr. John Fitzgerald. Their personal information is as follows:

Mr. Edward Thomas Pappert
DOB 10-17-39
SS# xxx-xx-xxxx

Mr. John J. Fitzgerald Jr.
DOB 9-27-35
SS# xxx-xx-xxxx

Please email the proper address and location so that we can insure they arrive in the right place at the right time. We really appreciate this generous opportunity, and please feel free to contact me anytime if you require any additional information.

Most Sincerely,
Tamara C. Darvish
Cell: 202-xxx-xxxx

The meeting took place in a small conference room in the Treasury building at 10:30 a.m. on Friday, July 31. Tom was accompanied by Jack and Rob who were cleared to attend as Mr. Pappert's "escorts." Bloom showed up a little after 10:30; Deese did not show at all.

Tom was given about three minutes to explain why the dealer reduction/brand consolidation plan on which Chrysler and GM were embarking would result in fewer sales for the car companies. Then, for the next seven minutes Bloom took the floor and proceeded to explain that, while his auto experience was not deep, it was broad. He extended both arms to make the point. He was once quoted saying, "Let me give you some advice. First, we are big believers in dentist-chair bargaining. For those of you not familiar with this approach, it is inspired by the story of the man who walks into his dentist's office, grabs the dentist by the balls and says, 'Now, let's not hurt each other.'"[26]

The Auto Team had consulted with "experts," stated Mr. Bloom, who went on to explain to this highly regarded Chrysler executive how wrong he was, despite Pappert's 30 years of experience. The meeting lasted all of 10 minutes when Bloom abruptly ended the discussion and left his three guests sitting in the conference room. The meeting that seemed too good to be true turned out to be exactly that.

Later that day, Pappert met with about two dozen Congressional staffers and some Congressmen to give his views on the subject. The audience was much more receptive than Bloom had been. We even picked up a couple more co-sponsors.

Our Momentum Stalls in the August Recess

Things cooled off significantly and our momentum stalled during the August recess. Intensely, we worked the phones during this time and sketched out a strategy for achieving victory in the Senate. Seeking face time with a busy group of officials, we were pursuing it at exactly the wrong time. In August 2009, legislators were returning to their districts, only to find—thanks to a rising tide of concern over the nascent national health care plan and the state of the nation's economy—wave after wave of angry constituents at various conferences, gatherings, and

---

[26] Bloom, Ron, Remarks to INSOL International Annual Regional Conference, Fairmont Scottsdale Princess, Scottsdale, AZ, May 21, 2006

"town hall" meetings. On the defensive, the senators we sought to meet with were far too preoccupied with responding to voters on other matters.

Still, we kept chipping away. I spent most of the month attempting to talk with Senate staffers. Alison and Jeremy set up conference-call appointments and recruited a dealer from the senator's state to be on the call. It's always more effective, in some cases mandatory, to have a constituent in the mix.

Meanwhile, Jack and Rob continued to "pound the pavement" on Capitol Hill. They were in and out of Senate offices on a daily basis to plead the case of the terminated dealers. They were well armed with reams of hard data prepared by Jack and his team.

Tammy was quite adept at communicating with the dealers who joined our efforts. While I was sending occasional e-mails to our members, Tammy did a wonderful job of keeping them informed on a regular basis. This was particularly important during the August recess. We wanted to regain the momentum we had built in July.

One of the most important allies we had was Tim Doran from the Automotive Trade Association Executives or ATAE (a group of 103 executive directors from different local, state and regional auto dealer associations.) Each member represents a variety of local dealers and their job is to know the politicians. Since we figured they could be very helpful, we immediately partnered with them back in June. It was especially fortuitous that I'd known Tim for more than 25 years. The year of 2009 was "his year" to run the organization and he played a key role in the "fly-in" lobbying in July. Earlier, he'd been active in the bankruptcy proceedings. He was solidly behind CRDR. Over the course of our many months of collaboration, we grew to appreciate his colorful, smart, and uniquely articulate ways.

But, as can sometimes be the case with powerful, driven personalities, we would soon have our own internecine battles to resolve.

CHAPTER 10

THE SCHISM—TRYING TO NEGOTIATE A SOLUTION

*Every ... house divided against itself
shall not stand.*

Matthew 12:25

GM and Chrysler were not without their own legislative supporters, of course. And after they suffered their setback in the House, a great deal of behind-the-scenes wrangling ensued. Most significantly, some leading legislators and their staffers consulted with GM and Chrysler and made it clear to the automakers that CRDR and our allies had the critical mass and momentum to get dealer terminations overturned. Their advice to the manufacturers: sit down with the dealers and cut a deal. Otherwise, Congress would pass the bill and that measure would have far less favorable terms.

Both GM and Chrysler agreed to negotiate—but not with our committee. Initially the companies refused to acknowledge our existence and took the position that they would only negotiate with NADA. Eventually, again after more pressure from our Congressional supporters, both companies acquiesced and CRDR was given a seat at the table. After all, wasn't the Committee to Restore Dealer Rights the only organization that represented the terminated dealers exclusively?

John Hughes, senior policy advisor to Steny Hoyer and a key member of his staff, and David Weaver, the chief of staff for Chris Van Hollen, were the point men from the House. On the Senate side, it was Albert Sanders from Dick Durbin's office. Sanders was no-nonsense, and I had enjoyed my earlier conversations with him. You didn't get doubletalk or political speak from Sanders. It was only straight talk. He immersed himself in these negotiations and I believed he could help us significantly. Surely the Senate was our Achilles heel. Hughes and Weaver appeared unwavering in their support for terminated dealers, although Weaver seemed a bit more steadfast. It's possible that was just a difference in personalities.

These Congressional leaders came to all of us—CRDR, NADA, the ATAE, and the North American Minority Auto Dealers (NAMAD)—and asked for our consensus regarding how they should approach these negotiations with the automakers. The meeting took place in Steny Hoyer's large offices on Aug. 3. And that's when our competing priorities started to surface.

With so many different cooks in the kitchen, it was only natural, I suppose, that there would be different opinions about how to proceed. What I hadn't anticipated was that the differences would be so large and the opinions so strongly held. Unfortunately, other commitments kept me from attending that pivotal Aug. 3 meeting. While I realized there were divergent views among us about the best approach to use in negotiating with the car companies, I assumed reasonable minds would prevail and we would hash out a proposal that everyone could live with. I quickly learned that our meeting, whose purpose was to come up with a unified offer to manufacturers, had ended in an acrimonious impasse. Soon after, my BlackBerry started to buzz with messages—some unprintable—from my colleagues about the failure to reach a compromise. The Type A personalities that helped us all succeed could sometimes make it more difficult to negotiate and compromise.

I later said to Alison, "I'm not going to miss one more meeting—the stakes are too high." Here we were, just trying to set the table for a round of non-legislatively driven negotiations with automakers and we couldn't even agree among ourselves.

There was consensus among us that binding arbitration by neutral third parties would be an acceptable compromise to the automatic reinstatement called for in the legislation. However, the various groups had very different notions of what metrics should be used for consideration by the arbitrators. We disagreed about the procedures for arbitration, the terms, the parameters, the scope—just about everything. In our opinion, NADA and Tim Doran seemed to give too much weight to the manufacturers' criteria defining which dealerships to cut. Were they trying to tacitly placate the manufacturers or did they just not want to stand up to them? I'd known Tim too long to believe that was the case with him. Nevertheless all sides remained intractable and a potential catastrophe loomed.

September 3: Our Détente

Exactly one month later, on September 3, with much more urgency, representatives of the four groups agreed to reconvene in Washington, D.C., to try to hash out a final agreement. This time, I made sure I was there. I wanted to see if I could help break this logjam . Alison, Tammy, Rob, Jack, Dan, and I joined Maryland and D.C. area trade execs Pete Kitzmiller and Gerry

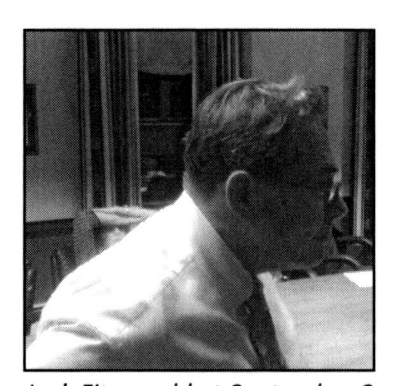

Jack Fitzgerald at September 3 negotiating session with four dealer groups. (Tensions were high).

Tammy Darvish listens during September 3 session with dealer groups

Murphy for a working lunch at Bullfeathers on Capitol Hill. Apparently, the restaurant was a popular choice on the Hill—our counterparts from NADA dined just a few tables away.

At 3 p.m. we gathered in the Majority Leader's conference room. But after a long and tiring afternoon, we had no results. After spinning our wheels for hours, we were at an utter impasse. There wasn't any name-calling, but I don't think we were all that far away from it, either.

We were stuck right where we'd been when the schism first hit in early August. Only now, time was running out. Without agreement on a unified proposal for these non-legislative negotiations, we were done. Cooked. Finished. There would be no negotiations. Our supporters in Congress insisted on *one* proposal. It would be back to the Senate to lobby for our legislation where we knew we were still fighting an uphill battle. We were wearing out our welcome in the halls of Congress and were about to be done in by our own infighting.

The temperatures in the room were near the boiling point and our time was up. We left the Majority Leader's offices and the whiff of failure was strong. Jack was adamant that we move forward with our committee's proposal. But as everyone stood outside, rather aimlessly, ready to go their separate ways in frustration, I said to my dealer partners, "Let's keep going. We *have* to keep talking. We can't leave it here. We have to keep going." Tammy agreed.

Reluctantly at first, we agreed to keep the dialogue going. NADA has offices on Capitol Hill and Tammy suggested we walk up there to continue the conversation and see if we could find common ground, hammer out an agreement, and present that crucial united front to the manufacturers. As we walked, I sidled up to Dan. "Dan," I said quietly, "you're the key here. You have the respect of everyone in these negotiations—and you're a great wordsmith, to boot. We need you to take control of these negotiations. You can be the catalyst, the broker who can pull us all together." He nodded in modesty and agreed to assume a leadership role to break this impasse.

Tim Doran hadn't been able to attend that day's session, having other commitments to attend to. Tim's was a very influential voice. I wasn't sure if his absence would possibly speed things along—only to have them sidetracked when he rejoined the process later. I knew no proposal would be submitted that he hadn't signed on to. He'd been unrelenting in his feeling that the arbitrations and appeals *had* to incorporate the manufacturers' criteria.

Ohio Automobile Dealers Association president Tim Doran was also chairman of the Automotive Trade Association Executives

Jack, meanwhile, felt that the quality of the vehicles was a huge and overlooked issue. He was insisting that data from *Consumer Reports* be included among the criteria. "If the quality of the product isn't there, then who, really, underperformed?" he said, not unpersuasively. He felt the manufacturers' criteria was fatally flawed and should have no weight whatsoever. Regardless, we had to keep going. And we did—until after 10 p.m. that night. That's when we finally reached an agreement. Predictably, we compromised somewhere between Tim's and Jack's positions.

The e-mail exchange below with my friend and fellow Wind Down dealer Craig Wierda from Holland, Michigan, characterizes the tension of the negotiations:

From: Craig Wierda
Date: Thu, 3 Sep 2009 20:06:46 -0400
To: Alan Spitzer
Subject: Today

Alan,
How did it go today?

From: Alan Spitzer
To: Craig Wierda
Sent: Thu Sep 03 20:19:08 2009
Subject: Re: Today

Met with legislative staff from 3:30—6:00. Could not get on same page with NADA. We adjourned to NADA offices and are still going at it.

From: Craig Wierda
Date: Thu, 3 Sep 2009 20:54:23 -0400
To: Alan Spitzer
Subject: Re: Today

I do not understand why they are there.
They do not have a dog in the fight.

From: Alan Spitzer
To: Craig Wierda
Sent: Thu Sep 03 21:25:34 2009
Subject: Re: Today

The problem is they have had a presence with the legislature for many years so it's hard to get them to see that. We did make a lot of progress. I think we may wear them out.

Thanks
AS

As is common in these kinds of situations, it seemed as if it really all came together in that final hour of negotiations. By deleting a phrase or two here and inserting a phrase or two there, we had the drafting done in less than 30 minutes. Soon, everyone was comfortable.

Our next task: send it to Tim, which we did that very night. David Regan, vice president of NADA's Legislative Affairs Group, made the call and we held our collective breath. Fortunately, and somewhat surprisingly, he was fine with our proposal. Alison and I then made our way to the airport for a very late flight home. As we flew back to Ohio, I had a moment to reflect on how difficult this all was. As a young student, I'd paid attention in civics classes, but I'd never realized just how much wrangling, negotiation, and compromise was required to move the wheels of government. Democracy can be a torturous and winding process.

The next morning, my phone rang—it was Tim.

"How'd you do that?" he wanted to know.

"Hey," I replied, "I told you I wouldn't miss any more meetings."

"Maybe it was a good thing I wasn't there."

"You think?" I replied with a laugh.

The fact was, even though we'd all been at loggerheads, Tim's approval was still crucial. While I liked to think that CRDR had a high profile, it was a fact that Congress had a decades-long relationship with NADA. And although Tim was technically not representing NADA in these discussions, that was a moot point. It was clear that NADA would never support a position that Tim opposed. His influence over the organization's leadership was that powerful. With our ducks lined up, we were ready to enter these high-stakes negotiations with the manufacturers—under the auspices and watchful eyes of numerous Congressional leaders.

Outline of Alternative Solutions
Offered by NADA, NAMAD, ATAE, and CRDR
September 3, 2009

1. Establishment of transparency for individual dealers
   a. Disclosure of the precise objective criteria/standards used to identify the wind down GM dealers with continuing brands and the rejected Chrysler dealers (collectively the "Affected Dealers") as applied to an individual Affected Dealer.

2. Procedure for reinstatement of dealers.
   a. Any disputes about wind down, termination or rejection will be resolved by an Arbitration Panel, including but not limited to reinstatement.
   b. An Arbitration Panel shall decide whether the decision to terminate/wind down was objective and fair, based substantially on: 1) the standard for termination of a franchise under state motor vehicle franchise laws; and 2) the dealer's financial viability. Other factors may be proposed by GM or Chrysler and the Affected Dealer, including demographic and geographic characteristics in the Affected Dealer's market.

THE SCHISM—TRYING TO NEGOTIATE A SOLUTION

    c. "Arbitration Panel" for any dispute herein means: 1) a balanced three-person panel composed of a manufacturer's representative, the Affected Dealer's representative, and a neutral party agreed to by the other parties; and 2) a binding proceeding based in the dealer's state, governed by the rules of the American Arbitration Association with decisions governed by the Federal Arbitration Act.

    d. GM and Chrysler will automatically offer reinstatement to any Affected Dealer that meets or exceeds the manufacturer's respective objective criteria/standards previously disclosed.

    e. Affected Dealers shall have the right of first refusal to reenter their respective relevant markets upon qualifying with the manufacturer's requirements. If denied such right, dealers may challenge the decision before an Arbitration Panel and seek damages.

3. For rejected, wind-down, and terminated Affected Dealers, compensation based on the following:

    a. Each dealer: $3,000 per vehicle sold in one of three calendar years 2006, 2007, or 2008, as specified by the dealer.

    b. Exigent circumstances: Includes, without limitation, costs paid by dealers at the urging of the manufacturers since January 1, 2005 to acquire real estate, improve facilities, or pay for the blue sky for another franchise.

    c. Payment to a GM Affected Dealer will be the greater of the wind down agreement payment or the compensation under 3a and 3b.

    d. Affected Dealers may appeal disputes about 3a and 3b to an Arbitration Panel.

4. GM agrees to address open issues related to the wind down dealers including allowing wind down dealers the following:

a. Continued ability to purchase vehicles at GM auctions;
   b. Continued ability to purchase "Warehouse" (unallocated) vehicles;
   c. Continued ability to make dealer trades;
   d. Ability to obtain delivery of "sold" orders;
   e. Ability to wind down earlier than January 1, 2010 and receive full payments;
   f. Continued ability of remaining GM franchises to receive parts for Pontiac on same terms and conditions; and
   g. The compensation described in item 3 shall be available to Saturn, Saab, and Hummer dealers in the event that those brands are not sold but are ultimately wound down by GM.
   h. Revision of the medium-duty truck wind down agreement (currently based on the Pontiac wind down agreement) to reflect the commercial truck business.

5. Agreement to support transitional tax package (LIFO relief, 1031 exchange, QFOBI relief, etc.) and other transitional issues (i.e., pension liability, product liability) for dealers that lost franchises.

6. Agreement by the Auto Task Force to work with GMAC and other TARP recipients to (i) remove barriers to floorplan financing, working capital, and retail financing for Chrysler and GM dealers; and (ii) end oppressive tactics like terminations not based on material defaults, audit fees, and noncompliance fees, or unfair enforcement of personal guaranties.

7. An affirmative statement from the Auto Task Force and from GM and Chrysler that dealers are the manufacturers' customers, that they are distribution and warranty service outlets generating sales for the manufacturers, and that they absorb virtually all of manufacturers' costs related to the retail distribution of motor vehicles.

Chapter 11

LET THE NEGOTIATIONS BEGIN

In union there is strength.

Aesop

On September 30, we were ready to meet face-to-face with representatives from the automobile manufacturers to negotiate a framework for arbitration and appeals. Dozens of people gathered in room H207 in the Capitol Building—the conference room adjacent to the office of House Majority Leader Steny Hoyer. There was to be one combined session with Chrysler and GM. Then, due to restraint of trade issues, each company would meet with us separately to discuss specific terms. Members of Congress were concerned that all parties meeting together would be illegal under the Sherman Anti-Trust Act of 1890.

There were 10 members of Congress seated at the table, including Steve LaTourette, who had achieved the near-miracle of getting his bill attached to an appropriation and passed by the

House; Chris Van Hollen from Maryland; Dan Maffei of New York; Maxine Waters from California; Frank Kratovil of Maryland; Corrine Brown from Florida; Sheila Jackson-Lee from Texas; Donna Edwards from Maryland and Hank Johnson from Georgia. Also present: Tim Doran, along with Jim Appleton and Bill Wolters from ATAE; Damon Lester, Desmond Roberts, and Todd Bullard from NAMAD; David Regan and John McEleney from NADA; Ken Cole, GM's vice president of public policy and government relations ; John Bozzella, senior vice president of external affairs and public policy for Chrysler; and and GM lawyer Joe Lines. There were also numerous staffers from various Congressional offices. All in all, it was a high-powered bunch of people.

Our group, the Committee to Restore Dealer Rights, also had seven people there: Tammy, Jack, and me; Dan Renberg and Mary Jo Dowd; Rob Smith; and Alison, who was still nursing her first child at the time. At one point, my wife, Pat, who was outside and in front of the Capitol watching Alison's daughter, Vera, turned to me during a break in the proceedings. "I can't believe how many powerful and important people are in the same room, working to make this right."

I had great optimism as the negotiations began. The dealers were excited because we expected the manufacturers to cooperate with us. We had a united front (albeit a very hard-fought one) in our negotiating position. Our hope was that Chrysler and GM would work with us to create more viable companies, and we had, in our hip pocket, a bill passed by the House that we felt was very strong negotiating leverage. Maybe Chrysler and GM would see the errors of their ways.

The room was ringed with House and Senate staffers. Also present was the infamous Brian Deese from the White House Task Force, one of the main architects of the dealer terminations.

Deese had been on the presidential campaign staff of Hillary Clinton. He joined the Obama campaign when Hillary dropped out. Shortly after the inauguration of President Obama, Deese was assigned to the Auto Team. Leading up to this meeting, we had become very familiar with Deese and his direct connection to the hasty decision to terminate dealers. Alison particularly was shocked by the power he wielded both at such a young age and with no prior experience. It was hard for her not to stare at Deese during the proceedings, being in the same room with this improbable architect, the man behind the proverbial curtain. She wondered if he had any idea of the devastation he had caused so many people throughout the country.

After all were properly assembled, in strode Steny Hoyer to call the meeting to order by announcing, only half in jest perhaps, that the meeting of the Board of Directors would come to order. The statement ironically had a ring of truth since the federal government now owned a controlling interest in GM and a large share of Chrysler. After Hoyer's opening remarks, the other members of Congress in attendance delivered opening statements. All were highly critical of the manufacturers' actions. One by one, they urged Chrysler and GM to negotiate with the dealers in good faith and find a solution to the devastation the terminations had wrought on the communities they represented. I particularly remember Rep. Hank Johnson from Georgia's 4th District telling everyone in the room that "the train is back in the station"—a pointed barb to those who, earlier in the year, had blithely dismissed our legitimate complaints by telling us that nothing could be done to help the terminated dealers because "the train had left the station."

Each of the four dealer groups (NADA, ATAE, NAMAD, and CRDR) also gave opening statements. The CRDR statement that follows was delivered by Dan.

**Statement of the Committee to Restore Dealer Rights
(September 30, 2009)**

The Committee to Restore Dealer Rights and its co-chairs, Jack Fitzgerald, Alan Spitzer, and Tammy Darvish, appreciate the opportunity to work toward restoring as many of the nearly 3,400 auto dealers as possible and preserving the jobs of 169,000 American workers.

CRDR represents many of the dealerships rejected by Chrysler or terminated by General Motors. CRDR was formed by volunteers to protect the rights of these affected dealers and to work toward their reinstatement. In our view, the actions taken earlier this year by GM, Chrysler, the Auto Task Force and the Bankruptcy Court have violated the affected dealers' property rights—one of the most basic rights since the founding of our Nation.

At the outset, we want to stress that we want Chrysler and General Motors to succeed and to regain lost market share. There is no alternate agenda. CRDR strongly believes that dealers are part of the solution, not part of the problem. As Tammy Darvish wrote recently, "Dealers are the heart, soul, and fiber of their communities." Dealers provide tens of thousands of local jobs, contribute millions in state revenues, and are particularly critical to rural economies. In our view, the manufacturers and the Auto Task Force wrongly assumed that Dealers cost the factory money and that closing down their loyal business partners would help them in their own recovery. In fact, there was already a market solution in place, as the dealer sector has been right-sizing naturally, without trampling on rights protected under state law.

Our voice at the table is the voice of a nationally renowned second generation woman dealer in the Detroit suburbs, whose two Chrysler stores were in the top 100 in sales for years. They won countless awards and employed 170 people. The stores are closed now, the buildings empty, no longer an economic driver in a part of the country where every job counts so much.

Our voice is the voice of a dealer in Houston who was profitable for 11 of 12 months prior to receiving the wind-down letter, with the only unprofitable month having occurred when the store was without power for 15 days due to a hurricane.

Our voice is the voice of profitable multi-generational family businesses that were loyal to General Motors and Chrysler, undertook renovations, built new facilities, and accepted vehicles at your companies' request, but had their stores taken away in many cases without compensation. One example is in Rockford, Illinois, where a Chevrolet dealer received a termination letter even though his dealer performance scores were well above the standard used by GM, even though he sold more than 500 new cars and trucks last year, has 260% more capital than required by GM, and was profitable all the way through July, 2009.

We are also the voice of dealers who have seen their franchises given to a competitor. We are particularly troubled that such reassignments continue to occur while both sides have been preparing for these negotiations. We urge both companies to cease such reassignments as a sign of good faith while we are negotiating.

We believe it is in your companies' best interests to reinstate immediately the dealers who were either erroneously terminated using your criteria, are economically viable, or who can demonstrate to a neutral party that they would not have been terminated under the dealer franchise laws of their States. Not all dealers will pursue reinstatement, but many CRDR supporters are ready to get back in the game and are watching these negotiations with a hopeful eye.

As noted earlier, we believe you need our points of sale to succeed. The massive reduction in dealers means there are nearly two domestic vehicles on the road for every one import vehicle and there are not enough dealerships to service those vehicles. We fear that the next time your customers are in the market for a new car, the service frustrations generated by the closure of 3,400 dealerships will lessen the chance they will purchase the same brand of vehicle they bought previously.

CRDR's willingness to show good faith and sign on to the dealers' unified proposal reflects our desire for prompt resolution of the dealer crisis. People are hurting. Livelihoods have been lost. Each of the co-chairs of CRDR gets daily reminders of the heart-wrenching stories of terminated dealers who have been so adversely impacted by the decisions of this Spring. That is what motivated us to come here today.

In conclusion, the parties in this room can restore hope and generate economic growth to the mutual benefit of manufacturers, dealers, and consumers. We look forward to the discussions that start with this opening session.

Thank you.

Powerful opening statements on behalf of the terminated dealers were also delivered by David Regan of NADA, Tim Doran of ATAE and Damon Lester of NAMAD.

John Bozzella gave the opening statement for Chrysler and Ken Cole spoke on behalf of GM. While the remarks from these vice presidents of the car companies were short on specifics, they sounded a conciliatory tone. A sense of optimism was in the air. Unfortunately, it was short lived.

The insincerity of the manufacturers' approach to these negotiations became apparent soon after we subsequently broke into separate sessions. Our first meeting was with Chrysler. Their negotiating team didn't even have a copy of our proposal with them. How could they come to Washington, D.C., and meet a room full of Congressmen to begin a crucial multi-billion-dollar negotiation and not even have a copy of what we were there to discuss in front of them? They had received our proposal more than two weeks earlier from John Hughes of Steny Hoyer's office. So we paused the meeting, to the annoyance of the congressional representatives, for someone to go out and make copies for members of the Chrysler team.

Their arrogance was not only stunning, but an insult to the assembled group of dealer advocates. This display also angered the many congressional aides and counsel in attendance. Our proposal extensively and carefully laid out formulas for monetary compensation and arbitration criteria. And we asked them to disclose the specific criteria they used for the Rejections/Wind Downs. To date, Chrysler had released no data at all regarding the basis for dealership terminations. GM offered criteria but often broke their own rules when deciding which dealers to terminate. Unfortunately, we didn't get too far. Instead—at this meeting and at the several subsequent meetings that followed over the following eight weeks—we saw nothing more than rhetoric, posturing, and bad-faith negotiations. The progress (if you could call it that) was glacial.

Alison was disappointed, as we all were, by the tone of condescension. "They keep saying how they shed tears over this, but it doesn't seem sincere," she said to me. "They get to go home and leave this work at the office. Plus how many of the people sitting across the table from us will still be working for the manufacturers this time next year?" Her thinking was eminently prescient. Bozzella and Cole would both "resign" before year's end.

Chrysler's first counteroffer was woefully inadequate. At that time, the company had approximately 100 of what are known as "open points"—vacant sales territories throughout the country where it wanted to open stores. They offered the 789 closed dealers the "right of first proposal" for these sales territories. This wasn't a reopening, a guarantee, or even any meaningful preference. It was simply a Congressionally coerced offer to *accept applications* first from Rejected dealers. Of course, the location of the proposed "open point" could possibly be in a completely different part of the country from where the Rejected dealer lived. No doubt, those applications would quickly be summarily rejected—probably using the same opaque and flawed logic of the closures—and Chrysler would continue on its merry way.

The absence of decision-makers that day and the tone of the offer made it clear that Chrysler was not adopting a serious negotiating posture. When I saw what Chrysler was offering, I knew we were in for a long haul that would likely produce some very unsatisfactory outcomes. Nevertheless, after that first meeting on September 30, all parties agreed to be very tight-lipped in our comments to the press, only to say that we were "still talking."

Unfortunately there was a leak. *Automotive News* ran a story in their online edition later that day by Washington bureau reporter Neil Roland with a blow-by-blow description of the negotiations. Members of Congress presiding over the negotiations were furious and properly scolded the group of about 20 at the next meeting. The leaks persisted to varying degrees throughout our negotiating sessions. We had our own version of "Deep Throat." Roland had recently joined the Washington bureau of *Automotive News*, having previously worked as a reporter for *Bloomberg News* and *The Miami Herald*. His ability to gather intimate knowledge from our closed door discussions from "reliable sources" made many of the participants uncomfortable. To keep our members apprised of the situation, we sent out an e-mail the next day.

From: Alan Spitzer
Sent: Thursday, October 01, 2009 11:35 AM
To: Alan Spitzer
Subject: CRDR Update

Dear CRDR Friends and Supporters:

Yesterday, CRDR Co-Chairs, Tammy Darvish, Jack Fitzgerald and I joined representatives from NADA, ATAE and NAMAD in Washington to meet with executives from both GM and Chrysler. The day was kicked off with an overall meeting led by House Majority Leader Steny Hoyer (D-MD). Members participating included Reps. Chris Van Hollen (D-MD), Steve LaTourette (R-OH), Maxine Waters (D-CA), H.R. 2743 sponsor Dan Maffei (D-NY), Frank Kratovil (D-MD), Corrine Brown (D-FL), Donna Edwards (D-MD), and Hank Johnson (D-GA). Each of the Members spoke eloquently on behalf of the disenfranchised dealers and, while strongly encouraging the parties to craft a non-legislative solution, made it clear that H.R. 2743/S. 1304 and the LaTourette Amendment continue to be viable options.

We then adjourned to separate breakout sessions, first with Chrysler then GM. These talks were facilitated by senior staff from House and Senate leadership. Each session lasted approximately two hours with no final resolution consequently we have nothing of substance yet to report to you. The talks are scheduled to resume with both carmakers on Friday again in separate sessions. We believe all four groups representing the dealers acquitted themselves very well and it was clear to all those present that we were unified.

Realistically we did not expect to resolve these issues in one session. It is certainly positive that the talks are continuing and the tone was fairly amiable. While we maintain a sense of cautious optimism for a positive outcome of these negotiations, please continue to contact members of the Senate and the House who have not cosponsored. Congratulations to the dealers from Minnesota and ATAE Scott Lambert for securing the co-sponsorship of Al Franken as #43.

Thank you for the contributions you have made and continue to make. They allow us to wage a very professional campaign with our team of highly competent professionals. We have had several compliments from House and Senate staff about the quality of our organization including our volunteers. We are grateful for any financial assistance you can give CRDR personally if you are able. If you know of other Affected or for that matter Going Forward or Accepted Dealers who have not yet contributed please ask them to contribute as well.

We will report any new developments as soon as we are able.

Best regards,
Alan Spitzer
Tammy Darvish
Jack Fitzgerald

Over the weekend, we were heartened when House Speaker Nancy Pelosi made her first public comments about the dealer terminations in an interview with David Shepardson of *The Detroit News*: "Pelosi said Congress might still pass legislation on dealers, 'If there isn't some fairness that is injected'."[27]

Sensing we might eventually be back in Congress pushing the legislation, we knew we were going to need some additional firepower. Anticipating a brawl in the Senate if these negotiations irretrievably broke down, Jack believed we needed additional lobbyists to help Dan. When Alison attended graduate school

---

[27] Shepardson, D., "Pelosi: Hands Off Auto Industry." *Detroit News*, Oct. 3, 2009.

at American University, she had interned with Cassidy & Associates, one of the most powerful lobbying firms in D.C. and still had contacts there. Unfortunately, they cited a conflict of interest that made it impossible for us to hire them. One of Alison's contacts, Marty Russo, referred us to Quinn Gillespie & Associates.

I knew of Jack Quinn from the contentious 2000 presidential election between George W. Bush and Al Gore. Jack had represented Gore in Florida during the infamous recount. He was on TV on a daily basis defending Gore in the court of public opinion. Alison set up a meeting with Quinn and Dave Hoppe, one of his associates with strong contacts in the Senate. In the late afternoon of Oct. 2, Alison and I joined Jack Fitzgerald and Rob at the offices of Quinn Gillespie at 1133 Connecticut Ave. NW, where we prepped them for what we foresaw would be a combative process once we hit the Senate—if our efforts to forge a compromise failed.

After our initial meeting with the manufacturers on September 30, we met several more times over the course of eight weeks. Each time, we met separately with Chrysler and then with GM in back-to-back sessions. Soon, of course, it became clear that the two automakers were talking to each other in collusive fashion. Too many lines of discussion and offers were too similar to be coincidental.

Between meetings, I attempted to keep the dialogue open. Almost every time we adjourned, I'd contact Cole or Bozzella for sidebar conversations. I also hoped to learn a little bit about their thinking that could help us. In effect, I used many of the same negotiation and conflict-resolution techniques that I'd employed just a month earlier during our own "schism." I sought to keep the channels open and remove the "chill." The content of these conversations varied, of course, but I tried to repeat our talking points in a more personal, less threatening way. I tried to show why they should be more flexible. Tammy and Jack ended up being our "bad cops." We didn't *plan* it that way—that's just the way it happened. It seemed at the time that all of our efforts would prove to be in vain.

THE NEXT INSULT

At one point during this arduous process in late October, we were once again seemingly and hopelessly bogged down. Our Congressional attendees encouraged us to continue to meet without their presence, if we thought that might defuse the situation and lower the tensions. So I called Bozzella and arranged a meeting at Chrysler's D.C. offices in Suite 700 at 1401 H St. NW. "Alan, I think we will have something you'll like," he said on the phone. So as Alison and I once again flew into the nation's capital, I was optimistic. Jack was not.

Hope came crashing down once the meeting began. Tammy, Jack, Rob, Dan, Alison, and I were there representing CRDR, along with David Hoppe from Quinn Gillespie. David Regan from NADA and Tim Doran were there. Damon Lester was out of town and attended by speaker phone. We walked into the conference room adjacent to Bozzella's office—where Gwen Young, Chrysler's outside counsel from the Denver law firm of Wheeler Trigg O'Donnell was also seated. After pleasantries, Bozzella got right to the point, passing out Chrysler's proposal to all in attendance. "We'd like to offer binding arbitration to any Rejected dealer who'd like to appeal his closure," he said.

We went through their proposal item by item. Soon we saw the deal breaker: There would be NO change in the evaluation criteria that Chrysler had used to make the closure decisions. Apparently, Chrysler thought that we'd be dazzled by the words "binding arbitration." But if arbitrators were ordered to use the same deeply flawed standards—how would it be possible to get different results? It was an absurd proposal. We were all insulted and deeply disappointed. "Guys, we're on the brink of an impasse," I said.

Ken Cole soon followed up with a similar proposal in our next meeting with GM. Jack, Tammy, and I felt that Cole was far more sincere and upfront in his efforts but that his hands were tied. Like Chrysler, GM was offering a dealer review (by GM employees, no less) that still used 100 percent of its previous criteria. By their own admission, the proposal from GM would only reinstate about 50 dealers at most.

Despite our pre-meeting plans to ask GM careful questions, Tammy soon zoomed in on the insincerity of the offer. "How much more would it cost GM to add one more dealer to the network?" she challenged Cole defiantly. An already tense meeting soon went downhill from there. Tammy's comment probably made no difference. For some reason, the heretofore statesman-like Cole entered the room visibly upset and irritated. Cole's response was unreasonable.

One example of the bad-faith standards was the accounting data that GM used to make closure decisions. Each month, dealers send in financial reports that, at the end of the year for income tax purposes, often use specific accounting techniques such as last-in, first-out (LIFO) adjustments for inventory. But those reports were wholly unsuited for closure analyses. Shockingly, GM often inadvertently had used tax-accounting statements (which are inherently designed to lower reported profitability, of course) to assess the profitability of dealers—a colossal error and breach of good faith. These financials artificially lowered the Dealer Performance Summary or "DPS" score GM was using in the termination selection process. I asked GM lawyer Joe Lines how they could use such flawed analyses and his only response to me was, "We got what we got." What they needed were fresh financial statements, more accurately reflecting the dealer's actual performance—but they just couldn't be bothered.

As Tammy, Jack, and I analyzed the situation, we kept striving to understand the automakers' position. It was apparent to us that they were seriously overlooking our strength and broad-based support in Congress. We knew they were stunned by our victory in the House, but nonetheless, they appeared unfazed by the prospect of their own potential failure in the Senate as well. They seemed very confident that the legislation would never pass the Senate. And now, they could say to wavering senators, "Look, we tried to negotiate with them. We even offered binding arbitration."

On November 11, 2009, the evening before Alison and I were set to board a plane to Washington for another round of negotiations that both of us anticipated would be fruitless, I sent an e-mail to Congressional staff who were attending our sessions. I held faint hope that Congress would somehow put pressure on the car companies to negotiate in good faith and actually offer the dealers something substantive:

> **From:** Alan Spitzer
> **Sent:** Wednesday, November 11, 2009 7:02 PM
> **To:** Albert Sanders; Bruce Andrews; John Hughes; David Weaver; Michele Stockwell; Kathy Nuebel; Kate Ostrander; Joe Guzzo
> **Cc:** tammy darvish; Jack Fitzgerald; Rob; Dan Renberg; Dowd, Mary Joanne; Alison Spitzer; Alan Spitzer; T Doran; D Regan; John Mceleney; EC Tonkin; Damon Lester; Ashley Spitzer; Dave Hoppe; Jack Quinn; Mike Hussey; M Ortiz
> **Subject:** CRDR Plea for Justice
>
> To our Friends on Capitol Hill:

Today is Veteran's Day and the eve of our next meeting with representatives of General Motors to arrive at a non-legislative solution to the "quiet crisis" that is occurring across this country. I am sending you e-mails of four scenarios below that we received **just today.** Two are Rejected Chrysler Dealers and two are General Motors Wind Down dealers with bizarre circumstances beyond the bizarre and un-American nature of the Wind Downs/Rejections themselves. These scenarios are a microcosm of the horrible, real-life accounts of the devastation of good peoples' lives that Tammy, Jack and I hear about on a daily basis. On one level we are witness to actions that, if allowed to stand, will adversely affect untold numbers of Americans, certainly well into the millions when you count family members. These adverse effects range from joblessness and divorce to bankruptcy and suicide.

On another level, the precedent set by these unconscionable actions, once again if allowed to stand, will go down as possibly the most insidious in the history of American business. It is completely unthinkable that companies funded with taxpayer dollars are doing this; it is equally unthinkable to hear their top executives make statements under oath to our Congress and Federal Bankruptcy Court that are at best disingenuous and at worst patently false.

We fervently hope to arrive at a just non-legislative solution with both companies very, very soon. Time is of the essence. You are our best hope. Thanks for all you have done to help rectify this egregious wrong!

Regards,
Alan Spitzer

Case 1:

Jack, Tammy, Alan,

Due to continued post-termination losses even if my franchises were given back I do not feel I have the financial stability to continue to weather the storm while supporting an idle inventory of dead CDJ merchandise ....without some type of compensation from the government or the factory. Thank you though for your continued work on this. Joe (Name and location provided on request)

Joe,

Do you mind if I share your story with Congressional staff and the dealer advocacy groups? AS

No. Go right ahead…and if I can provide anything else to explain in more detail let me know.

Case 2:

Dear Alan,

First let me say I appreciate all that you do. I'm a little embarrassed to ask this favor knowing how busy you must be. I'm a Rejected Dealer who can't survive as a used car, service, parts and body shop operation. We will be closing our doors 11/30/09. This email will no longer be valid. Could you please start using my new e-mail. I'm sorry to bother you with this. And still appreciate all that you do.

Sincerely

Tim (Name and location provided on request)

Tim,

Do you mind if we share your story with legislative staff and other dealer advocates?

Dear Alan,

Please do. All my staff that's left and even those that are no longer here would probably like to tell them what they think of our new socialistic society.

Sincerely,
Tim

Case 3:

Alan,

I am trying. It is getting very difficult. I have only 5 new cars left in stock. I have closed my GMC Truck store. GM is "stealing" money from me as it pertains to expenses that they bill my open account. There is nobody we can complain to....they just "take" the money. We are still open. The dealers around me are "dropping like flies". I am not giving up. I remain....

Most Dedicated,
John (Name and location provided on request)

John,

Are you telling me you are being charged by GM incorrectly?

Alan, Yes. They are (GM Dealer Equipment) is billing me for a T-1 line that I was paying GM $500 a month for.....similar to my GM sign lease. They forced me to close my GMC Truck store that was connected electronically to my Buick store through this T-1 line. They charged me $14,000 to cancel the line....which is outrageous!!! My billing on this connection should just stop. Also, GM has told us that we must pay some of the expenses to remove our GM sign including «grinding the base» to the ground level. We should be able to refit these signs with different panels. My stores are both closing not due to anything that I did. They also billed me for and sent special tools the «Very day» before I got my «doom» letter fully knowing that I was getting the letter....they had to «clear their shelves» of the special tools and «dumped them» on the Dealers....remember GM owns Kent-Moore which sells us the special tools. We have no recourse as if we «protest» we put our Wind-Down money in jeopardy. Anything they want to charge us for...they will with this «carte blanche» approach.

Case 4:

Thank you to you, Jack and Tammy,

I'm sure you know this but 2 Wind-Down dealers around me have been given packets along with about 30 other «candidates» (like they don't already know who they want to put in) to bid on being the dealers in their own points

One Wind-Down dealer's present facility is 500 feet outside of the one-mile radius that they deem as an open point.

I feel like I am living in another country. The sad thing is unless you are going through this no one else seems to really care.

Anyway, I will do all that I can do.

J (Name and location provided on request)

J,

Do you mind if I share this?

No absolutely. These dealers are up and operating and received a packet that they are invited to bid on their own points. As I said, the one dealer received a packet on their own store but the radius they want to put someone in place is 450 feet from their store (calculated coincidence). They worked 40 years to build up this point (just like us) and GM is going to give it away while they have to stand by and watch. The Wind Down dealers have no rights at all.

We received a packet to bid on a store 25 miles away. When I called the dealer to get some information they were very short with me until I told them I had no plans at all on bidding for their point. They could not believe that we received a packet that far away. Supposedly GM is opening more points that they deemed they did not need. I›m sure ours will be one of them, as the Saturn store next to us is now closed and someone would just move right in.

All these Wind Down dealers are buying inventory and fighting all the rumors etc. to try and stay open. We are all trying to keep people employed and trying to sell their product.

What they have done to people in 6 months is horrible. It›s like a horrible divorce. The new younger spouse gets it all, and the one who did all the work is left alone and broke.

In our case it will cost my brother and I $6 million to be a Chevy dealer for 18 months. They keep the guy 5 miles from us (whom we outsold in 2008 by 180 vehicles) who has an EEOC Federal indictment (In all the papers and on the major news stations and even in Automotive News) and get rid of us who is on a dealer row. The Government gave them the power to pick and choose who they wanted to keep.

Ok now I will shut up. It is just so hard to believe that in AMERICA that this is allowed to happen.

J

The negotiations were increasingly appearing to be at a dead end. We kept making concessions. We gave a mile, they gave an inch. It was a pointless eight weeks, it seemed to us. Neither company really had a true decision-maker from Detroit attend our Washington meetings. We felt that was a bad-faith move on their part. We knew that Bozzella and Cole weren't empowered to make final decisions. Congress had expressly instructed GM and Chrysler to make sure decision-makers were in the room, a request that was blithely ignored. (Chrysler's Pete Grady who has oversight of the "dealer network" attended a couple of our sessions which I thought was a positive sign. Apparently, it was a cosmetic gesture. We would later learn that he was intransigent on the issue of any terminated dealer reinstatements.)

By now, it was December 2009 and the negotiations had gone nowhere. In some ways, the manufacturers were acting like the tobacco giants—just continuing to delay and delay, biding their time while appearing to cooperate, in hopes of bleeding out our commitment and enthusiasm until we gave up. They were trying to run out the clock and that was a big mistake.

CHAPTER 12

BLACK THURSDAY

Obstacles are things a person sees when he takes his eyes off his goal.

E. Joseph Cossman

Finally, as the calendar turned to December, CRDR moved into "last-ditch mode." On December 2, I called Pete Grady from Chrysler. He was in charge of the dealer network and the Rejections fell under his bailiwick. In essence, I was asking him to "walk back" from these closures, to admit a massive mistake, something that is naturally difficult for anyone to do. We talked for about an hour and I kept looking for a crack of compromise, but I got nowhere with Pete. They were completely committed to their position and weren't budging.

Meanwhile, Jack, Tammy, and I were busily working with Dan drafting what we envisioned as our last and final offer in the non-legislative negotiations with GM and Chrysler. And it reflected the many compromises we'd agreed to over the previous eight weeks. Our plan: deliver this to Chrysler and GM as our ultimatum. If they failed to accept the proposal, we'd simply fall back to our previous strategy: passage of the appropriations bill (with our amendment) in the Senate.

Later that day, I received a telephone message from Pete. Clearly, Chrysler sensed we were ready to move on a final proposal—and they decided to pre-empt our move with one of their own. Before I could return Pete's call, an e-mail came in—an outrageous and infuriating message that nearly knocked the legs out from under us.

Chrysler's statement was a sterling example of the company's back-of-the-hand contempt for the hundreds of dealerships it was unfairly closing. The company also released an accompanying statement.

> **Statement Regarding Chrysler Group LLC's Agreement to Offer Binding Independent Review Process for Discontinued Dealers**
>
> Chrysler Group LLC appreciates the leadership that Senate Majority Whip Richard Durbin, House Majority Leader Steny Hoyer and their staffs have displayed in the effort to settle issues regarding discontinued dealers amicably.
>
> As a result of these discussions, Chrysler has agreed to provide a binding independent review process for discontinued dealers, with the understanding that this binding independent review is an alternative to federal legislation affecting Chrysler's dealer network. As a show of good faith, Chrysler is implementing the binding independent review process today. The appeal process provides:
>
> - Transparency on Chrysler's initial dealer determinations through face-to- face meetings with Chrysler executives
> - A binding review of those determinations by an independent 3-person panel
> - An opportunity to join the new dealer network if that independent review panel rules in the discontinued dealer's favor

The fundamental elements of the appeal process include the following:

- Provide each discontinued dealer the general criteria and standards used by the former Chrysler LLC in making its rejection decisions and the specific criteria considered and applied to the individual discontinued dealer's circumstances
- Offer of a meeting with the discontinued dealer's former Business Center to discuss the criteria, and ability for the dealer to present information to refute the rejection decision
- Right to call for a binding independent review if dealer believes its rejection was not warranted. Chrysler will abide by the decision of the independent review panel
- Two opportunities to join the new dealer network if the panel rules in the discontinued dealer's favor: first, to join the new network as a Genesis (Chrysler, Jeep® and Dodge) dealer in the previous market area or, if that is not possible, to be offered an opportunity to open a Genesis dealership in another market area from a list of available market areas

A detailed letter describing the offer will be mailed to all 789 discontinued dealers on or before December 10, 2009, and the process will begin at that time. This offer will be available in all states where Chrysler is legally permitted to offer these opportunities to join the dealer network.

Additional Chrysler efforts to provide a soft landing for discontinued dealers include:

- Chrysler has successfully found buyers for 100 percent of the discontinued dealers' outstanding eligible new vehicle inventory
- On November 9, 2009, Chrysler notified the 789 rejected dealers, per our commitment in June, that if they desire,

> the company would repurchase eligible parts inventory at $0.68 on the dollar, which was the average transaction price for eligible parts sold among dealers between June 9 and September 10, 2009. Dealers received the information in both email and letter form
>
> The road to recovery for Chrysler required the company to make some very difficult decisions and sacrifices in order to build a vibrant new company. While Chrysler has not closed the door to further discussion with the dealer groups, Chrysler believes that the process it offers today fully addresses concerns that Congress and the discontinued dealers have raised: it provides transparency, a right of appeal, and opportunities to join the new dealer network. Moving forward with this process today enables us to focus our efforts on the business of servicing our current dealer network and building and selling new Chrysler, Jeep, Dodge and Ram vehicles—our best way to repay the nation's support.

This "proposal" was nothing more than what we'd rejected in our October meeting in Chrysler's offices. It contained the words "binding independent review" that made it seem like a win for CRDR. The catch: it was a review using *their* criteria. Essentially, this was their walk-away strategy. The dead giveaway: the statement didn't include any other parties. This was not the "joint statement" indicative of agreement among the parties. It was a unilateral, take-it-or-leave it offer—"my way or the highway." Until that point, we didn't think the negotiations were over. But before we had the chance to deliver our final offer, the carmakers walked away from the table.

Twenty Minutes Later, GM Follows Suit

With an appearance of the kind of collusion that makes regulators wince, just 20 minutes later, I received an e-mail from GM vice president Ken Cole informing me that GM would also unilaterally offer binding arbitration—using GM's "stacked deck" of closure standards, of course.

In a sidebar conversation with Tim Doran just days earlier, Cole had confided, "We don't believe you can do it (pass the legislation)!" Tim had pleaded with Cole not to unilaterally break off the negotiations. But Cole was near tears when he responded that he had no choice.

From: Ken Cole
Sent: Thursday, December 03, 2009 2:37 PM
To: Alan Spitzer
Subject: GM Dealer Plan Announcement

Dear Alan:

I wanted to share with you a release that has just hit the newswire. GM is announcing a comprehensive plan to provide complete transparency and the opportunity for dealer reinstatement. I sincerely appreciate your thoughtful and constructive engagement on the issues over the past several months. This plan and the dealer network have benefitted greatly from your involvement.

GM will begin to implement this plan in mid-January.

Sincerely,

Ken W. Cole
GM Vice President
Public Policy and Government Relations

GM Announces Comprehensive Plan to Address Dealer Concerns Press release
media.gm.com
12-03-2009

Today, GM is announcing that it is prepared to implement a comprehensive plan that both resolves concerns raised by dealers regarding GM's dealer network restructuring activities and allows it to continue to move forward with a critical component of its long-term viability plan.

GM will begin to implement this plan in mid-January provided that legislation related to GM's dealer restructuring does not move forward. GM's plan offers a more certain and timely process and the appropriate alternative to address dealer concerns especially compared to proposed legislation that would raise a variety of legal and constitutional concerns. The GM plan, the result of several months of discussion and constructive engagement among dealer groups and Members of Congress, provides complete transparency, face-to-face reviews and binding arbitration, which together, will likely result in some dealers being reinstated.

"GM especially appreciates the leadership of Senator Durbin and House Majority Leader Hoyer and the contribution of other Congressional members. Their tireless efforts to facilitate the discussion among all parties to achieve a non-legislative resolution to address dealer concerns were critical to the development of GM's comprehensive plan," said Susan Docherty, GM Vice President, U.S. Sales.

"GM values its dealer body and recognizes the contributions they are making to the future viability of the company, the critical role they play in satisfying customers and their importance to communities across the country. We are prepared to implement this plan so GM and its dealers can channel our full focus on building and selling exceptional cars and trucks with the consumer experience to match," Docherty said.

"I would also like to thank the National Association of Minority Automobile Dealers (NAMAD) for their commitment to work through some very difficult and complicated issues involving GM's dealer network," Docherty said.

GM's plan includes:

- A commitment to advise all Chevrolet, Buick, GMC and Cadillac dealerships that received a complete wind-down agreement of the criteria used by GM in the selection of that dealership for wind-down.
- A face-to-face review process for all complete wind-down dealers who have not already terminated their dealer sales and service agreements with GM.
- If the complete wind-down dealer is not satisfied with the outcome of the face-to-face review process, he or she may elect to proceed to binding arbitration. The arbitration will expressly be limited to whether GM selected the dealer to receive the wind-down agreement on the basis of its business criteria.

Additional components include:

- Accelerated wind-down payments to dealers consistent with the terms of their wind-down agreements.
- A process to resolve open issues identified by dealers related to the operation of wind-down dealers.
- Agreement to support public policy issues of mutual interest identified by dealers.
- Agreement to work with appropriate policy makers regarding floor-plan and other financing issues that are important to dealers.
- Additional evaluation in limited circumstances for complete wind-down dealers who purchased stock, land or dealerships from GM in the last four years.

> - Reaffirmation of GM's long-standing commitment to try to increase the diversity of its dealer body.
> - In the limited circumstances where there are dealer re-establishments, area wind-down dealers will be given the opportunity to submit a proposal.
> - Market reevaluation to ensure GM has sufficient dealer representation across the country.
> - Placement assistance for service technicians and other dealership employees.

Like Chrysler, we didn't even get the courtesy of a *pro forma* phone conversation. The GM announcement essentially laid out the same offer. It was a railroading with a pre-determined outcome.

"Alan—they already told us that this arbitration would only reinstate anywhere from 39-51 dealers," Tammy told me on the phone. "What good is that? How stupid do they think we are—and Congress, too?" For my part, I wondered, how could they have an estimate that tight if these cases were going before an independent arbitrator? The question answered itself, of course.

Chapter 13

SHORT RESPONSE, LONG WEEKEND

Never, never, never, never give up.

Winston Churchill

GM and Chrysler, clearly acting in concert, had tried to snatch the momentum and leverage we'd painstakingly created and give wavering senators an excuse to reject our amendment to the appropriations bill. On the surface, it might have seemed like a good play at first. After all, Tammy, Jack, and I immediately started receiving congratulatory e-mails and calls from CRDR members from around the country.

"Congrats, Alan! You got binding arbitration!" was typical of the responses I was receiving.

"Hold your horses," I replied. "That's just what they want you to think." When I quickly explained to our supporters the true nature of what had been offered, they were, of course, very dispirited. We had to halt the spread of this misinformation before the perception "hardened" among Congress, the dealers, and other industry-watchers.

We didn't waste any time. On behalf of CRDR, Dan drafted and released a scathing, and completely appropriate, response that fully rejected the Chrysler and GM proposals. We had to be "fast and furious" to ensure that these phony proposals didn't gather any steam. Tim Doran and NADA also jumped in with their denunciations.

> **Statement of the Committee to Restore Dealer Rights Regarding General Motors and Chrysler Press Statements**
> **DECEMBER 3, 2009**
>
> We are greatly disappointed at today's unilateral decisions by General Motors and Chrysler to end negotiations with dealer representatives and to publicize indefensible so-called reinstatement plans. We would say that their plans are shams, but that is an insult to the word "sham" because the GM and Chrysler plans would at best reinstate only very, very few dealers, if any.
>
> We assure dealers, Members of Congress, and consumers that at no point in the negotiating process did General Motors or Chrysler present a plan that would realistically get more than a few dealers back in business. On the other hand, dealer groups have been willing to show flexibility on a non-legislative solution in order to get our colleagues back in business as soon as possible.
>
> We just could not in good conscience accept the GM or Chrysler plans when they rely so much on flawed criteria and would make a mockery of the arbitration process. Under their plans, a dealer would have had a better chance at winning the Powerball lottery than getting back in business.
>
> We will not foreclose future discussions with GM or Chrysler to resolve the dealer crisis. However, we intend to

> press forward with our numerous bipartisan supporters in Congress to ensure enactment of legislation to add back in dealers whose economic rights were trampled by GM and Chrysler.
>
> Alan Spitzer
> Jack Fitzgerald
> Tamara Darvish

> **NADA Statement on GM Plan to Address Dealer Closings**
>
> *McLEAN, Va. (December 3, 2009)—The following statement was issued by the National Automobile Dealers Association on the dealer rights issue:*
>
> "NADA appreciates the good faith and constructive dialogue we have had with GM as we try to build a consensus to ensure that GM and its dealer network are as successful as possible. GM's announced plan to address the issue of dealership closings is a positive step, but we do not believe it establishes a sufficiently meaningful appeals process that provides for a reasonable opportunity for dealer reinstatement. Our hope is that we can work expeditiously with GM to improve its proposal. We will also continue to work with Congress on the pending 'dealer rights' legislation in the event a non-legislative solution cannot be achieved on this important issue which affects thousands of people's lives and their communities. All the parties concerned have a mutual interest in strengthening the long-term viability of GM and its dealer network."

Our supporters and allies clearly saw through these bogus ploys by Chrysler and GM. We needed to rally them – especially those in the Senate, since the legislation containing our amendment was coming up for a vote very quickly. Rep. Chris Van Hollen from Maryland once again entered the fray on our behalf, issuing a strong statement of support later that evening.

Van Hollen Statement on Chrysler and GM Dealership Plans

Washington, D.C.—*Today Congressman Chris Van Hollen (D-MD) issued the following statement on Chrysler and General Motors Dealership Re-Instatement Plans:*

"The plans offered today by Chrysler and General Motors are a step in the right direction, but still fall short of what is needed to help re-instate profitable car dealers and put their employees back to work. Earlier this year, after receiving billions of dollars in taxpayer money, Chrysler and GM announced they were terminating more than 3,000 dealerships, many of them profitable small businesses employing thousands of people in communities all across the nation. Their logic didn't make sense then, and it still doesn't make sense today. Rather than costing money, profitable car dealers help a manufacturer's bottom line. In fact, Chrysler's former CEO Jim Press has acknowledged that terminating car dealerships will hurt, not help that company's recovery.

"Over the past several months, I have worked closely with Majority Leader Hoyer, Congressmen Kratovil and Maffei, and other Members of Congress to help reinstate profitable dealerships. The House of Representatives, by a wide margin, passed a measure earlier this year to restore terminated dealerships. However, in an effort to find a non-legislative resolution to this matter, we convened talks with the auto dealer groups and the manufacturers. While both sides offered significant concessions, these efforts have fallen short and the measures announced today by the two auto companies don't go far enough to help get profitable dealers re-instated and their employees back to work.

"I intend to re-double my efforts to enact legislation that will give auto dealers a fair and reasonable opportunity to get back into business, put people back to work, and help pump money back into America's car companies."

The next day—December 4—in Steny Hoyer's office, John Hughes got back to us with a crucial update. Since the manufacturers were, indeed, walking away and betting that they could prevail in the Senate, Hoyer and other leaders had consulted with key senators to determine if our language in the House bill would fly in the Senate. No dice. LaTourette's language was, in the Senate's eyes, a little too strong. Instead, Hughes drafted a 10-page substitute—and they needed our buy-in by the following morning if we wanted it in the appropriations bill.

Rep. Chris Van Hollen

That night, the 250-member Greater Cleveland Auto Dealers Association held its annual holiday party and was inducting a new chairman for 2010. Ironically, it was Bill Burke one of our company's general managers and a partner in Spitzer Lakewood Chrysler-Jeep, one of our company's Rejected dealerships. Throughout the party, between the appetizers, the laughter, and the camaraderie, I had to keep up a dizzying pace. I was on numerous conference calls, jumping back to the party for a few minutes to network with my colleagues. It seemed as if all I did was send BlackBerry e-mails, talk to Tammy, Jack, Rob, and Dan, and, in between, chat with people at the party. It was a blur.

Although the party broke up at a reasonable hour, the furious back and forth of the document review and editing went on well into the morning. Hughes e-mailed us at 3 a.m. wanting to know where we stood. Finally, we had everyone's approval and returned a marked-up version to Hughes in the wee hours of December 5. (My last e-mail was sent at 4:49 a.m.) This was language that we could share with the Senate. But that wasn't enough. As I had long since learned, we needed to press the issue with senators to convince them to agree. The one thing we wanted was to have this language locked down before the bill went to the Joint Conference Committee (which hashes out discrepancies between House and Senate versions of bills).

Dan e-mailed Tammy, Jack, Rob, and me, releasing the hounds, so to speak. The plan was to start applying some pressure to key senators. We wanted them to hear from Rejected dealers, employees, and customers to encourage them to accept the language we were presenting. Over the next 24 hours, Tammy and Rob arranged conference calls involving hundreds of CRDR members, during which we carefully explained the events that were about to unfold and stressed the importance of contacting the key Senators.

> **From:** Renberg, Dan
> **Sent:** Saturday, December 05, 2009 4:30 PM
> **To:** Tammy Darvish; Alan Spitzer; Jack; Rob Smith
> **Cc:** Dowd, Mary Joanne;
> **Subject:** Release the Hounds
>
> House leadership staff has blessed our putting the pressure on the Senate to accept the House substitute language, which offers a real, fair, and transparent binding arbitration process. The key players are Senators Reid (NV), Durbin (IL) Inouye (HI), Cochran(MS), Collins (ME), McConnell (KY), Grassley (IA), Rockefeller (WVA), Hutchison (TX), and other members of the Senate Approps Committee.
>
> Our message is simple:
>
> As a compromise to the LaTourette Amendment (which the Senate did not want), House leaders have developed a compromise amendment establishing a transparent arbitration process far more fair than GM and C offered. It does not rely on the manufacturer's criteria only, as they offered. It will happen swiftly and will always involve neutral arbitrators, not company officials. It offers all terminated, rejected, and wind-down dealers their chance for a fair hearing to get their franchises back.
>
> We need to tell all senators, but especially those noted above:

> "As part of the negotiations over the Financial Services Appropriations bill, the House has proposed a fair, transparent, balanced arbitration procedure open to all terminated dealers. It is critical that you (Senator X) urge Chairman Durbin, Senator Collins, and Senator McConnell, Chairman Inouye and Majority Leader Reid to accept the House substitute amendment without change. It is a reasonable compromise made necessary by the Senate's refusal to consider legislation like S. 1304. The House substitute amendment represents our best chance to get dealers back in business and to preserve many of the 169,000 jobs at risk from the terminations earlier this year. We will have the chance to review the termination criteria and to explain to an arbitrator why we should added or continued as part of the Chrysler or GM dealer network."
>
> Please contact the Washington and local staff immediately. We are advised that the Senate might respond tomorrow (Sunday) to the House proposal and this is best chance to influence outcome. Generate multiple calls and emails from employees and customers.
>
> It would have been great to get legislation that might have automatically reinstated dealers but there has not been sufficient support. This amendment offers perhaps a better chance ultimately to get back in business. Please use tonight and tomorrow to exert pressure on the Senate.

It was a challenge we relished. The goal line was in sight. We called and e-mailed all of the senators we could reach on such a short notice over the weekend. As the fateful week of Senate debate on the appropriations bill drew near, we were feeling good about our chances.

Chapter 14

THE FRAY IN THE SENATE

We must all hang together or most assuredly we shall hang separately.

Benjamin Franklin

On December 7, Alison and I were in Pittsburgh for a meeting of Toyota dealers regarding upcoming advertising plans. On that morning, I was feeling particularly good. The language in Hughes's 10-page amendment was particularly advantageous to dealers. We envisioned that a vast majority of Rejected dealers would get reinstated under this arbitration framework. The criteria were very favorable—simply demonstrate financial viability with sufficient working capital and show a dealer floor plan (bank financing for vehicle inventory). If they did that, the arbitrator would be instructed to reinstate the dealer. Our initial indication was that the Senate would accept the House language.

But the manufacturers came back very strongly. Our proposal called for all arbitrations to be completed by March 31, 2010, about 100 days from enactment. That would be a tall order for the carmakers. They managed to push the deadline back to June

15. But the real assaults started when they sought to add their own criteria. Their strategy was death by increments. Over the next two days, it was volley after volley. And backed by CRDR, our Congressional allies held firm.

One key change the carmakers sought concerned their business plan—the brand-consolidation efforts (Chrysler's "Project Genesis" and GM's so-called "Channel" strategy to combine its Buick and GMC brands as well as Chevrolet and Cadillac in selected markets). The problem with this was that the arbitrator could assign any weighting/significance to that particular metric. So, for example, if a Chrysler dealer didn't have a Genesis dealership, an arbitrator could weigh that heavily against him— or not at all. It was highly subjective, and therefore a real threat. If an arbitrator thought Genesis was important and the appealing dealer wasn't a Genesis dealer, it would be very difficult to make the case for reversal. Unfortunately we were unsuccessful in attempts to keep this criterion out of the legislation. While we were disappointed that this specific criterion remained in the bill, in the end it may have made no difference. Both dealers and car companies were permitted to "present any relevant information during the arbitration." Hence, the arbitrator still would have been able to consider the brand consolidation plans if he so chose.

At the 11th hour, it fell to Deese of Obama's Auto Team, to once again try to plunge the dagger into the heart of the Rejected dealers. He sought to add an eighth criterion for arbitrators to consider by redefining the terms of "financial viability" of, not the dealership, but *the car companies,* implying that the dealer cuts were vital to their survival:

> (8) the operational and financial impact on the covered manufacturer [Chrysler and GM] of renewing, assuming, or assigning the covered dealership.

We saw it as damaging and a tool for arbitrators to issue unwarranted denials. "Jack, this could be the death knell for the terminated dealers," I said. He agreed—and the three of us set out to quickly get that scrubbed out of the bill.

We started with the Senate—talking to key allies and aides there. Then, we prevailed upon our friends in the House to also lobby their Senate colleagues. Steve LaTourette, for one, was livid and once again threatened to file a protest over the inclusion of Deese's language. Tim was equally apoplectic. All of us put a full-court press on the staff of Sen. Dick Durbin (D-IL) and, as a result, were able to get Deese's language stripped back out of the bill. This was a huge win. Sen. Durbin's involvement was critical to our effort. Not only was he an ally and confidante of President Obama, as the Senate Majority Whip he was the second-highest ranking member of the Senate. I had sensed Durbin was sympathetic to the terminated dealers' plight back in July when I first talked with one of his key aides, Albert Sanders. Then, a few weeks later, a delegation of Illinois dealers led by Illinois Automobile Dealers Association President Pete Sander was successful in getting a face-to-face meeting with Sen. Durbin. I was communicating with Pete along with Rachel Bachrodt, who would also attend. The Bachrodt family was an integral part of our effort from the beginning. Their family and their employees were working hard every day to cultivate Congressional support for H.R. 2743/S. 1304 and help in any way they could.

Rachel was the family's designated contact with CRDR. Jack, Tammy, and I desperately wanted CRDR to have a presence in the meeting with Durbin. Rachel and Pete lobbied for CRDR to

Senate Majority Whip Richard Durbin

be permitted to send a delegate. Tony or I was prepared to fly to Springfield for the meeting. No dice. Durbin's staff insisted that there was limited space and all seats were to be occupied by his constituents, Illinois residents.

The night before the meeting Tony and I went to Plan B. We each spent about an hour on the phone with Pete and Rachel individually reviewing and rehearsing talking points in preparation for the meeting. The meeting didn't last as long as the dealers had hoped but I believe it was successful. My sense was the Sen. Durbin became even a stronger advocate from that point. Subsequent to that meeting, Durbin had sent a strongly worded letter to the CEOs of both companies threatening legislative action if our negotiations proved unsuccessful *(see sidebar)*.

Later that day, NADA sent out a broadcast e-mail seeking to rally the troops for our final push and encouraged all of its members to hit the phones and e-mail to urge their senators to support the revised LaTourette amendment of the appropriations bill so that it could get through the Conference Committee.

It paid off.

There was only one more hurdle: the House-Senate Conference Committee. This committee includes a small subset of representatives and senators whose sole task is to create a single, unified piece of legislation by hashing through the various subtle differences between the two versions of the bill approved by each chamber of Congress. Their influence is especially powerful because, when they finish and return with legislation to their respective chambers, representatives and senators can only vote yea or nay—without making any amendments.

On December 8, the Conference Committee met and we were ready for absolutely anything. I monitored the proceedings very carefully from afar while Tammy and Dan were on site

RICHARD J. DURBIN
ILLINOIS
―――
COMMITTEE ON APPROPRIATIONS
―――
COMMITTEE ON THE JUDICIARY
―――
COMMITTEE ON RULES
AND ADMINISTRATION
―――
ASSISTANT MAJORITY
LEADER

United States Senate
Washington, DC 20510-1304

309 HART SENATE OFFICE BUILDING
WASHINGTON, DC 20510-1304
(202) 224-2152
TTY (202) 224-8180

230 SOUTH DEARBORN, 38TH FLOOR
CHICAGO, IL 60604
(312) 353-4952

525 SOUTH EIGHTH STREET
SPRINGFIELD, IL 62703
(217) 492-4062

701 NORTH COURT STREET
MARION, IL 62959
(618) 998-8812

durbin.senate.gov

September 14, 2009

Mr. Frtiz Henderson
President and Chief Executive Officer
General Motors Company
P.O. Box 33170
Detroit, MI 48232-5170

Dear Mr. Henderson:

I write to urge General Motors to participate in a constructive dialogue with the key groups representing the hundreds of dealerships that received wind-down letters and are scheduled to close by October 2010. As you know, the National Automobile Dealers Association, the Automotive Trade Association Executives, the National Association of Minority Automobile Dealers, and the Committee to Restore Dealer Rights have raised a number of issues on behalf of the affected dealers concerning the implementation and impact of the dealership closures.

While I have not foreclosed the option of supporting a legislative solution to address these concerns, I believe very strongly that these issues can and should be resolved outside of the legislative process. At the negotiating table, the unique concerns of the affected dealerships and the commercial interests of GM can be articulated and resolved by those who know them best – the dealers and GM.

Now that GM has emerged from bankruptcy, it is critical that it return to profitability and viability as soon as commercially feasible. The company's current employees, remaining dealers, and customers, and the taxpayers who provided critical financial support during the bankruptcy proceeding, are relying on GM to once again be a vibrant, profitable leader in the automotive sector.

I understand that the road to recovery for GM required the company to make some very difficult decisions and sacrifices, including the elimination of some dealerships. It is my hope that GM and the dealer groups will work cooperatively to resolve the concerns the dealers have raised. I have communicated this same message to the groups representing the dealers. I hope that the parties will begin constructive conversations soon and update me on any progress that is made.

Sincerely,

Richard J. Durbin
United States Senator

RICHARD J. DURBIN
ILLINOIS

COMMITTEE ON APPROPRIATIONS

COMMITTEE ON THE JUDICIARY

COMMITTEE ON RULES
AND ADMINISTRATION

ASSISTANT MAJORITY
LEADER

United States Senate
Washington, DC 20510-1304

309 HART SENATE OFFICE BUILDING
WASHINGTON, DC 20510-1304
(202) 224-2152
TTY (202) 224-8180

230 SOUTH DEARBORN, 38TH FLOOR
CHICAGO, IL 60604
(312) 353-4952

525 SOUTH EIGHTH STREET
SPRINGFIELD, IL 62703
(217) 492-4062

701 NORTH COURT STREET
MARION, IL 62959
(618) 998-8812

durbin.senate.gov

September 14, 2009

Mr. Sergio Marchionne
Chief Executive Officer
Chrysler Group LLC
P.O. Box 21-8004
Auburn Hills, MI 48321-8004

Dear Mr. Marchionne:

I write to urge Chrysler to participate in a constructive dialogue with the key groups representing the 789 dealerships that were terminated earlier this year. As you know, the National Automobile Dealers Association, the Automotive Trade Association Executives, the National Association of Minority Automobile Dealers, and the Committee to Restore Dealer Rights have raised a number of issues on behalf of terminated dealers concerning the implementation and impact of the dealership terminations.

While I have not foreclosed the option of supporting a legislative solution to address these concerns, I believe very strongly that these issues can and should be resolved outside of the legislative process. At the negotiating table, the unique concerns of the terminated dealerships and the commercial interests of Chrysler can be articulated and resolved by those who know them best – the dealers and Chrysler.

Now that Chrysler has emerged from bankruptcy, it is critical that it return to profitability and viability as soon as commercially feasible. The company's current employees, remaining dealers, and customers, and the taxpayers who provided critical financial support during the bankruptcy proceeding, are relying on Chrysler to once again be a vibrant, profitable leader in the automotive sector.

I understand that the road to recovery for Chrysler required the company to make some very difficult decisions and sacrifices, including the termination of some dealerships. It is my hope that Chrysler and the dealer groups will work cooperatively to resolve the concerns these dealers have raised. I hope that the parties will begin constructive conversations soon and update me on any progress that is made.

Sincerely,

Richard J. Durbin
United States Senator

and ready to swing into action if necessary—but there were no speed bumps. Sec. 747 of H.R. 3288 sailed through the Conference Committee without any changes.

At last, we had our victory! Congratulatory messages poured in from dealers all over the country.

While the language in Sec. 747 as passed was not as favorable to the dealers as the original language in the House version, I don't believe it was possible to do any better, given the strong opposition from the White House and both car companies. Tammy, Jack, and I were convinced that if the arbitrators had an open mind, a high percentage of dealers would win reinstatement. Unfortunately, as we would later learn, in all too many instances, the arbitrators were biased in favor of Chrysler and GM.

We knew that once we emerged from the Conference Committee, we were home free. The House of Representatives passed the appropriations bill on December 10 and on Saturday, December 12, the Senate voted 60-37 to invoke cloture and end debate on the bill. On December 13, the Senate formally passed the same bill, sending it to President Obama for his signature.

Since there is no line-item veto, Obama had to sign the entire appropriations bill with our language in Sec. 747. And on December 16, that's exactly what he did. H.R. 3288—Consolidated Appropriations Act, 2010, was enacted into law. The dealer rights legislation was on the books as part of what was now *Public Law No: 111-117*. Finally, GM and Chrysler dealers received some measure of justice: binding arbitration, independent criteria, transparent standards, and an expedited process.

SEC. 747. (a) DEFINITIONS.—For purposes of this section the following definitions apply:

(1) The term "covered manufacturer" means—

    (A) an automobile manufacturer in which the United States Government has an ownership interest, or to which the Government has provided financial assistance under title I of the Emergency Economic Stabilization Act of 2008; or

    (B) an automobile manufacturer which acquired more than half of the assets of an automobile manufacturer in which the United States Government has an ownership interest, or to which the Government has provided financial assistance under title I of the Emergency Economic Stabilization Act of 2008.

(2) The term "covered dealership" means an automobile dealership that had a franchise agreement for the sale and service of vehicles of a brand or brands with a covered manufacturer in effect as of October 3, 2008, and such agreement was terminated, not assigned in the form existing on October 3, 2008 to another covered manufacturer in connection with an acquisition of assets related to the manufacture of that vehicle brand or brands, not renewed, or not continued during the period beginning on October 3, 2008, and ending on December 31, 2010.

    (b) A covered dealership that was not lawfully terminated under applicable State law on or before April 29, 2009, shall have the right to seek, through binding arbitration, continuation, or reinstatement of a franchise agreement, or to be added as a franchisee to the dealer network of the covered manufacturer in the geographical area where the covered dealership was located when its franchise agreement was terminated, not assigned, not renewed, or not continued. Such continuation, reinstatement, or addition shall be limited to each brand owned and manufactured by the covered manufacturer at the time the arbitration commences, to the extent that the covered dealership had been a dealer for such brand at the time such dealer's franchise agreement was terminated, not assigned, not renewed, or not continued.

(c) Before the end of the 30-day period beginning on the date of the enactment of this Act, a covered manufacturer shall provide to each covered dealership related to such covered manufacturer a summary of the terms and the rights accorded under this section to a covered dealership and the specific criteria pursuant to which such dealer was terminated, was not renewed, or was not assumed and assigned to a covered manufacturer.

(d) A covered dealership may elect to pursue the right to binding arbitration with the appropriate covered manufacturer. Such election must occur within 40 days of the date of enactment. The arbitration process must commence as soon as practicable thereafter with the selection of the arbitrator and conclude with the case being submitted to the arbitrator for deliberation within 180 days of the date of enactment of this Act. The arbitrator may extend the time periods in this subsection for up to 30 days for good cause. The covered manufacturer and the covered dealership may present any relevant information during the arbitration. The arbitrator shall balance the economic interest of the covered dealership, the economic interest of the covered manufacturer, and the economic interest of the public at large and shall decide, based on that balancing, whether or not the covered dealership should be added to the dealer network of the covered manufacturer. The factors considered by the arbitrator shall include (1) the covered dealership's profitability in 2006, 2007, 2008, and 2009, (2) the covered manufacturer's overall business plan, (3) the covered dealership's current economic viability, (4) the covered dealership's satisfaction of the performance objectives established pursuant to the applicable franchise agreement, (5) the demographic and geographic characteristics of the covered dealership's market territory, (6) the covered dealership's performance in relation to the criteria used by the covered manufacturer to terminate, not renew, not assume or not assign the covered dealership's franchise agreement, and (7) the length of experience of the covered dealership. The arbitrator shall issue a written determination no later than 7 business days after the arbitrator determines that case has been fully submitted. At a minimum, the written determination shall include (1) a description of the covered dealership, (2) a clear statement indicating whether the franchise agreement at issue is to be renewed, continued, assigned or assumed by the covered manufacturer, (3) the key facts relied upon by the arbitrator in making the determination, and (4) an explanation of how the balance of economic interests supports the arbitrator's determination.

(e) The arbitrator shall be selected from the list of qualified arbitrators maintained by the Regional Office of the American Arbitration Association (AAA), in the Region where the dealership is located, by mutual agreement of the covered dealership and covered manufacturer. If agreement cannot be reached on a suitable arbitrator, the parties shall request AAA to select the arbitrator. There will be no depositions in the proceedings, and discovery shall be limited to requests for documents specific to the covered dealership. The parties shall be responsible for their own expenses, fees, and costs, and shall share equally all other costs associated with the arbitration, such as arbitrator fees, meeting room charges, and administrative costs. The arbitration shall be conducted in the State where the covered dealership is located. Parties will have the option of conducting arbitration electronically and telephonically, by mutual agreement of both parties. The arbitrator shall not award compensatory, punitive, or exemplary damages to any party. If the arbitrator finds in favor of a covered dealership, the covered manufacturer shall as soon as practicable, but not later than 7 business days after receipt of the arbitrator's determination, provide the dealer a customary and usual letter of intent to enter into a sales and service agreement. After executing the sales and service agreement and successfully completing the operational prerequisites set forth therein, a covered dealership shall return to the covered manufacturer any financial compensation provided by the covered manufacturer in consideration of the covered manufacturer's initial determination to terminate, not renew, not assign or not assume the covered dealership's applicable franchise agreement.

(f) Any legally binding agreement resulting from a voluntary negotiation between a covered manufacturer and covered dealership(s) shall not be considered inconsistent with this provision and any covered dealership that is a party to such agreement shall forfeit the right to arbitration established by this provision.

(g) Notwithstanding the requirements of this provision, nothing herein shall prevent a covered manufacturer from lawfully terminating a covered dealership in accordance with applicable State law.

Chapter 15

EPILOGUE

Perseverance is a great element of success. If you only knock long enough and loud enough at the gate, you are sure to wake somebody.

Henry Wadsworth Longfellow

With the holidays rapidly approaching, the temptation was great for CRDR to relax a bit. We'd won—and won big in the face of skepticism and overwhelming odds. Opposed by two of the world's largest companies and numerous well-placed ideologues in the Obama administration (particularly in the Treasury Department), we'd managed to lay bare the half-baked excuses, lies, and poor decisions by both our federal government and the car companies. Hundreds of auto dealers across the country would now have a chance to make their case for reinstatement. But this opportunity for a fair shake might not happen unless we helped those dealers prepare for their day in court.

First, the carmakers had to go back to all of the Rejected/Wind Down dealers and inform them of their newly won right to independent binding arbitration. The legislation also stated that the communication to dealers had to describe the process, the deadlines, the reasons for their earlier rejection. Chrysler, unfortunately, largely failed to follow through on that directive. Perhaps that's because it didn't really have meaningful, structured standards and metrics for its closure decisions in the first place.

The deadline for filing for arbitration was Jan. 25, 2010—just a few weeks away. Tammy, Jack, Rob, Alison, and I recognized that CRDR's work was far from over. After the enactment, we felt a duty to encourage dealers to file for arbitration. Tammy arranged a webinar for members that was conducted by prominent dealer lawyer Mike Charapp on the basics of the arbitration process. This was especially helpful to those dealers who were going to arbitration *pro se* (without counsel), something our Committee vigorously discouraged.

Responding to a suggestion by Rachel Bachrodt, whose family was one of CRDR's strongest supporters, we quickly expanded the CRDR website, creating a secure message board for member communications called CRDRForum.com. We showed members what the criteria were and how to prepare the appeals. Many members shared what they'd learned as the various arbitrations hearings unfolded. We were able to blunt some of the main arguments the car companies were making across the country. Dealers could exchange ideas, share strategies, and anticipate many defenses used by the manufacturers based on feedback from dealers who had already completed their arbitrations. Several dealers who received successful arbitration determinations gave substantial credit to the CRDR Forum for their victories.

Post-enactment, one of the most meaningful changes was the appointment of Mark Reuss (pronounced Royce) as president

Jack Fitzgerald, Alan Spitzer, and Mark Reuss

of GM North America. Reuss had been managing director of GM Australia before being tapped to head up GM's worldwide manufacturing operations. His arrival and the departure of several other executives signaled a refreshing change of direction.

"The legislation that is happening is a good thing—to bring integrity and the right decisions for the companies and the families of our dealers across the land," he said. "It is an opportunity for all of us to make the right decisions and move on. The relationship of dealers and customers is my highest priority. Period."

I met Reuss at the launch of the Chevy Cruze at GM's Lordstown, Ohio, plant. He was GM's top "car guy" and an engineer. I thought that was particularly good—I believe GM, really any car company, should always have an engineer right at the top of its hierarchy. After all, it really is all about the product.

The whole posture of GM seemed to change when Reuss arrived. "Al, I couldn't believe the tone of just about everything in Detroit when I got there," he said. "Everyone was just angry with everyone else."

Before the arbitration deadline, more than 1,100 of GM's Wind Down dealers filed for arbitration. Rather than face the daunting task of responding to an overwhelming number of arbitration filings, on Friday, March 5, 2010, GM unilaterally agreed to reinstate more than 660 of those dealers—without a single arbitration hearing. It was gracious capitulation—and an implied acknowledgment that the Wind Down process of the previous year had been deeply flawed. In the days leading up to the arbitrations, GM continued its proactive approach and began individual negotiations with many of the remaining dealers. Some were reinstated. Others received additional financial consideration and withdrew their arbitration. Before the arbitrations began, GM was able to pare down the list to only 62 cases, prevailing in 39 of them with the dealers winning reinstatement in 23 of the hearings.

At Chrysler, it was a different story. The tone there didn't change much. A total of 409 dealers filed for arbitration. The company agreed to voluntarily reinstate 50 of those dealers. (It also claimed to have offered similar deals to 36 dealers earlier.) A total of 105 Rejected Dealers sought arbitration and Chrysler prevailed in 73 of those cases. Chrysler settled the bulk of them before the hearings occurred. A few were reinstated outside of arbitration. Other Rejected Dealers received financial compensation from Chrysler, which previously had offered nothing. Others simply went out of business.

In total, CRDR's grassroots advocacy was directly responsible for saving hundreds of dealerships and tens of thousands of jobs. I'm no economist, but the economic impact of our efforts surely reached into the tens of billions of dollars—an achievement of which our entire team is proud, of course.

But there's also the small matter of justice and fairness. CRDR, on behalf of the wrongfully railroaded auto dealers in this country, was vindicated by the Office of the Special Inspector General for the Troubled Asset Relief Program (SIGTARP), which conducted a thorough investigation into all of the events regarding dealer closures. Tammy and Rob met with the investigating team on behalf of CRDR. Our committee turned over about 1,000 pages of documents to them. The report laid bare the incompetence of the Auto Team, the flawed rationales, the pressures placed upon GM and Chrysler, and many other shortcomings.

The timing of the SIGTARP report was bothersome, coming just days after the last arbitration was complete. There's no question in my mind that, had the arbitrators had access to this scathing document—so critical of the Auto Task Force, GM, and Chrysler with respect to the dealer closures—during the hearings, many more determinations may have been rendered in favor of the dealer.

Did "Chicago politics" affect the selection of dealerships for closure? In other words, was this a "Blue State vs. Red State" event? Were "Democrat dealers" kept? Were "Republican dealers" cut? It's a tempting assumption and popular urban myth—but it's just not borne out by the evidence. There's no concrete proof that the White House itself was involved in the selection of who received Rejection/Wind Down notices and who didn't. After all, some loyal Democrats had dealerships terminated and were unsuccessful in arbitration hearings.

But that doesn't mean politics weren't involved—it's just that it appeared to be "car industry politics." There appeared to be a lot of internal score settling and vindictiveness that was troubling to any independent observer. Tammy, Jack, and I became aware of numerous examples of this, some of which have been detailed on these pages.

Also of great interest to passionate observers has been the sad events surrounding Steven Rattner, the man selected by the Obama administration to head up the Auto Team and dubbed the "car czar" by the media. In addition to the upbraiding by SIGTARP, Rattner faced much more serious charges from

Pat and Alan Spitzer with President and Mrs. Obama

the New York State Attorney General and the Securities and Exchange Commission. His private equity firm—the Quadrangle Group—was ensnared in a pension/kickback scheme that led to a multiyear ban from the securities industry and $6.2 million civil penalty from the SEC. It was so unseemly that, after he resigned from Quadrangle, his former partners felt compelled to issue a statement disassociating themselves from his unsavory actions. "We wholly disavow the conduct engaged in by Steve Rattner, who hired the New York State Comptroller's political consultant, Hank Morris, to arrange an investment from the New York State Common Retirement Fund. That conduct was inappropriate, wrong, and unethical."[28]

In a further entanglement with the law, Rattner settled a case brought by New York State Attorney General Andrew Cuomo

---

[28] Robbins, T., "Steve Rattner 'Unethical' Say Quadrangle and Cuomo." *The Village Voice*. April 15, 2010.

by paying a $10 million fine, but without an admission of guilt. (Innocent people voluntarily agree to pay $10 million fines all the time.)

Any potentially lingering reputation for fairness or ethics in his participation in the Auto Team was now fully gone. Try as he might, his attempt to spin the record in his book, *Overhaul*, could not adequately refute the evidence from the various investigations. The manner in which his book trivializes the actions of the Task Force to destroy the lives of so many by unnecessarily closing thousands of profitable small businesses owned by hard-working Americans shows a detachment that's almost beyond belief.

In the fall of 2010, I finally met with President Obama in person. During our time together, I thanked him for signing the legislation that established the arbitration process, yet made it very clear to him that I believed his Task Force made a huge mistake by calling for the termination of any dealers. His measured response: "We wanted to be sure the remaining dealers were profitable."

"The marketplace, Mr. President," I answered, almost involuntarily raising my right hand as if I was taking an oath. "The marketplace should be the judge of who lives and who dies!" I sensed in his tone of voice that he knew I was right. At any rate, he was very gracious, said he was sorry, and understood my point of view.

In the end, the CRDR journey was an amazing experience for all of us. Most experts both inside and outside the D.C. beltway predicted our effort would never get off the ground. Tammy, Jack, and I and countless others who supported us paid no attention to the naysayers. Sadly, it was not a complete victory. There were a number of casualties along the way. Many dealers were too financially strapped when the legislation was enacted to be able to get back in business. Others were victims of biased arbitrators.

In my opinion, these actions to terminate thousands of profitable businesses represent some of the darkest days in the history of American business. I was encouraged to write this book because many people believed it was a story that needed to be told. It is my fervent hope that, in some small way, it will help ensure future generations of Americans will never allow it to happen again.

AFTERWORD

You can't run away from trouble.
There ain't no place that far.

Joel Chandler Harris

Confidentiality agreements between the Spitzer organization and both General Motors and Chrysler prohibit detailed disclosure of the results of settlements between the parties. However, the results can be summarized as follows: There were 10 franchises involved—seven Chrysler and three GM. Eight of those were settled outside of arbitration. Six of the eight were reinstated. For the other two, Spitzer received compensation. The parties were unable to negotiate an acceptable settlement in two others and were forced to proceed to arbitration. Spitzer prevailed in one of them.

Alan believes the Spitzer organization today is as strong as it's ever been and stands ready to meet the many challenges the future will doubtlessly offer. He looks forward to working with his daughter, Alison, some of her siblings and other key members of the company to help guide the organization for years to come.

Jack Fitzgerald continues to preside over the very successful Fitzgerald Auto Mall chain from his Maryland headquarters. Fitzgerald's Countryside Chrysler-Jeep was successful in an arbitration proceeding and is back in the business of selling Chrysler products in Clearwater, FL. The Fitzgerald organization was able to satisfactorily resolve all outstanding issues with General Motors. Jack is also the leading advocate working with Congress to find an alternative to the job killing estate tax that has forced the sale of an untold number of small businesses and family farms. He has even formed another organization: Americans Standing for the Simplification of Estate Tax (ASSET). Not surprisingly, Tammy and Alan are united behind him in this effort. As always, Rob Smith is at his side every step of the way.

Tammy Darvish is still a perpetual motion machine. She has a leadership role in the large and highly respected DARCARS organization along with her involvement in a number of civic organizations. DARCARS was able to settle matters amiably with Chrysler and GM outside of arbitration. She will soon be publishing her own perspective of the events chronicled in this book. Tammy's book, tentatively entitled *Outrage,* is recommended reading.

Alison will soon deliver her second child, a boy to be named Archer Alan Swartz. When we became involved with the dealer rights initiative she was our company's Director of e-Commerce. She has since become Vice President – Director of Marketing and is poised to lead the fourth generation of our company. She does a remarkable job of balancing her duties as mother and business executive. Her husband, Jeremy Swartz, is at the helm of Spitzer Motor City, Inc. which represents the consolidated reinstatement of two Spitzer Chrysler dealerships. The dealership is destined to become one of the most important locations for Chrysler in Northeast Ohio.

Afterword

After so ably performing his dual role as chairman of the Automotive Trade Association Executives and president of the Ohio Automobile Dealers Association for a year, Tim Doran successfully shepherded the passage of a significant auto dealer law in the Ohio legislature that should become a model for other states to follow. Tim is in his fourth decade at the head of the Ohio dealer organization. Dealers in Ohio and across the country are fortunate to have such an articulate and passionate advocate.

The Committee to Restore Dealer Rights, LLC (CRDR) is still in existence although it faces an uncertain future. It has been suggested by many that the organization should continue to operate as a complement to the National Automobile Dealers Association (NADA). Was this an ad hoc organization whose mission has been accomplished or will it endure to face new challenges? Only time will tell!

As for GM and Chrysler, they aspire to be a 21st century Phoenix and "rise from the ashes." If they succeed, and we predict they will, it can't happen without a robust and aggressive dealer network. Brands come and brands go. In the past decade we have already seen the disappearance of once venerable brands like Plymouth, Oldsmobile, Pontiac and Mercury. Once heralded to be the "import fighter" that would help GM recapture lost market share, Saturn has disappeared after a little more than two decades.

Korean automakers Hyundai and KIA have gobbled up significant market share in what seems like a nanosecond. Global powers like China and India are eager to gain a presence in this country. Automakers from Europe, Japan and Korea have invested billions of dollars in US manufacturing plants, a trend that doubtlessly will continue.

Against this backdrop of uncertainty and arguably the most intense competition in the industry since at least World War II, two things seem abundantly clear. Quality is the price of admission. No longer will any car maker be able to exist for very long building substandard vehicles. And as the manufacturers battle for market share their respective dealer networks will become increasingly important to their success. One of the last bastions of entrepreneurship, the American car dealer, will persevere.

BIBLIOGRAPHY

"GM Settles Out of Court; to Award Nader $425,000." *The Harvard Crimson*. Aug. 14, 1970.

"It's time for GM to admit, finally, its $2 billion lie." *Automotive News*. Nov. 9, 2009.

1679-1681-R.P. Verbiest's Steam Chariot, History of the Automobile: Origin to 1900.

Banks, Cliff, "Chrysler's Valued Dealer List," *Ward's Dealer Business*. May 13, 2009.

DRP's patent No. 37435 (PDF, 561 kB, German) was filed Jan. 29, 1886 and granted Nov. 2, 1886, thus taking effect Jan. 29.

Georgano, G. N., *Cars: Early and Vintage, 1886-1930*. (London: Grange-Universal, 1985)

http://www.famoustexans.com/rossperot.htm

http://www.gm.ca/inm/gmcanada/english/about/OverviewHist/hist_auto.htm

http://www.juse.or.jp/e/deming/

Ingrassia, Paul, *Crash Course: The American Automobile Industry's Road from Glory to Disaster*, Random House, 2010.

Ingrassia, Paul and Joseph B. White, *Comeback: The Fall and Rise of the American Automobile Industry*, Simon & Schuster, 1994.

Krebs, M., "Chrysler Cuts 789 Dealer Agreements; GM Slashes Dealerships Friday." *Auto Observer*. May 14, 2009.

LaReau, J., "Mulally says he has work to do before retiring ." *Automotive News*. Jan. 18, 2010.

Levin, Doron and Jeff Green, "General Motors Chief Rick Wagoner Said to Step Down." Bloomberg.com. March 29, 2009.

Manwaring, L.A., *The Observer's Book of Automobiles* (12th ed.) 1966.

McLaughlin, D., "Chrysler Bankruptcy Judge Handled Enron, World Com." *The Wall Street Journal.* May 1, 2009.

Mercedes-Benz History. Edmunds.com.

Moore, T., "The GM System is Like a Blanket of Fog," *Fortune.* Feb. 15, 1988.

Perry, Mark, "Big 3 vs. Foreign Transplants," *The Wall Street Journal.* December 1, 2008.

Rattner, Steven, *Overhaul: An Insider's Account of the Obama Administration's Emergency Rescue of the Auto Industry,* Houghton Mifflin Harcourt, 2010.

Robbins, T., "Steve Rattner 'Unethical' Say Quadrangle and Cuomo." *The Village Voice.* April 15, 2010.

Sanger, D., "The 31-Year-Old in Charge of Dismantling G.M." *The New York Times.* May 31, 2009.

Shepardson, D., "Pelosi: Hands Off Auto Industry." *Detroit News,* Oct. 3, 2009.

Sherman, Joe, *In the Rings of Saturn,* Oxford University Press, 1994.

Sloan, Alfred P., Jr. *My Years With General Motors,* Doubleday, 1963.

Teather, David, "The Woman Who Built Financial 'Weapon of Mass Destruction' | Business." *The Guardian.* September 20, 2008.

Vlasic, B., "Choosing Its Own Path, Ford Stayed Independent." *The New York Times.* April 8, 2009.

Vlasic, Bill and Bradley A. Stertz, *Taken for a Ride: How Daimler-Benz Drove Off With Chrysler,* HarperCollins, 200

Wernle, B., "A Hero Falls, Hard." *Automotive News.* Oct. 26, 2009.

Wernle, B., "A Letter Comes—A Life's Work Is Shattered." *Automotive News.* May 18, 2009.

Wernle, Bradford, *Automotive News.* May 14, 2009.

"DETROIT 3" HISTORIES

by Gary Witzenburg

The pages that follow include brief histories of the companies formerly known as the Big Three: Chrysler, Ford and General Motors. They have been written by award-winning automotive writer Gary Witzenburg. Gary has been writing about automobiles, auto people and the auto industry since the 1980s. A former auto engineer, race driver and advanced technology vehicle development manager, his work has appeared in a wide variety of national magazines, including *The Robb Report, Playboy, Popular Mechanics, Car and Driver, Road & Track, Motor Trend, Automobile, Autoweek* and *Automobile Quarterly,* and he has authored eight automotive books. He is currently a columnist for AutoblogGreen, a contributing editor or correspondent to *Motor Trend, MT Classic* and *Truck Trend, Ward's Auto World, Kelley Blue Book* (www.kbb.com) and AutoMedia.com and a North American Car/Truck of the Year juror.

Appendix 1

THE HISTORY OF

GENERAL MOTORS

by Gary Witzenburg

General Motors owes its very existence to a handful of dreamers and inventors with vision and guts—vision to see the future and guts to reach out boldly for it. The first was Ransom Eli Olds, who said he invented an automobile because he couldn't stand the smell of horses on his father's farm. An expert machinist, he started building engines out of high school (around 1882) and four years later founded the Olds Gasoline Engine Works with his father.

By 1896, Olds attracted the attention of wealthy investors with a spindly, gas-powered buggy of his own design. They helped him incorporate the Olds Motor Vehicle Co. and move it from Lansing, Michigan, to Detroit. A lot more engines and a few (unprofitable) luxury cars were built in the next four years before he decided what America needed was a simple, inexpensive, single-cylinder runabout that almost any ordinary citizen could operate, understand and afford.

He labored day and night developing a prototype and blueprints until, one day early in 1901, his plant burned to the ground. No lives were lost and the prototype was saved, but the prints were gone. Olds started over, disassembled the car, made prints from the parts and more parts from the prints, and by the end of that year had sold 600 little toboggan-shaped, cart-springed, chain-drive "Curved-Dash" Oldsmobiles. And, as sales climbed to 2,500 in 1902, it became America's first mass-produced gas-engined car.

In 1903 Olds' sales hit 4,000, and his factory, which embodied the first tentative steps toward a moving assembly line, was touted as the world's largest auto plant. Some 5,500 cars were sold in 1904, but Olds' backers wanted to move into the more profitable luxury car field. He left the company, later to found a new one called REO, the founder's monogram. Oldsmobile moved back to Lansing and sold 6,500 Curved-Dash Runabouts in 1905, but it was primitive and underpowered by then, the pricier models were unprofitable, and the company was broke and deeply in debt.

Cadillac

At the turn of the century, Henry Martyn Leyland, a skilled gunsmith and toolmaker with very high standards of precision manufacture, was running Leyland and Faulconer, a successful Detroit company that built, among other things, engines for the infant auto industry. In 1902, he advised William H. Murphy to reorganize his failed Detroit Automobile Co. and build a new-design car using Leyland's high-quality engine. Murphy agreed, and the Cadillac Automobile Co. (named for the French explorer who founded the city of Detroit) was born.

The first Model A Cadillac was completed and displayed at the New York auto show that year, and initial orders were strong. But production problems, a fire in the plant, and other difficulties delayed deliveries. On Christmas Eve, 1904, Murphy and his partners persuaded a reluctant Leyland to take over management of their company along with his own, and the new organization was the Cadillac Motor Car Co.

Leyland applied his unusually precise manufacturing and assembly practices to the single-cylinder Cadillac cars, and in March, 1908 the two-seat Model K Runabout won the coveted British Dewar Trophy for engineering by demonstrating parts interchangeability superior to anything else at the time. That cemented Cadillac's quality reputation, and by the end of that year, more than 16,000 had been sold.

BUICK

David Dunbar Buick was a gifted tinkerer who in 1901 sold his profitable Detroit bathroom fixture firm and started tinkering with engines. His first design was a horizontally opposed twin, which was later improved with overhead valves. In May 1903, he built a car for the engine and founded the Buick Motor Car Co. But with debts rising and capital gone, he sold the company to a wagon maker in Flint, Michigan and moved there to manage it.

By the time the first production Buick, a 20-hp 2.6-liter Model B, was sold in August, 1904, the new investors had spent most of their money, and the struggling company was sold again to millionaire Flint carriage maker William Crapo Durant. Buick's excellent car became nationally famous, and Durant built the firm into one of America's largest automakers, with annual sales topping 8,000 by 1908. But David Buick, who found himself with a steadily decreasing management role and financial share as the company grew, left it that year.

General Motors

Born into a wealthy family, Durant started in business at age 16 and by 1900, at age 40, headed the nation's largest car- and carriage-making company. When he acquired the ailing Buick Motor Co., he figured that a single auto maker was dangerously dependent on fickle public taste, while a large organization of smaller companies offering a variety of products could prosper regardless of how the market winds shifted...and that in-house parts makers could supply components more cheaply and efficiently than outside suppliers could.

With Buick riding high in 1908, Durant arranged a meeting with the three other leading makers—Ransom Olds, Henry Ford, and Benjamin Briscoe of Maxwell Briscoe—to propose a merger. It almost came together, but Ford demanded $3 million in cash (instead of an exchange of stock) for his company, prompting Olds to do the same. With no way to raise that much on short notice, Durant decided to go it alone. On September16, 1908 he founded the General Motors Corp., which absorbed Buick, then he took over ailing Oldsmobile and 20 more companies, including Cadillac and struggling Pontiac, Michigan automaker Oakland. But he spent himself heavily into debt and soon proved better at building an empire than running one.

Two years later, Durant was forced into a bailout with a bankers' syndicate, lost control, resigned and returned to Flint to establish the Little Motor Car Co. He put a famous Swiss-born mechanic and race driver named Louis Chevrolet (who had worked for him at Buick) to work on a new high-priced, high-powered Durant-Chevrolet, then organized the Chevrolet Motor Co. in November, 1911. Both the $650 4-cylinder Little and the $2,150 6-cylinder Chevrolet were instant successes in 1912, with some 3,500 of the former and 2,999 of the latter sold.

GM II

Durant moved Chevrolet to Flint and set up additional assembly plants in other parts of the country, and when Louis Chevrolet returned from a trip abroad and saw what Durant was up to, he quit to pursue his own interests. Little folded in 1915, but Chevrolet thrived; and in September of that year, Durant consolidated his various enterprises into a new Chevrolet Motor Co. funded largely by the DuPont banking family. He and DuPont began exchanging Chevrolet stock five-to-one for GM shares—a very attractive proposition for GM shareholders, who had not seen a dividend in five years—and before long, he strode into the corporation he had founded, then lost and announced to everyone's shock that he controlled it again!

Cadillac, still being run by Leyland, was on a roll. In 1910, it was first to offer a standard closed body and the next year introduced the first practical electric ignition, lighting, and self starting system. The self-starter—a joint development with Charles F. "Boss" Kettering's Delco Laboratories—was a momentous breakthrough because it allowed nearly anyone to start and operate a motor vehicle without risking the bone-breaking crank. For this, Cadillac was awarded its second Dewar Trophy—the only automaker ever to win two. Kettering also helped develop the industry's first water-cooled V-8 engine, standard in all 1915 Cadillacs.

Buick, under president Walter P. Chrysler, produced an amazing 125,000 cars in 1916. Oldsmobile in 1910 introduced a car of colossal proportions (11.5-ft. wheelbase, 42-in. wheels, 11.6-liter 6-cylinder engine), and when one raced the famous 20th-Century Limited train from New York to Albany and won, its name was changed to Limited. And when Durant moved Chevrolet directly into competition with Ford's cheap and popular model T with a $490 model 490 in October, 1915, Chevrolet sales grew to 70,000 that year and nearly 126,000 the next.

In 1918, Chevrolet, the rest of the former General Motors Co. and some other Durant properties, including Delco and the Hyatt Roller Bearing Co., were absorbed into a new General Motors Corp. From Delco, it acquired super engineer Kettering, who would head its engineering and research departments, and from Hyatt came Alfred P. Sloan, Jr. the brilliant autocrat who would soon take its helm.

Durant then plunged into another spending and expansion spree, enlarging plants and building new ones, new research labs and a 15-story headquarters in Detroit, and acquiring additional companies, including Fisher body and refrigerator-maker Frigidaire. And he moved GM into the financing business by organizing General Motors Acceptance Corp. in 1919.

During and just after World War I, both Leyland and Chrysler left to found Lincoln and Chrysler, respectively, and when it became clear that Durant was driving GM into another financial collapse, Sloan almost quit. And when Durant was again forced into a banker bailout and resigned, banker Pierre S. du Pont became president and installed Sloan as executive vp.

Sadly, Durant plunged aggressively into the stock market after the 1929 crash attempting to demonstrate to the public his confidence in the market. The ploy failed when stock prices continued their precipitous decline. A few years later Durant would be forced into bankruptcy. He and his second wife lived on a small pension provided by Sloan. This larger than life entrepreneur whose vision was responsible for the creation of General Motors, world's largest corporation, spent his later years managing a bowling alley in Flint, Michigan.

Sloan (who would become GM's first CEO in 1923 and chairman of the board from 1937 to 1956) created the management system that saved GM: centralized management and budget control with committee decision-making and delegation of responsibility to the divisions. There would be "a car for every purse and purpose," with each division offering specific products for specific types of buyers, and a clear pecking order to encourage customers to step up from one to the next. And, recognizing that, other things being equal, people would buy the best-looking products, he hired California custom car designer Harley J. Earl to create the industry's first automotive styling department (and regular styling changes) in 1927.

Chevrolet became America's favorite car in 1929, Cadillac became "the standard of the world" among luxury cars, Oldsmobile and Buick thrived, and Oakland (which introduced the Pontiac car in 1926 and became Pontiac Motor Div. in 1932) slogged along with solid products.

Post World War II

Thus the stage was set for GM to grow into not just America's but the world's biggest automaker. In 1954, GM sold its 50 millionth U.S. car and generated $806 million net income on nearly

$10 billion net sales of 3.8 million vehicles worldwide (87 percent U.S.-built). A decade later, those figures were $1.7 billion on $17 billion sales of 6.1 million vehicles.

Most would agree that GM led the world in design (since 1958, under Earl successor William L. "Bill" Mitchell), technology and business savvy. And when the 1960s ushered in a "muscle car" era, GM led that as well, beginning with Pontiac's 1964 GTO. But the '60s also brought new concerns for auto safety, emissions and damageability, answered by huge government bureaucracies and blizzards of ever-tougher and more costly regulations.

Simultaneously, the world's biggest and most open auto market was being invaded by armies of aggressive off-shore competitors. New smaller, more fuel-efficient U.S. cars were developed in response, but most (including GM's 1960 Chevy Corvair, 1970 Vega and 1976 Chevette) were poorly built, hastily engineered, or both. On the positive side, GM developed the Positive Crankcase Ventilation valve, the industry's first vehicle emissions control device, led the way with engines that could run on low- or no-lead gasoline and in 1974 introduced the emissions-eating catalytic converter used ever since by automakers worldwide.

Following the 1973 Arab oil embargo, GM was first to downsize its entire U.S. vehicle fleet to increase fuel efficiency, ushering in a trend of ever-lighter and more aerodynamic designs across all model lines. It went well at first, but a second round of downsizing, a wholesale conversion to transverse-engine front-wheel drive and a chaotic corporate reorganization under 1980s CEO Roger B. Smith combined to kill GM's design leadership and severely damage its product quality, leading to a long, steady slide in sales and profits.

On top of that was piled relentless regulatory acceleration; growing government and media hostility; exploding labor costs (especially pensions and health care); over-taxation at every level of government; out-of-control litigation/lawsuit costs (a unique U.S. phenomenon); and, as a cumulative result, crippling levels of debt at all three U.S. automakers.

At GM, an all-new import-fighting Saturn brand was added in 1985, then starved of new product and promotion as GM's finances weakened. Bankruptcy was narrowly averted in the early 1990s, but profitability returned under new CEO Jack Smith. Then the struggling, 107-year-old Oldsmobile brand was killed in 2004.

In 2007, GM sold 9.4 million vehicles worldwide (second only to 9.6 million in 1978) but lost $38.7 billion and employed less than 270,000 people (vs. 839,000 in 1978). It also signed a historic agreement with the UAW to offload its hourly retiree healthcare cost to an independent trust and, in July 2008, announced a plan to cut costs by $10 billion and raise $5 billion through borrowing and asset sales. Nevertheless, the once-mighty world's biggest car company was financially unprepared to survive the massive economic collapse later that year.

With the U.S. (and much of the world's) economy in shambles, vehicle sales stalled and credit unavailable, GM was forced to go to the U.S. government, hat in hand, on Dec. 2, 2008 and beg for financial aid. Then, on June 1, it filed for Chapter 11 bankruptcy protection—from which it emerged (amazingly quickly) on July 10 a much smaller and leaner new company.

CEO Rick Wagoner was gone, replaced by former COO Fritz Henderson. In exchange for $50 billion in aid, the U.S. Treasury (taxpayers) would own 60.8 percent and the UAW health trust 17.5 percent. Half of its U.S. brands (Saturn, Pontiac, Hummer and Saab) would have to be sold or closed and 13 of its 47 plants shuttered by the end of 2011, U.S. employees cut from about 91,000 to 64,000 and dealer count slashed 40 percent from 6,000 to 3,600 (though about 725 of them would later regain their franchises after Congress passed a law requiring third party arbitration).

Since then, the new General Motors Company's horizons have brightened substantially. Its new leadership and structure (under CEO Dan Ackerson) appear to be working well. All of the newer products from its four remaining U.S. brands (Chevrolet, Buick, Cadillac and GMC) are selling strongly, some virtually sold out. Net income for 2010 was $4.7 billion on $135.6 billion U.S. sales—GM's first profit since 2004—even as the U.S. economy continues to struggle with high unemployment and fast-rising petroleum prices due to Middle East troubles.

If the U.S. government will only get out of the way and cooperate to begin reducing automaker regulation, taxation and litigation costs, it should be well positioned for the future.

Appendix 2

THE HISTORY OF

CHRYSLER

by Gary Witzenburg

Of the hundreds of automobile makers that came and went during the first century of U.S. automotive history, few survived more than a handful of years, and only three lived long enough to crash up against the economic tsunami of 2008. Of those three, latecomer Chrysler was born 22 years after Ford and 17 after General Motors was incorporated. And, like Ford, Chrysler was the creation of the one remarkable individual whose name it still bears.

Walter Percy Chrysler, born in Wamego, Kansas in 1875, went to work as an apprentice railroad engineer at the tender age of 17 and by 33 was a top manager. In 1908, he bought his first automobile (a Locomobile Phaeton), then took it apart and put it together several times to get to know its technology. In the process, he learned how to drive.

Four years later, Chrysler joined the automobile industry at the Buick Motor Co. in Flint, Michigan, a subsidiary of the General Motors Company. As production manager there, he raised production from 20 to 550 vehicles per day. On October 13, 1916, General Motors Corporation was incorporated under Delaware law and acquired all the stock of General Motors Company. Thereafter, Chrysler soon rose to Buick president and general manager. Under his leadership, Buick became GM's biggest money maker, and he took on additional responsibilities in 1919 as GM's first vice president, in charge of production.

But Chrysler resigned the following year over major "differences" with then-GM boss William C. Durant. A few months later, creditors of the struggling Willys-Overland Co. brought him in as executive vice president, with total operational control and an unheard-of salary of $1 million per year, and he turned that company around in just two years. At the same time, he was also reviving the Maxwell Motor Company, 90 percent owned by the Chalmers Motor Company. In 1921, Chrysler became chairman of Maxwell-Chalmers Co., which a year later was renamed Maxwell Motor Corporation.

Three years later, still head of Maxwell, he took a newly-created car bearing his name to the New York Auto Show. Because his "Chrysler Six" was not yet available for sale, he was denied access to the show but displayed it in the lobby of the nearby Commodore Hotel. With a seven-main-bearing crankshaft, aluminum pistons, forced lubrication and higher compression than anyone had thought possible, its 3.3-liter "L-Head" 6-cylinder engine delivered 68 hp at 3,000 rpm, while the car it powered boasted four-wheel hydraulic brakes and shocks and was sensationally fast at nearly 70 mph.

The Chrysler Six caused a media and industry sensation, and nearly 32,000 were sold in 1924, the best sales to date for a new

American launch. On June 6, 1925, the Maxwell Motor Corp. became Chrysler Corp. and posted a $4 million net profit for the year.

By 1926, the Chrysler range had expanded to three model series with names indicating their top speeds: the 4-cylinder Series 58 and 6-cylinder Series G-70 and G-80. Top of the line was the 92-hp E-80 Imperial, the first Chrysler luxury car with carburetor pre-heating and custom body work. A (1927-model) Series 60 was added mid-year as the new Chrysler Corporation moved to fifth place among American automakers, then to fourth in 1927.

The low-priced Plymouth brand was launched in 1928, followed by middle-priced DeSoto, both beginning with 1929 models. Powered by a 45-hp four cylinder and priced at just $670, the Plymouth was first in its class with four-wheel hydraulic brakes and rubber-mounted bodies. Six-cylinder DeSoto production began in July, and 100,000 were sold in its first 14 months—a new record for a newly launched automobile that would stand for 30 years.

Also that year, Chrysler acquired Dodge Brothers, Inc., a company five times its size. The 4-cylinder Chrysler Series 52, 6-cylinder Series 62 and 72 and Imperial Series 80 combined sold a record 160,670 units, and Chrysler became the third largest U.S. maker.

Chrysler's first 8-cylinder engine debuted in 1931 in the Chrysler Eight and Imperial, and the company introduced a revolutionary new "Floating Power" engine mount with a leaf spring under the transmission and rubber bearings to isolate the chassis from engine vibrations. In 1933, in the midst of a world economic crisis, Chrysler was the only American automaker to top its sales of boom year 1929.

In 1934, Chrysler launched controversial streamlined Chrysler and DeSoto Airflow automobiles with an optional automatic overdrive transmission. The following year, Walter P. Chrysler resigned as president but remained chairman, and K.T. Keller, who had moved to Chrysler from General Motors in 1926, replaced him as president. By 1936, annual production had reached a million vehicles per year.

In 1940, Chrysler built six each of its first experimental "Idea Cars," Thunderbolt and Newport dual cowl phaeton, and on August 18 of that year, founder Walter P. Chrysler passed away at age 65. In 1941, Chrysler launched its first Town & Country wagon, with a wood and steel body and visible wood ribbing, and introduced a four-speed semi-automatic transmission that shifted automatically between its two lower gears or its two higher gears.

In 1942, civilian vehicle production was suspended in favor of war production. Four years later, production of slightly modified prewar models resumed, along with new sedan, coupe and convertible versions of the Town & Country. In 1949, the first all-new Chrysler models were launched into a car-starved postwar U.S. market, and the company hired famed auto designer Virgil Exner away from Studebaker.

In 1950, K.T. Keller became chairman and Lester L. "Tex" Colbert president, and Chrysler introduced four-wheel disc brakes, industry-first electric power windows and the first of many Idea Cars from Italian design house Ghia. Chrysler's first V8 engine—boasting 180 horsepower from hemispherical ("Hemi") combustion chambers—and power steering arrived for 1951. Two years later came an innovative PowerFlite automatic transmission.

In 1954, entry-level Plymouths began offering optional V8s, and Chrysler engineers began testing a revolutionary gas turbine auto engine. Nineteen-fifty-five brought Virgil Exner's "Forward Look" styling and the C-300, the first in a long line of Chrysler "letter series" cars. The following year saw introduction of the "Magic Touch" pushbutton automatic transmission, followed for 1957 by a new-design "TorqueFlite." automatic.

In 1958, Chrysler bought into French automaker Simca and started importing Simca vehicles to North America. It grew the Hemi V8 to 5.9 liters, but new fuel injection in the 300D performance model proved problematic and was soon replaced by conventional carburetors. The Hemi V8 expanded again to 6.3 liters and was rated at a muscular 345 hp for 1959.

In response to growing sales of small imported cars, Detroit automakers introduced their first American "compacts" for 1960. Chrysler's entry was the Plymouth Valiant, powered by a new "Slant Six" engine that would come to be known for anvil-tough durability. Lester Colbert became chairman while retaining the title of president.

In 1961, George H. Love became chairman and Lynn A. Townsend president, and the 33-year-old DeSoto brand was dropped. In 1963, Chrysler introduced a bold five-year/50,000-mile powertrain warranty and built 51 custom-bodied gas-turbine-powered cars to be tested by selected customers. They performed fairly well but were far too expensive to be practical.

Ford's first Mustang hit the streets in April, 1964, but Plymouth's first sport-compact Barracuda (essentially a Valiant coupe with a unique fastback roofline) preceded it by a couple of weeks. In 1967, Townsend was appointed chairman and Virgil

E. Boyd president, and in 1970, Chrysler began importing small cars and trucks from its Japanese partner, Mitsubishi Motors Corp., and selling them under the Dodge and Plymouth labels.

John J. Riccardo became chairman and Eugene A. Cafiero president in 1975. Three years later, financially struggling Chrysler sold its European operations to Peugeot-Citröen and introduced the industry's first U.S.-built small front-wheel-drive cars, the Dodge Omni and Plymouth Horizon. In 1979, with the company in seriously bad financial straits, Riccardo named Lee A. Iacocca (recently fired by Ford chairman Henry Ford II) Chrysler president.

Iacocca succeeded Riccardo as chairman the following year and named J. Paul Bergmoser president, then admitted in an interview (with this writer) that, had he fully understood how bad things were, he never would have taken the job. But he managed to secure $1.5 billion in U.S. government-guaranteed loans, enough to keep the company afloat to begin a badly-needed product transformation led by a series of all-new front-drive "K-cars."

Those first K-cars, the Dodge Aries and Plymouth Reliant, arrived for 1982 and sold well enough to aid a fast financial recovery, and in 1983 Chrysler proudly paid back its federally-guaranteed loans seven years ahead of schedule. The following year, the company created what would become a hugely popular new U.S. market segment with introduction of K-car-based Dodge Caravan and Plymouth Voyager minivans. Also in 1984, Chrysler Corp. was reorganized as a holding company consisting of Chrysler Motors, Chrysler Financial, Chrysler Technologies and Gulfstream Aerospace, and Harold K. Sperlich was named president.

In 1985, Chrysler and Mitsubishi established Diamond-Star Motors, a joint venture to build small cars in Normal, Illinois. The next year brought a seven-year/70,000-mile powertrain warranty and seven-year/100,000-mile corrosion protection.

In 1987, Chrysler bought the struggling American Motors Corp., America's fourth largest automaker, along with its iconic Jeep brand, and launched a new Eagle brand. (In 1963, Willys-Overland, maker of the original military Jeeps, had become the Kaiser-Jeep Corp., which had been purchased by American Motors in 1970.) In 1988, Chrysler bought Italian exoticar-maker Lamborghini and signed an agreement with Italy's Fiat to sell Alfa Romeos in North America, and Diamond-Star Motors launched vehicle production.

In 1989, Chrysler sold Chrysler Technologies, partnered with GM to establish New Venture Gear, the first joint venture between two U.S. automakers, and implemented a $1 billion cost-cutting and reorganization program. The next year saw a re-launch of the Town & Country as a new Chrysler luxury minivan.

In 1991, Chrysler broke ground on a $1 billion Technology Center in Auburn Hills, Michigan, sold its Mitsubishi shares, ended its agreement with Fiat and hired top auto exec Robert A. Lutz away from Ford to be its new president. But Iacocca didn't get along with Lutz, so the following year he bypassed Lutz and hired GM of Europe chief Robert J. Eaton as vice chairman, chief operating officer and heir apparent. Meanwhile, Lutz created the Dodge Viper, a high-performance V10-powered two-seat sports car and the first Chrysler product designed by a platform team.

In 1993, Eaton replaced the retiring Iacocca, and Chrysler sold Lamborghini. Then it launched the Chrysler Concorde, Dodge

Intrepid and Eagle Vision, an attractive new line of family cars with innovative "cab-forward" design. Sales hit 2.5 million cars and trucks that year, a 14 percent increase over 1992, and 1994 net earnings were a record $3.7 billion.

Chrysler opened its new Auburn Hills world headquarters and technical center in 1996 and in 1997 introduced the '98 mid-size Dodge Durango SUV and second-generation Chrysler Concordes and Dodge Intrepids, and announced that it would drop the Eagle brand at the end of '98. Chrysler's U.S. market share improved to 14.9 percent vs. 13.1 percent in 1992.

Thomas T. Stallkamp became president in 1998, and the company launched the '99 Chrysler LHS and 300M sedans, the latter continuing the legacy of the 1955 to 1965 "letter series" cars, and the '99 Jeep Grand Cherokee. But that year's major development was a takeover by German automaker Daimler-Benz, initially billed as a "merger of equals," which saw Chrysler Corp. become Chrysler Group, a business unit of the new DaimlerChrysler AG.

In 1999, James P. Holden replaced Stallkamp as president, then in 2000 Dr. Dieter Zetsche was appointed Chrysler Group president and CEO. The following year, the 73-year-old Plymouth brand was discontinued. Production of a new 5.7-liter HEMI V8 for '03 Dodge Ram Heavy Duty trucks began in 2002, and in 2003, Chrysler formed a Global Engine Manufacturing Alliance (GEMA) with Mitsubishi and Korea's Hyundai Motor Co. to produce a new series of dual-overhead-cam, 16-valve, dual-variable-valve-timing four-cylinder engines.

Chrysler's all-new, rear-drive 2005 full-size 300 sedan and Dodge Magnum wagon hit the streets in late 2004 and were praised for bold styling and surprising dynamics. Most everyone else had been doing smaller, more fuel efficient front-drive sedans for decades, so Chrysler was boldly running counter-trend. And it worked. That '05 Chrysler 300 won numerous awards (including Motor Trend and North American "Car of the Year"), sold well and polished the brand's image, and the 300C and Magnum RT performance models were the first passenger cars to offer a 5.7-liter HEMI V8 with efficiency-enhancing cylinder deactivation.

Zetsche returned to Germany as DaimlerChrysler's chairman and head of its Mercedes Car Group. In 2005, Tom LaSorda was appointed Chrysler Group president and CEO, and the Global Engine Manufacturing Alliance began volume production of its new world engines in Dundee, Michigan. In 2007, Chrysler unveiled all-new 2008 Chrysler Town & Country and Dodge Grand Caravan minivans, and the first diesel-powered U.S.-market Jeep Grand Cherokee.

But the company was again in dire financial straits. Zetsche said "all options are on the table" and unveiled a Recovery and Transformation Plan designed to return it to profitability and sustain long-term success. DaimlerChrysler sold 80.1 percent of Chrysler Group to investment firm Cerberus Capital Management, Cerberus executive Bob Nardelli was appointed chairman and CEO, and LaSorda became vice chairman and president. Then long-time Toyota top U.S. executive Jim Press stunned the auto world by joining LaSorda as co-vice chairman and co-president.

The year 2008 brought three significant new '09 products, a Dodge Journey mid-size crossover utility (CUV), a 300-based, retro-look Dodge Challenger sport coupe and an all-new, vastly-improved line of Dodge Ram pickups. And it ended with the U.S. economy and auto sales in freefall and both Chrysler and GM—unable to secure private credit, as Ford had two years earlier—begging an arrogant and auto-ignorant U.S. Congress for federal loans.

Chrysler received a $4 billion government loan in 2009 to help it weather the ongoing economic crisis, then joined Italy's Fiat in a non-binding agreement to establish a global strategic alliance. Daimler relinquished its remaining 19.9 percent, and Cerberus (along with Nardelli, LaSorda and Press) exited stage left as Chrysler entered into a government-brokered Chapter 11 bankruptcy and shotgun marriage to Fiat.

Under Fiat/Chrysler CEO Sergio Marchionne and new Chrysler Group LLC chairman C. Robert Kidder, the company announced a post-bankruptcy restructuring to a leaner, flatter organization, separated its truck line from Dodge cars under a new Ram brand and presented a five-year business plan to rebuild into a "vibrant and competitive" auto company. The government "task force" also forced abrupt termination of 789 of Chrysler's 3,181 dealers. On the product front, the 2010 Ram 2500/3500 Heavy Duty pickups were named Motor Trend "Truck of the Year."

In 2010, Laura J. Soave was appointed Head of the Fiat Brand for North America to lead the 2011 U.S. launch of Fiat's tiny 500 car line, and Chrysler launched production of an all-new 3.6-liter Pentastar V6 engine at a new plant in Trenton, Michigan.

As this is written, the new Chrysler is on a strong product roll. Beginning with an all-new 2011 Jeep Grand Cherokee and followed by an equally new Dodge Durango SUV and thoroughly upgraded Dodge Journey, Challenger and Avenger, Chrysler 200 (formerly Sebring) and Dodge Caravan and Chrysler Town and Country minivans, nearly every car and truck the company makes—including most Jeeps—was made thoroughly competitive, or better, in an amazingly short period of time. The very appealing all-new Chrysler 300 and Dodge Charger sedans also arrived in early 2011, then the surprisingly likeable Fiat 500.

Given growing uncertainty over oil prices, regulatory issues and other factors, no one knows where America's economy or auto sales might go in 2011 and beyond, but the new Chrysler Group LLC, under Fiat leadership, appears well equipped to survive and prosper.

APPENDIX 3

THE HISTORY OF

FORD MOTOR COMPANY

by Gary Witzenburg

Of the three surviving American automobile companies, Ford Motor Company, the one with the longest history, is one of two whose founders' names are still prominently displayed on their products and facilities worldwide. But it is the only one whose founder's family remains heavily involved in its ownership and management.

Henry Ford was born on a farm in Dearborn, Michigan, near Detroit, in 1863, when the American Civil War was still going on. Soon after he married Clara Bryant, a local Dearborn girl, at age 25, he moved to Detroit for a job as a night-time engineer at the Edison Electric Illuminating Co., owned by inventor Thomas Edison, who would later become Ford's close friend and mentor. He and Clara had just one child, a son they named Edsel, after a friend.

Ford had big ideas about making life easier for people by developing not only a horseless carriage but also a farm tractor, and in 1896 he bolted together his first example of the former in an old carriage house behind his apartment. This box on wheels, which he called a Quadricycle, wasn't the world's (or America's) first or best automobile, but it was the modest beginning of what would become his life's work. If he could build one, why not thousands?

Ford was soon involved with the start-up Detroit Automobile Co., but that failed in 1901. He built some race cars and formed his own Henry Ford Corp., which later evolved into the Cadillac Motor Co. Finally, after his cars had won some races, investors convinced him to start a new company, which he did: The Ford Motor Co., incorporated on June 16, 1903. With Ford as director and general manager, it began building automobiles in a converted wagon factory on Mack Ave. in Detroit and sold its first "Model A" car to a Detroit doctor on July 20.

As its products' reputation and sales blossomed, the company soon outgrew its Mack Ave plant and in 1904 built a much larger facility on Piquette Ave., where production increased from 25 to 100 cars per day by 1906. Also that year, Henry acquired a majority of the company's stock, promoted himself to president and commissioned famed industrial architect Albert Kahn to design a much larger plant in Highland Park, Michigan, just north of Detroit.

The succession of Ford "alphabet" models moved from that early A through B, C, E, F, K, N and, by 1907, R and S, each built with increasingly efficient assembly processes. Then, on October 18, 1908, Ford unveiled the durable, versatile and lovable Model T that would become one of the world's most popular cars. Available in a variety of body styles, it would also be one of the world's first global cars as Ford expanded distribution beyond Canada to France, England, China and such remote new markets as Indonesia, Siam and the Dutch East Indies. And in 1911, the company opened its first overseas assembly plant in Manchester, England.

In addition to its other attributes, the Model T offered controls in easy reach on the steering column and floor pedals to help drivers keep both hands on the wheel. On October 7, 1913, Ford made history with the world's first moving automobile assembly line at Highland Park. The following January brought Ford's famous $5 eight-hour work day, which attracted thousands of job applicants at a time when factory workers were typically paid less than half that for nine or more hours of labor.

Ford's millionth Model T rolled off the line on December 10, 1915 as sales and production virtually doubled each year—from 10,660 in 1908-09 to more than two million in 1923. Ford's first truck (the Model TT) and the world's first mass-produced tractor arrived in 1917, as did Henry Ford II, Edsel and Eleanor Ford's first son.

At the beginning of 1918, construction began on a massive new Rouge River auto manufacturing complex south of Detroit that would advance "vertical integration" to the nth degree. The plan was to build virtually every part of every automobile on site. Raw materials would be shipped in and complete cars shipped out.

Edsel Ford succeeded his father as president on January 1, 1919, and the company re-incorporated in Delaware that July 9. Two days later, Henry Ford bought out all other stockholders and redistributed the stock: 55 percent to himself, 42 percent to Edsel and three percent to Clara.

In 1922, the company founded Ford of Belgium and bought the Lincoln Motor Co. Overseas operations expanded to Italy the following year, Japan in 1925 and Egypt in 1926. On May 26, 1927, Henry and Edsel drove the 15 millionth and last (U.S.-built) Model T off the line at Highland Park. Total world Model T production by the end of that year: 15,458,781.

But the fact that its replacement, an all-new Model A, was not ready nearly sank the company. Fortunately, after production began at the Rouge plant more than five months later on November 1 and the car was publicly introduced on Dec. 2, it proved very popular.

Ford built its 20 millionth car on April 14, 1931, its first V8-powered car on March 9, 1932 and its 25 millionth car on January 18, 1937. The mid-range Mercury line was launched on October 6, 1938 and the first Lincoln Continental on October 3, 1939.

With the U.S. at war, Ford built the first military general purpose (G.P. or "Jeep") vehicle (a Willys Overland design) at the Rouge plant on March 1, 1941 and shifted to full military production on February 1, 1942. When Edsel died at just 49 on May 26, 1943 founder Henry re-assumed the presidency. The following January 22, grandson Henry II was elected vice president (the U.S. Navy agreed to release him early because the government feared for the company's future) and three months later, executive vice president. Civilian production resumed on July 3, 1945, and on September 21, 28-year-old "Hank the Deuce" was named Ford president.

Still privately owned and run by Henry I and his thug lieutenant, Harry Bennett, the post-war Ford was in terrible shape. The old man wanted Bennett to take over but eventually agreed (with his family) to name Henry II president, and his grandson's first big decision was to fire Bennett. Henry I died on April 7, 1947, at the age of 83.

Then he set about hiring people with experience in cars and business, beginning with Bendix Aviation President Ernest R. Breech, who had been a top executive at General Motors and knew a lot of GM's best people. Breech convinced a number of his former colleagues to come over from GM, giving Ford a cadre of knowledgeable mid-career auto people to help him organize the company.

And he brought in a group of former Army Air Force officers to join the ex-GMers as the core of a new Ford Motor Company management. Because none had much knowledge of the automobile business going in, they asked so many questions that they soon became known as "Quiz Kids," which later changed to "Whiz Kids." Six of them would become Ford vice presidents, and two would be presidents.

In 1948, Hank's younger brother Benson was elected vice president and general manager of the Lincoln-Mercury division. Production of the post-war '49 Ford began on April 26, and a third brother William Clay (Bill) was elected to the board of directors. The first two-seat Ford Thunderbird arrived in October, 1954, and Breech was elected board chairman in January, 1955.

Later that year, Breech gave ex-GMer Louis Crusoe the challenge of creating a Ford Div. to take on GM's Chevrolet. Then he set about trying to match GM by creating a division for every brand. Whiz Kid Bob McNamara was chosen to head up Ford Div., Ben Mills Lincoln, Jack Reith Mercury, Bill Ford Continental (the '56 Continental Mark II was introduced in October) and Dick Crafee a new Edsel Div., all under Crusoe.

But the most significant event was the initial sale of Ford common stock beginning on January 17, 1956. After decades of private ownership, the company was going public, though the family retained control through special voting rights. On September 26, a new Central Office Building (later renamed Ford World Headquarters) was dedicated in Dearborn. Continental was folded into Lincoln; and, in 1957, Lincoln and Mercury were re-combined and a new controversially-styled, medium-priced Edsel line introduced.

Ford built its 50 millionth vehicle on April 29, 1959, introduced a compact Falcon line on October 8 and canned its two-year-old Edsel line (and division) due to dismal sales on November 19. On July 13, 1960, Breech resigned as board chairman and was succeeded by Henry II. McNamara was named president in November, then left a month later to become President John F. Kennedy's secretary of defense. Henry reacquired the title, then handed it off to John Dykstra on April 12. On October 3, the UAW called its first company-wide strike against Ford, which ended October 20 with a three-year contract. Arjay Miller, was elected president on May 1, 1963.

On April 17, 1964, Ford introduced the industry's first sport compact, the Falcon-based Mustang, which created a hot new "pony car" class, and sold its millionth Mustang less than two years later. Another UAW strike hit on September 6, 1967 and lasted through October 22. Semon E. "Bunky" Knudsen became president on February 6 and introduced a new Continental Mark III on April 5. The next year brought a new compact Maverick and, on September 11, a top management reorganization that elevated Lee Iacocca to president of Ford North America.

The subcompact Pinto arrived in 1970, and Iacocca was promoted to company president. Three years later, reacting to growing import competition, a crippling Arab oil embargo and a barrage of emissions, safety, bumper and fuel economy regulations, Ford introduced a much smaller Pinto-based Mustang II. The following January, Edsel Ford II (Henry II's son) joined the company as a product analyst.

Another top-level reorganization established a three-member Office of the Chief Executive in April, 1977 with an eye toward Henry II's impending retirement. Iacocca continued as president, but Philip Caldwell was named vice chairman. The following year saw Caldwell elevated to deputy CEO, then president after HF II fired Iacocca over strong differences. On October 1, 1979, HF II stepped down as CEO and named Caldwell to succeed him, and his nephew, William Clay Ford, Jr. joined the company as a product planning analyst. On March 13, 1980, Caldwell also became board chairman and Donald Petersen was elected president.

The Ford Motor Co. of 1980 was again in serious trouble. Its products' styling was awful, their quality shoddy, and their reputation dismal. So Caldwell and Petersen set out to fix all that. They reached a historic cooperative labor agreement with the UAW in February, 1982, and their first new product hits were the aerodynamically stylish '83 Ford Thunderbird and Mercury Cougar coupes, followed by Ford Tempo and Mercury Topaz compact coupes and sedans, a Continental Mark IV and new generations of popular and profitable Ford trucks.

Ford lost record sums of money during the first three (downmarket) years of its new leadership, but the auto market eventually recovered, its quality improved, its new products sold well, and profitability returned. Petersen succeeded the retiring Caldwell on February 1, 1985, and at the end of that year, the company introduced aerodynamic new mid-size '86 Ford Taurus and Mercury Sable sedans and wagons that would become U.S. best-sellers.

The company's 1988 worldwide earnings hit a record $5.3 billion for 1988, and William Clay (Bill) Ford Sr. retired the following April 1. On September 25, 1989, Ford announced it would purchase 75 percent of British exoticar maker Aston Martin. Just two days later, Henry Ford II died at the age of 70. On January 14, 1990, the founder's great grandsons, Edsel II and Bill Ford, Jr. were elected to the board of directors.

Ford bought British luxury-sport maker Jaguar on February 28, and the very next day, Petersen resigned and was replaced as chairman by Harold "Red" Polling, while Philip Benton, Jr. was elected president. A new '91 Ford Explorer sport utility vehicle (SUV) was unveiled in March, 1990 and would become another huge seller.

In 1992, Ford bought 50 percent of Japanese maker Mazda, and its F-Series pickup was the U.S.-market's best-selling vehicle for the 10th straight year. The F-Series was again the best-selling vehicle in 1993, Taurus was the best-selling car, three other Ford products were among the top eight U.S. best sellers, and Englishman Sir Alex Trotman succeeded Poling as chairman.

On January 1, 1995, Trotman initiated a "Ford 2000" restructuring plan that merged North American and European operations into a single Ford Automotive Operations (FAO). Ford's two-hundred-fifty-millionth vehicle was built on October 8, 1996, and 1997 brought another earnings record at $6.9 billion.

When Trotman retired on January 1, 1999, Bill Ford, Jr. was elected chairman and Jacques Nasser president. Ford purchased Swedish automaker Volvo and British Land Rover, and a new compact Ford Focus won the prestigious 1999 European Car of the Year award. When the North American version launched a year later, it was named 2000 North American Car of the Year, the first vehicle to receive both awards.

But the first decade of the new millennium would be a troubled and turbulent one for all three U.S. automakers and the industry in general. Nick Scheele was named president and COO on October 30, 2001, the once-legendary Lincoln Continental was discontinued in 2002, and the company celebrated its 100th anniversary in 2003.

In 2004 came the Escape Hybrid, the industry's first gas-electric hybrid SUV, and all-new F-150 pickups. For 2005, a retro-style redesigned Mustang revived Ford's iconic pony car, and new Ford Five Hundred and Freestyle and Mercury Montego full-size sedans and crossover utilities (CUVs) put the Mercury Sable out to pasture and demoted the aging Ford Taurus to rental car, taxi, and other fleet sales.

The old Taurus ceased production in 2006 after a 20-year run, while new mid-size Ford Fusion, Mercury Milan and Lincoln Zephyr sedans were introduced. But with the company struggling and losing boatloads of money, Bill Ford announced a "Way Forward" major restructuring, then brought in Boeing executive vp Alan Mulally as President and CEO.

One of Mulally's first moves was to mortgage the company's assets, including its buildings and the logos on them, to raise $23.6 billion for much-needed product development during its restructuring. This was seen by most everyone, including the automotive press, as extremely risky … but would enable Ford to avoid the embarrassment of Chapter 11 bankruptcy and government help when the economy crashed in 2008.

In 2007, Ford introduced the Ford Edge and Lincoln MKX mid-size CUVs and reported a $12.7 billion loss for 2006. At

Mulally's direction, the Ford Five Hundred and Freestyle and Mercury Montego nameplates were dropped and the previously-retired Taurus and Sable labels slapped onto freshened versions of the large sedans, while the Freestyle CUV became the Taurus X. Aston Martin was sold and plans announced to sell Jaguar and Land Rover.

Unlike its Detroit rivals, Ford was able to survive the 2008 economic tsunami and severe sales downturn thanks to Mulally's 2006 loans, the image boost it enjoyed from avoiding bankruptcy and continuing launches of appealing new products. Over the next three years, these would include a Fusion hybrid, Ford Flex and Lincoln MKT three-row CUVs, an all-new Taurus and Lincoln MKS sedans and an all-new, Taurus-based Ford Explorer SUV.

In 2009, Ford announced that it would bring more of its European products to North America, beginning with the Turkish-built Transit Connect compact van and a new Ford Fiesta subcompact. In 2010, Volvo was sold and a new 2012 compact Ford Focus was unveiled. It launched in North America in early 2011 and will be built—along with electric, hybrid and C-Max compact minivan versions—in the refurbished Michigan Assembly Plant in Wayne, Michigan.

Like most surviving automakers around the world, Ford Motor Co. has seen major ups and disastrous downs through its 108-year history. As this is written, it remains a strong second to GM and well ahead of Chrysler—both recovering from their 2009 bankruptcies—among U.S. makers and appears very well led and positioned to compete in what is certain to be a volatile industry.

Appendix 4

GM RESTRUCTURING PLAN

February 17, 2009

General Motors Corporation

GM

2009 – 2014 Restructuring Plan

Presented to U.S. Department of the Treasury
As Required Under Section 7.20
of the Loan and Security Agreement
Between General Motors and the
U. S. Department of the Treasury
Dated December 31, 2008

February 17, 2009

GENERAL MOTORS RESTRUCTURING PLAN HIGHLIGHTS

- **GM's Plan details a return to sustainable profitability in 24 months**
  - Demonstrates GM's viability under conservative economic assumptions
  - Expands and accelerates the Plan submitted on December 2
  - Lowers the Company's breakeven to a U.S. market of 11.5-12.0M units annually
- **GM is comprehensively transforming its business, globally**
  - Brands, nameplates and dealer networks streamlined and focused
  - Productivity and flexibility gains enabling more facility consolidations
  - Shared global vehicle architectures creating substantial cost savings
  - Unprofitable foreign operations addressed
- **GM's Plan emphasizes the Company's continued focus on great products**
  - "Fewer, better" vehicles in U.S. supporting Chevrolet, Cadillac, Buick and GMC
  - Renewed commitment to lead in fuel efficiency, hybrids, advanced propulsion
  - All major U.S. introductions in 2009-2014 are high-mileage cars and crossovers
- **GM's Plan calls for considerable sacrifice from all stakeholders**
  - Bondholders and other debtors
  - Hourly and salaried employees, executives and retirees
  - Dealers and suppliers
  - Shareholders
- **GM's Plan addresses the requirements of the loan agreement with the United States Department of the Treasury**
  - Competitive product mix and cost structure
  - Compliance with Federal fuel efficiency and emissions requirements
  - Domestic manufacturer of advanced technology vehicles
  - Rationalization of costs, capitalization and capacity
  - Major progress made with the UAW and hourly employees; considerable progress made with bondholders; additional work under way to achieve term sheet requirements and savings targets
  - Positive net present value (NPV)
  - Repayment of Federal loans
- **Reflecting further deterioration in economic, industry and credit markets since December 2, GM's Plan details need for additional Federal funding**
  - Restructuring actions accelerated to mitigate this need
  - Partial repayment of Federal funding still slated to begin in 2012
- **General Motors is vital to a robust U.S. economy, and a revitalized GM will greatly advance America's technology leadership and energy independence**
  - Highly focused on a U.S. supply base and U.S. R&D, design and engineering
  - Directly and indirectly supports 1.3 million U.S. jobs
  - Committed to investing in advanced technologies and high-tech "green" jobs
  - A sound investment for U.S. taxpayers that will be repaid fully

**General Motors Corporation
2009-2014 Restructuring Plan
February 17, 2009**

1. Introduction

On December 2, 2008, General Motors submitted a Restructuring Plan for Long-Term Viability to the Senate Banking Committee and the House of Representatives Financial Services Committee. The Plan was a blueprint for a new General Motors in the United States, one that is lean, profitable, self-sustaining and fully competitive. Key elements of the December 2nd Plan included:

* A dramatic shift in the Company's U.S. product portfolio, with 22 of 24 new vehicle launches in 2009-2012 being fuel-efficient cars and crossovers;
* Full compliance with the 2007 Energy Independence and Security Act, and extensive investment in a wide array of advanced propulsion technologies;
* Reduction in brands, nameplates and dealerships to focus available resources and growth strategies on the Company's profitable operations;
* Full labor cost competitiveness with foreign manufacturers in the U.S. by no later than 2012;
* Further manufacturing and structural cost reductions through increased productivity and employment reductions; and
* Balance sheet restructuring and supplementing liquidity via temporary Federal assistance.

The net effect of these and other operational and financial restructuring elements was a plan to restore GM North America (GMNA) to profitability on an adjusted Earnings Before Interest and Taxes (EBIT) basis at U.S. industry sales rates of 12.5-13.0 million units, well below both actual sales levels experienced in the past several years and consensus projections for 2010-2014.

Reflecting a dramatic deterioration in economic and market conditions during 2008, new vehicle sales declined rapidly, falling to their lowest per-capita levels in 50 years. General Motors' revenues fell precipitously, in part reflecting escalating public speculation about a potential GM bankruptcy, consuming liquidity that one year prior was considered adequate to fully fund the Company's restructuring efforts. To bridge to more normal market conditions, General Motors requested temporary Federal assistance totaling $18 billion, comprised of a $12 billion term loan and a $6 billion line of credit (as a provision for the Downside scenario) to sustain operations and accelerate implementation of the Restructuring Plan. Given the Baseline industry outlook contained in the December 2 submission to Congress, General Motors planned to begin repayment of the requested Federal loan in 2011.

Subsequent to December 2, the United States Department of the Treasury and General Motors entered into negotiations for the requested Federal loans, reaching agreement on

GM RESTRUCTURING PLAN

December 31, 2008. This agreement provides General Motors with up to $13.4 billion in 3-year term loans to sustain operations through the 1st Quarter of 2009, providing necessary liquidity support while the Company finalizes its Restructuring Plan. In consideration for this temporary loan facility, General Motors is required to submit to the U.S. Department of the Treasury, by February 17, a detailed restructuring plan for the period 2009-2014 that demonstrates long-term viability.

Specifically, as Chart 1 below highlights, Section 7.20 of the loan agreement sets forth key restructuring targets that GM's Plan needs to address in the February 17th and March 31st submissions to the U.S. Department of the Treasury.

Chart 1: Loan Agreement Requirements

Federal Loan Requirements	February 17 Restructuring Plan Status	March 31 Progress Report Status
• Product Mix & Cost Structure Competitiveness	• Detailed Plan Submitted	• Implementation Progress to be Provided
- Competitive Labor Cost Agreement	• JOBS Program Suspended • Major Progress Made Related to Competitive Gap Closure	• Targeting Final Agreement on Competitive Gap Closure
• Compliance with Federal Fuel Efficiency and Emission Requirements	• Compliance Confirmed in Plan	• Status Update
• Domestic Manufacture of Advanced Technology Vehicles (Section 136 Applications)	• Two Applications Submitted to Department of Energy • Third Application Being Developed	• Status Update
• Rationalization of Cost, Capitalization and Capacity	• Detailed Plan Submitted	• Status Update
- Agreement on 50% VEBA Equitization	• Negotiations Under Way; Confirming Letter Contained in Appendix G	• Targeting Final Agreement
- Agreement on Conversion of 2/3rds Unsecured Public Debt to Equity	• Negotiations Under Way; Confirming Letter Contained in Appendix G	• Targeting Commencement of Bond Exchange Offer
• Financial Viability (Positive NPV)	• Positive NPV Demonstrated in Plan	• Status Update
• Repayment of Federal Loans	• Under Baseline Scenario, Repayments Begin in 2012	• Status Update

The Plan is to include evidence of progress related to both labor cost competitiveness and debt reduction. Specifically, the loan documents require "best efforts" related to the achievement of hourly and salaried wage compensation and work rule competitiveness by December 31, 2009; conversion of at least half of future VEBA payments to equity; and a reduction in unsecured public indebtedness by at least two-thirds by December 31, 2009 (with the actual exchange offer having commenced by March 31).

This Restructuring Plan addresses the requirements set forth in the loan documents executed with the United States Department of the Treasury on December 31, 2008.

2. Executive Summary

The automotive industry has been the backbone of U.S. manufacturing and a leading investor in research and development for nearly a century. It is a significant factor in the

U.S. economy, employing 1 in 10 workers and a major purchaser of U.S.-made steel, aluminum, iron, glass, plastics and electronics. It is an industry undergoing massive change, and one that can be key to both transforming the U.S. economy and creating high-tech, "green" jobs that support a healthy and growing middle class. Appendix A presents key facts about the role of the automotive industry on the U.S. economy.

For most of this decade, General Motors has been pursuing a major transformation of its business, working to improve the consumer appeal, quality, safety, and fuel efficiency of its cars and trucks; to achieve cost competitiveness or advantage in labor, manufacturing, product development, procurement and staff functions; and to address the Company's huge legacy cost burden. As noted in the December 2 submission, the Company has made significant progress in all of these areas and, even after rising oil prices and a slowing economy in mid-2008 cut automotive volumes by more than 20%, GM was confident in its ability to self-fund its continuing transformation.

In the last six months of 2008, housing price declines accelerated, foreclosures rose, credit markets froze, job losses skyrocketed, and consumer confidence tumbled. As the economic crisis intensified, automotive sales fell to their lowest per-capita levels in half a century, putting automakers under enormous financial stress. All automotive manufacturers have been severely affected, with most reporting significant losses in the recent quarter. Under these extraordinary conditions, GM's liquidity fell rapidly to levels below those needed to operate the Company, and GM was compelled to turn to the U.S. Government for assistance.

Since December 2, economic conditions have continued to deteriorate globally. This, combined with public speculation about GM's future, has further reduced the Company's volumes, revenues, and cash flows. In addition, the weakening financial markets have significantly reduced the value of GM's large pension fund assets.

The Company has responded aggressively to these worsening economic and industry circumstances, accelerating, and adding to, the restructuring elements contained in the Company's December 2 Plan (Chart 2 below presents key Plan changes). The revised Plan comprehensively addresses GM's revenues, costs, and balance sheet for its U.S. and foreign operations, and is based on conservative assumptions. It also results in a business that will contribute materially to the national interest by developing and commercializing advanced technologies and vehicles that will reduce petroleum dependency and greenhouse gas emissions, and drive national technological and manufacturing competitiveness.

Chart 2: Restructuring Plan – Summary of Key Changes

Plan Element	December 2	February 17
2009 U.S. GDP Forecast (%)	(1.0)	(2.0)
2009 U.S. Industry Volumes		
Baseline	12.0M	10.5M
Upside	12.0M	12.0M
Downside	10.5M	9.5M
2012 Market Share		
U.S.	20.5%	20.0%
Global	13.1%	13.0%
Labor Cost Competitiveness Obtained	2012	2009
2012 U.S. Manufacturing Plant Count	38	33
2012 U.S. Salaried Headcount	27k	26k
U.S. Breakeven Volume (Adjusted EBIT Basis)	12.5-13.0M	11.5-12.0M
U.S. Brand Reductions Completed	No Date	2011
Foreign Operations Restructuring Comprehended		
Sweden (Saab)	No	Yes
Germany and Europe	No	Yes
Canada	No	Yes
Thailand and India	No	Yes
Financial Projections Through	2012	2014

The revised Plan restructures the Company's business in the U.S. by concentrating on GM's three strongest global brands (Chevrolet, Cadillac and Buick) and its premium truck brand (GMC); by restructuring the retail distribution channel to achieve a strong, healthy dealer network while preserving GM's historical strength in rural areas; by basing the product plan on "fewer, better" entries; and by continued commitment to be a quality leader. The Company is accelerating the timetable to achieve competitive costs and work rules to 2009, in line with Federal loan requirements. The Company will close additional facilities and reduce employment beyond the December Plan targets, and will continue to leverage already highly efficient manufacturing and product development operations.

GM will also pursue accelerated restructuring of its Canadian, European, and certain Asia-Pacific operations. While the Company intends to retain its global approach to conducting business, additional funding will be required to sustain certain operations outside the U.S., given the global economic slowdown also impacting these markets. The Company is also in discussions with many foreign governments for funding support. Significant restructuring of the Company's liabilities and balance sheet are also vital parts of this Plan, and detailed negotiations related to restructuring of VEBA obligations and unsecured public debt are progressing.

Since the December submission, the Company has been engaged with the UAW, regarding competitive costs/work rules and restructuring VEBA obligations, and advisors to an unofficial committee of major bondholders with regard to conversion of unsecured public debt to equity. As of February 17, the Company and the UAW have made significant progress on costs/work rules, which represent major steps in narrowing the competitive gap. However, these revisions do not achieve all of the labor cost savings comprehended in the Company's financial projections.

GM plans to report this progress to the U.S. Secretary of Labor who must certify GM's competitiveness relative to the U.S. transplants. Management will continue to work with the UAW with regard to competitiveness, and will work on additional initiatives to ensure GM achieves the cost reductions and financial targets comprehended in the Plan.

With regard to both the VEBA and bondholder negotiations, while discussions and due diligence are underway, restructuring agreements have not yet been finalized with either party at this point. Negotiations will continue with the objective of achieving successful resolution of these matters no later than March 31, 2009.

The net effect of all Restructuring Plan initiatives is a further reduced breakeven point, allowing for profitable operations in North America (on an adjusted EBIT basis) with a U.S. industry sales rates as low as 11.5-12.0 million units, compared to 12.5-13.0 million units in the December Plan. The Company's operating and balance sheet restructurings are expected to generate positive adjusted EBIT and positive adjusted operating cash flow for its North American operations in 2010 (with a U.S. industry volume of 12.5 million units), with significant improvements occurring over the 2010-2014 period.

Globally, positive adjusted EBIT will also be achieved in 2010, with adjusted operating cash flow approaching breakeven in 2011. Partially offsetting these results are restructuring costs (including provisions for resolution of Delphi), debt retirements, and additional contributions to the Company's U.S. pension plans that may be required in 2013 and 2014.

Financial Viability—One important measure of determining long-term financial viability is whether the Company has positive Net Present Value (NPV). Based on the assumptions and methodology set forth in Section 5.3 and Appendix J, the Enterprise Value of GM under the Baseline Scenario is estimated between $59 billion and $70 billion. After deducting the Net Obligations of the Company and adjusting for the pro-forma effects of the two-thirds reduction in public unsecured indebtedness and 50 percent reduction in the UAW Hourly VEBA obligations (per the requirements of the U.S. Department of the Treasury loan agreement), the NPV of the Baseline Scenario of the GM Restructuring Plan is estimated in the range of approximately $5 billion to $14 billion.

Presently, there are additional restructuring initiatives in process inside and outside the U.S. that when successfully concluded, are anticipated to have a further positive effect on the Baseline Scenario NPV range. In the Upside Sensitivity Scenario, in which U.S. industry volumes return to more historical trendline levels by 2014, the NPV analysis yields a range of $30 billion to $41 billion. Further elaboration of the Baseline Scenario and both Upside and Downside sensitivities can be found in Appendix J.

Federal Funding Request—While the accelerated restructuring efforts have, for the most part, offset the massively negative effects of volume and revenue deterioration, Federal support beyond that requested in December will be required to complete the Company's renewal. In the December 2 submission, the Company indicated that General Motors needs to retain the level of targeted global cash balances (approximately $11-$14 billion) to support the normal conduct of business and under a U.S. Downside volume sensitivity, GM would need funding support of approximately $18 billion. In addition, it should be noted that in its December 2 submission, the Company had assumed that the $4.5 billion U.S. secured bank revolver credit facility would be renewed and fully drawn again in 2011.

In the current Baseline forecast, near-term U.S. industry volumes are similar to the December 2 Downside scenario and the Company has not assumed, based upon credit market conditions, that it will be able to rollover and draw the full $4.5 billion secured bank revolver in 2011. On this basis, GM is requesting Baseline federal funding support of $22.5 billion (i.e., the $18 billion prior Downside funding request plus the $4.5 billion incremental required). If the new, even lower Downside volume sensitivity scenario occurs, GM will require further federal funding, estimated currently at an additional $7.5 billion, which could bring total Government support up to $30 billion by 2011.

Under the Company's Baseline outlook, repayment of Federal support is expected to begin in 2012 and be fully repaid by 2017. Additional financial support might be required in 2013 and 2014 if U.S. pension fund contributions are required (as is currently estimated) but, at this time it is premature to plan for such additional funding support until alternatives to address pension funding status are fully explored.

During the 2009-2014 timeframe, General Motors is also requesting funding support from certain foreign governments. Notably, the Company is presently in discussions with the Governments of Canada, Germany, United Kingdom, Sweden and Thailand, and has included an estimate of up to $6 billion in funding support to provide operating liquidity specifically for GM's operations overseas and additional amounts beyond the $6 billion to mitigate legacy obligations.

The dramatic change in the Company's financial outlook over the past 6 months demonstrates the industry's acute sensitivity to volume. As discussed previously, the Company's U.S. industry assumptions are conservative compared to other forecasts, well below levels experienced for most of this decade of approximately 17 million units, and below scrappage rates, estimated to be around 12.5 million units. If industry volumes recover more quickly, as a result of general economic stimulus or industry-specific measures (such as sales tax holidays), U.S. Federal TARP funding support could decline from $18 billion in mid-2009 to $13 billion in 2011, and be fully repaid by 2014.

The GM Restructuring Plan, complete with appendices and tables, can be found in its entirety at: http://www.scribd.com/doc/12561377/GM-Restructuring-Plan

Appendix 5

CHRYSLER RESTRUCTURING PLAN

eecutive Summary
2-17-09

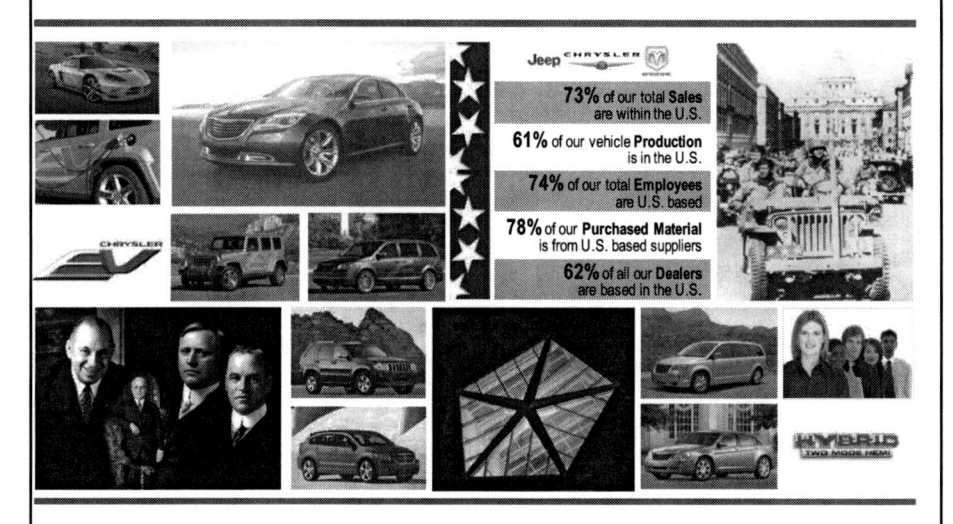

Chrysler Restructuring Plan for Long-Term Viability
Executive Summary

February 17, 2009

CHRYSLER

TABLE OF CONTENTS

	Page
Introduction	2
Restructuring Plan Assumptions and Key Metrics	4
Restructuring Actions	7
Strategic Alliance	10
Commitment to Energy Security and Environmental Sustainability	12
Compliance with Fuel Economy Regulations	13
Compliance with Emissions Regulations	14
Achieving a Competitive Product Mix and Cost Structure	15
Conclusion	18

List of Tables

1. Revenue Impact of U.S. SAAR Levels 4
2. Request for Government Loan 5
3. Key Operating Metrics of the Restructuring Plan 6
4. Net Present Value 7

List of Figures

1. Status of Restructuring Actions 8
2. Improvement of Fuel Economy Using Powertrain and Portfolio Opportunities with Fiat 10
3. Expansion through Current Geographic (Percent Sales by Region) 11
4. Chrysler's Electric Vehicle Product Portfolio 12
5. 2008 Harbour Report (Manufacturing Efficiency) 15
6. Chrysler Total Quality Improvement 16
7. Customer Promoter Score (CPS) / Appeal of New Dodge Ram 17

Chrysler Restructuring Plan for Long-Term Viability

Introduction

On December 2, 2008, Chrysler LLC ("Chrysler" or "the Company") submitted its Plan for Short-Term and Long-Term Viability to Congress as part of its request for a $7 billion working capital loan from the U.S. government to support its short term restructuring and long term viability. On January 2, 2009, Chrysler received an initial $4 billion loan from the United States Department of the Treasury, the terms of which require the Company to submit a restructuring plan to achieve and sustain long-term viability, international competitiveness and energy efficiency.

The restructuring plan presented demonstrates Chrysler's ability to meet those requirements through its continued focus on implementing cost reductions and modifications to its capital structure to improve its balance sheet, and on developing a fuel-efficient product portfolio that meets customer expectations and governmentally imposed environmental requirements. Chrysler's management believes that this restructuring plan, which assumes achievement of concessions from all constituents, Chrysler Financial maintaining adequate retail and wholesale financing capacity, and incremental funding from the U.S. Treasury can be successfully implemented and will result in the Company's long-term viability, international competitiveness and energy efficiency.

Due to the continued deterioration in the economy which has led to an unprecedented decline in the automotive sector since our December 2nd plan submission, in addition to the $7 billion original request, $4 billion of which has been received, Chrysler is requesting an additional $2 billion, for a total of $9 billion to support ongoing operations.

CHRYSLER

The availability of credit for automotive customers and dealers is the single most important element of Chrysler's viability. Because of the credit market crisis and subsequent rating agency actions, restrictions were placed on Chrysler Financial's credit conduits. Because of these restrictions, Chrysler Financial was forced to greatly reduce the level of retail and wholesale financing support for customers and dealers in the U.S., Mexico and Canada. Most significant was the complete discontinuation of lease financing in the U.S. and Canada in August 2008, which led directly to reductions in total sales volumes of 20% and 50% for the U.S. and Canada, respectively.

Chrysler Financial received a U.S. Treasury loan of $1.5 billion in mid January, 2009 to support retail financing, and it was estimated that this amount would provide adequate financing capacity through March 31, 2009. However, this is not a long-term solution. Because of the continued lack of liquidity in the credit markets, several follow-on proposals have been submitted by Chrysler Financial to the U.S. government for a long-term solution to ensure its financing capacity. It is critical that these requests be resolved, as adequate retail and wholesale financing capacity for Chrysler Financial is a requirement for Chrysler's viability.

The Company's standalone restructuring plan demonstrates viability which could be further enhanced with a strategic alliance that more effectively utilizes its manufacturing capacity and positions the Company for growth. Chrysler and Fiat S.p.A. have signed a non-binding letter of intent that is conditioned upon Chrysler meeting all restructuring targets set forth in Chrysler's U.S. Treasury Loan Agreement Department. If completed, this partnership would greatly improve Chrysler's long-term viability.

It is essential that Chrysler achieve the concessions and planned balance sheet restructuring identified in its restructuring plan, including the receipt of incremental government funding. If the requisite concessions are not achieved by the government's March 31st funding deadline, management believes the only alternative would be to immediately plan for an orderly wind down of all operations through a court-supervised liquidation. This is clearly not an alternative Chrysler would prefer, but is one that the Company is prepared to implement if required.

CHRYSLER

Chrysler has had discussions with each of its constituents and believes that it has made substantial progress in seeking concessions from its dealers, suppliers, 2nd lien lenders, shareholders and the UAW. In order to complete its restructuring plan, the Company requires further concessions of $5 billion of additional liability and interest burden relief from its creditor groups[1].

The Company has engaged in discussions with its creditor groups[1] and believes it is possible to reach agreement on the terms and conditions of required concessions. With the continuing participation and diligent effort of all creditor groups[1], and support from the President's Designee and the Presidential Task Force on Autos, Chrysler will be in a position to finalize its restructuring plan and receive additional government funding, by March 31, 2009.

1) Restructuring Plan Assumptions and Key Metrics

Due to the continued lack of consumer credit, which has prevented interested customers from purchasing new vehicles and has prevented dealers from securing financing to support continued wholesale orders, Chrysler has revised its Seasonally Adjusted Annual Rate (SAAR) forecast covering the next four years. Chrysler's restructuring plan is based on conservative SAAR assumptions that reflect the reality of a declining automotive industry. The restructuring plan projects, commencing in 2009, a SAAR level of 10.1 million units, and for years 2009 through 2012, an average SAAR level of 10.8 million units. This represents a reduction from the Company's original December 2, 2008 submission to Congress of 7.2 million units, or on average, 1.8 million units annually over the four years.

Table 1 – Revenue Impact of U.S. SAAR Levels (millions)

	2009	2010	2011	2012
December Submission	11.1	12.1	13.7	13.7
Current Restructuring Plan	10.1	10.6	11.1	11.6
Change	(1.0)	(1.5)	(2.6)	(2.1)
Cumulative Change	**(1.0)**	**(2.5)**	**(5.1)**	**(7.2)**
Estimated Revenue Impact on Chrysler (a)	$ (2,500)	$ (6,250)	$ (12,750)	$ (18,000)
Estimated Cash Impact	$ (500)	$ (1,250)	$ (2,550)	$ (3,600)

(a) Based on assumed market share of 10%

Footnote 1: Creditors include the 1st lien lenders, the U.S. Government and the UAW-VEBA

CHRYSLER

For Chrysler, this represents a sales decline of approximately 720,000 units, assuming a 10% market share, and approximately $18 billion in lost revenue and a $3.6 billion decline in cash inflow over the four years.

As the Company indicated in its December 2nd Congressional testimony, the availability of credit to automotive consumers and dealers is the single most important element of Chrysler's viability. The continued credit market turmoil has resulted in rejection of consumer loan applications and lost sales to dealers, which in turn has led to reduced wholesale orders for Chrysler vehicles and further vehicle production cuts.

This chain of events has created a rapidly declining SAAR trend which directly and immediately reduces cash inflow in a manner that cannot be addressed adequately through even the most aggressive restructuring actions. These softer-than-expected market conditions during the 4th quarter have continued into the 1st quarter of 2009 resulting in an industry-wide decline in automotive sales. As a result, Chrysler now requires an additional $2 billion in cash beyond that anticipated in Chrysler's December submission, bringing its total request to $9 billion.

Table 2 below summarizes Chrysler's initial and current funding request:

Table 2 – Request for Government Loan

	Funding To Date ($Billions)
Funded to Date	$ 4
Remaining	$ 3
Total Original Requested	**$ 7**
Additional Request	$ 2
TOTAL Funds Requested	**$ 9**

Chrysler proposes to repay the U.S. Treasury Loan with interest, fees and out-of-pocket expenses beginning in 2012. The fees to be paid are in lieu of warrants, given Chrysler is a private company.

CHRYSLER RESTRUCTURING PLAN

CHRYSLER

Chrysler's restructuring plan includes the benefit of restructuring actions and concessions that management believes will be reached with its core constituents including: the UAW, dealers, suppliers, shareholders, 2nd lien lenders and other creditor groups. These benefits are reflected in the restructuring plan in fixed costs savings, improved EBITDA and improved cash flow.

The restructuring plan shows that the Company will have adequate liquidity throughout the planning period while making significant loan amortization payments. The chart below summarizes the key operating metrics of the restructuring plan on the pro forma basis and reflects what the Company believes to be a conservative outlook.

	2008 Unaudited	2009 Plan	2010 Plan	2011 Plan	2012 Plan	2013 Plan	2014 Plan	2015 Plan	2016 Plan
U.S. Industry SAAR (Mills) (Light Duty Only)	13.2	10.1	10.6	11.1	11.6	12.1	12.6	13.1	13.7
Worldwide Shipments (000 units)	2,065	1,618	1,775	2,085	2,120	2,175	2,227	2,281	2,345
U.S. Market Share (Retail & Fleet) *	10.8%	10.4%	10.7%	10.7%	10.7%	10.7%	10.7%	10.7%	10.7%
U.S. Dealer Inventory (000 units)	398	355	312	306	306	306	306	306	306
Material Cost Savings	(1.1%)	0.25%	0.25%	0.25%	0.25%	0.50%	0.50%	0.50%	0.50%
Net Pricing	(1.0%)	(0.5%)	(0.5%)	(0.5%)	(0.5%)	(0.25%)	(0.25%)	(0.25%)	(0.25%)
Capital Expenditures (Bils)	$2.3	$2.3	$2.3	$2.6	$2.6	$2.6	$2.5	$2.5	$2.5
Fixed Cost excluding VEBA (Bils)	$10.9	$10.2	$10.2	$10.2	$10.2	$10.1	$10.1	$10.1	$10.1
EBITDA (Bils)	$0.3	$2.9	$5.0	$3.9	$3.9	$4.4	$4.7	$5.2	$5.6
Cash - Year End Balance (Bils)	$2.5	$9.0	$10.6	$10.8	$11.4	$11.3	$11.4	$12.2	$13.4

Table 3 - Key Operating Metrics of the Restructuring Plan

The restructuring plan shows that Chrysler achieves a positive net present value of $17.3 billion after taking into account all existing and projected costs, including repayment of 100% of the U.S. Treasury Loan and implementation of the restructuring plan.

For the seven years prior to the 2008 industry turn down (2001-2007) Chrysler's market share was flat compared to GM and Ford whose market share declined 17% and 25% respectively

CHRYSLER

Table 4 – Net Present Value

	2009	2010	2011	2012	2013	2014	2015	2016
Free Cash Flows to Equity	$ 6.5	$ 1.7	$ 0.1	$ 0.6	$ (0.1)	$ 0.1	$ 0.8	$ 1.2

Terminal Value		
EBITDA at 2016	$	5.6
Multiple		5.0
Terminal Value (Before Debt)	$	28.0
Less Debt:		(13.7)
Terminal Value (Net of Debt)	$	14.3

NPV Discount Rates

	5%	10%	15%	20%
	$ 9.7	$ 6.7	$ 4.7	$ 3.3
NPV of Free Cash Flows at 1/1/2009	9.7	8.7	8.0	7.5
NPV of Net Terminal Value	9.7	6.7	4.7	3.3
NPV of Chrysler Cash Flows	$ 19.4	$ 15.4	$ 12.7	$ 10.8
Plus: Cash at 1/1/2009	1.9	1.9	1.9	1.9
NPV per Section 7.20 of UST Loan	$ 21.3	$ 17.3	$ 14.6	$ 12.7

2) Restructuring Actions

Upon becoming an independent company on August 3, 2007, Chrysler took immediate action to redesign its business model, enhance its product portfolio and create a more competitive cost structure. In response to deteriorating economic conditions, Chrysler initiated additional measures to reduce costs and improve competitiveness which included:

- Workforce reduction of 32,000
- Capacity reduction of 1.2 million units (over 30% of total capacity)
- Reduction of 12 manufacturing shifts
- Discontinuation of 4 models
- Sale of $700 million in non-earning assets

Figure 1: Status of Restructuring Actions (2008 and 2009)

Action	Complete	Target
Workforce Reduction	32,000	35,000
Models Discontinued	4	7
Shift Reduction	12	13
Capacity Cuts	1.2 Million Units	1.3M
Sales of Non-Earning Assets	$700M	$1B

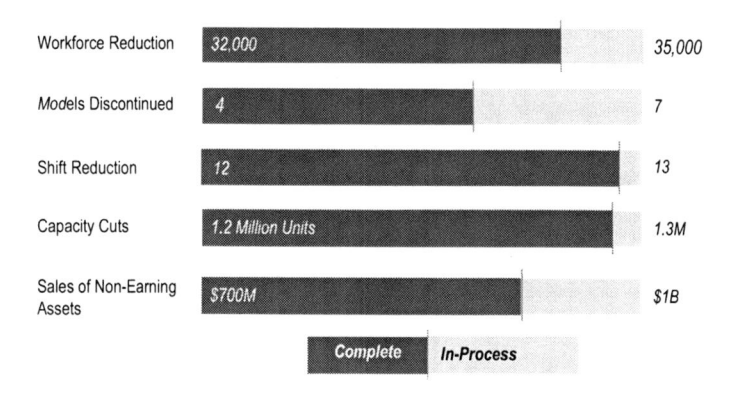

In developing its restructuring plan, Chrysler has worked closely with all key constituents to explore additional concessions. The identified concessions that management believes can be implemented by March 31, 2009 include:

- **Executive/Management Concessions** – Chrysler will fully comply with the restrictions established under section 111 of EESA relative to executive privileges and compensation. In addition, the company has suspended the 401K match, performance bonuses, merit increases, and eliminated retiree life insurance benefits.
- **Dealer Concessions** – Chrysler will achieve cost savings and improved cash flow through a number of initiatives including reduced dealer margins, elimination of fuel fill reimbursement, and reduction of service contract margins.
- **Union Concessions** – The term sheets for the Labor Modifications and VEBA modifications fundamentally comply with the requirements of the U.S. Treasury Loan and once realized, will provide Chrysler with a workforce cost structure that is competitive with the transplant automotive manufacturers. The VEBA modifications term sheet however is conditioned on, among other things, further due diligence and satisfactory debt restructuring. Chrysler will continue to work diligently with its labor unions and retirees' class counsel in structuring and negotiating concessions necessary to

the Company's continued viability and look forward to the assistance of the U.S. Treasury in that effort.
- **Supplier Concessions** – The Company has initiated a dialogue with its suppliers and believes that it will be able to obtain substantial cost reductions from suppliers that will result in achieving targeted savings. Chrysler also supports the supplier associations' proposals which would provide a government guarantee of OEM accounts payables.
- **2nd Lien Debt Holders Concessions** – The holders of the 2nd Lien Debt have expressed a willingness to convert 100% of their debt to equity.
- **Shareholders** – Current shareholders have also indicated a willingness to relinquish their current equity position to support Chrysler's viability plan.

Additionally, the viability plan includes a further reduction of outstanding obligations from certain creditor groups by $5 billion. In addition to strengthening the Company's balance sheet for the long-term, this reduction will also provide immediate cash flow via interest savings of between $350 - $400 million annually.

CHRYSLER RESTRUCTURING PLAN

3) Strategic Alliance

The written and oral testimony Chrysler submitted to the U.S. House and Senate in 2008 stated the Company's intent to seek the benefits of global partnerships and alliances. Chrysler has signed a non-binding agreement to pursue a strategic alliance with Fiat which represents an attractive opportunity for significant strategic and financial benefits.

Figure 2: Improvement of Fuel Economy Using Powertrain and Portfolio Opportunities with Fiat

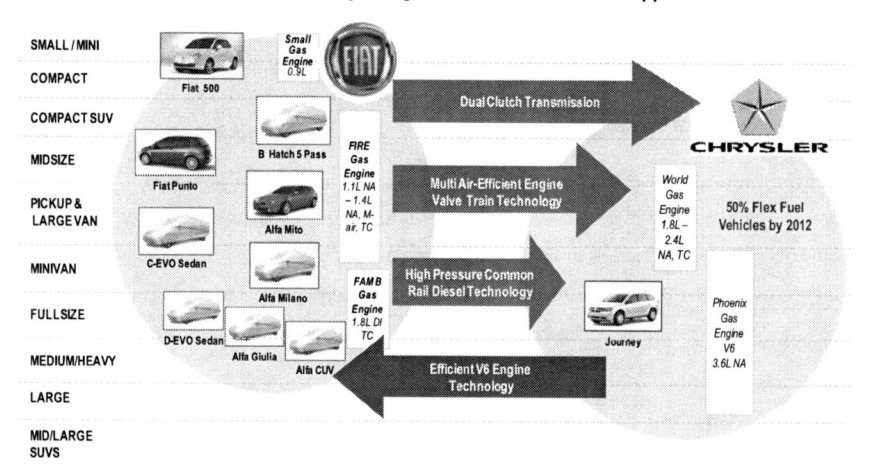

The proposed Fiat alliance would enhance Chrysler's restructuring plan, provide customers with access to competitive fuel-efficient vehicle platforms, provide Chrysler with substantial cost saving opportunities and provide Chrysler with distribution capabilities in key growth markets. The alliance would also help stabilize the U.S. automotive market and enhance Chrysler's ability to more quickly repay the U.S. Treasury loan.

Figure 3: Expansion through Current Geographic – Percent (%) Sales by Region

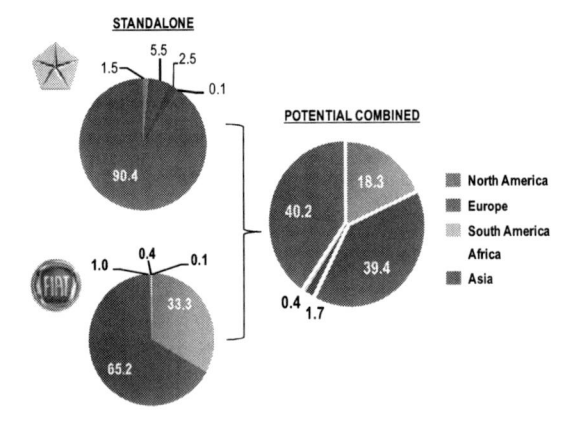

STANDALONE
- 90.4
- 5.5
- 2.5
- 1.5
- 0.1

- 65.2
- 33.3
- 1.0
- 0.4
- 0.1

POTENTIAL COMBINED
- 40.2
- 39.4
- 18.3
- 1.7
- 0.4

Legend:
- North America
- Europe
- South America
- Africa
- Asia

Chrysler's intent is to build on its product alliances or form global alliances to enhance its viability. The Company has proposed that a percentage of its new equity be retained in a trust controlled by the Presidents Designee to facilitate these alliances in the future. This provision will avoid a redistribution and reallocation of Chrysler equity in the future.

CHRYSLER

4) Commitment to Energy Security and Environmental Sustainability

In 2008, Chrysler offered six vehicles with highway fuel economy of 28 miles per gallon or better. The 2009 product lineup offers improved fuel economy with 73% of its vehicles showing improved fuel economy compared with the prior year's model. Fuel economy will continue to improve in 2010 with the introduction of the all-new Phoenix V-6 engine, which will provide fuel efficiency improvements of between 6-to-8 percent. A two-mode hybrid version of the Company's best-selling vehicle, the Dodge Ram is scheduled for 2010.

The first Chrysler electric-drive vehicle is also scheduled to reach the market in 2010. It will be followed by other electric-drive vehicles, including Range-extended Electric Vehicles, in order to further reduce fuel consumption and greenhouse gas emissions in Chrysler's mainstream vehicles.

Figure 4: Chrysler's Electric Vehicle Product Portfolio

	2009	2010	2011	2012	2013	2014
Battery Electric Vehicle (NEV, CEV, BEV)	GEM/Peapod Renewal NEV >200 mpg	ENVI #1 BEV >200 mpg	ENVI #2 CityEV >200 mpg			
Range-Extended Electric Vehicles (ReEV)				ENVI #3 ReEV (or HEV) 55-65 mpg	ENVI #4 ReEV >45 mpg (alternative)	ENVI #5 ReEV 60-70 mpg / ENVI #6 ReEV 40-50 mpg
Hybrid Electric Vehicles (HEV)		Dodge RAM 1500 HEV Gen 1 25-27 mpg		HEV 28-30 mpg	In DOE Plan → ENVI #4 HEV 40-45 mpg	Dodge RAM 1500 HEV Gen 2 26-28 mpg

NOTE: ● Denotes inclusion in Chrysler's 10Nov2008 ATVM Loan Program Submission to DOE

The proposed Fiat alliance would further help the Company achieve fuel economy improvements as Chrysler gains access to Fiat's smaller, fuel efficient platforms and powertrain technologies.

CHRYSLER

This alliance would enable Chrysler to reduce its capital expenditures while supporting the Company's commitment to develop a portfolio of vehicles that meet the country's energy security and environmental objectives.

5) Compliance with Fuel Economy Regulations

Chrysler is committed to meeting Federal Corporate Average Fuel Economy (CAFE) requirements. The restructuring plan supports the company's compliance with all federal fuel economy standards as set forth in the Energy Independence and Security Act of 2007. Going forward, Chrysler supports the development of a uniform national standard that reflects the input of all constituents.

Included in the main report are estimates of Chrysler's required minimum CAFE levels in model years 2008 to 2011, based on a pre-publication draft of the NHTSA Final Rule for model years 2009 to 2015 that became available earlier this year. The Appendix contains a series of charts showing the specific technologies to be used in each vehicle to achieve CAFE compliance, along with the timing of the deployment of the technologies. This description of specific actions demonstrates that Chrysler will comply with the CAFE standards throughout the term of the U.S. Treasury loan and beyond.

Pursuant to California Assembly Bill 1493 ("AB 1493") the California Air Resources Board ("CARB") has also adopted vehicle emissions standards to control greenhouse gas ("GHG") emissions, chiefly carbon dioxide. The GHG standards include sales-weighted fleet average requirements using a formula that requires increases in fuel economy, because the only current available technology to reduce carbon dioxide emissions from gasoline- or diesel-powered vehicles is to reduce fuel consumption. Thirteen other States and the District of Columbia have adopted the California GHG standards. These states comprise approximately 50% of the United States vehicle market during model years 2012-2016.

13

If the California GHG standards take effect, Chrysler will try its best to comply using available technology, however, as a last resort it may be necessary to restrict the sales of certain vehicle models in order to comply with the GHG fleet average requirements in each jurisdiction that has adopted them and that has decided to enforce the fleet average requirements. The ultimate effect of the California standards on Chrysler's product plan depends on a number of developments as indicated in the Appendix.

6) Compliance with Emissions Regulations

The United States EPA and the CARB enforce regulations to control hydrocarbons and nitrogen oxides, the two vehicular air emissions aimed at reducing smog. Chrysler vehicle engine systems and catalytic converters oxidize and reduce these emissions to regulatory levels, and control emissions of other compounds subject to other EPA and CARB regulations. EPA and CARB also enforce "on board diagnostic" ("OBD") regulations governing vehicles onboard computer, which among other things optimize the performance of the catalytic converter and determine if emissions-related components are properly functioning.

Chrysler pre-production and post-production vehicles must pass rigorous testing, after which vehicle certification to a specific set of EPA and CARB emissions standards is obtained. Chrysler also must warrant that its vehicles will pass such testing when properly maintained and used.

The Appendix includes materials that show that Chrysler will comply with emissions standards as expressed, per the regulations, as a weighted average of the various categories of emissions requirements versus fleet sales volumes for cars and trucks established by EPA and CARB for the time period relevant to the loan agreement. The Appendix also shows Chrysler's compliance with CARB's "zero emission vehicle" ("ZEV") requirements, which are promulgated for model years 2009 through 2010, and Chrysler's best understanding of the as yet unpromulgated ZEV requirements for model years 2011 and later.

7) Achieving a Competitive Product Mix and Cost Structure

As noted above, Chrysler has taken a number of actions over the past several years to improve its cost competitiveness. According to the Harbour Report, Chrysler has improved its manufacturing productivity by 32% over the past seven years to equal that of Toyota, making Chrysler and Toyota the most productive automakers in North America in terms of hours of assembly per vehicle.

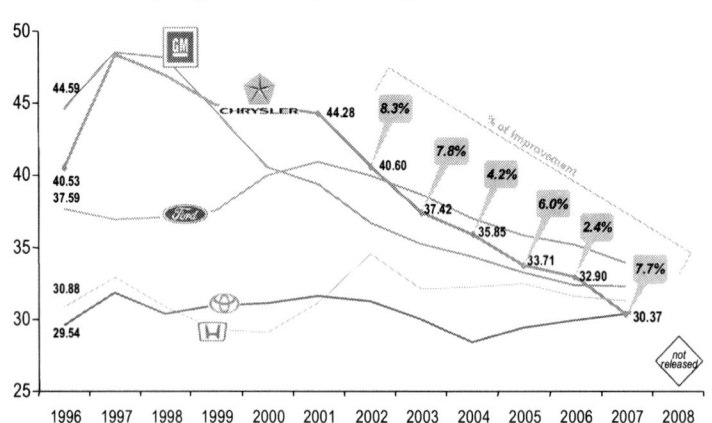

Figure 5: 2008 Harbour Report (Manufacturing Efficiency)

Having achieved world class hours of assembly time per vehicle, assuming the implementation of new wage rates consistent with the government mandated labor modifications, Chrysler will be on par with transplants from a manufacturing cost perspective.

Since becoming a standalone company on August 3, 2007, Chrysler has made quality a major focus. In its first 60 days as an independent automaker, Chrysler management approved more than 260 product enhancements representing an investment of $500 million. Hundreds of additional engineering improvements were made in the following months to enhance the interior quality, fit and finish, and the driving performance of many Chrysler products. In the 2008 J.D.

Chrysler Restructuring Plan

Power and Associates Initial Quality Survey, the Company's vehicles improved scores by an average of 5 points. In addition, in 2008 Chrysler achieved the lowest warranty claim rate in its history – a 30% improvement compared to the prior year. And, among the seven major auto manufacturers, Chrysler had the lowest number of vehicles recalled in 2008 as measured by NHTSA.

Figure 6: Chrysler Total Quality Improvement

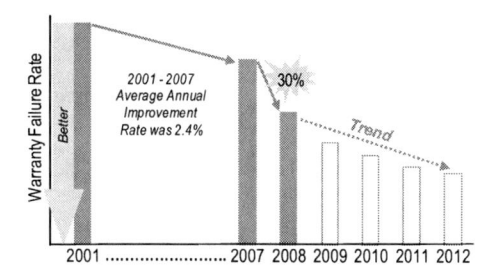

Chrysler was the first company in the industry to appoint a Chief Customer Officer devoted to improving real and perceived quality. As part of this initiative, Chrysler has formed cross-functional customer satisfaction teams that act as problem solvers on new vehicles as they are being developed and launched.

Figure 7: Customer Promoter Score (CPS) Confirms Consumer Appeal of New Dodge Ram

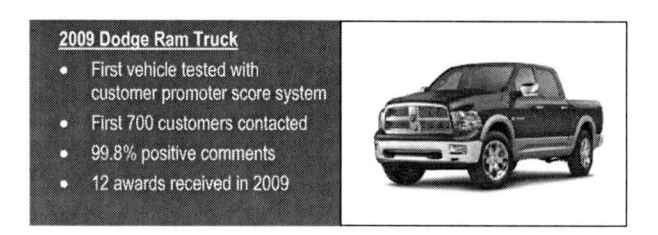

2009 Dodge Ram Truck
- First vehicle tested with customer promoter score system
- First 700 customers contacted
- 99.8% positive comments
- 12 awards received in 2009

Chrysler's product line is a key component to its restructuring plan. Next year Chrysler will launch revisions to four of its previously highly successful platforms: Jeep Grand Cherokee, Dodge Charger, Dodge Durango and Chrysler 300. The Chrysler 300C has become the most

CHRYSLER

awarded car in automotive history since its launch in 2005. This launch will be followed by a new, bolder, more intimidating Dodge Charger and an all new unibody Dodge Durango.

Chrysler will continue to work with its dealer body to rationalize the number of dealerships to enhance the long-term profitability of all dealers. Through Project Genesis, Chrysler is committed to facilitating the ability to offer each of Chrysler's three product brands under one roof, creating an enhanced buying and service experience for the consumer and supporting the viability of Chrysler dealers in communities across the country. The proposed alliance with Fiat would allow Chrysler to broaden its product offerings – bringing the American consumer a broader selection of cars to meet their needs - and providing Chrysler dealers with an expanded product line and opportunity for improved profitability.

8) Conclusion

We believe Chrysler's restructuring plan, as approved by its Board of Directors, demonstrates that, with constituent concessions, adequate retail and wholesale capacity for Chrysler Financial, a restructuring of our liabilities resulting in a $5 billion reduction in debt and debt service requirements and additional governmental assistance, Chrysler can achieve and sustain long-term viability, international competitiveness and energy efficiency. The Company's viability can be further enhanced through strategic alliances and partnerships. However, in order to weather the current economic crisis, in addition to the original $7 billion, $4 billion of which has been received, Chrysler is requesting an additional $2 billion, for a total of $9 billion, to support ongoing operations due to the continued deterioration in the economy, which has led to an unprecedented decline in the automotive sector since the Company's December 2nd plan submission.

While this is a substantial investment of taxpayer funds, Chrysler believes the requested loan is the least costly available alternative and will provide an important stimulus to the U.S. economy that will eventually deliver positive returns for the American taxpayer.

Respectfully submitted,

Chrysler LLC

**The entire Chrysler Restructuring Plan (177 pages) can be found at:
www.media.chrysler.com/dcxms/assets/attachments/Restructuring_Plan_for_LongTerm_Viability.pdf**

APPENDIX 6

GM VIABILITY DETERMINATION

March 30, 2009

Determination of Viability Summary
General Motors Corporation

March 30, 2009

<u>**GM February 17 Plan**</u>
Viability Determination

Summary

The Loan and Security Agreement of December 31, 2008 between the General Motors Corporation and the United States Department of the Treasury ("LSA") laid out conditions that needed to be met by March 31, including the approval of Labor Modifications, VEBA Modifications, and the commencement of a Bond Exchange (all as defined in the LSA).

As of the date of this memo, the above steps have not been completed, nor are they expected to be completed by March 31. As a result, General Motors has not satisfied the terms of its loan agreement. Additionally, after substantial effort and review, the President's Designee[1] has concluded that the GM plan, in its current form, is not viable and will need to be restructured substantially while GM operates under an amendment to the existing LSA. It is strongly believed, however, that such a substantial restructuring will lead to a viable GM.

This determination of viability was based on a thorough review, as conducted by the Task Force and its outside advisors and as summarized below, of the Company's submitted plan and prospects. While there were many individual considerations, no single factor was critical to the assessment. Rather, the ultimate determination of viability was based upon a total consideration of all relevant factors, taken as a whole.

General Motors is in the early stages of an operational turnaround in which the Company has made material progress in a number of areas, including purchasing, product design, manufacturing, brand rationalization and its dealer network. Despite these steps, a great deal more progress needs to be made, and GM's plan contemplates initiatives that will take many years to complete. In the end, GM's plan is based on a number of assumptions that will be very challenging to meet without a more dramatic restructuring in which many of its planned changes are accelerated. A few highlights:

- **Market Share:** GM has been losing market share to its competitors for decades, yet its plan assumes only a very moderate decline, despite reducing fleet sales and shuttering brands that represent 1.8% of its current market share.
- **Price:** The plan assumes improvement in net price realization despite a severely distressed market, lingering consumer quality perceptions, and an increase in smaller vehicles (where the Company has previously struggled to maintain pricing power).
- **Brands/Dealers:** The Company is currently burdened with underperforming brands, nameplates and an excess of dealers. The plan does not act aggressively enough to curb these problems.
- **Product mix:** GM earns a large share of its profits from high-margin trucks and SUVs, which are vulnerable to a continuing shift in consumer preference to smaller vehicles. Additionally, while the Chevy Volt holds promise, it will likely be too expensive to be commercially successful in the short-term.
- **Legacy liabilities:** In GM's plan, its cash needs associated with legacy liabilities grow to unsustainable levels, reaching approximately $6 billion per year in 2013 and 2014.

Moreover, even under the Company's optimistic assumptions, the Company continues to experience negative free cash flow (before financing but after legacy obligations) through the projection period, failing a fundamental test of viability.

In short, while the Company has made meaningful progress in its turnaround plan over the last few years, the progress has been far too slow, allowing the Company to continue to lag the best-in-class competitors. As a result, the President's Designee has found that General Motors' plan is not viable as it is currently structured. However, because of GM's scale, franchise and progress to date, we believe that there could be a viable business within GM if the Company and its stakeholders engage in a substantially more aggressive restructuring plan.

Determination of Viability Summary March 30, 2009
General Motors Corporation

Detailed Determination

The Loan and Security Agreement of December 31, 2008 between the General Motors Corporation and the United States Department of the Treasury ("LSA") laid out various conditions that needed to be met by March 31, including:

(a) Approval of the Labor Modifications (Compensation Reductions, the Severance Rationalization and the Work Rule Modifications) by the members of the Unions;

(b) Receipt of all necessary approvals of the VEBA Modifications other than regulatory and judicial approvals; provided, that the Borrower must have filed and be diligently prosecuting applications for any necessary regulatory and judicial approvals; and

(c) The commencement of an exchange offer to implement a Bond Exchange.

As of the date of this memo, none of the above steps has been completed. As a result, General Motors has not satisfied the terms of its loan agreement.

The LSA also requires that the President's Designee review the Restructuring Plan Report in order to determine whether General Motors has taken all necessary steps to achieve and sustain the long-term viability, international competitiveness and energy efficiency of the Company and its subsidiaries

Since receiving the Company's plan on February 17th, the Government has engaged in substantial efforts to assess its viability. This work has involved staff from the Department of the Treasury, National Economic Council, Council of Economic Advisors as well as the numerous other Cabinet agencies involved in the President's Task Force on the Auto Industry. The working group has also worked extensively with several dozen individuals at industry-leading consulting, financial advisory and law firms. Numerous outside experts and affected stakeholders have been consulted. As a result of this work, the President's Designee has concluded that the General Motors plan, in its current form, is not viable and will need to be restructured substantially in order to lead to a viable General Motors. It is strongly believed, however, that such a substantial restructuring will lead to a viable General Motors.

While the President's Designee considered many factors when assessing viability, the most fundamental benchmark was the following: for a business to be viable, it must be able – after accounting for spending on research and development and capital expenditures necessary to maintain and enhance the company's competitive position -- to generate positive cashflow and earn an adequate return on capital over the course of a normal business cycle.

Progress to date:

General Motors is in the early stages of an operational turnaround in which GM has made material progress in a number of areas:

- o Purchasing: GM has organized its purchasing globally, with its purchasing organization taking advantage of GM's global scale, and has put into place a rigorous, metric-oriented approach to drive supplier quality and cost improvements.
- o Product design: GM has refined its product design process to create global vehicle platforms, thus allowing GM to reduce engineering costs and improve the content of its cars. These global platforms leverage the scale of the business and allow GM to amortize product development costs over a large range

Determination of Viability Summary   March 30, 2009
General Motors Corporation

of models. GM has also, since 2005, focused on customer needs, interior designs, styling and quality to provide more attractive products. Examples of successes of this initiative include the 2008 North American Car of the Year Chevy Malibu and the 2008 Motor Trend Car of the Year Cadillac CTS (though they constitute a modest share of GM's portfolio today).
- o Manufacturing: GM has worked to create greater flexibility within its facilities, allowing for increased capacity utilization and an enhanced ability to spread its significant fixed costs across a broader car base.
- o Brand rationalization: The recently announced decisions to divest or shut down Saab, Saturn and Hummer, while late, were important steps in reducing the Company's brand portfolio and allowing it to focus its financial and human resources on a smaller number of higher quality brands.
- o Dealer network: GM has been eliminating dealers from markets where it is oversaturated, as well as eliminating dealers who are either unprofitable or create a poor customer experience.

However, it is important to recognize that a great deal more progress needs to be made, and that GM's plan is based on fairly optimistic assumptions that will be challenging in the absence of a more aggressive restructuring.

- The plan contemplates that each of its restructuring initiatives will continue well into the future, in some cases until 2014, before they are complete.
    - o The slow pace at which this turnaround is progressing undermines the Company's ability to compete against large, highly capable and well-funded competitors. GM's plan forecasts it to catch up to (and, in some cases, surpass) its competitors' current performance metrics; however, its key competitors are constantly working to improve as well, potentially leaving GM further behind over time.
- Given the slow pace of the turnaround, the assumptions in GM's business plan are too optimistic.
    - o Market Share
        - GM has been losing market share slowly to its competitors for decades. In 1980, GM's US market share was 45%; in 1990, GM's US share was 36%, in 2000, its share was 29%. In 2008, its share was 22%. In short, GM has been losing 0.7% per year for the last 30 years.
            - Yet, in its forecast, GM assumes a much slower rate of decline, 0.3% per year until 2014, even though it is reducing fleet sales and shuttering brands which represent a loss of 1.8% market share, of which only a fraction will be retained. Management's plan to achieve this is driven by a reduction in nameplates and an ensuing increase in marketing spend per nameplate.
            - Furthermore, in the current plan, GM has retained too many unprofitable nameplates that tarnish its brands, distract the focus of its management team, demand increasingly scarce marketing dollars and are a lingering drag on consumer perception, market share and margin.
    - o Price
        - In 2006 and 2007, GM North America achieved a 30.4% contribution margin. Then, the plan assumes, despite a severely distressed market, that margins increase to 30.8% in 2009 and 30.7% in 2010. These figures remain at 30.9% in 2013 and 30.3% in 2014, despite GM's plan to increase its focus on passenger cars and crossovers, which have traditionally earned lower margins.
        - Fundamentally, the lingering consumer perception is that GM makes lower-quality cars (despite meaningful improvements in the last few years), which in turn leads to greater discounting, which harms GM's price realizations and depresses profitability. These lower price points are an important impediment to enhanced GM profitability and need to be reversed over time in order for GM to bring its margins into line with its best-in-class peers.

3

Determination of Viability Summary   March 30, 2009
General Motors Corporation

- Brands/dealers
    - GM has been successfully pruning unprofitable or underperforming dealers for several years. However, its current pace will leave it with too many such dealers for a long period of time while requiring significant closure costs that its competitors will not incur. These underperforming dealers create a drag on the overall brand equity of GM and hurt the prospects of the many stronger dealers who could help GM drive incremental sales.
- Europe
    - GM's European operations have experienced negative results for at least the last decade with a sharp decline in market share from 12.9% to 9.3% between 1995 and 2008, leaving the Company with high fixed costs and low capacity utilization.
    - The European business is seeking additional capital beyond the funds requested from the Treasury. These funds have not been allocated and thus represent a risk to the viability of GM's current plan.
- Product mix and CAFE compliance
    - GM earns a disproportionate share of its profits from high-margin trucks and SUVs and is thus vulnerable to energy cost-driven shifts in consumer demand. For example, of its top 20 profit contributors in 2008, only nine were cars.
    - GM is at least one generation behind Toyota on advanced, "green" powertrain development. In an attempt to leapfrog Toyota, GM has devoted significant resources to the Chevy Volt. While the Volt holds promise, it is currently projected to be much more expensive than its gasoline-fueled peers and will likely need substantial reductions in manufacturing cost in order to become commercially viable
    - Absent the successful introduction of a number of new-generation nameplates, as described in the Company's plan, GM's product portfolio is more vulnerable to CAFE standard increases than the portfolios of many of its competitors (although GM is in compliance today with current standards). Many of its products fail to meet the minimum threshold on fuel economy and rank in the bottom quartile of fuel economy achievement.
- Legacy liabilities – cash costs
    - As GM moves through its forecast period, its cash needs associated with legacy liabilities grow, reaching approximately $6 billion per year in 2013 and 2014. To meet this cash outflow, GM needs to sell 900,000 additional cars per year, creating a difficult burden that leaves it fighting to maximize volume rather than return on investment.
- Even under the Company's optimistic assumptions, the Company remains breakeven, at best, on a free cash flow basis throughout the projection period, thus failing the fundamental test of viability.
    - Under its own plan, GM generates $14.5bn of negative free cash flow over its 6 year forecast period. Even in 2014, on its own assumptions, GM generates negative free cash flow after servicing legacy obligations.
    - Given the highly challenging current market, the Company is already behind plan in its overall volume expectations and market share for calendar year 2009.
    - Since the Company has built a plan with little margin for error, even slight swings in its assumptions produce significant and ongoing negative cash flows. For example, a 1% share miss in overall global sales, all else being equal, in 2014 would lead to a $2 billion cash flow reduction in that year.

In short, while the Company has made meaningful progress in its turnaround plan over the last few years, the progress has been far too slow, allowing the Company to continue to lag the best-in-class competitors. Furthermore, even if the projected plan is achieved, the cash flow forecast is quite modest, leaving the Company little margin for error in what will

4

Determination of Viability Summary
General Motors Corporation

March 30, 2009

be a very difficult turnaround. As a result, the President's Designee has found that General Motors' plan is not viable as it is currently structured. However, given the improvements that have been made to date, and the path on which these improvements place GM, we believe that there could be a viable business within GM if the Company and its stakeholders engage in a substantially more aggressive restructuring plan.

Appendix 7

CHRYSLER VIABILITY DETERMINATION

March 30, 2009

Determination of Viability Summary
Chrysler, LLC

March 30, 2009

Chrysler February 17 Plan
Viability Determination

Summary

The Loan and Security Agreement of December 31, 2008 between Chrysler, LLC and the United States Department of the Treasury ("LSA") laid out various conditions that needed to be met by March 31, including the approval of Labor Modifications, VEBA Modifications, and the commencement of a Debt Exchange (all as defined in the LSA).

As of the date of this memo, the above steps have not been completed, nor are they expected to be completed by March 31. As a result, Chrysler has not satisfied the terms of its loan agreement. Additionally, after substantial effort and review, the President's Designee[1] has concluded that the Chrysler plan is not likely to lead to viability on a standalone basis, and that Chrysler must seek a partner in order to achieve the scale and other important attributes it needs to be successful in the global automotive industry while Chrysler operates under an amendment to the existing LSA.

This determination of viability was based on a thorough review, as conducted by the Task Force and its outside advisors and as summarized below, of the Company's submitted plan and prospects. While there were many individual considerations, no single factor was critical to the assessment. Rather, the ultimate determination of viability was based upon a total consideration of all relevant factors, taken as a whole.

The Plan that was submitted by Chrysler on February 17, 2009 reflects some progress that has been made under current management but ultimately is insufficient due to several structural issues that Chrysler, as a standalone entity, is highly unlikely to overcome. In particular, Chrysler's limited scale in an increasingly capital-intensive global business, the inferior quality of its existing product portfolio and its heavy truck mix leave the Company poorly positioned. Chrysler's plan to address these issues is based on overly optimistic assumptions that are inconsistent with its current products and its resources. A few key challenges:

- **Scale:** Chrysler cannot afford to dedicate enough R&D to each product platform to maintain competitiveness, suffers from having a smaller supply purchasing base and amortizes its significant fixed costs over a much smaller base of vehicles than its competitors
- **Quality:** While the Company is committed to improving quality, its current quality scores significantly lag competitors. Chrysler admits that improving quality and associated brand perception will take a number of years.
- **Product Mix:** Chrysler does not have a product pipeline to cover the smaller car segments which are projected to grow in share of the overall car market and will struggle to meet proposed fuel-efficiency standards.
- **Manufacturing:** In contrast to best-in-class OEMs, as well as both GM and Ford, Chrysler has not invested significantly in common architectures and flexible plant manufacturing capacity, which will be critical to long-term profitability.
- **Geographic Concentration:** Unlike many of its competitors, Chrysler's business is heavily weighted to North America, which makes the Company more vulnerable to local economic fluctuations and less able to take advantage of developing markets.

While the Company has made meaningful changes to its cost structure in the last few years, the combination of a fundamentally disadvantaged operating structure and a limited set of desirable products make standalone viability for the business highly challenging. As a result, the President's Designee has found that Chrysler's plan is not viable as currently structured. However, to the extent Chrysler can develop a partner who would improve Chrysler's scale, bolster its product development, and allow it to enter the small car market with a robust set of products, Chrysler has some prospects for long term viability.

Determination of Viability Summary March 30, 2009
Chrysler, LLC

Detailed Determination

The Loan and Security Agreement of December 31, 2008 between the Chrysler Corporation and the United States Department of the Treasury ("LSA") laid out various conditions that needed to be met by March 31, including:

(a) Approval of the Labor Modifications (Compensation Reductions, the Severance Rationalization and the Work Rule Modifications) by the members of the Unions;

(b) Receipt of all necessary approvals of the VEBA Modifications other than regulatory and judicial approvals; provided, that the Borrower must have filed and be diligently prosecuting applications for any necessary regulatory and judicial approvals; and

(c) The commencement of an exchange offer to implement a Debt Exchange.

As of the date of this memo, the above steps have not been completed. As a result, Chrysler has not satisfied the terms of its loan agreement.

The LSA also requires that the President's Designee review the Restructuring Plan Report in order to determine whether Chrysler has taken all necessary steps to achieve and sustain the long-term viability, international competitiveness and energy efficiency of the Company and its subsidiaries

Since receiving the Company's plan on February 17th, the Government has engaged in substantial efforts to assess its viability. This work has involved staff from the Department of Treasury, National Economic Council, Council of Economic Advisors as well as the numerous other Cabinet agencies involved in the President's Task Force on the Auto Industry. The working group has also worked extensively with several dozen individuals at industry-leading consulting, financial advisory and law firms. Numerous outside experts and affected stakeholders have been consulted. Based on this work, the President's Designee has concluded that the Chrysler plan is not likely to lead to viability on a standalone basis, and that Chrysler must seek a partner in order to achieve the scale and other important attributes it needs to be successful in the global automotive industry.

While the President's Designee considered many factors when assessing viability, the most fundamental benchmark was the following: for a business to be viable, it must be able – after accounting for spending on research and development and capital expenditures necessary to maintain and enhance the company's competitive position -- to generate positive cashflow and earn an adequate return on capital over the course of a normal business cycle.

The Plan that was submitted by Chrysler on February 17, 2009 reflects some progress that has been made under current management but ultimately is insufficient due to several structural issues that Chrysler, as a standalone entity, is highly unlikely to overcome:

Progress to date:

- Chrysler has made meaningful progress, and identified a great deal more opportunity, in reducing its cost structure as part of a major operating restructuring:
    - **Structural costs**: The Company plans to reduce structural costs by 29% from 2007 to 2009. These improvements are driven largely by aggressive reductions in salaried headcount, which is expected to fall by 60% from 2000 to 2010.

Determination of Viability Summary   **March 30, 2009**
Chrysler, LLC

- - **Capacity utilization**: The plan contemplates the reduction of manufacturing capacity by 1.3M units in order to respond to a depressed global auto market. The manufacturing capacity will be eliminated mainly through the closure of two assembly plants and five engine plants from 2009 to 2014.
  - **Wage rate rationalization**: The Company projects that its US hourly wage rate will reach benchmark levels by 2010. These assumptions are based on current negotiations, which have yet to be finalized.
- Chrysler's plan also focuses on improving product quality, which has historically lagged at Chrysler:
  - Since the formation of Chrysler LLC, there has been a renewed effort to increase the quality and interior content of vehicles, although quality often takes many years to significantly improve and the perception of quality can lag still further. Importantly, current market research by independent experts does not suggest any significant improvement in customers' perception of Chrysler product quality.

In short, Chrysler's current management team has made meaningful progress in addressing the areas under which they have the most control, particularly on a short-term basis. However, Chrysler suffers from a number of structural disadvantages that can not be addressed on a standalone basis. In particular, Chrysler's limited scale in an increasingly capital-intensive global business, the poor quality of its existing product portfolio and its heavy truck mix leave the Company poorly positioned. Chrysler's plan to address these issues is based on overly optimistic assumptions that are inconsistent with its current products and its resources.

- Chrysler's smaller scale has broad implications for its business, both at the top line as it seeks necessary improvements in its product portfolio and at the bottom line as it seeks to improve its cost structure.
  - **Product Development:** Chrysler's scale limits its product development budget overall, and particularly limits the amount the Company can spend developing each platform. Chrysler currently dedicates only 50% as many engineers to each platform, on average, as GM does. Furthermore, Chrysler has much lower volume platforms, on average, than most of its competitors, and these lower volume platforms mean that Chrysler must amortize its R&D and capital expenditures over a much smaller base. This, of course, limits the Company's ability to innovate and develop new product.
  - **Purchasing:** Due to its limited scale, the Company is unable to exert leverage on suppliers to reduce its cost of goods. For example, GM's average yearly global buy is ~$90B, whereas Chrysler's is ~$20B.
  - **Fixed costs:** Chrysler's more limited scale means that some of its fixed costs are spread over a smaller base. As a result, Chrysler has a significant disadvantage on fixed costs (estimated at approximately 3-4% of revenue), which translates into several hundred dollars per car of reduced profit.
- Chrysler's products have also historically underperformed in terms of quality, which remains a significant challenge:
  - **Quality Ratings**: Chrysler has low quality scores across all of its brands, and perceived quality lags the best-in-class OEMs (2008 IQS of 147 for Chrysler versus 105 for Toyota). Moreover, every single one of Chrysler's brands are in the bottom quartile based on JD Power APEAL scores. Finally, a recent Consumer Reports article listed Chrysler last in terms of the number of recommended nameplates in its portfolio (zero Chrysler nameplates were recommended). By contrast, all of GM's continuing brands outperform Chrysler on an IQS basis and, on average, substantially outperform on APEAL scores.
  - **Timeframe**: While there has been a renewed focus on quality since January 2008, Chrysler admits that improving quality and associated brand perception will take a number of years, as about 40% of quality issues (IQS/100 vehicles) are design related and are typically not addressed until a new product is developed.

3

Determination of Viability Summary
Chrysler, LLC
March 30, 2009

- The Company is burdened with an unfavorable product mix, which may create further disadvantage in the evolving marketplace:
    - **Market tastes and shifts**: Chrysler does not have a product pipeline to cover the smaller car segments which are projected to grow in share of the overall car market. Chrysler's shares of the small and medium car markets are 3% and 7%, respectively (while each category represents 21% and 25% of the market, respectively), and has been declining in each segment.
    - **Current focus**: In the near term, Chrysler is planning to lift profitability by focusing on its more profitable truck and SUV segments. Given the potential variability in fuel prices, Chrysler's volume assumptions for these cars may be at risk.
    - **CAFE standards**: Chrysler's product strength is in the pickup, SUV, and minivan segments – all of which are relatively low in fuel efficiency. On a standalone basis, Chrysler will struggle to comply with increasing fuel efficiency standards, and it may even have to restrict the sale of certain models to make sure it is in accordance with proposed standards.

The limitations imposed on Chrysler by its smaller scale permeate its ability to manage its business and hinder its hopes of improving its fortunes. For example:

- Given Chrysler's limited financial resources, it can not make the necessary catch-up investments in R&D required to refresh its portfolio and bring it up to par with its competitors. So, while Chrysler's declining competitive position demands that it makes substantial investments in new products and a more diversified mix of products, its own plan projects the following:
    - **Limited new products**: The 2009 through 2014 product plan delivers only four new nameplates under the current Chrysler umbrella, with potential for additional nameplates only through a partnership.
    - **Powertrain development**: While Chrysler is investing in newer powertrain development, as are all the OEMs, its limited resources lead it to project spending just over 3% of revenue on R&D over the next five years, versus 4-5% for General Motors, Toyota and Honda.
    - **Small cars**: Chrysler's standalone plan does not provide for a substantial entrance into the small car segments – an area that will be increasingly important to automotive manufacturer profitability if potential gasoline price hikes meaningfully increase demand for smaller, more fuel-efficient cars and as CAFE standards demand a higher mix of small cars.

- Chrysler also lags its competitors in terms of manufacturing flexibility:
    - Virtually all industry observers and outside experts agree that increasing flexibility in the manufacturing footprint is critical to driving long-term profitability in the global automotive industry. In contrast to other best-in-class OEMs, as well as both GM and Ford, Chrysler has not invested significantly in common architectures and flexible plant manufacturing capacity to build multiple platforms in a given plant.
    - Chrysler is planning to invest in more flexible capacity but is behind both the transplants and GM in this capability. This lag increases Chrysler's risk to market segment shifts and individual product acceptance. For example, of the nine plants Chrysler is targeting to have by 2013, only two will be flexible across multiple platforms (compared to ~80% of GM plants).

Given these substantial obstacles, the assumptions in Chrysler's business plan are too aggressive:

- **Market share**: Chrysler's plan assumes that it maintains its current market share, although the Company has consistently lost share over the last decade

Determination of Viability Summary   **March 30, 2009**
Chrysler, LLC

- o Chrysler has lost five percentage points of market share since the height of its share, at 16.2%, in 1998. This loss has occurred across all segments, even within its historically strong minivan offerings, where share has declined from 39% to 33% since 2006.
- o The plan projects market share to stabilize at 10.7% and assumes that Chrysler will be able to find partnerships to launch new products in a very competitive market. Continued share erosion in line with recent history would translate into several billion dollars of increased losses over time.
- o Unlike GM, which has had a number of successful recent product introductions and has developed a new global product development process that has promise, there are few tangible signs that Chrysler can reverse its share erosion. In fact, the gap in perceived brand quality for Chrysler, Dodge and Jeep relative to their competitors has increased meaningfully over the last several years, suggesting that Chrysler's market share, if not for significantly increased incentives that have further eroded profitability, is even more vulnerable than history suggests.
- **Financing**: The viability plan relies on Chrysler's captive financing arm to provide a significant amount of financing, which may prove challenging:
  - o In general, Chrysler's customer mix is skewed to a lower FICO score buyer (in the first quarter of 2008, approximately 34% of buyers were subprime or near-subprime), so the current financing environment disproportionately hurts traditional Chrysler buyers' ability to purchase a new car.
  - o Given the separation and independence of Chrysler Financial and increased credit standards, it is unlikely that demand will return to the robust levels of recent years in the near term.
  - o In 2008, 48% of financing for Chrysler buyers was provided by Chrysler Financial. The captive finance unit has substantial financing challenges of its own in the current financing environment, so future demand may depend on Chrysler finding alternate lending sources.
- **Price realization**: Chrysler also assumes only a modest decline in price realization despite entering highly competitive segments:
  - o Given the quality gap from which Chrysler suffers, it will be challenging to maintain pricing as projected.
  - o Even more importantly, the Company projects providing lower incentives than it has provided in its recent history – at a level of more than 25% less than the recent historical average. If the incentives were "normalized", based on the average of 2006 - 2007 incentives, the Company will lose consistently between $500 million and $1 billion per year from 2010 to 2014 on an EBIT basis. This is inconsistent with the Company's recent history with regard to incentives, in which increasingly larger incentives still translated into continued share erosion.
- **Variable margin**: The plan also includes a constant variable margin assumption, despite a shift to producing lower margin vehicles. The primary drivers of this assumption are improved price realization and a reduction in cost of goods fueled by material cost management and supplier concessions of 3%, which may prove difficult given Chrysler's limited scale and distressed supply base.

While the Company has made meaningful changes to its cost structure in the last few years, the combination of a fundamentally disadvantaged operating structure and a limited set of desirable products make standalone viability for the business highly challenging. As a result, the President's Designee has found that Chrysler's plan is not viable as currently structured. However, a partnership with another automotive company, such as Fiat or another prospective partner, which addresses many of these issues could lead to a path to viability for Chrysler.

Appendix 8

GM NETWORK ANALYSIS

GM Conducted Dealer Network Analysis to Establish the Size of a Viable Dealer Network

- GM's Approach to Dealer Network Planning
  - Competitive Dealer Throughput
  - Competitive Dealer Return on Investment
  - Customer Convenience better than targeted competitor (drive time analysis)
  - Market Demographics and how they change over time
- From this data we created an "Ideal" Dealer Blueprint
  - This analysis yielded an "ideal" dealer blueprint of 3,380 dealers
  - We determined that a subjective process of eliminating dealers to achieve this optimal footprint would not be fair or consistent with our past business practices
  - Therefore, we selected objective dealer performance criteria to stratify the dealers between performing dealers that we would want in our long-term dealer network and those dealers that are underperforming in today's market
  - Using this objective performance criteria yielded approximately 4,100 dealers vs. 3,380

Dealer Network Restructuring

- Plan enables competitive dealer throughput and Return on Assets (ROA) opportunity in the metro markets
- Despite reductions GM would maintain extensive hubtown (i.e. 25-50k population) and small town footprint as strategic advantage
- Chrysler plan rejected and immediately terminated a portion of the dealers
- GM's plan offers a "wind-down" agreement to facilitate vehicle and parts inventory sell-down, and customer migration in an orderly way over the next 12 – 17 months
- Dealers not accepting the "wind-down" agreements will be rejected (similar to Chrysler). It is highly unlikely that any GM dealers will fall into this category.
- GM is responsible for vehicle inventory of terminated dealers who are floored through GMAC (approximately 80% of inventory)
- Approximately 4,100 dealers will be offered a continuing assignment agreement to include:
  – Sales, inventory, and image performance
  – Essential brand elements (requirements)
  – No non-GM duals
  – Waive right to protest
- It is projected that 3,500 – 3,800 dealers will accept the continuing assignment agreement and move forward with the new GM

Dealer Performance Score

Overall Score

Each of the four Category Scores is added together to total an *Overall Score* for the portfolio (DPS Score). The Category Minimums are listed as a reference for each of the four specific measurement categories and the overall performance. Dealers with a DPS score less than 70 received a wind-down agreement.

They include:

- Sales – Weighted at 50% measured against appropriate average for size of market (i.e. measuring relative share performance against dealers in similar size markets in the state)
- Customer Satisfaction Index – Weighted at 30% measured against regional average (GM has 5 regions in U.S.)
- Capitalization – Weighted at 10% measured against dealer's needed working capital standard
- Profitability – Net profits before taxes weighted at 10%
- Overall – A score of 100 is average; below 100 indicates a performance issue with 70 or below indicating extremely poor performance

Note: Wind-down agreements were given to stores with sales less than 50 per year. Additional wind-downs may have included dealers with Non-GM Brands under the same roof and performance issues, phased out brands such as Pontiac or dealers in an unprofitable position 3 years in a row with inadequate working capital

Wind Down Dealers by State

State	# Dealers	State	# Dealers	State	# Dealers
Alabama	33	Louisanna	10	Ohio	79
Alaska	0	Maine	14	Oklahoma	17
Arizona	11	Massachusetts	29	Oregon	21
Arkansas	17	Maryland	21	Pennsylvania	90
California	65	Michigan	58	Rhode Island	3
Colorado	15	Minnesota	39	South Carolina	24
Connecticut	11	Missouri	38	South Dakota	16
Deleware	2	Mississippi	14	Tennessee	30
Florida	35	Montana	16	Texas	55
Georgia	24	Nebraska	21	Utah	6
Hawaii	2	Nevada	3	Vermont	8
Idaho	8	New Hampshire	6	Virginia	26
Illinois	66	New Jersey	33	Washington	18
Indiana	48	New Mexico	10	West Vergina	25
Iowa	46	New York	60	Wisconsin	50
Kansas	29	North Carolina	36	Wyoming	6
Kentucky	23	North Dakota	6		

4

What a Dealer Gets if Dealer Agreement is Rejected in Bankruptcy Proceedings

- In a nutshell, the dealer has a general unsecured claim which likely is valueless
- If the rejection is approved by the bankruptcy court, dealer agreement is terminated and the dealer has to abruptly shut down the dealership operations because it no longer has a license or the legal ability to sell or service vehicles
  - Once rejected, the manufacturer is not required to repurchase the new vehicles, parts and tools under the dealer agreement because the agreement no longer exists
  - Thus, the dealer is stuck with vehicles and parts it can not sell to customers in the normal course of business and must find a way to dispose of at wholesale or distressed prices -- probably at huge discounts from what the dealer paid
  - In addition, the dealer would have to address its employees
  - While obviously harsh this would be the normal outcome in bankruptcy proceedings as we are observing with Chrysler. It is exactly because of these harsh outcomes that GM is offering wind-down agreements to GM dealers.
  - For GM dealers that floorplan with GMAC, if the dealer agreement is rejected we expect that the dealer would turn-in its new vehicle inventory to GM-GMAC which GM would then re-distribute.

What a Dealer Gets if Dealer Signs Participation Agreement

- If a dealer signs this agreement they are assigned to NewCo
- If for whatever reason the dealer later decides to voluntarily terminate the dealer agreement, all the repurchase obligations of the dealer agreement would apply requiring GM to repurchase eligible new vehicles (current model year) parts and tools

What Dealer Gets if Dealer Signs Wind-Down Agreement

- The Dealer's Wind-Down Agreement would be assumed by NewCo
- In return for the money paid and the assignment to NewCo, the dealer waives all future termination assistance rights under the dealer agreement with respect to new vehicles, parts and tools
- Dealer is allowed up to 16 months in order to wind down its business and to sell its existing inventory to retail customers at normal transaction prices
  - Dealer participates in GM's normal marketing support programs
  - Dealer may not order new vehicles
- Existing parts inventories can be used during this period to do warranty and other service
- The dealer should make money on these operations plus receiving GM's payments to assist in the wind down of operations
- Dealer will have access to the GM auction to acquire used vehicles which are a tremendous source of profit
- Dealer will be able to plan and work with involved employees to transition from employment over time
- GM's wind down agreements are significantly better for the dealers than in normal bankruptcy proceedings where there is an abrupt rejection with no financial assistance, time to plan or ability to make money in a wind down mode

History of Direct Dealer "Support" Programs

- Historically, during the time period when GM experienced annual market share and volume increases, the dealer network expanded to support the growing demand for GM vehicles
  - Dealers enjoyed vigorous margins and profits, and direct dealer support payments were not necessary
- During the 70's and 80's, GM witnessed a consistent and steady decline in market share, but the size of the dealer network contracted little
  - Dealer profitability began to suffer
  - Direct dealer support programs were introduced
- Although the last few decades saw further gradual reductions in the number of dealers, it was at a significantly slower pace than the rate of GM market share decay, thereby creating intense pressure on dealer profitability
  - Currently, a majority of GM dealers are unprofitable despite the highest-ever level of dealer support payments
- **Dealer attrition in 2009 is averaging 80 GM dealers per month. This rate would imply attrition of 1,280 dealerships through October, 2010 or approximately the same number of dealers that have been offered wind-down agreements.**

Direct Dealer "Support" Savings Potential

- A right-sized dealer network will allow GM to systematically reduce virtually all direct dealer support programs, which today cost GM approximately $2.1* Billion
  - Gross savings potential of $928,000 per rooftop completely phased out from GM's network (through wind-down, attrition, or brand sale or phase-out)

Dealer Margin (1% Market Support)	~$810 M
Incentives Paid Directly to Dealer	~$380 M
Standards For Excellence	~$350 M
New Vehicle Inspection	~$350 M
Factory Wholesale Floorplan Support	~$140 M
Fuel Fill	~$120 M
Total	~$2,150 M

Estimated number of rooftops no longer in GM's dealer network ~2,300

Direct Dealer Incentive Savings per Closed Rooftop ~$928,000

* Based on 3.1M GM Sales Volume

Direct GM Structural Cost Savings Potential

- In addition, dealer network reductions enable an estimated $415M in GM gross structural cost savings potential
  - Gross savings of $180,000 per rooftop no longer in GM's dealer network

• Local Dealer Advertising Assistance	~$200 M
• Funding for Dealer Channel Network Alignment	~$125 M
• Number of Sales & Service Consultants	~$40 M
• Funding for Dealer Website & Lead Mgmt Tools	~$30 M
• Dealership Employee Product & Service Training	~$10 M
• Funding for Dealer IT Systems & Support	~$10 M
Total	~$415 M

Estimated number of rooftops no longer in GM's dealer network	~2,300
Direct GM Structural Cost Savings per Rooftop	~$180,000

APPENDIX 9

CONGRESSIONAL RECORD

(LEGISLATIVE HISTORY)

LEGISLATIVE HISTORY

CONFERENCE REPORT ON SECTION 747, H.R. 3288, CONSOLIDATED APPROPRIATIONS ACT, 2010

FROM THE CONGRESSIONAL RECORD

CONFERENCE REPORT ON H.R. 3288, CONSOLIDATED APPROPRIATIONS ACT, 2010—(House of Representatives - December 10, 2009)

I am now pleased to yield 2 minutes to the gentleman from Ohio (Mr. LaTourette).

Mr. LaTOURETTE. I thank the gentleman for yielding. I am going to break the mold here and say something nice about five pages of the bill, this bill in front of me--I think those pages are right here--and say something nice about Mr. Obey as well, and Mr. Serrano is waving in the back.

By way of history, people know that the auto industry in this country got into trouble, and this administration made a decision to use leftover TARP funds to bail out Chrysler and General Motors. Both car companies submitted reorganization plans in February of this year and both were rejected by the auto task force.

The auto task force was kind of a strange collection of people that didn't have any experience in the auto industry at all. Most of them didn't own cars. Those that did own cars owned foreign cars, but they determined that the car companies had to be more aggressive when it came to dealerships. As a result, about 800 Chrysler dealers were closed and about 2,000 GM dealers. The problem with that is, with rampant unemployment, about 60 people work at each car dealership across this country. Car dealerships don't cost the car companies any money, and it was a strange way to do business and potentially take 200,000 people and put them on the street.

A couple of young, fresh-faced Democrats, Mr. Maffei of New York and Mr. Kratovil of Maryland, launched a legislative effort. But as a grizzled veteran, having been here for the last 15 years, I know that the one piece of legislation or pieces of legislation that have to leave town are the appropriations bills. We drafted some language and put it in Mr. Serrano's bill, and Mr. Obey took it. They didn't have to--they probably got in trouble for taking it--but that became the 800-pound gorilla that had to be dealt with as General Motors and Chrysler have moved forward on how to deal with this dealer situation.

I also want to say something nice about the majority leader, Mr. Hoyer. He took up the mantle and said we are going to solve this problem. As a result, the five pages that are here in the bill indicate that those aggrieved dealers now have the opportunity for binding arbitration, and the facts need to be brought forward, and hopefully fairness will prevail. But that wouldn't happen without something good and bipartisan happening in the United States Congress.

Mr. VAN HOLLEN. Mr. Speaker, I rise today to express my appreciation that language has been included in the Financial Services Appropriations Conference Report that will give automobile dealers around the nation a fair and reasonable shot at getting back into business. For the past several months, I have been pleased to join with Majority Leader *Hoyer*, Congressmen *Kratovil* and *Maffei*, and others to ensure that profitable car dealers have every opportunity to contribute to our economic recovery and put their employees back to work.

Profitable and viable dealers should have never been terminated in the first place, and I was proud to join the fight to have these short-sighted decisions reversed. Automobile manufacturers won't be able to get back on their feet without a strong dealer network, and Congress is committed to ensuring that such a network exists. I salute the tenacity and determination of these small business owners, many of whom have been selling cars and supporting the American auto industry for decades. Under the provision we are approving today, these terminated dealers will have an opportunity, once again, to do what they do best--sell and service cars. And that is good for our economy, for job creation and for the American car industry.

It would have been my preference that we would not need to legislate on this matter. We convened talks with the auto dealer groups and the manufacturers and while both sides offered significant concessions, efforts to achieve a non-legislative solution failed when auto manufacturers offered plans that fell short of what was needed to add dealers to their dealer networks and put their employees back to work.

As 2009 comes to a close, the federal government still maintains a substantial financial stake in Chrysler and General Motors and therefore in the United States automobile industry. Clearly, it is in the national interest to have the domestic automobile industry regain profitability and maintain sufficient dealerships to meet consumer demand.

Section 747 of the Financial Services Appropriations division of this bill recognizes the valuable role that dealers play in the auto industry and our local economies. Automobile dealers are essential to the success of automobile manufacturers because at no material cost to the manufacturers, they facilitate distribution, sales, and servicing of hundreds of millions of vehicles annually. This legislation is premised on the notion that it is in the best interest of automobile manufacturers, the automotive industry, dealers and the public to have an extensive and competitive automobile distribution network throughout the country, including in urban, suburban and rural areas.

Section 747 mandates that manufacturers promptly provide covered auto dealers in writing the specific criteria and supporting data relied upon by a manufacturer in its decision to end or wind down the dealership relationship. In the spirit of cooperation and to ensure an efficient process as this legislation is implemented, we expect that the manufacturers will provide the information in a format that is user friendly, clearly identifies facts, readily accessible, and understandable by the dealer and that the data may be transmitted either by mail or electronically. We intend that this process provide transparency and avoid the excessive costs and delays of litigation and discovery disputes. The manufacturers should provide their respective covered dealers with each and every detail and criterion related to the evaluations of the dealership and the decisions to terminate, not assign, not renew or discontinue. It is anticipated that the manufacturers will be cooperative and forthcoming and that all relevant information will be provided promptly.

It further provides such dealers with the opportunity to participate in a neutral arbitration process designed for the dealer to make the case for being added to the manufacturer's dealer network. Congress has included specific timeliness for this process and we expect both parties to the arbitration to act in good faith and expeditiously so that added dealers can return to full-fledged operations quickly.

Section 747 expressly permits the manufacturer and dealer to present any kind of relevant information during the arbitration and provides that the arbitrator shall decide whether the dealer should be added to the manufacturer's dealer network based on a balancing of the interests of the dealer, the manufacturer, and the general public. The public interest includes reasonably convenient access for consumers to a dealer who can service their vehicles, which is of particular concern in rural areas where many dealers were terminated in 2009. It has been well-reported that more and more individuals have to drive substantial distances to obtain service from an authorized dealer of a specific brand because of a dealer termination.

Congress has provided seven enumerated factors for the arbitrator to consider, but this list is not exhaustive because the legislation provides that the parties can introduce "any relevant information." For example, we expect that arbitrators should consider relevant State laws, which provide a context for analyzing franchise agreements and the obligations of dealers and manufacturers.

A couple of these enumerated criteria merit additional explanation. For example, Congress has directed that the demographic and geographic characteristics of the market are taken into account. This reflects our intention that the arbitrator should pay special attention to the concerns expressed by some terminated dealers that there are factors in their market areas or States that affect their performance and render some measurements, such as State averages, less than accurate in portraying the true picture of a dealer's operations.

Another one of the factors involves the dealer's performance under the franchise agreement terminated in 2009. In considering this factor and related factors, it is important for arbitrators to recognize that state law is part and parcel of and modifies auto dealer franchise agreements. To look only at a franchise agreement, in other words, misses an important contextual element. Accordingly, it is anticipated that the arbitrators will consider State law elements of good faith and fair dealing in this process and that, for example, the franchise agreement's performance standards and a dealer's performance under the original agreement will be evaluated in accordance with State law.

Another factor is the historic profitability of the dealership. During the legislative process, Congress learned that some dealers, for tax planning reasons or other reasons use a variety of legitimate, widely recognized accounting conventions, such as LIFO, that could, depending on the date a snapshot is taken, affect materially whether the dealership appears profitable. It is important that arbitrators recognize such accounting conventions when considering the profitability of a dealership so a fair and accurate picture is obtained.

With respect to being added back to a dealer network, it is the intent of Congress that notwithstanding the preference of a manufacturer to have several brands in the same dealership, in the case of a dealer seeking to be added to a dealer network but with fewer than all of the preferred brands, the dealer nonetheless will be eligible to be added.

It is worth noting that pursuant to subsection (f), manufacturers and dealers may, of their own volition, decide to enter into legally binding agreements with one another instead of going through the arbitration process. It is the intent of Congress that for this subsection to apply, the legally binding agreements shall be consensual, non-coercive resolutions of the issue between the dealer and the manufacturer entered into or ratified after the date of enactment. Coercive agreements should not be upheld.

In conclusion, I want to recognize the tireless efforts of dealers from around the Nation who worked to develop and implement a truly historic grassroots effort over the past seven months. Groups such as the Committee to Restore Dealer Rights, the Automobile Trade Association Executives, National Automobile Dealers Association and the National Association of Minority Auto Dealers, were instrumental in bringing about the legislation we are approving today.

Mr. CONYERS. Mr. Speaker, I would like to thank the Conferees for including section 747, which regulates the relationship between automobile manufacturers and automobile dealerships. I, along with Majority Leader Steny Hoyer, and Representatives Chris Van Hollen, Daniel Maffei, Frank Kratovil, Steven LaTourette, Jackie Speier, Robert Brady, Betty Sutton, and Bob Etheridge have worked together to create legislation that will best serve the interests of the automobile industry, including manufacturers and dealerships, and the citizens who have a significant portion of their tax dollars invested in the success of this critical industry. The following is a description of the legislation.

Section 747 of the Conference Agreement includes language establishing an arbitration process to determine whether previously terminated, non-assigned, non-renewed, or non-continued auto dealerships should be added to dealership networks of automobile manufacturers that received federal assistance under the TARP program, or that are partially owned by the Federal Government. This provision replaces Section 745 of the House bill, which also addressed concerns regarding terminated auto dealerships.

It is in the national interest to protect the substantial federal investment in automobile manufacturers by assuring the viability of such companies through the maintenance of sufficiently sized dealership networks to meet consumer demand for sales and servicing nationally. In addition to facilitating the maintenance and growth of industry market share among manufacturers that benefitted from TARP funds, and in which the taxpayers have a significant financial investment, it is in the national interest to ensure that dealerships and manufacturers are each treated fairly in their business relationships based on their respective economic interests.

Evidence obtained over the course of numerous Congressional hearings in 2009 demonstrates that the automobile industry is integral to the health of the United States economy as a whole. Automobile manufacturers have been among the largest and most successful corporations in the United States, providing significant numbers of jobs and producing valuable goods for consumers. Automobile dealerships are also essential businesses in most communities nationally, providing many jobs to local residents and facilitating the distribution, sales, and servicing of millions of vehicles annually. Our investigations have made clear that it is in the best interest of the automobile industry, automobile manufacturers, dealerships and the public to have a competitive and economically viable domestic automobile distribution network throughout the country, including urban, suburban, and rural areas.

This provision was included because we also believe that by providing a process for working out the relationship between automobile manufacturers and dealerships that ensures transparency and review by a neutral arbitrator according to an equitable and balanced standard, taking into account the interests of all affected parties, the property and due process rights of manufacturers and dealerships will be safeguarded.

Section 747 establishes a procedure by which an automobile dealership that had a franchise agreement for a vehicle brand that was not assigned to a covered manufacturer, or that was terminated in a manner not consistent with applicable state law, on or before April 29, 2009, may seek continuation or reinstatement of the franchise agreement, or seek to be added as a franchisee to a dealership network of the covered manufacturer who manufactures the vehicle brand of the covered dealership, with such franchisee being located in the geographic area where the covered dealership was located when its franchise agreement was terminated, not assigned, not renewed, or not continued. Absent such election by the covered dealership, no such binding arbitration would occur.

In order to provide a covered automobile dealership with the information useful to determine whether to elect to enter into binding arbitration, the dealership will receive in writing notice from the covered manufacturer detailing the specific criteria pursuant to which such dealership's franchise agreement was terminated, was not renewed, or was not assumed and assigned to a covered manufacturer. This notice must be provided within the 30-day period beginning on the date of the enactment of this Section. This transparency is a vital step in giving dealerships the opportunity to understand why their franchise agreements were terminated, not renewed, or were not assumed and assigned to a covered manufacturer. It is our expectation that this transparency will obviate the need for unnecessary arbitration. It is also our expectation that this transparency will encourage informal agreements between covered dealerships and manufacturers without recourse to the more formal procedures provided in this Section. We expect that the written transmittal letter will also provide appropriate contact information, including an e-mail address, to enable the dealership to contact the manufacturer should the dealership have specific questions about the dealership's information and individual criteria contained in such letter.

The Conference Agreement provides such dealerships with the opportunity to elect to participate in a neutral arbitration process designed to permit the dealership to present information in support of its addition to the manufacturer's dealership network, and for the manufacturer to present information against such addition based on its business plan and future economic viability. The arbitrator in each case shall balance the interests of the covered dealership, the covered manufacturer, and the public and will decide based on that balancing whether or not the covered dealership should be added to the dealership network of the covered manufacturer. These are the only remedies the arbitrator may provide. The Conference Agreement specifically prohibits the awarding of compensatory, punitive, or exemplary damages to any party.

The Conference Agreement sets out seven specific factors that the arbitrator should consider in ruling on each case. The list is not exclusive, and the arbitrator would have the discretion to consider all the relevant facts on a case-by-case basis. In considering whether adding the covered dealership to the covered manufacturer's dealership network is in the public interest, the arbitrator should consider, among other factors, the need for reasonable access for consumers to a dealership that can service their vehicles, which is of particular concern in rural areas. The arbitrator should also consider the impact on the viability of the manufacturer of adding the dealership to the manufacturer's network, the length of experience of the dealership, the dealership's historical profitability and current economic viability, and demographic and geographic characteristics of the market.

It is our understanding that the General Commercial Rules of the American Arbitration Association shall apply to the arbitration proceeding, except to the extent that a rule is inconsistent with any provision of this Section.

Subsection (f) addresses negotiations between a covered manufacturer and a covered dealership, whether acting individually, as a group, or through an organization acting on behalf of one or more covered dealerships. The provision is intended to ensure that any legally binding agreement, such as a memorandum of understanding, resulting from a voluntary negotiation between a covered manufacturer and a covered dealership, a group of covered dealerships, or an organization acting on behalf of one or more covered dealerships will not be disturbed by this section. It also makes clear that once a covered dealership is party to such an agreement, such covered dealership would not be eligible for the arbitration remedy in this section.

It is not the intent of Congress to bar a covered dealership from the provisions of this section if the covered dealership accepted a standard form contract prepared by the covered manufacturer and offered on a "take-it-or-leave-it" basis, even if the agreement was entered into voluntarily. As a consequence, a covered dealership that accepted a "wind-down" agreement drafted by a covered manufacturer would be able to avail itself of the provisions of this section. An agreement between a covered manufacturer and a covered dealership, whether acting individually, as a group, or as part of a group of dealerships acting through an organization, will be considered voluntarily negotiated if the agreement between the parties reflects a compromise based on written or oral discussions, even if one party to the negotiation is the principal or primary drafter of the agreement.

We chose this approach because binding arbitration by a neutral arbitrator is the most appropriate means of resolving the differences between covered dealerships and manufacturers, and to protect the taxpayers, and the broader economy. For this reason, the Conference Agreement sets out a procedure for ensuring that a neutral arbitrator conducts the arbitration according to a clear standard with factors the arbitrator must weigh.

Due to the time sensitive nature of this situation, the Conference Agreement provides that a covered dealership must elect to pursue arbitration no later than 40 days of the date of enactment of this section, that such arbitration must commence as soon as practicable and must be submitted to the arbitrator for deliberation not later than 180 days of such date. The arbitrator is given the flexibility to extend that period for up to 30 days for good cause. The arbitrator then has seven business days after the arbitrator determines that the case has been fully submitted to issue a written opinion.

Section 747 expressly permits the manufacturer and dealership to present any kind of relevant information during the arbitration. As an additional means of ensuring efficiency and economy in the arbitration process, the provision prohibits depositions and limits discovery to documents specific to the covered dealership.

Section 747 also makes clear that a manufacturer may terminate a covered dealership in accordance with applicable state law.

[End Insert]

I yield back the balance of my time.

DEPARTMENTS OF TRANSPORTATION AND HOUSING AND URBAN DEVELOPMENT, AND RELATED AGENCIES APPROPRIATIONS ACT, 2010--CONFERENCE REPORT—(Senate - December 13, 2009)

Ms. STABENOW. Mr. President, I would like to discuss with the chairman of the Financial Services and General Government Appropriations Subcommittee, Senator Durbin, as manager of the Financial Services Subcommittee section of the bill before the Senate, language included in the bill that creates a binding arbitration process for auto dealers associated with General Motors and Chrysler whose contracts were terminated as part of the manufacturers' restructuring efforts this year.

The difficult decisions made during the last year have highlighted the interconnectedness of the industry and have shown the impact that these companies have in every State in the country. I particularly understand how difficult this situation has been for Michigan auto dealers. My father and grandfather ran the Oldsmobile dealership in Clare, MI, where I grew up. My very first job was washing cars on that lot.

Thousands of employees, either directly employed by the companies or through the thousands of dealerships and suppliers, depend on the viability of the auto manufacturers. Without the manufacturers, there is no dealer network, and small businesses across the country would close, adding more devastating job losses as our economy is trying to recover. What we do here must continue to ensure a healthy future for the auto companies as they work towards a profitable future. When negotiating an agreement for arbitration was it the Chairman's intent that the dealers entitled to this arbitration process would only be the dealers that were terminated as a result of the bankruptcy?

Mr. DURBIN. Yes, it is my understanding that the only dealerships entitled to arbitration are those dealerships that were terminated as a result of the manufacturers' bankruptcy, rather than those that may have closed for other business reasons.

Ms. STABENOW. The statutory language for the arbitration process provides criteria that will be used to review each case. Is it the Chairman's goal that by considering the economic interest of the public at large the arbitrator should focus on maximizing the return of taxpayer dollars that have been invested in the company?

Mr. DURBIN. Yes, the economic interest of the public at large must be considered to ensure that the investments will be recovered as quickly as possible.

Ms. STABENOW. Additionally, when reviewing the cases, does the statutory language ensure arbitrators take into consideration the stability and protection of the existing dealer network?

Mr. DURBIN. Yes, the statutory language will allow arbitrators to review the potential impact of reinstating a dealership on the existing dealer network for the covered manufacturer, as well as on any dealer retained by the covered manufacturer in a given market territory.

Ms. STABENOW. I thank the Chairman for these clarifications and for his ongoing efforts to ensure a fair process for all stakeholders as the auto industry continues to restructure.

Mr. LEVIN. Mr. President, I would like to discuss with the chairman of the Financial Services and General Government Appropriations Subcommittee, Senator Durbin, as manager of the Financial Services Subcommittee section of the bill before the Senate, two aspects of the provision included in that bill that establishes an arbitration process for review of decisions made by Chrysler and GM to terminate or wind down auto dealerships earlier this year. Under the process laid out in this provision, an arbitrator is to balance the economic interests of the covered dealership, the covered manufacturer, and the public at large by considering a number of factors. Those factors include the covered dealership's profitability, the covered manufacturer's overall business plan, the covered dealership's satisfaction of the performance objectives of the franchise agreement, and the covered dealership's performance in relation to the criteria used to terminate the dealership.

Is it the chairman's understanding that in looking at these factors, and in particular in looking at the dealership's profitability and the manufacturer's overall business plan, that the arbitrator will consider the profitability of the dealership with respect to the new vehicles sales of the covered manufacturer?

Mr. DURBIN. Yes, that is my understanding. In making decisions about the makeup of the dealership network, profitability in terms of new vehicles sales for that manufacturer is what is critically important to the long-term financial health of the manufacturer. That manufacturer's long-term health is also vitally important to the Federal Government because of the significant taxpayer investment in these companies.

Mr. LEVIN. I thank the chairman for his assurances and his clarification.

I would also like to raise a question about the arbitration process established in this bill. The statutory language could be interpreted to allow for potentially as many as hundreds or thousands of arbitrators each involved in individual reviews of dealership decisions. I am concerned that a very large number of arbitrators would be unduly burdensome and impractical to the point of being unworkable. The statutory language requires that arbitrations be conducted in the State where the covered dealerships are located. It is my hope that the arbitration process could be managed in a given State so that there would be one arbitrator or a small manageable panel of arbitrators within any given State. Does the chairman believe that the statutory language would allow for management of arbitration in this way?

Mr. DURBIN. Yes, the statutory language would allow for that. The primary intent of this provision is to ensure that covered dealerships have a fair and impartial review of the termination decision. I agree with the Senator from Michigan that we should try to avoid a situation where there would be hundreds or even thousands of individual arbitrators.

Mr. LEVIN. Mr. President, I want to highlight several provisions of the legislation now before us that I believe will provide important benefits to Michigan and the Nation, and one that I think does not serve the Nation's interests.

The Consolidated Appropriations Act of 2010 contains provisions that will improve our health care system, ensure that contracting dollars do not flow to companies avoiding income taxes by incorporating overseas, improve Federal oversight of our financial system, and improve educational opportunity for our citizens.

I am especially pleased to see an increase in funding for health information technology, HIT. This bill will provide $61 million to the Office of the National Coordinator for Health Information Technology. These funds will help increase administrative efficiency and move our current system away from paper-based organization. This will help ensure that doctors and patients have the necessary information easily accessible when working together to make important health care decisions and ensure that health records of individuals remain confidential. Improving the interoperability of our HIT systems will not only enhance the quality of care, experts believe that improved HIT will reduce health care costs for all Americans, streamlining billing practices and reducing administrative costs that waste so many billions of dollars.

I strongly support the bill's language continuing the prohibition on Federal contracts with "inverted" corporations. Corporate inversions--the practice of incorporating some or all of a U.S.-based company's businesses overseas--are transparent tax-avoidance schemes. There is no reason we should provide taxpayer dollars to firms that dodge their tax obligations, and I am pleased that we will continue to bar such companies from Federal contracting unless doing so would damage national security.

The bill also includes an increase of $151 million in funding for the Securities and Exchange Commission. This increased funding will support enhanced enforcement, capital market oversight, and investor protection activities, including investigations of accounting fraud, market manipulation, insider trading, and investment scams that target seniors and low-income communities. This is a wise investment in protecting our citizens and our economy from those who seek to profit by fraud or from taking excessive risks that endanger the financial system.

Also included are a number of important education provisions. The legislation would increase the maximum Pell grant award by $200, to $5,500; provide funding for disadvantaged, disabled and first-generation college students; and restore $1.5 billion in title I funding for disadvantaged public school students. Of particular importance is $11.5 billion in funding for Individuals with Disabilities Education Act programs, which marks a historic Federal commitment to education of those with disabilities.

There are also important measures that will help boost Michigan's economy and its future. I am pleased that this bill includes $1 million I requested for the Thunder Bay National Marine Sanctuary and Underwater Preserve in Alpena. Part of the National Oceanic and Atmospheric Administration's sanctuary system, the Thunder Bay Sanctuary protects well-preserved shipwrecks that are a valuable piece of Michigan's history and our Nation's. The funding provided in this bill will allow for expansion of the Great Lakes Maritime Heritage Center to include a Science Hall and other facilities that will allow more people to explore and learn about Michigan's maritime history.

The bill also includes important language that will bring the Woodward Avenue Light Rail Project closer to reality, an important economic development project in the heart of metropolitan Detroit. The conferees retained language regarding the Woodward Avenue project similar to language I authored for the Senate bill.

These all are important provisions worthy of support. But I am disappointed that the legislation includes a provision requiring General Motors and Chrysler to submit to binding, third-party arbitration in disputes with auto dealerships closed as part of those companies' restructuring efforts.

There is widespread agreement among auto industry analysts that GM and Chrysler needed to consolidate their dealer structure in order to compete. The Federal Government has made a substantial--and wise--investment in these companies, which are key components of our manufacturing sector. Submitting to arbitration of decisions already approved in bankruptcy court risks hampering the recoveries these companies and their workers are fighting so hard to achieve. My vote in favor of this act follows reassurances I received from the chairman of the Financial Services and General Government Appropriations Subcommittee, Senator Durbin, in response to my concerns about a number of provisions in the arbitration language.

Appendix 10

SIGTARP – 1

FACTORS AFFECTING THE DECISIONS OF GENERAL MOTORS AND CRYSLER TO REDUCE THEIR DEALERSHIPNETWORKS

July 19, 2010

SIGTARP | Office of the Special Inspector General for the Troubled Asset Relief Program

Advancing Economic Stability Through Transparency, Coordinated Oversight and Robust Enforcement

Factors Affecting the Decisions of General Motors and Chrysler to Reduce their Dealership Networks

SIGTARP-10-008
July 19, 2010

SIGTARP
Office of the Special Inspector General for the Troubled Asset Relief Program

July 19, 2010

Factors Affecting the Decisions of General Motors and Chrysler to Reduce their Dealership Networks

Summary of Report: SIGTARP-10-008

Why SIGTARP Did This Study

For the U.S. automotive industry, the quarter ending June 30, 2009, was dominated by the bankruptcy filings of Chrysler LLC ("Chrysler") and General Motors Corporation ("GM"). As part of the bankruptcy proceedings, Chrysler terminated 789 dealerships on June 10, 2009, and GM planned to wind down 1,454 dealerships by October 2010.

The Department of the Treasury ("Treasury"), through the Troubled Asset Relief Program ("TARP"), has played a key role in the financing of GM and Chrysler, both before and during their bankruptcies. To date, Treasury has committed $80.7 billion to the two automakers under TARP's Automotive Industry Financing Program ("AIFP"). On February 15, 2009, President Obama announced the creation of an interagency Presidential Task Force on the Auto Industry ("Task Force") that would review the Chrysler and GM restructuring plans submitted as a requirement of their loan agreements. In addition, the Administration created a Treasury Auto Team ("Auto Team"), which reports to the Task Force and had the responsibility, among other things, of evaluating the companies' restructuring plans and negotiating the terms of any further assistance.

Questions arose as to how GM and Chrysler selected dealerships for termination and what benefit, if any, the companies gained from terminating the dealerships. SIGTARP received Congressional requests to conduct an audit on the dealership terminations from Senator Jay Rockefeller, Chairman of the Senate Committee on Commerce, Science, and Transportation, and Representative David Obey, Chairman of the House Appropriations Committee. This report addresses (1) the role of Treasury's Auto Team in the decision to reduce dealership networks, (2) the extent to which GM and Chrysler developed and documented processes for deciding which dealerships to terminate and which to retain, and (3) to what extent the dealership reductions are expected to lead to cost savings for GM and Chrysler.

SIGTARP interviewed key GM and Chrysler officials regarding the process and criteria used to analyze whether dealers would be terminated or retained and analyzed GM and Chrysler data to determine if the companies consistently followed their criteria. We also interviewed Treasury's Auto Team officials, auto industry experts, automobile dealers, and representatives from several dealer advocacy groups. Our work was performed in accordance with generally accepted government auditing standards.

In commenting on a draft of this report, Treasury stated that it strongly disagrees with many of the statements, conclusions and lessons learned of the report, and may respond more fully at a later date. A fuller description of Treasury's response is included in the *Management Comments and Audit Response* section of this report.

What SIGTARP Found

Pursuant to their loan agreements with Treasury, as a condition of receiving additional TARP funding, GM and Chrysler were required to submit restructuring plans to the Treasury Auto Team in February 2009. GM's restructuring plan explicitly spelled out its plan to reduce its dealership network gradually, by approximately 300 dealers per year over the next five years. In March 2009, Treasury's Auto Team rejected both companies' restructuring plans. In GM's case, the Auto Team specifically highlighted GM's planned "pace" of dealership closings as one of the obstacles to its viability. In response to the Auto Team's rejection of their restructuring plans and in light of their intervening bankruptcies, GM and Chrysler significantly accelerated their dealership termination timetables, with Chrysler terminating 789 dealerships by June 10, 2009, and GM announcing plans to wind down 1,454 dealerships by October 2010.

The Auto Team's view about the need for GM and Chrysler to reduce their dealership networks and do so rapidly was based on a theory that, with fewer dealerships (and thus less internecine competition), like their smaller networked foreign competitors, the remaining dealerships would be more profitable and thus would permit the dealerships to invest more in their facilities and staff. For GM and Chrysler, the theory goes, this would mean better brand equity and would allow the manufacturers over time to decrease their substantial dealership incentives. In addition, the Auto Team felt the companies' best chance of success required "utilizing the bankruptcy code in a quick and surgical way" and noted further that it would have been a "waste of taxpayer resources" for the auto manufacturers to exit bankruptcy without reducing their networks.

Only time will tell whether and to what extent the rapid reduction of the number of dealerships will improve the manufacturer's profitability over time; SIGTARP's audit found that there are several aspects of how the Auto Team came to have this view about dealership reductions that are worth noting. One, although there was broad consensus that GM and Chrysler generally needed to decrease the number of their dealerships, there was disagreement over where, and *how quickly*, the cuts should have been made. Some experts questioned whether it was appropriate to apply a foreign model to the U.S. automakers, particularly in small markets in which the U.S. companies currently have a competitive advantage, and one expert opined that closing dealerships in an environment already disrupted by the recession could result in an even greater crisis in sales. Two, job losses at terminated dealerships were apparently not a substantial factor in the Auto Team's consideration of the dealership termination issue. Although there is some controversy over how many jobs will be lost per terminated dealership, it is clear that tens of thousands of dealership jobs were immediately put in jeopardy as a result of the terminations by GM and Chrysler. Finally, the acceleration of dealership closings was not done with any explicit cost savings to the manufacturers in mind.

Chrysler decided which dealerships to terminate based on case-by-case, market-by-market determinations, and did not offer an appeals process. SIGTARP did not identify any instances in which Chrysler's termination decision varied from its stated, albeit subjective selection criteria. GM's approach, which was conducted in two phases, was purportedly more objective, and it offered an appeals process. However, SIGTARP found that GM did not consistently follow its stated criteria and that there was little or no documentation of the decision-making process to terminate or retain dealerships with similar profiles, or of the appeals process.

Lessons Learned

Although perhaps it is inevitable that public ownership of private companies will have the effect of blurring the Government's appropriate role, the fact that Treasury was acting in part as an investor in GM and Chrysler does not insulate Treasury from its responsibility to the broader economy. Treasury should have taken special care given that the Auto Team's determinations had the potential to contribute to job losses, particularly given that one goal of the loan agreements was to "preserve and promote jobs of American workers employed directly by the automakers and subsidiaries and in related industries." This audit concludes that before the Auto Team rejected GM's original, more gradual termination plan as an obstacle to its continued viability and then encouraged the companies to accelerate their planned dealership closures in order to take advantage of bankruptcy proceedings, Treasury (a) should have taken every reasonable step to ensure that accelerating the dealership terminations was truly necessary for the long-term viability of the companies and (b) should have at least considered whether the benefits to the companies from the accelerated terminations outweighed the costs to the economy that would result from potentially tens of thousands of accelerated job losses. Moreover, in light of the way in which the companies selected dealerships for termination, in the future, to the extent that Treasury takes action with respect to a TARP recipient that has the potential to affect so many jobs in so many different communities, Treasury should monitor the recipients' actions to ensure that they are carried out in a fair and transparent manner.

Special Inspector General for the Troubled Asset Relief Program

OFFICE OF THE SPECIAL INSPECTOR GENERAL
FOR THE TROUBLED ASSET RELIEF PROGRAM
1801 L STREET, NW
WASHINGTON, D.C. 20220

JUL 19 2010

MEMORANDUM FOR: The Honorable Timothy F. Geithner, Secretary of the Treasury

SUBJECT: Factors Affecting the Decisions of General Motors and Chrysler to Reduce their Dealership Networks (SIGTARP-10-008)

We are providing this audit report for your information and use. It discusses the decisions made by General Motors and Chrysler to reduce the number of auto dealerships in their dealership networks, identifies the role of the Treasury Auto Team in that process, considers the estimated cost savings that would result from decreasing the number of dealerships in each company's network, and lessons learned from this review. The Office of the Special Inspector General for the Troubled Asset Relief Program ("SIGTARP") conducted this audit under the authority of Public Law 110-343, as amended, which also incorporates the duties and responsibilities of inspectors general of the Inspector General Act of 1978, as amended.

We considered comments from the Department of the Treasury when preparing the final report. The comments are addressed in the report, where applicable, and a copy of Treasury's response to the audit is included in the Management Comments Appendix D of this report.

We appreciate the courtesies extended to the staff. For additional information on this report, please contact Shannon Williams (Shannon.Williams@do.treas.gov / 202-927-8732) or Kurt Hyde (Kurt.Hyde@do.treas.gov / 202-622-4633).

Sincerely,

Neil M. Barofsky
Special Inspector General
for the Troubled Asset Relief Program

Table of Contents

Introduction 1

In Response to the Auto Team's Determination that GM's Proposed Pace for Closing Dealerships Was Too Slow and an Obstacle to Its Viability, GM Accelerated Its Dealership Closures; Chrysler Also Accelerated, and at a Faster Pace 7

Criteria Used by GM and Chrysler To Identify Dealerships to Close 16

Dealership Termination Decisions Were Not Based on GM's and Chrysler's Cost Savings Estimates 25

Conclusions and Lessons Learned 28

Management Comments and Audit Response 33

Appendices

    A. Scope and Methodology 34

    B. Acronyms and Definitions 36

    C. Audit Team Members 37

    D. Management Comments 38

    E. Additional Tables 39

Introduction

For the U.S. automotive industry, the quarter ending June 30, 2009, was dominated by the bankruptcy filings of General Motors Corporation ("GM") and Chrysler LLC[1] ("Chrysler"). As part of their bankruptcies, GM and Chrysler each planned to reduce dramatically the number of dealerships in their dealer networks. On June 2, 2009, GM announced plans to "wind down"[2] 1,454 (26 percent) of its 5,591[3] dealerships by October 2010, and Chrysler terminated 789 (25 percent) of its 3,181 dealerships on June 10, 2009. GM and Chrysler maintained that their pre-existing dealership networks were too large and needed to be reduced for the companies to become viable. The companies' leaders stated that a smaller network would result in greater sales *per dealership*, which would make the dealerships more profitable and thus enable them to invest in their facilities to meet GM and Chrysler standards and retain top-tier sales and service staffs.

In June 2009, the Senate Committee on Commerce, Science, and Transportation held a hearing on the dealership terminations. Subsequently, Senator Jay Rockefeller sent a letter to SIGTARP noting that the hearing demonstrated substantial confusion, even amongst dealers, as to how GM and Chrysler selected dealerships for termination and what benefit, if any, the companies gained from terminating the dealerships. Senator Rockefeller requested that SIGTARP review how GM and Chrysler decided which dealerships to terminate. Representative David Obey, Chairman of the House Committee on Appropriations, also sent a letter to SIGTARP asking for a review of GM and Chrysler's decision-making processes.

Consequently, SIGTARP began a review to meet the following objectives:

- to determine the role of the U.S. Department of the Treasury ("Treasury") Auto Team in the decisions to reduce dealership networks
- to determine the extent to which GM and Chrysler developed and documented processes for deciding which dealerships to terminate and which to retain
- to determine to what extent the dealership reductions are expected to lead to cost savings for GM and Chrysler

For a discussion of this audit's scope and methodology, see Appendix A. For definitions of the acronyms used in this report, see Appendix B. For the audit team members, see Appendix C. For management comments, see Appendix D. For additional tables, see Appendix E.

---

[1] Chrysler's corporate name was Chrysler LLC during much of the time period covered by this report. The automaker's current iteration is Chrysler Group LLC.
[2] GM issued "wind-down agreements" to 1,289 dealerships carrying GM's core brands (GMC, Chevrolet, Buick, and Cadillac), allowing them to operate until the agreement expires in October 2010, and to 165 standalone Pontiac and GMC Medium Duty dealerships, brands that were eventually phased out. GM also issued "partial" wind-down notifications to 2,385 dealerships that would no longer be able to sell one or more core GM brands. GM would later offer to restore dealer status to 216 complete wind-downs and 450 partial wind-downs, as discussed later in this report.
[3] This figure includes the 165 standalone Pontiac and GMC Medium Duty dealerships.

Background

In recent years, the American automotive industry has faced challenges related to changing consumer preferences and perceptions, growing legacy costs, rising fuel prices, and ceding of market share to foreign competitors. During the recession, these factors coalesced into a historic crisis that threatened the survival of the domestic auto manufacturers. According to testimony from Ron Bloom, a Senior Advisor at the U.S. Treasury Department, in 2008 alone, the domestic auto industry lost 50 percent of its sales volume and over 400,000 jobs. Near the end of 2008, the financial conditions of GM and Chrysler were seriously deteriorating, and the two companies were virtually closed out of the private capital markets, meaning that they were not able to secure the day-to-day funding they needed to function and remain in business. Without assistance, both companies faced liquidation bankruptcies that would have resulted in substantial job losses and would have had a dramatic impact on the broader American economy.

As part of the Troubled Asset Relief Program ("TARP"), the Automotive Industry Financing Program ("AIFP") was created on December 19, 2008, to permit Treasury to invest in the automakers and their financing arms. The program's stated goal was to prevent a significant disruption of the American automotive industry that would pose a systemic risk to financial market stability and have a negative effect on the U.S. economy. To date, Treasury has committed $80.7 billion[4] through AIFP to facilitate restructuring and to support the automotive manufacturing companies and their financing arms to "avoid a disorderly bankruptcy of one or more automotive companies." On February 15, 2009, President Obama announced the creation of an interagency Presidential Task Force on the Auto Industry ("Task Force") that would review the Chrysler and GM restructuring plans submitted as a requirement of their loan agreements. Co-chaired by Treasury Secretary Timothy Geithner and National Economic Council Director Lawrence Summers, the Task Force has 21 members, including a number of *ex-officio* designees and Government staffers.

In addition to the Task Force, the Administration created a Treasury Auto Team (the "Auto Team"), which reports to the Task Force and had the responsibility of evaluating the companies' restructuring plans and negotiating the terms of any further assistance. Leading the Auto Team were two advisors: Ron Bloom, a former investment banker and head of collective bargaining for the United Steelworkers Union, and Steven Rattner, the co-founder of the Quadrangle Group, a private-equity firm.[5] The Auto Team had a staff of 15 people who conducted analyses in order to determine GM and Chrysler's viability. The Auto Team included Treasury employees who reported to Mr. Bloom and Mr. Rattner, who in turn reported to Secretary Geithner and Mr. Summers.[6] Although this group was responsible for managing AIFP, none of the Auto Team leaders or personnel had any experience or expertise in the auto industry.

---

[4] The $80.7 billion figure represents the funds provided directly to the companies and does not include commitments made under the Auto Warranty Commitment Program or the Auto Suppliers Support Program.
[5] Mr. Rattner left the Treasury Auto Team on July 13, 2009, leaving Mr. Bloom as the head of the Auto Team.
[6] For more information, please see the September 2009 Congressional Oversight Panel report, *The Use of TARP Funds in Support and Reorganization of the Domestic Automotive Industry*.

TARP Assistance to General Motors and Chrysler

Under AIFP, Treasury committed to provide GM and Chrysler with financing from TARP funds.[7] Pursuant to the loan agreements, which were both dated December 31, 2008,[8] the financings were intended to accomplish the following goals:

- enable the automakers and subsidiaries to develop viable and competitive businesses that minimize adverse effects on the environment
- enhance the ability and the capacity of the automakers and subsidiaries to pursue the timely and aggressive production of energy-efficient, advanced-technology vehicles
- preserve and promote jobs of American workers employed directly by the automakers and subsidiaries and in related industries
- safeguard the ability of the automakers and subsidiaries to provide retirement and health care benefits for their retirees and retirees' dependents
- stimulate manufacturing and sales of automobiles produced by GM and Chrysler

The loan agreements, set to expire in December 2011 for GM and January 2012 for Chrysler, included other conditions such as executive compensation limits, compliance with Federal fuel efficiency and emissions requirements, and in the case of GM, the provision of warrants to Treasury of non-voting stock and in the case of GM and Chrysler, additional notes.

Under their loan agreements, GM and Chrysler were required to submit to Treasury restructuring plans to show how they would use the assistance from the Government to achieve "long-term viability," which was defined as "positive net present value...taking into account all current and future costs, and can fully repay the government loan."[9] The restructuring plans were intended "to achieve and sustain [the automakers'] long-term viability, international competitiveness and energy efficiency," the loan agreements specified. President George W. Bush said that ensuring viability would require "meaningful concessions from all involved in the automotive industry," including employees, dealers, suppliers, and creditors. Some of these meaningful concessions related to issues such as wages, benefits, health care, and reductions in capacity and dealership networks.

On February 17, 2009, both companies submitted their restructuring plans. GM's plan called for reducing the number of plants from 47 to 32 by the year 2014, and the number of employees from 92,000 to 72,000 by the year 2012. GM's restructuring plan also called for eliminating the

---

[7] Ultimately, Treasury committed $49.5 billion to GM and $12.5 billion to Chrysler. In addition, GMAC LLC, GM's financing arm, received $17.2 billion, and Chrysler Financial, Chrysler's financing arm, received $1.5 billion, for a total of $80.7 billion. As part of the companies' bankruptcies, a substantial portion of the TARP loans were converted into common stock, and, as a result, Treasury now owns 60.8 percent of GM's common stock (plus $2.1 billion in preferred) and 9.9 percent of Chrysler's. Again, the $80.7 billion figure does not include commitments made under the Auto Warranty Commitment Program or the Auto Suppliers Support Program.
[8] The effective date of Chrysler's agreement was amended to January 2, 2009.
[9] Please see COP report referenced above.

Saturn, Saab, and Hummer brands and terminating 1,650 dealerships (approximately 300 per year) by 2014, as shown in Table 1.

Table 1—Planned Dealership Reductions in GM's Restructuring Plan Submitted to Treasury in February 2009

Type of Dealership	2009	2010	2011	2012	2013	2014	Planned Reduction Number	Reduction as a Percentage of 2009 level
Metro[a]	1,890	1,640	1,570	1,400	1,250	1,100	790	41.8
Hubtown[b]	1,210	1,160	1,030	1,000	950	825	385	31.8
Rural[c]	2,650	2,500	2,400	2,300	2,200	2,175	475	17.9
Total	5,750	5,300	5,000	4,700	4,400	4,100	1,650	28.7

[a] GM defines "Metro" as a large metropolitan area
[b] GM defines "Hubtown" as a midsize market that is growing and attracts customers from surrounding areas
[c] GM defines "Rural" as a small market with "no significant retail draw"
Note: Table includes both core and phased-out or sold brands
Source: SIGTARP analysis of GM Restructuring Plan

GM announced in its restructuring plan that, from 2009 to 2014, the company would "accelerate the right-sizing and re-shaping of its dealer network in major markets, increasing volume throughput in better locations." Having fewer, better-located dealerships would increase dealer profits, allowing for recruitment and retention of the best retail talent and more effective local marketing initiatives, GM's plan said. Improving the profitability of GM's independent dealers would help the company, GM said in the plan, by increasing sales, attracting private investment, and driving greater customer loyalty. "The Company's objective is to have the right number of dealers in the right locations operated by the right entrepreneurs," the restructuring plan said.

GM's right-sizing efforts had been under way for decades. From 1970 to 2008, GM reduced the dealership network by over 6,000 dealerships as a result of normal attrition, consolidation of franchises in smaller markets, and the discontinuation of the Oldsmobile brand. GM planned to continue reducing its network and also announced the phase out or sale of its Saturn, Saab, and Hummer brands which would achieve 502 (30 percent) of the 1,650 planned dealer closings by 2014. GM assumed that the remaining reductions would be achieved by three actions:

- consolidating dealerships in metro and suburban areas
- consolidating GMC, Pontiac, and Buick brands in the same dealerships (GM later phased out Pontiac and GMC Medium brands)
- normal attrition of dealerships

On February 17, 2009, Chrysler submitted its own restructuring plan to Treasury, which proposed measures to improve vehicle quality and fuel efficiency, as well as the overall product mix. The plan presented three scenarios for the future of Chrysler:

- Chrysler could continue as a standalone company with the help of $11 billion in loans from the Government.

- Chrysler could pursue a non-binding agreement already signed with the Italian automaker Fiat S.p.A. ("Fiat") and, with additional Government assistance, aim to sell more fuel-efficient cars to a wider range of markets.
- Chrysler could file for bankruptcy and embark on an orderly wind-down of the company.[10]

In contrast to GM's plan, the Chrysler restructuring plan did not contain any specific details about planned dealership closures, such as how many dealerships would close or what factors would be considered in deciding which dealerships to retain. However, the plan referred to Project Genesis, an ongoing Chrysler effort to reduce the number of Chrysler dealerships and to have each surviving dealership sell all three of its brands — Chrysler, Dodge, and Jeep.

As discussed in detail in the following section, the Auto Team reviewed the companies' proposals and rejected them, noting, among other things, that GM's proposed "pace" of closing dealerships was too slow and was an obstacle to its viability. Ultimately, Chrysler filed for bankruptcy on April 30, 2009, and GM followed on June 1, 2009. During their bankruptcies, GM and Chrysler accelerated the dealership termination process; the section beginning on page 16 details the companies' decision-making processes and the effects of the Consolidated Appropriations Act of 2010, which mandated arbitration for terminated dealers desiring such arbitration. The final section of this report, beginning on page 25, discusses the companies' estimates for how much money would be saved through the reduction of their dealership networks.

---

[10] Eventually Chrysler accomplished a combination of the second and third scenarios: Chrysler declared bankruptcy with additional Government assistance and Fiat purchased Chrysler's assets.

Figure 1 shows a timeline of key events discussed in this report from the formal announcement of the Task Force in February 2009 and the signing of the Consolidated Appropriations Act of 2010 in December 2009.

Figure 1: Key Dates Regarding Dealership Terminations

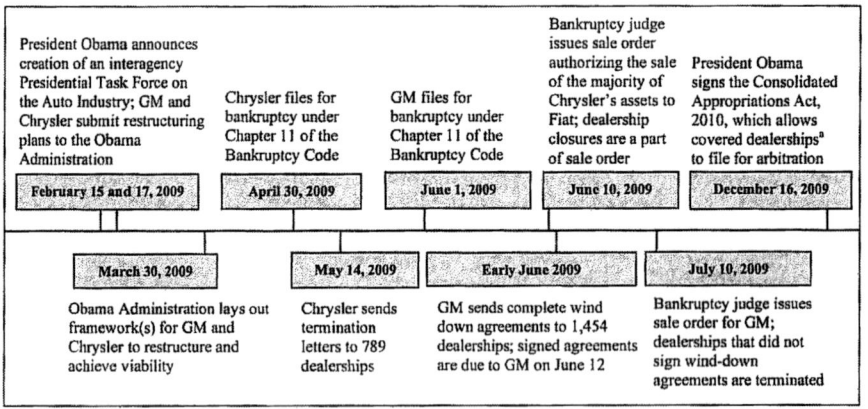

February 15 and 17, 2009	April 30, 2009	June 1, 2009	June 10, 2009	December 16, 2009
President Obama announces creation of an interagency Presidential Task Force on the Auto Industry; GM and Chrysler submit restructuring plans to the Obama Administration	Chrysler files for bankruptcy under Chapter 11 of the Bankruptcy Code	GM files for bankruptcy under Chapter 11 of the Bankruptcy Code	Bankruptcy judge issues sale order authorizing the sale of the majority of Chrysler's assets to Fiat; dealership closures are a part of sale order	President Obama signs the Consolidated Appropriations Act, 2010, which allows covered dealerships[a] to file for arbitration

March 30, 2009	May 14, 2009	Early June 2009	July 10, 2009
Obama Administration lays out framework(s) for GM and Chrysler to restructure and achieve viability	Chrysler sends termination letters to 789 dealerships	GM sends complete wind down agreements to 1,454 dealerships; signed agreements are due to GM on June 12	Bankruptcy judge issues sale order for GM; dealerships that did not sign wind-down agreements are terminated

Source: SIGTARP

[a] According to the Consolidated Appropriations Act, 2010, "The term 'covered dealership' means an automobile dealership that had a franchise agreement for the sale and service of vehicles of a brand or brands with a covered manufacturer in effect as of October 3, 2008, and such agreement was terminated, not assigned in the form existing on October 3, 2008 to another covered manufacturer in connection with an acquisition of assets related to the manufacture of that vehicle brand or brands, not renewed, or not continued during the period beginning on October 3, 2008, and ending on December 31, 2010."

In Response to the Auto Team's Determination that GM's Proposed Pace for Closing Dealerships Was Too Slow and an Obstacle to Its Viability, GM Accelerated Its Dealership Closures; Chrysler Also Accelerated, and at a Faster Pace

This section discusses the role of the Auto Team and its advisors in the decision-making process to terminate dealerships.

In response to Treasury's finding that GM's "pace" of planned dealership terminations was too slow and an obstacle to its viability, GM substantially accelerated its terminations. In its restructuring plan, GM initially proposed closing 1,650 dealers by 2014, but following the Auto Team's response, it instead identified 1,454 dealerships to be wound down by 2010 during its 2009 bankruptcy proceedings. Chrysler also accelerated its dealership terminations – it had planned to reduce its network from 3,181 in 2009 to about 2,000 dealerships by 2014 through Project Genesis (its effort at consolidating dealerships) and instead immediately terminated 789 dealerships during bankruptcy proceedings. The Auto Team encouraged network reduction for both companies based on advice they received from some industry experts that smaller dealership networks would allow GM and Chrysler to improve sales volume and better compete with import companies such as Toyota and Honda, as well as improve brand equity and the overall health of the remaining network. The Auto Team also encouraged the companies to terminate dealerships during bankruptcy proceedings, which provided the opportunity to close dealerships outside of state franchise laws, which could have made involuntary dealer closings more difficult and costly for the two companies.

Between February 17, 2009, the date that the auto companies released their restructuring plans, and March 30, 2009, the date that Treasury released its Viability Determinations in response to the plans, the Auto Team conducted a review of GM and Chrysler's submitted plans and prospects. According to the Viability Determinations, there were many individual considerations and no single factor was critical to the assessment, and the ultimate determination of viability was based upon a total consideration of all relevant factors, which differed for each company. Future Government assistance to GM and Chrysler was conditional on their resubmitting plans that demonstrated they could be viable.

For GM, the five key factors for the company's viability identified by Treasury were: adopting a more realistic assumption of GM's market share, which had been declining in recent years; improving pricing; improving the mix of products to steer the company away from trucks and sport utility vehicles ("SUVs"), which had high margins but were declining in popularity; reducing legacy liabilities such as employee pensions and health care costs; and reducing the number of brands and dealerships.

For Chrysler, the five key factors that Chrysler had to improve to ensure the company's viability were: dedicating more research and development to each platform; increasing product quality scores; improving the product mix (for example, adding more fuel-efficient autos); increasing manufacturing capability; and expanding outside of North America to take advantage of developing markets.

For help in assessing the companies' plans, the Auto Team contracted with Boston Consulting Group ("BCG"), an advisor on business strategy, and the Rothschild North America ("Rothschild"), a financial advisor, to assess the automotive sector and to help evaluate GM's restructuring plan and the proposed Chrysler alliance with Fiat. Treasury specified in the contract with BCG that BCG have extensive auto industry expertise.[11] The contract with Rothschild likewise stipulated that "[t]he Treasury Secretary needs to acquire specialized financial analysis and advice for the automobile industry that is beyond the purview and expertise of Treasury Department personnel."[12] BCG provided data comparing average number of vehicles sold per dealership for GM, Chrysler and their competitors. Rothschild provided the Auto Team with information that included its projections of the overall growth in auto sales in the United States from 2009 to 2014 and GM's projected share of that market.

Treasury Auto Team Reviewed Restructuring Plans With the Help of Outside Experts

Following the submission of the February 17 restructuring plans, the Treasury Auto Team, along with their external advisors, developed Viability Determinations for each company based on their review of the plans. The Viability Determinations, released on March 30, 2009, reflected the Auto Team's evaluation of the extent to which the restructuring plans would, if followed, allow GM and Chrysler to become viable companies. BCG and Rothschild were contracted to provide the Auto Team with feedback on the financial viability of the two companies. Following its Viability Determinations, the Auto Team also conducted its own research about potential job losses resulting from dealership closures and a study of the impact of terminations in Montana. Much of the information that the Auto Team received about the benefits for dealership determinations was based on the "Toyota Model," which suggested that smaller dealership networks would reduce competition among dealerships and increase sales volume for the remaining dealerships. It was believed that this would then allow the dealerships to invest more in their facilities, thus improving the brand equity of GM and Chrysler.

Rothschild created a Cost Benchmarking Analysis presentation in December 2008 that provided detailed information about GM, Chrysler and Ford's dealership network size and productivity measured against their top foreign competitors Toyota, Nissan, and Honda. An appendix to the presentation identified that, although the domestic manufacturers have significantly larger dealership networks, dealership network productivity data for 2007 U.S. new car and light truck

---

[11] Treasury signed its contract with Boston Consulting Group on April 3, 2009, and the contract was to run through October 2, 2009. The overall guaranteed minimum for this contract was $50,000 and the overall maximum for this contract was $7,000,000. According to the contract, its objectives were to provide management consulting services to: a) assist in Treasury's continued assessment of the automotive sector generally; b) assist in Treasury's work with GM to develop and evaluate a comprehensive restructuring and business plan acceptable to the government; and c) advise Treasury on the viability of the announced alliance between Fiat and Chrysler.

[12] Treasury engaged Rothschild through an Interagency Agreement with the Pension Benefit Guarantee Corporation ("PBGC"). The Interagency Agreement was signed by Treasury on February 25, 2009, and terminated on December 11, 2009. The total value of the agreement was $7,770,000.

sales per franchise shows that "foreign transplant [dealer] networks are significantly more productive" than their U.S. counterparts.

In March 2009, BCG provided Treasury with an analysis that compared the average annual sales of GM and Chrysler dealerships with those of their foreign competitors from 2005 through 2008. This analysis showed that on average GM and Chrysler dealerships sold fewer than 500 new vehicles per year, while Toyota and Honda dealerships averaged more than 1,000 new vehicles per year, as shown in Figure 2.

Figure 2: Average Annual Sales for GM, Chrysler Dealerships and Their Competitors (2005-2008)

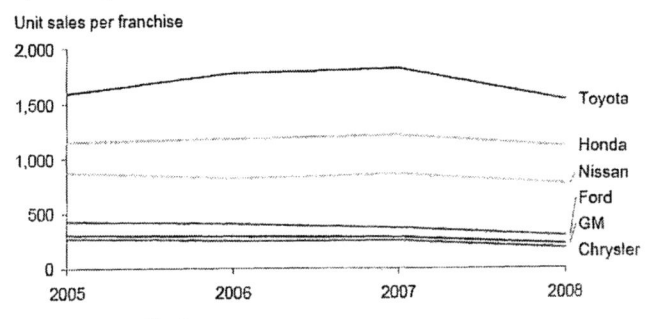

Source: Boston Consulting Group

In an interview with SIGTARP staff, a BCG managing director said that, in theory, if GM and Chrysler reduced the number of dealerships, the average sales at the remaining dealerships should increase, which would make them more profitable and enable them to invest more in their facilities. According to an Auto Team memo dated May 11, 2009, five weeks *after* it wrote its Viability Determination, dealership reductions generally involve near-term sacrifice and long-term gain. The memo notes that, according to BCG, the remaining dealerships typically recapture only 75 percent of the business of the terminated dealerships in year 1. By year 3, the Auto Team estimated, the sales would have returned to 100 percent. By year 5, the long-term gain would materialize as sales in the remaining dealerships would reach 125 percent of sales accomplished with the larger network as the benefits of a healthy dealership network start to materialize.

Rothschild provided the Auto Team with information that showed the anticipated growth in overall auto sales in the United States and GM's projected U.S. market share from 2009 to 2014. Rothschild assumed that overall new vehicle sales would grow from 10.5 million in 2009 to 16.8 million in 2014, but that GM's U.S. market share would fall from 19.5 percent to 18.3 percent during this period, as shown in Table 2.

Table 2—Projected U.S. Auto Sales and GM's U.S. Market Share 2009-2014

Category	2009	2010	2011	2012	2013	2014
U.S. Market (SAAR[1]) (units in millions)	10.5	12.5	14.3	16.0	16.4	16.8
GM Market Share (percent)	19.5%	18.9%	18.6%	18.4%	18.5%	18.3%
GM Sales — U.S. Market (SAAR) (units in millions)	2.0	2.4	2.7	2.9	3.0	3.1
Increase in GM Sales (percent)	-	20%	12.5%	7.4%	3.4%	3.3%

[1] Seasonally Adjusted Annual Rate
Source: SIGTARP analysis of data provided by Rothschild

Therefore, GM's U.S. market share would continue to decline, but its overall sales would increase, based on the assumption that overall new vehicle sales would substantially increase. Following the release of the Viability Determinations, Rothschild and BCG continued to provide updated information to the Treasury Auto Team regarding modifications to GM's restructuring plan and Chrysler-Fiat due diligence, focusing on products, new product development, brands, technology, and turnaround practices.

The Auto Team also consulted with automotive financial industry experts from Bain Consulting, UBS, A.T. Kearney, JP Morgan, Deutsche Bank, Barclays Capital, Roland Berger, and Auto Nation. Mr. Bloom stated that these conversations were not limited to dealership terminations, but also covered issues related to the overall viability of GM and Chrysler. Mr. Bloom noted that these were off-the-record conversations and were not documented. However, according to Mr. Bloom, the experts supported dealership terminations as a necessary part of GM and Chrysler's restructuring.

Experts from four of the firms offered SIGTARP the following observations about reducing the number of dealerships:

- A UBS official stated that terminating GM and Chrysler dealerships was necessary to increase the companies' profitability. Dealerships tend to carry "buffer stock" or excess stock when competing with nearby dealers of the same brand. Fewer dealerships would lead to reduced inventory levels which, in turn, would reduce the amount of floor plan financing.
  The reduction in floor plan financing and the corresponding manufacturer assistance needed by all dealerships would increase the profitability of the overall network and the manufacturer as well. An expert from Bain Consulting also stated many dealerships have too much inventory relative to their market area, particularly in smaller markets or

  > **Floor Plan Financing**
  > Revolving lines of credit used to finance inventories of items, in this case, autos.

  markets where there are more dealers than necessary, because they have to have sufficient diversity in their inventory to cover the manufacturer's entire portfolio and to meet varied customer needs. This leads to higher floor plan financing costs per vehicle. In addition, because it is difficult for a smaller dealership to match its mix of inventory with actual customer demand, they end up with higher quantities of slow moving inventory that can lead to a need for increased customer and dealer incentives to sell their vehicles.

- An official from A.T. Kearney said that the large networks have resulted in more dealerships competing for a smaller share of the auto market, which keeps prices lower. An expert from UBS also stated that reducing the number of dealerships will reduce inter-brand competition, and would result in the dealerships being able to sell new vehicles more quickly, which would increase the profitability of the whole network.

- An expert from JP Morgan noted that although GM and Chrysler have lost significant market share over the past few decades, the size of their dealership networks has not decreased accordingly. The expert also noted that some dealerships derive a large portion of revenue from used cars, service, and parts — not from new vehicle sales — and therefore do not invest in facilities to support new vehicle sales. As a result, some dealerships have improperly trained sales people and poor facilities, which can affect customer service. Having better facilities and trained staff will improve the overall image of the dealerships and the brands they sell. The official stated that the most significant anticipated benefit of the closures will be an increase in brand equity.[13]

Based on the analysis provided by the contractors and conversations with industry experts, the Auto Team issued its Viability Determination that GM's proposed "pace" of closing dealerships was too slow and was an obstacle to its viability, and GM and Chrysler accelerated their planned dealership closures. SIGTARP found that the Auto Team was not involved in determining which dealerships to terminate.

According to Mr. Bloom, of the experts that he consulted, only one — from the Center for Automotive Research — voiced opposition, as noted below, to dealership terminations. However, SIGTARP interviewed that expert and one from J.D. Power and Associates, who was not consulted by the Auto Team. Both experts said that while metro areas were oversaturated with GM and Chrysler dealerships and reductions were needed in these areas, this was not the case in rural areas where GM and Chrysler had an advantage over their import competitors.

Those two experts told SIGTARP that import dealerships such as Toyota, Honda, and Nissan are not generally located in rural areas. The representative from the Center for Automotive Research disputed the Auto Team's assumption that closing rural dealerships would not affect sales in rural areas.[14] He noted that it was not likely that someone would drive 80 miles to buy a Cadillac when they could simply buy another vehicle at a closer dealership.

---

[13] The interview with the JP Morgan official was conducted on November 16, 2009.

[14] In August 2009, well after issuing its Viability Determinations, and in response to a meeting with U.S. Senator Jon Tester of Montana, the Auto Team analyzed the impact of dealership terminations in Montana. They concluded that the average drive to a GM dealership for a Montana resident, including residents of extremely remote areas, was 21.9 miles prior to the dealership terminations and increased only to 24.6 miles after terminations. Based on this analysis, the Auto Team said, GM and Chrysler would not be giving up market share even if they closed rural dealerships, although the Auto Team did not validate this study to determine if average driving distance can predict future auto brand loyalty, nor did they replicate this study in any other state.

He also noted that although sales volume in small towns may be lower, the cost of operating dealerships in small towns is lower as well. In addition, closing dealerships in small towns could ruin the "historic relationship" that GM has had with residents in small towns and force buyers to drive to metro areas, where there are more competitors. In the worst case, the loss of market share in small and medium-sized markets could "jeopardize the return to profitability" for GM and Chrysler, the representative said. Representatives from the National Automobile Dealers Association also concurred that dealership terminations would cause GM and Chrysler to lose market share in rural areas.

A former Chrysler Deputy CEO told SIGTARP that the "Toyota model" studied by the Auto Team — that fewer dealerships, located mostly in metro areas, would lead to higher sales and profitability for the remaining dealerships — would not work for Chrysler. This is because Chrysler sells trucks in rural markets as well as cars in Midwestern states where imported cars are less popular. He said that Chrysler will "never" get to the same throughput level as its import competitors. The former Chrysler Deputy CEO likened applying the Toyota model to Chrysler to "trying to turn our sons into daughters."

Some automotive industry experts also disagreed with the Auto Team's position. The representative from J.D. Power and Associates, for example, said that Chrysler's decision to terminate 789 dealerships within three weeks in an environment that was already disrupted by the poor economy could bring about an even greater crisis in sales. Although he did not disagree from a business standpoint that terminating some dealerships was necessary, he asked why Chrysler would want to "create a wave of chaos amidst [an economic] crisis." Indeed, in September 2009, Chrysler officials themselves told SIGTARP that closing dealerships too quickly would have an adverse effect on sales. Chrysler officials said that they expected that their rapid terminations would result in lost sales in the short term, that Chrysler will take several years to recover lost sales, and that future increases in market share will depend on penetrating new markets.

Auto Team Determined that GM's and Chrysler's Restructuring Plans Were Not Viable; Companies Entered Bankruptcy and Terminated Dealerships

Based on the input from the experts it consulted and its own research, the Auto Team found that GM's overall plan was "not viable as it is currently structured," in part because GM relied on overly optimistic assumptions about the recovery of the company and the economy. In its Viability Determination dated March 30, 2009, Treasury listed five areas in which GM needed to improve its restructuring plan in order to become a viable company: more realistic assumption of its cash needs associated with legacy liabilities, reassessment of its market share assumption, improvement in prices, improved mix of products to steer the company away from high-margin trucks and SUVs, and an excess of brands and dealers.

Specifically with regard to GM dealerships, the Auto Team indicated that the automaker should accelerate the pace of dealership closings:

GM has been successfully pruning unprofitable or underperforming dealers for several years. However, its current pace will leave it with too many such dealers for a long period of time while requiring significant closure costs that its competitors will not incur. These underperforming dealers create a drag on the overall brand equity of GM and hurt the prospects of the many stronger dealers who could help GM drive incremental sales.

GM was given 60 days to submit a "more aggressive plan" overall, including planning for their dealership terminations, and was provided an additional $6 billion of TARP funds as working capital.

Treasury also listed five challenges for Chrysler in a separate Viability Determination: too small of a scale to dedicate enough research and development to each platform; low quality scores; insufficient product mix (for example, too few fuel-efficient autos); inflexible manufacturing capability; and too much geographic concentration in North America, which prevented Chrysler from taking advantage of developing markets. The Viability Determination for Chrysler did not address dealership terminations. The Auto Team concluded that Chrysler could succeed only if it developed a partnership with another automotive company.

Mr. Bloom stated that GM and Chrysler could use the terms of bankruptcy to eliminate dealerships quickly, and that it would have been a "waste of taxpayer resources" for the auto manufacturers to exit bankruptcy when they knew the networks would still have to be rationalized. Mr. Bloom referred to this as "taking the pain and getting past it."
Mr. Bloom also said that the Auto Team considered dealership reductions to be "consistent with overall industry thinking." He told SIGTARP that the Auto Team assumed that GM's and Chrysler's remaining dealerships would perform better and that the brand equity for both companies would improve if GM and Chrysler terminated dealerships.

A Treasury document summarizing the efforts of the AIFP noted that, although Chrysler and GM were on two different paths, "their best chance of success may well require utilizing the bankruptcy code in a quick and surgical way." According to Treasury, this would not entail liquidation or a conventional bankruptcy. Instead a "structured" bankruptcy would function as a tool to "make it easier for Chrysler and General Motors to clear away old liabilities." One effect of this strategy is that dealerships could be closed more quickly. In an internal memo, Auto Team officials reiterated that their goal was to take advantage of the bankruptcy code to reject dealership franchise agreements without significant up-front costs.

However, Treasury officials knew that there might be difficulties with closing dealerships quickly. According to an internal Auto Team memo, "(t)he decision to terminate such a large number of distribution points in a very short time is arguably the most challenging component of the revised plan...Despite the significant execution risk, the management team believes it is imperative that the company capitalize on this unique opportunity to reconfigure the dealer network outside the confines of restrictive state franchise law."

The impact of job losses was not a significant factor in the Auto Team's findings that GM's proposed pace would be an obstacle to its viability. Indeed, it was only after the decision was made that the Auto Team considered the impact its decision would have on job losses. In an internal memo dated April 20, 2009, the Auto Team estimated that GM dealership terminations would result in a short-term loss of 43,081 jobs and a long-term loss of 25,597 jobs. The memo also assumed that Chrysler would go out of business completely, resulting in 72,620 jobs lost in the short term and 43,580 jobs lost over the long term.

The memo notes that the average dealership employs 52 employees. The memo assumes that, at closed dealerships, about half of these employees (namely, the service professionals) would find other work quickly. Sales, managerial, and clerical staff, however, would have a more difficult time finding new jobs or would be permanently displaced. A Chrysler official cited a National Automobile Dealers Association statistic that 50 jobs might be lost for each dealership terminated, but also said that service or technical staff would find re-employment easily. GM officials disputed the NADA figure because many of the low-performing dealerships it terminated had fewer than 50 employees.

As a result of the comments in the Viability Determination, GM officials said their conclusion was to "move now" and quickly to "right-size" the dealership network. GM officials stated that it was their own decision to make the cuts by December 2010. GM accelerated its planned closings of dealerships during bankruptcy proceedings in June 2009 when it announced plans to close 1,454 dealerships by October 2010, rather than its originally planned closure of approximately 450 in the same time period. GM initially planned to close 1,650 dealers through 2014 (see Figure 3).

Figure 3: Planned GM Dealership Reductions Pre- and Post-Bankruptcy

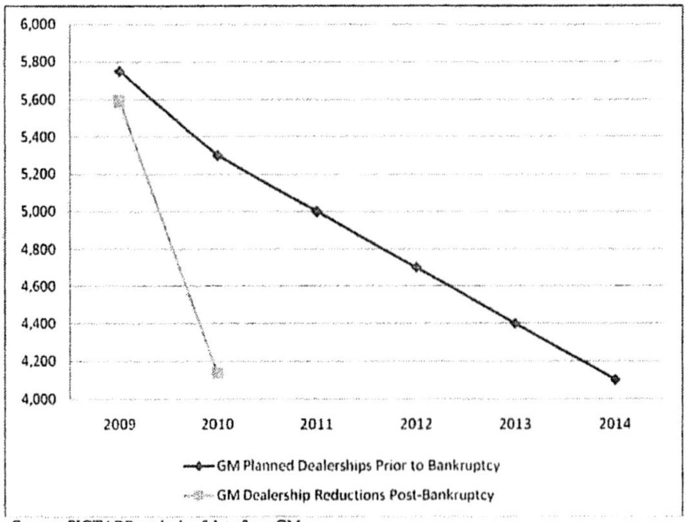

Source: SIGTARP analysis of data from GM

In response to verbal feedback from the Auto Team, Chrysler also accelerated its dealership closings. Chrysler officials said that bankruptcy offered Chrysler the opportunity to speed up their plans for Project Genesis by reducing costs through closing dealerships. Prior to bankruptcy, the officials said that they had a difficult time closing dealerships because of state franchise laws. During its 2009 bankruptcy proceedings, Chrysler eliminated 789 of 3,181 dealerships — almost 25 percent of its dealership network. Chrysler officials also noted that bankruptcy offered an opportunity to speed up the existing strategic plan to consolidate its three brands (*i.e.*, Chrysler, Dodge, and Jeep) within one dealership, Project Genesis. Under Project Genesis, Chrysler had planned to reduce its network over time to about 2,000 dealerships by 2014. Chrysler asserted that the percentage of dealerships that sold all of its three brands increased from 62 percent to 84 percent as a result of eliminating 789 dealerships. The retained dealerships had generated 86 percent of new vehicle sales in 2008.

Criteria Used by GM and Chrysler to Identify Dealerships to Close

This section describes the processes that GM and Chrysler used to identify dealerships to terminate, GM's appeals process, and the status of the arbitration process for both GM and Chrysler.

In June 2009, GM notified 1,454 dealerships that they would be wound down (terminated) in October 2010, and Chrysler notified 789 dealerships that they would be wound down in 22 days. GM allowed dealerships to appeal the wind-down decision; Chrysler did not allow appeals. In December 2009, legislation was enacted to allow dealerships to file for arbitration regarding these decisions.

GM Wind-Down Decisions Were Made in Two Phases

In April 2009, before entering bankruptcy, GM officials met to determine the size and scope of dealer network reductions. GM's Dealership Network Planning and Investments team developed the methodology used to select which dealerships to wind down and which to retain. As part of this process, the Dealership Network Planning and Investments team also worked in coordination with executive leadership, legal counsel, regional managers ("zone" managers), and other GM personnel working for each brand (for example, Chevrolet, Buick, GMC, and Cadillac). According to testimony given by GM officials and documents presented during that testimony, the company's approach to reducing the dealership network involved applying "objective performance criteria" such as dealership sales, profitability, customer convenience, and market demographics. Excluding the reduction from the sale or phase out of Saab, Saturn and Hummer, GM sought to reduce its remaining dealership network from 5,591 dealerships to 4,137. GM expected that normal attrition would eventually lead to an "ideal" network of approximately 3,300 dealerships.

GM selected dealerships that would receive complete wind-down notices in two phases, but all the dealerships were provided wind-down agreements at the same time. During phase one in May 2009, GM identified 1,071 dealerships that it would not likely include in its network going forward.[15] These dealerships were notified of GM's intent in letters dated May 14, 2009, but did not receive official wind-down agreements until the following month. GM officials stated that these dealerships were selected to receive the May 14 letter (and subsequent wind-down) based on one of two criteria that provided an objective framework to evaluate all 5,591 dealerships:

---

[15] Of 1,096 dealerships initially identified for termination in phase one, 14 of the termination decisions were reversed before the official wind-down agreements were sent out, and 11 dealers voluntarily terminated before bankruptcy. The remaining 1,071 dealerships received wind-down agreements in June 2010.

- Dealer Performance Summary Score ("DPS") of less than 70

Or

- annual sales of less than 50 new vehicles in 2008

GM officials noted that the DPS score has been used since 2002 as a measure of dealership performance and that dealerships can access their score on the same website they use to order vehicles and perform other sales-related functions. Our review confirmed that dealerships could access their scores through the website. SIGTARP found that only 26.1 percent of terminated dealerships viewed their DPS score on the website in 2008, and 47.5 percent did so in 2009. The DPS score is the sum of four weighted category scores: sales, customer satisfaction, capitalization, and profitability. GM arrived at each category score by applying a weighting to the ratio of actual performance to the expected performance, as described in Table 3:

Table 3—GM DPS Score Categories

Category	Weighting	Description
Retail Sales Index (RSI)	50 percent	Ratio of actual sales to expected sales. GM calculates expected sales[a] based on a segment-adjusted state average.
Customer Satisfaction Index (CSI)	30 percent	Ratio of actual score to expected score. GM calculates expected score based on a regional average.
Capitalization	10 percent	Ratio of actual working capital to standard working capital. GM calculates standard by averaging a dealership's needs for working capital over a year.
Profitability	10 percent	Ratio of actual dealer return on sales to expected return on sales. GM calculates expected return based on a regional average.

[a] GM calculates expected annual sales, CSI, capitalization, and profitability, based on vehicle registrations, industry averages, and other historical data
Source: SIGTARP analysis of GM data

GM determined that dealerships with a DPS Score of 100 were average performers; those below 70 were considered poor performers and would not be retained. SIGTARP noted, however, that GM did not uniformly apply the phase one criteria to the entire network. For example, our analysis found that two of the wind-down dealers did not meet either criterion. Furthermore, we found that, of the dealerships that met only one of the two criteria:

- GM retained 355 (or approximately 41 percent) of the 858 dealerships that had a DPS score below 70.[16]
- GM retained 9 of the 394 dealerships that sold fewer than 50 new vehicles in 2008.[17]

---

[16] An additional 10 dealerships with a DPS score below 70 were in phase two wind-downs.

GM officials attributed these inconsistencies primarily to a desire to maintain coverage in certain rural areas where they have a competitive advantage over import auto companies that are not typically located in rural areas, although ultimately close to half of all of the GM dealerships identified for termination were in rural areas. Other dealerships were retained because they were recently appointed, were key wholesale parts dealers, or were minority- or woman-owned dealerships.

On June 1, 2009, GM filed for bankruptcy. As indicated earlier in this report, bankruptcy would permit GM to accelerate the process without the restriction of state franchise laws. Bankruptcy laws supersede various state franchise laws, which could have required litigation or arbitration. GM management had also determined that the company would need to wind down more dealerships than those designated in phase one to get close enough to the "ideal network size" of 3,380 dealerships.

In early June 2009, GM initiated phase two of their wind-down process and identified an additional 383 dealerships to wind down. By this point, GM management had decided to eliminate the Pontiac and GMC Medium Duty Truck brands as part of the restructuring, and, as a result, 144 of the 383 dealerships identified in phase two were ones that sold only those brands.[18] GM officials stated that they also used a "more aggressive" set of criteria in phase two than in phase one to select the remaining 239 dealerships for wind-down and bring the phase two total to 383. GM used the following criteria to select the 239 dealerships for wind-down:

State Franchise Laws

Franchise laws, which vary from state to state, are designed to protect the rights and interests of a franchise purchaser by requiring the franchisor (in this case Chrysler or General Motors) to follow specific guidelines in order to terminate the franchise agreement. For example, under Delaware law, a franchisor is prevented from unjustly terminating, failing to renew a franchise, or refusing to deal with a franchisee with whom the franchisor has been dealing with for at least two years, without good cause or in bad faith. Franchisors are required to provide notice before terminating, or electing not to renew, a franchise agreement. Franchise laws also provide franchise purchasers with a legal remedy if a franchisor unjustly terminates, or threatens to or attempts to unjustly refuse to renew a franchise.

- DPS of 80 or less; or
- Unprofitable in 2006, 2007, and 2008; or
- Retail Sales Index below 70; or
- Non-GM brands in same facility and DPS below 100; or
- Buick-GMC or Cadillac dealership network viability[19]

SIGTARP found that GM did not wind down all the dealerships meeting the aforementioned criteria. For example, although 992 dealerships with a DPS below 80 were selected for closure, another 763 with a DPS below 80 were retained.[20] Similarly, for dealerships with a DPS of 100

---

[17] The balance of the 1,071 dealerships that were terminated met both criteria.
[18] A total of 165 wind-downs were related to discontinued brands (GMC Medium Duty Trucks and Pontiac). In phase one, 21 Pontiac dealerships received wind-downs; in phase two, 15 Pontiac dealerships received wind-downs. Also in phase two, 129 GMC Duty Trucks received wind-downs.
[19] *Buick-GMC dealership network viability* refers to GM's efforts to combine standalone Buick and GMC dealerships under one dealership. *Cadillac dealership network viability* refers to the reduction of the overall size of the Cadillac network to better compete with other luxury vehicle brands, such as Lexus and BMW.
[20] Of the dealerships with a DPS below 80, 15 additional were standalone dealerships that sold only the phased out Pontiac brand.

and a non-GM brand in the same facility, 226 were phase one wind-downs, 43 were phase two wind-downs, and 299 were retained.[21] Additionally, SIGTARP noted that 39 wind-down dealers in phase two did not meet any of the performance-based criteria (DPS, RSI, new vehicles sold, non-GM dual). During the time these decisions were made, GM did not document why some dealerships meeting the criteria were retained while others were wound-down. GM officials responded to questions about these inconsistencies by stating that they made case-by-case decisions to determine whether to issue a wind-down agreement to dealerships that met any one of the criteria. Officials also stated that two of the criteria, Buick-GMC and Cadillac dealer network activities, required review of individual market factors. Therefore, GM officials had to contact various regional or field representatives over several weeks to obtain their reconstruction of the impetus for decisions made several months prior.

SIGTARP also found that GM was missing data to evaluate some of the dealerships based on the established criteria. GM was missing at least one of the following criteria for 308[22] dealerships: DPS score, RSI, or 2008 retail sales. We determined that a total of 61 dealerships that lacked at least one of these criteria were terminated, and 247 were retained.[23] GM officials stated that the criteria were missing for 308 dealerships because the dealerships had not provided it or the dealership was new. To make wind-down or retention decisions for dealerships that were missing DPS scores, GM officials said they instead considered RSI and new vehicles sold.

During the first week of June 2009, GM sent wind-down agreements to 1,454 dealerships to end their franchise agreements in October 2010. To receive compensation as part of bankruptcy, dealerships were required to sign the wind-down agreements and submit them to GM by June 12, 2009. The wind-down dealerships were allowed up to 16 months to terminate the business and sell existing inventory to retail customers; however, these dealerships could not order new vehicles.

GM agreed to provide $587 million in compensation to wind down dealerships. Compensation for each dealership was determined using a formula that considered dealership rent, sales, and new vehicle inventory in late May 2009. The dealerships were provided with an initial payment of 25 percent of the total compensation, and the dealerships will receive the remaining 75 percent of the total compensation on the completion of various milestones. As of May 1, 2010, a total of 409 dealerships in wind-down sought to close their GM dealerships before October 2010.

GM Allowed Dealers to Appeal Wind-Down Decisions

Subsequent to announcing the dealership closures and declaring bankruptcy, GM set up an appeals process. Dealers were instructed to submit appeals to GM, but they still had to sign and submit their wind-down agreements by June 12, 2009. For the appeals process, GM created an appeals review team and an Executive Review Committee, but did not establish criteria for the

---

[21] For dealerships with a DPS of 100 and a non-GM brand in the same facility, 12 additional dealerships were standalone dealerships that sold the phased-out Pontiac brand and no other GM brands.
[22] An additional three dealerships were missing data but were standalone dealerships that sold phased-out brands.
[23] A total of 172 dealerships that lacked all three of these criteria were retained, and four received wind-downs; 61 dealerships missing DPS scores received wind-downs, and 247 were retained.

review or for the reversal of wind-down decisions. GM officials stated the appeals review was based on a second look at the same data used in the original wind-down decisions. The appeals process opened on June 4, 2009, and closed on August 7, 2009.

GM received 935 appeals related to complete wind-downs and granted 64 reversals.[24] GM did not document the reasons for reinstating dealerships. When SIGTARP requested explanations of the reversals, GM contacted various field representatives to obtain their undocumented recollections of the reasons for reinstatements. The reasons provided to SIGTARP included the desire to maintain market coverage in rural areas, recent facility upgrades, corrections of erroneous score data, GM legal advice, and GM leadership review. Without proper documentation from GM, SIGTARP could not validate the reasoning or consistency of appeal decisions.

GM did not provide guidance on the specific data that dealerships were to submit as part of the appeals process. Our review of 323 appeals packages found that dealers submitted a variety of information that they deemed relevant. For example, some provided updated financial data, and others submitted letters from members of the community, as shown in the following excerpts from the appeals packages:

> We have not heard back from anybody. We have just moved into a brand new dealership 04/14/2009. We do not understand this letter. We would like to appeal this. Please look at our investment. We have moved to the corner of two major highways and invested over 2 million dollars. We feel you might not be aware of our new dealership since it was addressed to our old address and name.

GM reversed this dealership's closure, but did not document why the appeal was granted. However, GM officials stated that this appeal was granted after its DPS score data was corrected and its facility upgrades were considered.

The following excerpt is from a dealership appeal that was rejected. GM did not document why the appeal was rejected.

> As a recipient of GM's May 14th letter of anticipated contract non-renewal and the Wind-Down Agreement dated June 1, 2009, we request that you review and reconsider the decision to abandon the market of 80,000...in light of the enclosed information. Our continued partnership is truly best for our mutual clientele, the current and future GM customers in this vital area....In an overwhelming show of support from the community, we have received nearly 300 letters and emails, most within a 24-hour period last week due to a grass-roots effort by customers....We would be happy to provide all these letters if you wish to review them....We respectfully request an opportunity to review the details

---

[24] GM received a total of 1,316 appeals related to both complete and partial wind-downs, and granted 86 reversals. 22 of the reversals were for dealerships that received partial wind-downs, 935 of the appeals were received from dealerships selected for complete wind-down, and 381 of the appeals were received from dealerships selected for partial wind-down, which involved eliminating one or more brands from a dealership, but keeping the dealership open.

of our situation in person with an appropriate GM representative at your earliest convenience.

The following excerpt is from another appeal that was rejected. GM officials did not document why the appeal was rejected.

We started out by getting very involved in the community and establishing our own brand as you would. Sponsorships ranging anywhere from the local high school football teams and cheerleaders, softball teams of all levels, Little League and Pee Wee Football...How can General Motors encourage and approve a dealer to make an investment in a franchised dealership and then in just 15 months after all of our investment tell us that there is no longer a market for the amount of dealers in this market. I could understand if that would have been 5 years later but not 15 months and two and a half million dollars later. Furthermore the commitment to our facility which was a 15-year lease with an option to purchase the facility at the end of 5 years is also a major factor that all parties were aware of at the time of the transaction. Could General Motors please tell me why we would be allowed to enter into this type of an arrangement when we are talking about just 15 months in business? My exposure on this facility is in excess of 4.5M over the next three and half years. I made the commitments and the investments based on your approval and your desire to have a dealer in this market.

Chrysler Evaluated Dealerships Market by Market

Before filing for bankruptcy, Chrysler had been implementing a plan known as Project Genesis to consolidate dealerships and have each dealer sell all three of its brands—Chrysler, Dodge, and Jeep. The plan was scheduled to be completed in 2014. Chrysler's Network Operations-Dealer Operations team developed and executed a market-by-market dealership review that incorporated the goals of Project Genesis. During bankruptcy, Chrysler accelerated this plan and decided to terminate 789 dealerships within 22 days without providing any financial assistance to these dealerships. Chrysler officials noted that prior to bankruptcy, state franchise laws made it difficult to close dealerships and stated that the goal was to close dealerships quickly and to have the terminations coincide with the effective date of the bankruptcy sale. Unlike GM, Chrysler did not have an appeals process.

Chrysler used the following primary criteria to select dealerships to retain or terminate: whether the dealer's location was a desirable one targeted by Chrysler; which brands were offered; the number of new vehicle sales; and the Minimum Sales Responsibility ("MSR").[25] Chrysler also considered customer convenience, financial stability of the dealership's company, condition of the dealership's buildings and lots, and capacity of the facility's buildings and lots. Chrysler identified target locations using a market analysis performed by Urban Science, a consulting group. The analysis compared the number of dealerships and corresponding sales to competitors in 1,712 markets across the United States. To demonstrate how it applied the analysis, Chrysler provided SIGTARP with market maps detailing the target areas, number of dealerships and new

---

[25] Minimum Sales Responsibility is a ratio of the actual sales to the average number of vehicle registrations in a state. One hundred is considered average. The state average is broken down by market share and market segment (small, midsize, *etc.*).

vehicle sales for each competitor brand. The analysis also detailed Chrysler's percentage of market share in each area.

SIGTARP's analysis of terminations in 13 markets found that Chrysler's rationale for termination focused on implementing Project Genesis, retaining dealerships with higher sales and premium facilities and retaining those located in target areas. In two of the markets reviewed (see Table 10 in Appendix E), Chrysler terminated all of the dealerships because their performances were below average. Chrysler plans to seek new owners to replace the dealerships in these markets. Chrysler also identified at least 27 other terminated dealerships nationwide that they intend to replace with dealerships under new ownership. For a summary of the 13 markets, see Table 10 in Appendix E.

Table 4 below shows the rationale Chrysler used in its decision-making process for one market.

Table 4—Example of Chrysler's Decision-Making in One Market

Dealership	Brands	In Target Location	2008 MSR	2008 New Vehicles Sold	Terminated	Chrysler Rationale
Dealer A	Jeep	Yes	442%	486	Yes	Blocking the addition of Jeep franchises in three other sales areas.
Dealer B	Dodge, Chrysler	Yes	172%	477	No	In target area, above-average sales performance. Jeep brand to be added in August 2009.
Dealer C	Chrysler, Dodge, Jeep	Yes	103%	390	No	In target area, above-average sales performance. New 2007 dealer and in line with project Genesis.
Dealer D	Dodge	Yes	445%	378	No	In target area, above-average sales performance. Jeep brand to be added in August 2009.
Dealer E	Chrysler, Dodge	Yes	162%	190	No	In target area, above-average sales performance.
Dealer F	Chrysler, Jeep	Yes	82%	145	Yes	Below-average sales performance, not profitable, undercapitalized.
Dealer G	Chrysler, Jeep	Yes	29%	45	Yes	Below-average sales performance, under-capitalized on finance hold, nearby dealership has above-average sales.
Dealer H	Dodge	No	87%	41	Yes	Not in target area, below-average sales performance, not profitable.

Source: SIGTARP analysis of Chrysler data

Three of the four terminated dealerships among these examples (F, G, and H) in Table 4 had the lowest MSR and lowest number of new vehicles sold. However, Dealer A, which had the highest sales and MSR, was terminated because the dealership was preventing Chrysler from adding the Jeep brand to surrounding dealerships, thus preventing Chrysler from implementing Project Genesis. The retained dealerships in this market accounted for 67 percent of the new vehicles sold and had an average MSR of 233 percent. The terminated dealerships accounted for 33 percent of the new vehicles sold and had an average MSR of 160 percent.

Chrysler asserted that the elimination of 789 dealers increased the percentage of dealerships that sold all three brands from 62 percent to 84 percent. In addition, retained dealers generated 86 percent of Chrysler's new vehicle sales in 2008.

Arbitration and Reinstatement Offers

Following the GM and Chrysler dealership closure announcements, Members of Congress held hearings in the House and Senate at which auto manufacturing executives and auto dealers testified. According to an August 2009 Congressional Research Service ("CRS") report, "…some Members of Congress were sympathetic to the concerns of the dealers, citing instances in their districts and states where long-standing dealers had been notified of termination." During the summer of 2009, several legislative proposals were introduced which sought to reinstate dealerships terminated by GM and Chrysler. One amendment to the Government Appropriations Act, 2010 (H.R. 3170) offered by Representative Steven C. LaTourette required reinstatement of the terminated dealerships because "the closing of these dealerships was punitive and secretive." Ultimately, on December 8, 2009, House Majority Leader Steny Hoyer and Assistant Senate Majority Leader Dick Durbin announced compromise legislative language requiring binding arbitration to address the "ongoing dispute between GM, Chrysler, and dealerships that were closed during the companies' restructuring." The compromise language was included in the Consolidated Appropriations Act, 2010.

On December 16, 2009, President Obama signed the Consolidated Appropriations Act, 2010, into law (Public Law No. 111-117). Under the act, affected dealerships had to file for arbitration by January 25, 2010. According to data provided by the auto companies, 1,169 GM dealerships and 418 Chrysler dealerships filed for arbitration. The law requires cases to be submitted to the arbitrators by June 15, 2010, but allows arbitrators to extend this deadline by 30 days if necessary. The deadline has now been extended to July 15, 2010.

In March 2010, both GM and Chrysler decided to offer reinstatement to a limited number of dealerships that filed for arbitration. Officials from both GM and Chrysler told SIGTARP that the decision to offer reinstatement to some dealerships was in response to the legislation and the realization that it would not be a prudent use of company resources to go through arbitration with every dealership that filed. Furthermore, the companies' officials expressed doubt that all the arbitration cases could be completed by the deadline of June 15, 2010. On March 5, 2010, GM announced that it would be sending Letters of Intent ("LOI") offering reinstatement to 666 dealers that filed reinstatement claims, including to 216 complete wind-down dealerships and 450 partial wind-downs,[26] as shown in Table 5. GM officials said they did not believe that the reinstatements will negatively affect the dealership network, stating that economic conditions are better now than they had anticipated at this time last year and that they have a "sense they can support the new network." Ultimately officials stated that they did not believe the reinstatements would be detrimental to the network.

---

[26] GM offered LOIs to 148 dealerships that had been identified in phase one and to 68 dealerships that had been identified in phase two.

Table 5—GM Letters of Intent Offered to Dealers

Type of Wind-Down	Metro	Hub	Rural	Total
Complete	41	54	121	216
Partial	34	220	196	450
Total	75	274	317	666

Source: SIGTARP analysis of GM data

GM officials stated that dealerships receiving LOIs were selected based on the dealership's RSI, CSI, and the geographical impact on existing dealerships. The Letter of Intent allows a dealership to be reinstated after complying with its terms, which require the dealership to meet capitalization requirements, secure wholesale floor plan financing within 60 days and, if a non-GM brand was added after receipt of the wind-down agreement, the dealership must remove that brand.

On March 26, 2010, Chrysler announced that it would offer LOIs to 50 of the 789 dealerships that had been terminated. According to Chrysler, 46 of these dealerships were in rural markets; the other four were in metro and secondary markets. Chrysler officials stated that dealerships that were provided LOIs were in areas where no other dealership could protest the addition of other Chrysler brands, and were not likely to harm sales in the remaining network.

Dealership Termination Decisions Were Not Based on GM's and Chrysler's Cost Savings Estimates

This section discusses the cost savings that the auto companies estimated would result from terminating auto dealerships.

GM reported that dealership terminations could yield cost savings of $2.6 billion (about $1.1 million per closed dealership); Chrysler expected to save $35.8 million ($45,501 per closed dealership). GM's estimate was significantly higher than Chrysler's because it included anticipated savings from reduced incentive payments to dealerships, which Chrysler did not include in its estimate. However, GM and Chrysler officials, along with Auto Team officials, emphasized that these estimates were not considered in their decisions to terminate dealerships, but were developed in response to congressional inquiries and in preparation for congressional testimony in June 2009, *i.e.*, after the terminations.

Indeed, key members of the Auto Team — including Messrs. Rattner and Bloom — stated that they did not consider cost savings to be a factor in determining the need for dealership closures. Nevertheless, GM officials stated that they developed the cost-savings estimate shown in Table 6 after being "pressed" during meetings with congressional representatives to explain the cost savings that would result from the dealership terminations. A Chrysler official said that the cost savings estimates had been originally developed in 2006 and 2007, before the issue of dealership terminations arose, and were updated based on SIGTARP's request. GM officials reiterated that the plan to reduce dealerships was based on making the remaining dealership network more profitable by increasing their sales volume. In fact, when asked by SIGTARP what GM will save by closing any particular dealership, one GM official stated the answer is usually "not one damn cent."

Furthermore, a GM official stated that removing a dealership from the network does not save money for GM—it might even cost GM money—and that savings cannot be attributed or assigned to any one dealership. According to one GM official, it was a "math exercise" to assign a savings amount to one dealership; it was difficult to estimate savings for a particular dealership because the savings are expected to be achieved when the entire dealership network plan is accomplished. GM's Dealer Network and Investments team said the cost savings estimate was their effort to quantify savings in response to the negative reaction to GM's plan to terminate dealerships and to the congressional "drumbeat" of statements that "this is a bad plan."

Estimated Cost Savings

GM's and Chrysler's estimated savings can be grouped into two categories: incentive savings and structural or administrative savings, as shown in Table 6.

Table 6—GM and Chrysler Estimated Cost Savings from Dealership Closures

Category of Savings Estimate	GM[a] Per dealership	Total	Chrysler[b] Per dealership	Total
Incentive Savings	928,000	2,150,000,000	0	0
Structural/Administrative Savings	180,000	415,000,000	45,501	35,900,289
Total Savings		**$2,565,000,000**		**$35,900,289**
Savings Per Dealership		**$1,108,000**		**$45,500**

[a] GM's total is based on a reduction of 2,300 dealerships
[b] Chrysler's total is based on a reduction of 789 dealerships
Source: SIGTARP analysis of data provided by GM and Chrysler

GM's savings estimate is significantly higher because it includes $2.1 billion in anticipated incentive payment reductions that it currently pays to dealerships. GM's incentive savings are based on the assumption that once excess dealerships have been eliminated, sales and profitability for remaining dealerships will increase. GM believed that as dealership profitability improved, it would be able to reduce the incentives to dealerships to sell new vehicles. GM's savings estimates are also based on two other assumptions — that GM's new vehicle sales will increase from the current level of 1.5 million per year to 3.1 million by 2014, and that GM will eliminate about 800 additional dealerships through normal attrition and consolidations during the same time period.

Approximately 80 percent of GM's estimated total savings are classified as reductions in the anticipated incentive payments that it currently makes to dealerships. The total estimated savings include:

- $810 million by reducing the dealership discount on vehicles GM sells to its dealerships

- $380 million by lowering other incentives paid directly to dealerships (for example, GM anticipates that significantly lower dealership inventory levels in 2010 will reduce the need to use incentives to encourage dealerships to reduce their vehicle inventory)

- $350 million by reducing payments for Standards for Excellence, a program that provides payments to dealerships if they meet certain criteria, such as selling more new vehicles in the current year than in the comparable period of the prior year

- $350 million by reducing the incentive that GM currently pays dealerships to inspect vehicles when they are delivered from the manufacturer-(GM plans to reduce the current payment to 15-20 percent)

- $140 million by reducing current levels of wholesale floor plan support, which provides a payment to dealerships to help them manage the cost of financing daily operations and purchasing new vehicle inventory

- $120 million by reducing reimbursement to dealerships by 15 to 20 percent for a full tank of gas for each new vehicle sold

Chrysler did not include incentive savings in its estimate. One Chrysler official noted that Chrysler did not project any incentive savings, and further stated it would be difficult to isolate savings derived from reduced incentives in a market where various dynamics can influence vehicle sales and the incentives that an auto manufacturer must offer.

GM and Chrysler also projected administrative savings from reducing the number of dealerships, as shown in Table 7.

Table 7—Estimated Structural/Administrative Cost Savings

Category of Savings Estimate	GM[a] Per dealership	Total	Chrysler[b] Per dealership	Total
Local Advertising	86,957	200,000,000	0	0
Dealer Channel Network Alignment	54,347	125,000,000	0	0
Sales and Service Consultants/Field Staff	17,391	40,000,000	3,802	3,000,000
Dealer Website/IT Expenses	17,391	40,000,000	4,183	3,300,000
Training	4,348	10,000,000	6,337	5,000,000
Corporate Administration	0	0	18,504	14,600,000
Transportation	0	0	10,139	8,000,000
Other	0	0	2,535	2,000,000
Total Savings		**$415,000,000**		**$35,900,000**
Savings Per Dealership		**$180,434**		**$45,500**

[a] GM's total is based on a reduction of 2,300 dealerships
[b] Chrysler's total is based on a reduction of 789 dealerships
Source: SIGTARP analysis of data provided by GM and Chrysler

GM's administrative savings estimate was higher primarily because it included savings from local advertising assistance and expenses associated with wind-down compensation provided to dealerships, which were not included in Chrysler's estimate. For example, GM estimated it would save $200 million in local advertising assistance, a dealer assistance program that GM intends to reduce over time when all of its planned wind-downs are completed. GM also estimated $125 million in savings for Dealer Channel Network Alignment, which refers to GM's historical expenses incurred to date to close dealerships, which will not be required at the same level once the wind-down process is complete.

Chrysler's largest cost savings estimate was $14.6 million in a reduction in administrative expenses from a smaller dealership network. Chrysler also anticipated that a smaller network would allow them to decrease training expenses, and that fewer delivery points for its parts distribution centers would reduce transportation expenses.

Conclusions and Lessons Learned

In response to the Treasury Auto Team's rejection of GM's and Chrysler's restructuring plans and its explicit comment that GM's "pace" of dealership closings was too slow and an obstacle to its viability, GM and Chrysler substantially accelerated their dealership termination timetables. In GM's case, instead of gradually reducing its network by approximately 300 dealerships per year through 2014, as GM had proposed in the plan initially submitted to Treasury, GM responded to the Auto Team's decision by terminating 1,454 dealerships' ability to acquire new GM vehicles and giving them until October 2010 to wind down operations completely; for Chrysler (which also had originally planned to terminate dealers over five years), its acceleration was even more abrupt, with Chrysler terminating 789 dealerships (25 percent of its network) within 22 days.

The Auto Team's view about the need for GM and Chrysler to reduce their dealership networks and do so rapidly was based on a theory that, with fewer dealerships (and thus less internecine competition), like their foreign competitors, the remaining dealerships would be more profitable (through more sales volume and less floor plan financing costs) and thus would permit the dealerships to invest more in their facilities and staff. For GM and Chrysler, the theory goes, this would mean better brand equity (*i.e.*, better consumer perception through more attractive facilities and better customer service) and would allow the manufacturers over time to decrease their substantial dealership incentives. In addition, the Auto Team felt the companies' best chance of success required "utilizing the bankruptcy code in a quick and surgical way" and noted further that it would have been a "waste of taxpayer resources" for the auto manufacturers to exit bankruptcy when they knew the networks would still have to be reduced. The Auto Team was so convinced of the need for the acceleration of dealership closings that it highlighted GM's proposed pace of dealership closings (approximately 300 a year over five years) as one of the primary obstacles to its continued viability, and required GM to revise its proposal to address the Auto Team's concerns as a condition for receiving the additional TARP support that GM believed it needed to survive. Not surprisingly, GM's and Chrysler's plans for accelerated terminations soon followed.

Perhaps only time will tell whether and to what extent the Auto Team's theory proves valid; however, there are several aspects of the theory and how the Auto Team came to have this view about dealership reductions that are worth noting.

- One, although there was broad consensus that GM and Chrysler generally needed to decrease the number of their dealerships, there was disagreement over where, and *how quickly*, the cuts should have been made. Some experts that SIGTARP spoke to in connection with this audit questioned whether it was appropriate to apply the foreign model to the U.S. automakers, particularly in small markets in which the U.S. companies currently have a competitive advantage, a concern apparently not substantially considered by the Auto Team when they adopted this theory. The conclusion that the manufacturers should close dealerships more rapidly than originally planned was also criticized as being potentially counterproductive; one expert opined, for example, that closing dealerships in an environment already disrupted by the recession could result in an even greater crisis in sales. Chrysler officials similarly told SIGTARP that closing dealerships too quickly would have an adverse effect on sales from which it would take several years to recover, and, even then, only if new markets were penetrated by opening new dealerships. The fact that, after the mandatory arbitration legislation was passed, GM offered to reinstate 666 dealerships[27] and Chrysler offered to reinstate 50 dealerships with a senior GM official stating that the final number of dealerships won't damage GM's ability to recover or grow the company, suggests, at the very least, that the number and speed of the terminations was not necessarily critical to the manufacturers' viability. It is worth noting that GM's top rival among U.S. automakers, Ford Motor Company, which is also carrying out plans to "aggressively restructure to operate profitably," is closing dealerships at a rate similar to that in GM's original restructuring plan which was rejected by Treasury.[28]

- Two, job losses at terminated dealerships were apparently not a substantial factor in the Auto Team's consideration of the dealership termination issue. Although there is some controversy over how many jobs will be lost per terminated dealership (the National Automobile Dealer Association's estimate of approximately 50 per dealership is challenged by the manufacturers as too high), it is clear that tens of thousands of dealership jobs were immediately put in jeopardy as a result of the terminations by GM and Chrysler. In the face of the worst unemployment crisis in a generation and during the same period in which the Government was spending hundreds of billions of dollars on a stimulus package to spur job growth, the Auto Team rejected GM's original plan (which included gradual dealership terminations), expressly indicated that GM's pace of terminations was too slow, and then encouraged the companies' use of bankruptcy to accelerate dealership terminations. These decisions — all based on the Auto Team's theory that GM and Chrysler would be better off by accelerating dealer terminations — contributed to the accelerated loss of potentially tens of thousands of jobs. Although the restructuring of GM and Chrysler inevitably required an overall reduction in their own workforces (and the termination of a certain number of poorly performing dealerships), it is not at all clear that the greatly accelerated pace of the dealership closings during one of the most severe economic downturns in our Nation's history was either necessary for the sake of the companies' economic survival or prudent for the sake of the Nation's economic recovery.

- Finally, the acceleration of dealership closings was not done with any explicit cost savings to the manufacturers in mind. Again, the anticipated benefits to GM and Chrysler from a smaller dealership network were far more amorphous — a better "brand

---

[27] Of these 666 dealerships, 216 were complete wind-downs, and 415 were partial wind-downs.
[28] According to Ford's 2009 annual report, concentrating efforts in its largest 130 metropolitan market areas, Ford closed an average of 200 Ford, Lincoln, and Mercury dealerships per year in calendar 2006, 2007, and 2008, and another 250 in calendar 2009, leaving a total of 3,550 dealerships at the beginning of 2010. Ford has a goal of an average of 1,500 vehicle sales per year for Ford dealerships and 600 per year for Lincoln Mercury dealerships. By focusing on closing dealerships located in metropolitan areas, Ford reflected its philosophy that "our dealers are a source of strength...especially in rural areas and small towns where they represent the face of Ford." This echoed comments industry experts made to SIGTARP advising that GM and Chrysler had less need to reduce the number of rural dealerships and instead should focus on closing dealerships in metropolitan areas.

equity" and the potential ability to decrease dealership incentives over time. GM prepared its cost savings estimate only at the request of Congress and only after the decisions to accelerate terminations had already been made. Chrysler provided Congress with estimated cost savings that had been developed three years prior. The disparity in the companies' cost-savings estimates are telling. Chrysler estimated a savings of only $45,500 per terminated dealership. GM, however, estimated cost savings of $1.1 million per terminated dealership. The difference in these estimates alone casts doubt on their credibility. Moreover, despite the fact that Treasury rejected GM's even less optimistic assumptions about their market share and profitability in its Viability Determination, GM's estimate was based on a projection that GM's sales would *double* by 2014. GM acknowledged that its cost savings (assuming the decreases in incentives could be realized) could only be calculated across its entire network and could not be calculated for a single particular closed dealership. Indeed, one GM official emphasized this point by telling SIGTARP that GM would usually save "not one damn cent" by closing any particular dealership.

Once the decisions to accelerate the dealership terminations were made, Chrysler decided which dealerships to terminate based on case-by-case, market-by-market determinations that examined whether the dealership's location was a desirable one, whether it offered all three of Chrysler's brands, the dealership's volume of new vehicle sales, and the dealership's score for Minimum Sales Responsibility, a ratio based on actual sales versus vehicle registrations broken down by market share and market segment. Chrysler did not offer an appeals process. Perhaps not surprisingly in light of the case-by-case nature of the process, SIGTARP did not identify any instances in which Chrysler's termination decision varied from its stated, albeit subjective selection criteria.

GM's approach, which was conducted in two phases, was purportedly more objective. In the first phase, GM claimed that the dealerships subject to termination were those meeting at least one of these criteria: a Dealer Performance Summary ("DPS") Score (a score based on a dealership's sales, customer satisfaction, capitalization and profitability) of less than 70; or annual sales of fewer than 50 new vehicles in 2008. In the second phase, GM stated that dealerships subject to termination were those meeting at least one of these criteria: those with a DPS of 80 or less; those that were unprofitable in 2006, 2007 and 2008; those with a retail sales index (a ratio of actual sales to expected sales based on a market average) below 70; those with non-GM brands in the same facility and a DPS of less than 100; or those interfering with GM's Buick-GMC Truck or Cadillac dealership network restructuring plans.

However, SIGTARP's review demonstrates that GM did not consistently follow its stated criteria. In the first phase, for example, two of the terminated dealerships did not fit into either termination category, and GM retained 364 dealerships that potentially qualified for termination. In phase two, GM terminated 39 dealerships that did not meet any of the objective criteria and retained more than 1,062 dealerships that met one or more criteria for termination. Just as troubling, there was little or no documentation of the decision-making process to terminate or retain dealerships with similar profiles, making it impossible in many cases for SIGTARP to determine the causes of deviations from the supposedly objective criteria. Similarly, although GM did have an appeals process and granted 64 reversals in cases of dealerships that would have been completely wound down, it failed to set the criteria or process for appeals or to document its reasoning for granting or denying appeals.

Lessons Learned

Although the auto dealership termination process is beginning to come to a close, several of the lessons from the process should be considered in the event Treasury once again is compelled to make decisions that directly affect the businesses in which it has invested. Although perhaps it is inevitable that public ownership of private companies will have the effect of blurring the Government's appropriate role, the fact that Treasury is acting in part as an investor in GM and Chrysler does not insulate Treasury from its responsibility to the broader economy. In particular, Treasury should have taken special care given that its determinations had the potential to lead to job losses, particularly given that one goal of the loan agreements was to "preserve and promote jobs of American workers employed directly by the automakers and subsidiaries and in related industries."

Here, before the Auto Team rejected GM's original, more gradual termination plan as an obstacle to its continued viability and then encouraged the companies to accelerate their planned dealership closures in order to take advantage of bankruptcy proceedings, Treasury (a) should have taken every reasonable step to ensure that accelerating the dealership terminations was truly necessary for the long-term viability of the companies and (b) should have at least considered whether the benefits to the companies from the accelerated terminations outweighed the costs to the economy that would result from potentially tens of thousands of accelerated job losses. The record is not at all clear that Treasury did either. The anticipated benefits to the companies of accelerated terminations were based almost entirely on the not-universally-accepted theory that an immediate decrease in dealerships would make them similar to their foreign competitors and therefore improve the companies' profitability, and the theory arguably did not take into account some of the unique circumstances of the domestic companies' dealership networks. Although Treasury consulted with several experts on the subject, it undertook no market studies to test the counterintuitive theory until after making its Viability Determination. More importantly, there was no effort even to quantify the number of job losses that the Auto Team's decision would contribute to until after the decision was made, and the effect on the broader economy caused by accelerated dealership terminations similarly was not sufficiently considered.

Stated another way, at a time when the country was experiencing the worst economic downturn in generations and the Government was asking its taxpayers to support a $787 billion stimulus package designed primarily to preserve jobs, Treasury made a series of decisions that may have substantially contributed to the accelerated shuttering of thousands of small businesses and thereby potentially adding tens of thousands of workers to the already lengthy unemployment rolls — all based on a theory and without sufficient consideration of the decisions' broader economic impact. That the automakers have offered reinstatement to hundreds of terminated dealerships in response to Congressional action without any apparent sacrifice to their ongoing viability further demonstrates the possibility that such dramatic and accelerated dealership closings may not have been necessary and underscores the need for Treasury to tread very carefully when considering such decisions in the future.

Furthermore, although it was certainly understandable for Treasury to defer to the automakers' management in selecting the criteria for closing dealerships, its decision not to monitor the process that they employed is far more questionable. In the absence of effective oversight, GM purportedly employed objective criteria but then deviated from such criteria, making termination decisions with little or no transparency and making a review of many of these decisions impossible; Chrysler's process did not even include an opportunity for dealerships to appeal the termination decision. In the future, to the extent that Treasury takes action with respect to a TARP recipient that has the potential to affect so many jobs in so many different communities, Treasury should monitor the recipients' actions to ensure that they are carried out in a fair and transparent manner.

Management Comments and Audit Response

Treasury responded preliminarily to a draft of this audit by letter dated July 16, 2010, which is reproduced in Appendix D. In its response, Treasury states that it "strongly disagree[s] with many of your statements, your conclusions and the lessons learned." Treasury notes in particular, among other things, that "[i]n the absence of government assistance, both GM and Chrysler faced almost certain failure and liquidation, which would have resulted in the loss of hundreds of thousands of jobs across multiple industries," and that "the outcome under the restructuring plans is far better than the likely alternatives had the Administration not stood behind the companies." Treasury goes on to say that it will continue to review the report and may respond more fully at a later date.

SIGTARP looks forward to Treasury's more complete response to the audit. It is important to note that Treasury was provided an opportunity to review a discussion draft of the report and provide comments. Treasury did so, changes were made to the report as appropriate, and, at the end of that process, Treasury offered no material factual objections with that draft audit report. Treasury might not agree with how the audit's conclusions portray the Auto Team's decision making or with the lessons that SIGTARP has drawn from those facts, but it should be made clear that Treasury has not challenged the essential underlying facts upon which those conclusions are based.

More importantly, SIGTARP does not dispute that Government assistance was necessary to prevent the failure of GM and Chrysler, and nothing in the audit suggests otherwise. Treasury's letter seems to imply that Treasury was faced with the decision either to encourage the acceleration of dealership terminations substantially, as it did, or let the companies fail altogether. This is a false dilemma with no factual support: no one from Treasury, the manufacturers or from anywhere else indicated that implementing a smaller or more gradual dealership termination plan would have resulted in the cataclysmic scenario spelled out in Treasury's response; indeed, when asked explicitly whether the Auto Team could have left the dealerships out of the restructurings, Mr. Bloom, the current head of the Auto Team, confirmed that the Auto Team "could have left any one component [of the restructuring plan] alone," but that doing so would have been inconsistent with the President's mandate for "shared sacrifice." That the scale of terminations was not vital to the companies' survival has since been further demonstrated by the fact that the companies have offered reinstatement to hundreds of dealerships without concerns that such reinstatements will threaten their viability.

In any event, Treasury's criticism does not address SIGTARP's lessons learned — that Treasury (a) should have taken every reasonable step to ensure that accelerating the dealership terminations was truly necessary for the long-term viability of the companies and (b) should have sufficiently considered whether the benefits to the companies from the accelerated terminations outweighed the costs to the economy that would result from potentially tens of thousands of accelerated job losses in the midst of the greatest recession in generations.

Appendix A—Scope and Methodology

We performed the audit under the authority of Public Law 110-343, as amended, which also incorporates the duties and responsibilities of inspectors general under the Inspector General Act of 1978, as amended. It was completed from July 2009 to July 2010 (Project No. 012). These were the audit's specific objectives:

1) Determine the role of the Treasury Auto Team in the decision to reduce dealership networks.
2) Determine the extent to which GM and Chrysler developed and documented processes for deciding which dealerships to terminate and which to retain.
3) Determine to what extent the dealership reductions are expected to lead to cost savings for GM and Chrysler.

We performed work at the Department of the Treasury in Washington, D.C. We also performed field interviews in New York, Michigan, and Virginia. The scope of this audit covered GM's and Chrysler's entire dealer networks—both terminated and retained populations.

To determine the role of the Auto Team in the decision to reduce dealerships, we interviewed members of the Auto Team, reviewed available documentation, and interviewed officials from GM and Chrysler. We also interviewed industry experts who were consulted by the Auto Team.

To determine the extent to which GM and Chrysler developed and appropriately documented consistent processes for deciding which dealerships to retain or terminate, we interviewed auto dealers and officials involved in the decision-making processes at GM and Chrysler. We analyzed the criteria and data used by both companies to make their decisions, and we determined whether or not dealerships met the criteria for termination or retention. We also analyzed a judgmental sample of GM retained and terminated dealerships and reviewed their Dealer Performance Summary scores, including the retail sales, customer satisfaction, and supporting financial data, including profitability and net working capital. For Chrysler, we analyzed a judgmental sample of retained and terminated dealerships and reviewed their sales performance, brand offering, and financial information (profitability and working capital). For Chrysler, we also selected markets across the United States and reviewed the decision-making process for each dealership in each market, with a specific focus on understanding the geographic/Project Genesis factor. Regarding GM's appeals process, we reviewed emails and appeals for the 86 reversals, along with general appeals emails.

To determine the extent to which the reductions would lead to cost savings for the auto manufacturers, we interviewed GM and Chrysler officials, auto industry analysts, and automobile dealers, and we reviewed any analyzed cost savings estimates provided by GM and Chrysler.

This performance audit was performed in accordance with generally accepted government auditing standards. Those standards require that we plan and perform the audit to obtain sufficient, appropriate evidence to provide a reasonable basis for our findings and conclusions based on our audit objectives. We believe that the evidence obtained provides a reasonable basis for our findings and conclusions based on our audit objectives.

Limitations on Data

GM did not document the meetings during which decisions were made about dealerships in their networks. GM did not document the rationale for granting or denying appeal requests from dealerships. Chrysler did not document meetings held to determine dealership closures. The Auto Team did not document some of the meetings it held with auto industry analysts.

Use of Computer-Processed Data

This audit did not use computer-processed data.

Internal Controls

This audit did not address internal controls.

Prior Coverage

No audits have been performed on dealership terminations with the same or similar objectives as this audit.

Appendix B—Acronyms and Definitions

Acronym	Definition
AIFP	Automotive Industry Financing Program
Auto Team	Treasury Auto Team
BCG	Boston Consulting Group
BMW	Bavarian Motor Works
CEO	Chief Executive Officer
CSI	Customer Satisfaction Index
DPS	Dealer Performance Summary
GM/GMC	General Motors/General Motors Company
LOI	Letter of Intent
MSR	Minimum Sales Responsibility
NADA	National Automobile Dealers Association
RSI	Retail Sales Index
SAAR	Seasonally Adjusted Annual Rate
SIGTARP	Special Inspector General for the Troubled Asset Relief Program
Task Force	Presidential Task Force on the Auto Industry

Appendix C—Audit Team Members

This report was prepared and the review was conducted under the direction of Kurt Hyde, Director of Audits, Office of the Special Inspector General for the Troubled Asset Relief Program. The staff members who conducted the audit and contributed to the report include: Michael Kennedy, Shannon Williams, Leah DeWolf, and Sarah Reed.

Appendix D—Management Comments

DEPARTMENT OF THE TREASURY
WASHINGTON, D.C. 20220

ASSISTANT SECRETARY

July 16, 2010

Neil M. Barofsky
Special Inspector General
Office of the Special Inspector General for the Troubled Asset Relief Program
1500 Pennsylvania Ave., NW, Suite 1064
Washington, D.C. 20220

RE: SIGTARP Official Draft Audit Report

Dear Mr. Barofsky:

Thank you for providing the U.S. Department of the Treasury (Treasury) with a copy of your official draft audit report regarding the factors affecting the decisions of General Motors and Chrysler to reduce their dealership networks.

While we have conducted only a preliminary review of the report at this time, we strongly disagree with many of your statements, your conclusions, and the lessons learned. In the absence of government assistance, both GM and Chrysler faced almost certain failure and liquidation, which would have resulted in the loss of hundreds of thousands of American jobs across multiple industries. Instead, both companies worked with their stakeholders and underwent fair, open, and successful bankruptcies.

Today, both GM and Chrysler have emerged as stronger global companies. Of course, this process was not easy. It required deep and painful sacrifices from all stakeholders—including workers, retirees, suppliers, dealers, creditors, and the countless communities that rely on a vibrant American auto industry. Nonetheless, the outcome under the restructuring plans is far better than the likely alternatives had the Administration not stood behind the companies. The Administration's actions not only avoided a potentially catastrophic collapse and brought needed stability to the entire auto industry, but they also saved hundreds of thousands of American jobs and gave GM and Chrysler a chance to reemerge as viable, competitive American businesses.

Thank you again for the opportunity to review your report. We will continue to review it in detail and may respond more fully to your findings at a later date.

We look forward to continuing to work with you and your team as we continue our efforts to stabilize our financial system.

Sincerely,

Herbert M. Allison, Jr.
Assistant Secretary for Financial Stability

Appendix E—Additional Tables

Table 8—GM and Chrysler Distribution of Dealership Networks Before and After Terminations

Market Description	Dealer Count Before Terminations GM	Dealer Count Before Terminations Chrysler	Number of Terminated Dealers GM	Number of Terminated Dealers Chrysler	Dealer Count After Terminations GM	Dealer Count After Terminations Chrysler
Metro	1,671	869	465	275	1,206	594
"Hubtown"[a]/Secondary	1,330	619	275	190	1,055	429
Rural	2,590	1,446	714	263	1,876	1,183
Non-Designated[b] (Chrysler Only)	N/A	247	N/A	61	N/A	186
Totals	5,591	3,181	1,454	789	4,137	2,392

[a] Term used by GM to describe a mid-size market that is growing and attracts consumers from surrounding areas
[b] A non-designated market has been determined to be unable to support a full-line dealer in the future. A dealer in a non-designated market is allowed to stay until it voluntarily terminates, or its performance warrants taking action
Source: SIGTARP analysis of data provided by GM and Chrysler

Table 9—Status of GM Wind-Down Dealership Funds as of 12/01/2009[a]

	Total Amount	25% Payment	75% Payment
Total Amount[b]	$587,060,628.00	$146,765,157.00	$440,295,471.00
Amount Paid	$159,306,755.50	$143,225,733.25	$16,081,022.25
Amount Owed	$427,753,872.50	$3,539,423.75[c]	$424,214,448.75

[a] This data pertains to 2,520 partial wind down dealerships and 1,840 complete wind down dealerships, and does not include dealerships that were rejected in bankruptcy
[b] 2,470,640 of the total amount is under dealership eligibility review
[c] 25 percent payment amount owed figure includes approximate 25 percent for Hummer
Source: SIGTARP analysis of data provided by GM

Table 10—Summary of Dealership Sales Statistics for 13 Chrysler Markets Reviewed by SIGTARP

Market	Status	Average Minimum Sales Responsibility (MSR)	New Vehicle Sales (units)	Percent of Total Sales (Retained and Terminated)
1	Retained	129%	3840	82%
	Terminated	58%	855	18%
2	Retained	110%	5,235	69%
	Terminated	104%	2,302	31%
3	Retained	139%	2,420	79%
	Terminated	89%	663	21%
4	Retained	71%	3,043	59%
	Terminated	79%	2,151	41%
5	Retained	108%	1,011	92%
	Terminated	21%	93	8%
6		All dealerships were below average and terminated; new appointment selected		
7	Retained	223%	1,435	67%
	Terminated	160%	717	33%
8	Retained	122%	4,435	68%
	Terminated	80%	2,113	32%
9		All dealerships were below average and terminated; new appointment selected		
10	Retained	150%	5,042	65%
	Terminated	70%	2,764	35%
11	Retained	85%	3,020	79%
	Terminated	47%	827	21%
12	Retained	78%	6,451	79%
	Terminated	68%	1,673	21%
13	Retained	135%	46,562	74%
	Terminated	103%	16,044	26%

SIGTARP Hotline

If you are aware of fraud, waste, abuse, mismanagement, or misrepresentations associated with the Troubled Asset Relief Program, please contact the SIGTARP Hotline.

By Online Form: www.SIGTARP.gov   *By Phone:* Call toll free: (877) SIG-2009

By Fax: (202) 622-4559

By Mail: Hotline: Office of the Special Inspector General
for the Troubled Asset Relief Program
1801 L Street., NW, 4th Floor
Washington, D.C. 20220

Press Inquiries

If you have any inquiries, please contact our Press Office:

Kristine Belisle
Director of Communications
Kris.Belisle@do.treas.gov
202-927-8940

Legislative Affairs

For congressional inquiries, please contact our Legislative Affairs Office:

Lori Hayman
Legislative Affairs
Lori.Hayman@do.treas.gov
202-927-8941

Obtaining Copies of Testimony and Reports

To obtain copies of testimony and reports, please log on to our website at www.sigtarp.gov.

Appendix 11

SIGTARP – II

Office of the Special Inspector General for the Troubled Asset Relief Program

Quarterly Report to Congress

October 26, 2010

SIGTARP

Office of the Special Inspector General for the Troubled Asset Relief Program

Advancing Economic Stability Through Transparency, Coordinated Oversight and Robust Enforcement

Quarterly Report to Congress
October 26, 2010

Factors Affecting the Decisions of General Motors and Chrysler to Reduce their Dealership Networks

On July 19, 2010, SIGTARP released its audit report, "Factors Affecting the Decisions of General Motors and Chrysler to Reduce their Dealership Networks." Conducted in response to a request by Senator Jay Rockefeller and Representative David Obey, this report addressed (1) the role of Treasury's Auto Team in the decision to reduce the dealership networks for General Motors Corporation ("GM") and Chrysler LLC ("Chrysler"), (2) the extent to which GM and Chrysler developed and documented processes for deciding which dealerships to terminate and which to retain, and (3) the extent to which the dealership reductions are expected to lead to cost savings for GM and Chrysler.

Pursuant to their loan agreements with Treasury, as a condition of receiving additional TARP funding, GM and Chrysler were required to submit restructuring plans in February 2009 to Treasury's Auto Team, a body created by the Administration and responsible for, among other things, evaluating the companies' restructuring plans and negotiating the terms of any further assistance. In March 2009 the Auto Team rejected both companies' plans and highlighted GM's planned "pace" of dealership closings as too slow and one of the obstacles to its viability. In response to the Auto Team's rejection of their restructuring plans, GM and Chrysler significantly accelerated their dealership termination timetables. In GM's case, instead of gradually reducing its network by approximately 300 dealerships per year through 2014, as it had proposed in the plan initially submitted to Treasury, GM responded to the Auto Team's decision by terminating 1,454 dealerships' ability to acquire new GM vehicles and giving them until October 2010 to wind down operations completely. For Chrysler (which also had originally planned to terminate dealers over five years), its acceleration was even more abrupt, with Chrysler terminating 789 dealerships (25% of its network) within 22 days.

The Auto Team's view about the need to reduce dealership networks and do so rapidly was based on a theory that, as in the case of GM and Chrysler's foreign competitors, with fewer dealerships producing less internecine competition, the remaining dealerships would be more profitable (through more sales volume per dealership and lower floor plan financing costs). This greater profitability would permit the dealerships to invest more in their facilities and staff. For GM and Chrysler, the theory went, this would mean better brand equity and would allow the manufacturers, over time, to decrease their substantial dealership incentives. In addition, the Auto Team felt the companies' best chance of success required "utilizing the bankruptcy code in a quick and surgical way" and noted further that it would have been a "waste of taxpayer resources" for the auto manufacturers to exit bankruptcy without reducing their networks. While perhaps only time will tell whether and to what extent the rapid reduction of the number of dealerships will improve the manufacturers' profitability, SIGTARP's audit found that there were several aspects of how the Auto Team came to this view about dealership reductions worth noting.

- First, although there was broad consensus that GM and Chrysler generally needed to decrease the number of their dealerships, there was disagreement over where, and how quickly, the cuts should have been made. In conversations with SIGTARP, some experts questioned whether it was appropriate to apply a foreign model of fewer dealerships located predominantly in metropolitan areas to the U.S. automakers, particularly in smaller and rural markets in which the U.S. companies currently have a competitive advantage, and one expert opined that closing dealerships in an environment already disrupted by the recession could result in an even greater crisis in sales. Similarly, Chrysler officials told SIGTARP that closing dealerships too quickly would have an adverse effect on sales from which several years would be required to recover — and even then, only if new markets were penetrated by opening new dealerships. The facts that, after the mandatory arbitration legislation was passed, GM and Chrysler offered to reinstate 666 and 50 dealerships, respectively, and that a senior GM official stated that the final number of dealerships would not damage GM's ability to recover or grow the company suggest, at the very least, that the number and speed of the terminations were not necessarily critical to the manufacturers' viability. Indeed, after the audit's release, GM Chairman and former Chief Executive Officer ("CEO") Ed Whitacre acknowledged both to the Detroit Press and to SIGTARP that GM may have tried to cut too many dealers in its initial reaction to Treasury's rejection of its viability plan. As he said to SIGTARP, "In my judgment, [cutting that many dealers] was not necessary."
- Second, job losses at terminated dealerships were not a substantial factor in the Auto Team's consideration of the dealership termination issue. In the face of the worst unemployment crisis in a generation and during the same period in which the Government was spending hundreds of billions of dollars on a stimulus package to spur job growth, Treasury's Auto Team rejected GM's original plan (which included gradual dealership terminations), expressly stated that GM's pace of terminations was too slow, and then encouraged the companies' use of bankruptcy to accelerate dealership terminations. Although the restructuring of GM and Chrysler inevitably required an overall reduction in their own work

forces (and the termination of a certain number of poorly performing dealerships), it is not at all clear that the greatly accelerated pace of the dealership closings during one of the most severe economic downturns in our nation's history was either necessary for the sake of the companies' economic survival or prudent for the sake of the nation's economic recovery.

- Finally, the acceleration of dealership closings was not done with any explicit cost savings to the manufacturers in mind. Again, the anticipated benefits to GM and Chrysler from a smaller dealership network were far more amorphous — a better "brand equity" and the potential ability to decrease dealership incentives over time. Indeed, one GM official emphasized this point by telling SIGTARP that GM would usually save "not one damn cent" by closing any particular dealership.

Once the decisions to accelerate the dealership terminations were made, Chrysler decided which dealerships to terminate based on case-by-case, market-by-market determinations. Chrysler did not offer an appeals process. Perhaps not surprisingly in light of the case-by-case nature of the process, SIGTARP did not identify any instances in which Chrysler's termination decision varied from its stated, albeit subjective, selection criteria. GM's approach, which was conducted in two phases, was purportedly more objective. However, SIGTARP found that GM did not consistently follow its stated criteria, nor did it set the criteria or process for appeals or document its reasoning for appeals decisions.

SIGTARP identified several important lessons that should be learned from the circumstances surrounding the Auto Team's encouragement of GM and Chrysler to accelerate their planned termination of dealerships. Although the dealership termination process is near its conclusion, these lessons should be considered in the event Treasury once again is compelled to make decisions that directly affect the businesses in which it has invested. Here, before the Auto Team rejected GM's original, more gradual termination plan as an obstacle to its continued viability and then encouraged the companies to accelerate their planned dealership closures in order to take advantage of bankruptcy proceedings, Treasury (a) should have taken every reasonable step to ensure that accelerating the dealership terminations was truly necessary for the viability of the companies, and (b) should have at least considered whether the benefits to the companies from the accelerated terminations outweighed the costs to the economy that would have resulted from potentially tens of thousands of accelerated job losses. The record is not at all clear that Treasury did either. It made no effort even to quantify the number of job losses to which the Auto Team's decision would contribute until after the decision was made, nor did it sufficiently consider the effect on the broader economy caused by accelerated dealership terminations.

Stated another way, at a time when the country was experiencing the worst economic downturn in generations and the Government was asking its taxpayers to support a $787 billion stimulus package designed primarily to preserve jobs, Treasury made a series of decisions that may have substantially contributed to the accelerated shuttering of more than 2,000 small businesses, thereby potentially adding tens of thousands of workers to the already lengthy unemployment rolls — all without sufficient consideration of the decisions' broader economic impact. There is no evidence that implementing a smaller or more gradual dealership termination plan would have materially increased the companies' risk of failure. That the automakers have offered reinstatement to hundreds of terminated dealerships in response to Congressional action without any apparent sacrifice of their ongoing viability further demonstrates the possibility that such dramatic and accelerated dealership closings may not have been necessary and underscores the need for Treasury to tread very carefully when considering such decisions in the future.

Furthermore, although it was certainly understandable for Treasury to defer to the automakers' management in selecting the criteria for closing dealerships, its decision not to monitor the process that they employed is far more questionable. In the absence of effective oversight, GM purportedly employed objective criteria but then deviated from them, making termination decisions with little or no transparency and making a review of many of these decisions impossible; Chrysler's process did not even include an opportunity for dealerships to appeal the termination decision. In the future, to the extent that Treasury takes action with respect to a TARP recipient that has the potential to affect so many jobs in so many different communities, Treasury should monitor the recipient's actions to ensure that they are carried out in a fair and transparent manner.

In a July 16, 2010, response to this audit report, Treasury stated that it "strongly disagree[s] with many of your statements, your conclusions, and the lessons learned." The response asserted that absent Government assistance, GM and Chrysler would have faced the prospect of failure and liquidation, resulting in the loss of hundreds of thousands of jobs across multiple industries. Treasury argued that "[t]he Administration's actions not only avoided a potentially catastrophic collapse and brought needed stability to the entire auto industry, but they also saved hundreds of thousands of American jobs and gave GM and Chrysler a chance to reemerge as viable, competitive American businesses." On August 19, 2010, Treasury submitted a follow-up letter. Both letters are reproduced in Appendix H: "Correspondence."

The second letter, in Treasury's words, "provide[s] responses to certain statements in the report which we believe are materially inaccurate or incomplete." It is important to note that Treasury was provided an opportunity to review a discussion draft of the report and provide comments. Treasury did so, changes were made to the report as appropriate, and, at the end of that process, Treasury offered no material factual objections to that draft audit report. The August 19, 2010, letter, while quoting numerous statements from the audit report, fails to identify a single factual assertion in the report as inaccurate. Treasury might not agree with how the audit's conclusions portray the Auto Team's decision making or with the lessons that SIGTARP has drawn from those facts, but it should be made clear that Treasury has not challenged the essential underlying facts upon which those conclusions are based. Instead, Treasury's objections to the audit's conclusions and lessons learned amount to little more than the erection of a series of straw men that appear to be designed to distract the reader from the lack of any meaningful substantive response.

Treasury's specific comments are summarized below, followed by SIGTARP's response.

- Treasury contends that certain statements in the report "overstate one factor of the restructurings and demonstrate a misunderstanding of Treasury's decision-making process." In particular, Treasury disagrees with SIGTARP's criticisms of the Auto Team for insufficiently taking job losses at terminated dealerships into account, pointing out that without steps to attain viability, both GM and Chrysler faced almost certain liquidations, which would have resulted in the loss of hundreds of thousands of jobs across multiple industries, including auto dealerships. In Treasury's view, it did not have either the "mandate to study how to best preserve jobs for one group of stakeholders given the enormity of the risk to the industry and the limited time in which a plan had to be implemented," or the time to conduct studies without "requir[ing] the Administration to continue to fund the companies with billions of taxpayer dollars in the absence of approved viability plans." Treasury further notes that employment losses since June 2007 for auto dealers have not been as severe as for the rest of the auto industry, and that "over the past year since GM and Chrysler emerged from bankruptcy, employment at auto dealers has actually increased."

Notably absent from these objections is any meaningful defense against the core criticism of the audit report — that the Auto Team's failure to seriously consider job losses at terminated dealerships was a fundamental flaw in its evaluation of the automakers' restructuring plans. SIGTARP does not dispute that Government assistance was necessary to prevent the failure of GM and Chrysler, and notwithstanding Treasury's attempt to erect this straw man criticism of the report, nothing in the audit suggests otherwise. Further, Treasury does not and cannot support its implication that had dealership closings not been dramatically accelerated, GM and Chrysler would have failed. None of the experts that SIGTARP interviewed supported such a proposition. Indeed, a senior member of the Auto Team, Ron

Bloom, when asked explicitly whether the Auto Team could have left dealerships out of the restructurings, affirmatively told SIGTARP that it "could have left any one component [of the restructuring plan] alone." Furthermore, that the companies have subsequently offered reinstatement to hundreds of dealerships without any impact to their ongoing viability in the U.S. suggests, at a minimum, that the speed and scale of the terminations were not essential to the companies' survival. Particularly telling are the statements of Whitacre, who not only acknowledged that the cuts before reinstatements were "not necessary," but also pointed out the value of preserving dealerships: "I thought from the start that if you had more good dealers then you can sell more good cars and that is what we are in the business of doing. I still believe that it is a much better idea to have more good dealers."

Treasury's reference to labor statistics, which demonstrate that from 2009 to 2010, depending on the month selected, there was a slight increase or slight decrease in the number of employees at all of the country's auto dealerships, foreign and domestic, used and new, likewise misses its mark. As an initial matter, whatever the current employment levels at auto dealerships, they are simply irrelevant to the audit's conclusion that Treasury should have at least considered whether the benefits to the companies from accelerated terminations outweighed the costs to the economy from potentially significant accelerated job losses. In other words, even if Treasury's actions did not significantly contribute to job losses, that fortuitous outcome would not have been the result of careful analysis, given Treasury's failure to consider the broader impact of its decision. In any event, the cited statistics fail to support Treasury's suggestion that the dealership closings in question have had no adverse impact on jobs. First, those statistics cover all auto dealerships, and so tell us little about the impact of GM and Chrysler dealership closings. Second, in response to Congressional action and other factors that softened the blow of Treasury's decision, GM and Chrysler significantly reduced the number of planned dealership closings originally approved by the Auto Team. Third, as Treasury is well aware, the statistic is potentially misleading because GM will not complete its dealership closings until the end of October 2010, so the mid-summer numbers do not reflect the impact of a substantial number of GM closings.

Finally, Treasury's claimed lack of any "mandate" to consider job preservation or time to conduct meaningful studies exposes its other arguments for what they are — efforts to distract from its failure to conduct meaningful analysis in support of well-founded, well-judged decisions that balance the benefits and costs for all stakeholders appropriately. The audit nowhere suggests that the Auto Team should have delayed its decision making for an extended period. Indeed, Treasury accomplished its after-the-fact analysis of job impact within weeks of its initial decision. In the face of the worst unemployment crisis in a generation, and in the context of one of the most severe economic downturns in our nation's history, Treasury certainly could have used some of the time it spent consulting its dozen experts considering the broader impact of its decision.

- Treasury contends that SIGTARP inaccurately "argues that the decisions of GM and Chrysler to accelerate dealership closures were based entirely on Treasury's written viability plan determination." Treasury asserts that it did not "direct" the companies to terminate specific dealers or accelerate dealer closings in particular. Rather, it determined that each company's initial viability plans failed to aggressively effectuate the entire restructuring across several different criteria. The companies determined that the only way to restructure their debt obligations was through a bankruptcy proceeding, which provided an opportunity for an extensive restructuring of other liabilities, including those concerning facilities, suppliers, environmental liabilities, and the dealer network. The restructuring of all liabilities minimized the amount of taxpayer money that had to be injected into each company.

Here Treasury has erected and attacked a new straw man. The audit report nowhere contends that the decisions of GM and Chrysler were based "entirely" on Treasury's written viability plan determination. Nor does the report state that Treasury "directed" GM and Chrysler to terminate specific dealers. Indeed, the report specifically stated otherwise. But to the extent that Treasury is trying to disclaim any responsibility for the accelerated closing plans, its position strains credulity. Treasury rejected both companies' initial restructuring plans, emphasizing (in writing to GM and orally to Chrysler) the importance to their long-term viability of accelerated dealership closings. Not surprisingly, particularly given that their ability to tap more TARP funds was contingent on Treasury's approval of the restructuring plans, GM and Chrysler both responded by amending their plans to accelerate dealer closings in conformance with Treasury's wishes. SIGTARP does not dispute Treasury's claim that the prospect of a bankruptcy proceeding made accelerated dealership closings more attractive, but that concept was not the companies' alone, and Treasury officials acknowledged to SIGTARP that they strongly encouraged the auto manufacturers to use bankruptcy to shed dealerships, in order to get around the laws that the states had enacted to protect these small businesses. In the words of an internal Auto Team memo concerning GM, the "team believes it is imperative that the company capitalize on the unique opportunity to reconfigure the dealer network outside the confines of restrictive state franchise laws."

- Treasury objects that SIGTARP failed to acknowledge the benefits of early implementation of planned dealership closings. It also disagrees with the criticism that the Auto Team embraced "not-universally-accepted" theories on the benefits of dealer terminations and did not perform explicit cost savings analyses before recommending acceleration of dealership closings. In Treasury's view, SIGTARP chose to downplay an almost unanimous consensus among industry experts that GM and Chrysler should reduce their dealership networks while emphasizing the views of one or two experts who, in part, disagreed. Treasury notes that GM and Chrysler had planned dealership closures on their own, irrespective of Treasury's guidance, in order to improve brand equity, sales throughput, and the dealer network's overall health. In Treasury's view, it would have been irresponsible not to use the bankruptcy process as a quicker, less expensive way to effect reductions in their dealer networks.

The audit report fully and accurately described the range of expert opinion on the benefits and costs of dealership closings. Contrary to Treasury's intimation, the report acknowledged the "broad consensus" that GM and Chrysler, in a general sense, needed to decrease the number of their dealerships. The report also noted, as Treasury seems reluctant to concede, that there is important disagreement over where, and how quickly, the cuts should have been made, and whether such cuts were necessary to the viability of GM and Chrysler. As noted above, some experts, as well as a former Chrysler deputy CEO, questioned whether it was appropriate to apply to U.S. automakers a foreign model of fewer dealerships overall, with a significantly reduced presence in smaller or rural markets (GM increased its planned termination of rural dealerships from 475 to 714 in response to Treasury's reaction to its initial plan), particularly when the U.S. companies held a competitive advantage in such markets. And, of course, even GM's chairman and former CEO believed that the cuts before reinstatement, which were made at Treasury's encouragement, might have been too drastic and "not necessary." A more thoughtful process from Treasury might have avoided such a conclusion.

- Treasury objects to SIGTARP's observation that because GM and Chrysler offered to reinstate hundreds of dealerships after Congress passed mandatory arbitration legislation, the number and speed of the terminations were not necessarily critical to either company's viability. Treasury contends that the report misunderstood the situation the companies faced after Congress acted, and notes that nearly 70% of the subsequent arbitration proceedings were decided in favor of the manufacturers.

The arbitration statistics cited by Treasury are wholly unrelated to the fundamental point at issue — that the Auto Team failed to adequately justify its conclusion that an aggressive acceleration of dealership terminations was necessary to the manufacturers' viability. That the manufacturers offered reinstatement to so many dealers without any threat to their viability, whatever the reason, undermines any such conclusion. In any event, Treasury's citation to the results of termination cases actually arbitrated is potentially misleading as well as irrelevant. Only 170 of the 1,584 arbitration claims filed actually proceeded through arbitration to a ruling. The vast majority of filings (approximately 89%) were resolved in other ways, including offers of reinstatement and financial settlements accepted by the dealer. In light of these facts, it is not surprising that those few that were not offered reinstatement or settlements did not ordinarily succeed in arbitration. Given the number of dealerships reinstated without any apparent threat to the companies' viability, the previously noted opinion of GM's chairman and former CEO that the initial cuts were likely too deep, and the current head of the Auto Team's acknowledgment that the accelerated dealership closings, as with any other single factor, were not essential for viability, it is curious that Treasury still clings to the contrary opinion.

- In Treasury's view, SIGTARP unfairly concluded that Treasury should have done more to monitor the process that the automakers employed in implementing their dealership closure plans. Treasury asserts that its role, as mandated by the President, was to take a broad commercial approach to these restructurings and refrain from intervening in day-to-day decisions. This policy was intended to preserve the long-term viability of GM and Chrysler and their ability to repay the Government's investment. In Treasury's words, "[t]he Government's role was not to run the companies."

Here again, Treasury misses the point. SIGTARP's report did not suggest that Treasury should involve itself in examining individual closure decisions. Rather, it made the commonsense suggestion that Treasury, having put in motion an aggressive dealership closing plan, should have monitored the process by which closure decisions were made to ensure that the process was both fair and transparent. Doing so would hardly have been more invasive than the Auto Team's approach to assessing the need to dramatically accelerate dealership closings, or a host of other business decisions, from plant closings to brand removal to leadership choices.

Having examined Treasury's objections, SIGTARP stands by its earlier findings.

Appendix 12

AMERICAN ARBITRATION ASSOCIATION

Report to Congress

November, 2010

A REPORT TO CONGRESS ON THE

Automobile Industry Special Binding Arbitration Program

*Administered By The American Arbitration Association
Under Authority Of Section 747 Of Public Law 111-117*

NOVEMBER, 2010

American Arbitration Association
Dispute Resolution Services Worldwide

"ECONOMY, SPEED, AND JUSTICE"

American Arbitration Association
Dispute Resolution Services Worldwide

I am pleased to present this comprehensive report on the Auto Industry Special Binding Arbitration Program.

This remarkable program, established by Congress and administered by the American Arbitration Association, demonstrates the positive potential for the use of alternative dispute resolution. In just seven months, nearly 1,600 businesses were provided recourse to address their concerns.

At the same time, the arbitration program did not add to the burdens of the nation's courts, and not one dollar of direct taxpayer funds was expended.

The Association here expresses its profound and continuing thanks to Congress for its trust in choosing the AAA to administer this seminal program.

William K. Slate II
President and CEO,
American Arbitration Association

354   GRAND THEFT AUTO

American Arbitration Association®
Dispute Resolution Services Worldwide

Automobile Industry Special Binding Arbitration Program

December 2009	January 2010	February 2010	March 2010	April 2010	May 2010	June 2010	July 2010

AAA Program Development and Management: AAA develops program rules, website, forms, state arbitrator panel development and screening, party and attorney outreach, communications systems development, hearing logistics, etc.

Dealers notified about Program

Cases filed with AAA

Mediation/settlement discussions/negotiations encouraged by AAA

Party review, selection, appointment of arbitrator

Arbitrator orientation/logistics discussions

Preliminary and regular hearings scheduled and held

Arbitrators issue determinations

2,789 eligible dealerships

1,575 Total Cases Filed

Case Disposition/Outcomes
In accordance to statutory timeframes

- Cases Withdrawn By End of Program: 493 (31.3%)
- Cases Settled By End of Program: 803 (50.9%)
- Cases Closed By End of Program: 113 (7.2%)
- Determinations in Favor of Dealership: 55 (3.5%)
- Determinations in Favor of Manufacturer: 111 (7%)

THE AAA, ESTABLISHED...

in 1926, is a not-for-profit public service organization with a long history of assisting government in the design and implementation of alternative dispute resolution and prevention programs.

CREATION OF PROGRAM

Section 747 of Public Law 111-117 authorized the creation of this program, the Automobile Industry Special Binding Arbitration Program, which provided a successful and efficient forum for the resolution of 1,575 disputes at no direct cost to taxpayers.

EXECUTIVE SUMMARY

In December 2009, Congress passed and President Barack Obama signed legislation directing the establishment of a legislatively tailored alternative dispute resolution (ADR) mechanism, under the auspices of the American Arbitration Association® (AAA), to resolve disputes related to the termination of thousands of automobile dealerships. Section 747 of Public Law 111-117 authorized the creation of this program, the Automobile Industry Special Binding Arbitration Program, which provided a successful and efficient forum for the resolution of 1,575 disputes at no direct cost to taxpayers.

The genesis of the program lay in the economic downturn and subsequent termination of a large number of dealerships by General Motors (GM) and Chrysler as part of their restructuring under bankruptcy protection. Because the bankruptcy process provides for quick and comprehensive organizational change, the terminated dealerships had no avenue to contest their closures or seek redress. Congress considered several measures to address the concerns of the dealerships and manufacturers, and ultimately developed an innovative compromise, whereby the auto dealerships could appeal the manufacturers' decisions through a process of alternative dispute resolution, including binding arbitration, administered by the Association.

In accordance with the Congressional mandate, and drawing upon its institutional expertise, the AAA® developed and implemented this fair, user-friendly, and efficient ADR program. In the end, 2,789 dealerships, with no recourse prior to Congressional action, were given an opportunity to seek reinstatement, and 1,575 of those availed themselves of that opportunity. Over half of the disputes filed under this program were resolved through negotiation and voluntary settlement. In just over seven months, the AAA provided a forum through which 1,575 claims were resolved without the use of appropriated or direct taxpayer funds.

Program Totals by Case Disposition	
Status	Final Program Total
Total Cases Filed	1,575
Withdrawn	493
Settled	803
Administratively Closed	113
Arbitral Determination	166
• *Dealer*	*55*
• *Manufacturer*	*111*

INCEPTION OF THE PROGRAM

Economic Decline and Bankruptcy

The economic downturn that began in 2007 had global consequences, including a serious impact on a wide range of private industries in the United States. One key domestic industry was hit particularly hard – auto manufacturing.

Two major U.S. auto manufacturers, Chrysler and General Motors, were especially affected. In response to the likely widespread impact on the broader economy which the failure of a major domestic manufacturer could precipitate, the federal government actively sought to address the problems affecting the automotive industry. According to the Department of Treasury's Special Inspector General's report on the Troubled Asset Relief Program (TARP), through the creation of its "Auto Team," the Department of the Treasury sought "to prevent a significant disruption of the American automotive industry that would pose a systemic risk to financial market stability and have a negative effect on the U.S. economy." As a condition of its investment of over $80 billion in both manufacturers through the Automotive Industry Financing Program (AIFP), a component of TARP, the Treasury Department required the two manufacturers to develop and submit restructuring plans, but it ultimately rejected those plans, in part because the pace of downsizing the dealership networks was deemed to be not quick enough. Having rejected the manufacturers' proposals, the Treasury Department's Auto Team determined that bankruptcy was the only feasible option left to prevent insolvency and protect the ailing economy from further disruption.

Chrysler and General Motors filed for Chapter 11 bankruptcy protection on April 30 and June 1, 2009, respectively, in the United States Bankruptcy Court for the Southern District of New York. As part of their efforts to downsize and reorganize under bankruptcy procedures, both manufacturers terminated a significant number of local dealerships across the U.S. In total, the contracts of 2,789 dealerships, 2,000 from General Motors' network and 789 from Chrysler's, were terminated.

Congressional Action and Intervention

Following the termination of these franchise agreements, Congress began to explore different proposals related to the dealership closures. Legislation was introduced, for example, that would have restored closed dealerships and required the manufacturers to work through state courts using applicable state laws to cancel dealership agreements, bypassing the federal bankruptcy courts and laws. Other members of Congress argued that the federal government should not involve itself directly in this issue. Nevertheless, leadership in both the House and Senate became actively involved in seeking a compromise that would balance the interests of the government, the public, manufacturers, and terminated dealerships.

After House Majority Leader Steny Hoyer mentioned his desire to find a "credible appeals process" during a September, 2009 press conference, the AAA volunteered to assist with its alternative dispute resolution services and expertise. Over the course of the next several months, lawmakers from all parts of the political spectrum explored various options and mechanisms, ultimately developing legislative provisions to authorize an impartial and

---

NOTED

"We want a credible appeals process…"

– *House Majority Leader Steny Hoyer*

> **NOTEWORTHY**
>
> This was a bipartisan effort. Representative LaTourette observed, for example, that this program would not have been created "…without something good and bipartisan happening in the United States Congress."

> " We intend that this process provide transparency and avoid the excessive costs and delays of litigation and discovery disputes."
>
> – *Representative Christopher Van Hollen*

binding process administered by the AAA that balanced the interests of both terminated dealerships and the manufacturers. Eventually, Representative Hoyer in the House and Senator Richard Durbin in the Senate drafted and guided through their respective chambers legislation to establish a process that would "provide transparency and avoid the excessive costs and delays of litigation and discovery disputes," as described by Representative Christopher Van Hollen on the House floor. Incorporated as Section 747 of H.R. 3288, the Consolidated Appropriations Act of 2010, Congress succeeded in creating the appeals process for which it was searching. Noteworthy, this was also a bipartisan effort. Representative Steven C. LaTourette observed, for example, that this program would not have been created "…without something good and bipartisan happening in the United States Congress."

In Section 747 and the legislative history, Congress clearly articulated objectives for this new program. The binding arbitration provision was included, according to House Judiciary Committee Chairman John Conyers, because:

> "…By providing a process for working out the relationship between automobile manufacturers and dealerships that ensures transparency and review by a neutral arbitrator according to an equitable and balanced standard, taking into account the interests of all affected parties, the property and due process rights of manufacturers and dealerships will be safeguarded."

Congress also sought to promote ADR's traditional emphasis on mediation and voluntary settlement. In creating an alternative dispute resolution mechanism, which includes a final step of binding arbitration rendered by an impartial, neutral arbitrator, Congress included provisions intended to facilitate and encourage voluntary settlement. These goals were ultimately successfully achieved, with over half the cases being resolved through voluntary settlement.

IMPLEMENTATION BY THE AAA

Fulfilling its Public Service Mission

With President Obama's signing of the Consolidated Appropriations Act of 2010 on December 16, 2009, Section 747 became law. The AAA immediately mobilized to create the Automobile Industry Special Binding Arbitration Program. With nearly 3,000 potential parties and a statutory seven-month timeframe for completion of all cases, the scope of this project was potentially daunting. Senior AAA staff with expertise in case management, legal and procedural issues, legislative affairs, and government ADR system design convened to lay the foundation of this *sui generis* program crafted by Congress in partnership with the AAA.

Although the Automobile Industry Special Binding Arbitration Program incorporated a number of innovative elements, the designation of the AAA to develop and implement it was not unprecedented. The AAA's extensive experience in partnering with government to develop ADR programs, combined with its status as a not-for-profit public service organization, place it in a singular position to design and administer such a program. Governments know of, and rely on, the AAA's strict adherence to principles of independence, neutrality, and integrity, as well as its technical capabilities and capacity to handle a large volume of disputes. As a consequence, the AAA has been named in hundreds of statutes, regulations, ordinances, and orders throughout the United States. The AAA has been specifically written into a number federal statutes, regulations, and orders pertaining to such governmental entities as the Centers for Medicare & Medicaid Services, the Federal Communications Commission, the Federal Reserve System, the Department of the Interior, and the Environmental Protection Agency. The AAA also provides its services at the state and local levels, assisting states, counties, and municipalities to resolve tens of thousands of disputes under government mandate. Furthermore, the AAA has a proven track record in quickly developing and deploying the necessary staff and technological resources to provide large-scale ADR programs, as it did in the aftermath of Hurricanes Katrina and Rita, when the states of Louisiana and Mississippi designated the AAA to provide alternative dispute resolution programs to resolve claims disputes. Because of the flexible nature of ADR, government agencies working with the AAA are able to create equitable and customized programs to allow for the speedy resolution of a wide range of disputes. *See Appendix IV for more extensive information regarding the AAA's government programs.*

SECTION 747

On December 16, 2009, Section 747 became law. The AAA immediately mobilized to create the Automobile Industry Special Binding Arbitration Program.

Program Specifications

The Automobile Industry Special Binding Arbitration Program was based on specific requirements and guidelines included in Section 747 and the pertinent legislative history. The legislation included specific deadlines. For example, from enactment to final decision, all claims had to be resolved within seven months.

Section 747 applied to automobile manufacturers ("covered manufacturers"), that had received government assistance under the Emergency Economic Stabilization Act of 2008 or in which the federal government had an ownership stake—namely, Chrysler and General Motors. Section 747 also clearly defined which terminated dealerships ("covered dealerships") would be eligible to participate in the program. As House Judiciary Committee Chairman John Conyers noted on the House floor, such a remedy was necessary because "It is in the national interest to protect the substantial federal investment in automobile manufacturers by assuring the viability of such companies through the maintenance of sufficiently sized dealership networks…"

GM-National Association of Minority Automobile Dealers Memorandum of Understanding

Although Section 747 did not allow the awarding of other remedies in arbitration, it did permit manufacturers and dealerships to reach voluntary settlement (through mediation, negotiation, and other mechanisms) satisfactory to all parties. For example, the National Association of Minority Automobile Dealers (NAMAD) and General Motors signed a memorandum of understanding (MOU) which provides for mediation and arbitration of certain issues and disputes for dealers not seeking reinstatement.

Section 747(c) mandated that the manufacturers provide to covered dealerships, no later than thirty days after enactment of the legislation, a written summary of the criteria used in determining whether a covered dealership's contract was terminated or not renewed. Within forty days from enactment (ten days later), covered dealerships had to decide whether to file for binding arbitration with the American Arbitration Association. Section 747 further required that the overall arbitration process must be completed within 180 days after enactment of the legislation. The statute did, however, provide the arbitrator discretion to grant an extension of up to thirty days.

THE LEGISLATION INCLUDED...

specific deadlines. For example, from enactment to final decision, all claims had to be resolved within seven months.

NOTED

"It is in the national interest to protect the substantial federal investment in automobile manufacturers by assuring the viability of such companies through the maintenance of sufficiently sized dealership networks…"

– *House Judiciary Committee Chairman John Conyers*

Program Development and Rollout

Because of the program's unprecedented nature, scope, and time constraints, the American Arbitration Association immediately began to prepare special educational materials for the dealers and manufacturers. Customized resources were created and made available through the AAA's website, including program information, simplified filing forms, and access to substantial amounts of relevant background material. Additional information—accessible to all parties, counsel, and neutrals—was made available through a secure section of the Association's website. Concurrently, the AAA began to assemble panels of highly qualified arbitrators for each state affected by the Automobile Industry Special Binding Arbitration Program. Drawing on its pool of over 6,000 neutrals, the AAA's roster of arbitrators for this program included former judges, members of the Large, Complex Case (LCC) panel, and others with relevant expertise and knowledge to handle these important cases. As part of its program initiation process, the AAA began extensive education efforts to ensure that all of the elements of Section 747 were understood by parties, counsel, AAA staff, and arbitrators. This was done by means of special, program-specific web pages, the secure website area, and administrative webcast conferences for each state. Establishing precise rules, procedures, and methods specific to this program early in the process was a critical element to the program's success because it allowed parties and counsel to understand and more effectively participate in the program. These resources also set the tone of appropriate transparency for a program of this nature.

With Section 747, Congress succeeded in achieving its goal — the creation of an appeals process for the terminated dealerships. In so doing, Congress provided the equivalent of "steps to the courthouse" that were previously unavailable and upon which a settlement could be reached. Expedited and balanced proceedings, the availability of highly qualified impartial decision-makers empowered to make binding and final determinations, and specific timeframes were key elements of the ADR system. Now dealerships would have the opportunity to have their claims addressed.

Although the program mandated by Congress was based predominantly on the AAA's standard Commercial Arbitration Rules and Mediation Procedures, Section 747 contained a number of supplemental elements and criteria, including several that proved significant to the program's efficacy. For example, under the statute, the arbitrators were directed to take into consideration the following specific factors: (1) the dealership's profitability; (2) the manufacturer's business plan; (3) the dealership's economic viability; (4) the dealership's satisfaction of performance objectives; (5) the demographic and geographic characteristics of the dealership's market territory; (6) the covered dealership's performance in relation to the manufacturer's criteria for termination or non-renewal of franchise agreements; and (7) the dealership's experience. The law prohibited depositions in the proceedings and discovery beyond documents specific to the covered dealerships and required that all proceedings—conducted in-person, electronically, or telephonically—take place in the state where the covered dealership was located.

Although the statute required that the proceedings be conducted in the state where the dealership was located, the AAA had to determine the venues where the cases would be heard. The AAA sought to balance the interests of both the manufacturers and dealerships with respect to the venue selection and determination process. Mindful of these interests, as well as the strict deadlines and its administrative capacity, the AAA chose the venues strategically and in a manner that considered the interests of the parties, arbitrator accessibility, and other logistical factors.

DESIGNATED HEARING VENUES

MAP KEY

- AAA Office & Hearing Location
- Hearing Location

12 AUTOMOBILE INDUSTRY SPECIAL BINDING ARBITRATION PROGRAM

Additionally, the overall alternative dispute resolution process implemented by the AAA was made more efficient by extensive use of the AAA's WebFile online resources, which allows parties and counsel to carry out a number of functions electronically, including arbitrator selection, document filing, and final determination transmittal. The efficiencies of this technology benefited parties, counsel, arbitrators, and case managers and were widely utilized by parties. For example, 75% of arbitrators were selected electronically by the parties.

Responsibilities of the Arbitrators

The legislation specified that the arbitrators were to be selected by mutual consent of the parties using the Association's cadre of arbitrators and, if agreement could not reached, the AAA would select an arbitrator. While some parties mutually agreed to an arbitrator after having received a state-based list of candidates and their qualifications from the Association, many waited and selected neutrals by means of a more limited strike-and-rank list in accordance with the AAA's Rules. In the end, a total of nearly 350 arbitrators were mobilized and assigned cases under the auspices of this program. Another singular element of Section 747 was the mandate that the arbitrator weigh not only the interests of the directly affected parties (the manufacturer and the dealer) but also the interest of the public. The statute further required the arbitrator to include in his/her determination: (1) a description of the covered dealership; (2) whether the franchise agreement was to be renewed, continued, or assumed by the manufacturer; (3) the key facts used by the arbitrator in making the decision; and (4) an explanation of how the balance of economic interests supported the determination. According to Section 747(e), the arbitrator was unable to award either party "compensatory, punitive, or exemplary damages," limiting the outcome to issuing a determination "indicating whether the franchise agreement at issue is to be renewed, continued, assigned, or assumed" by the manufacturer. Congress further mandated that if the arbitrator found in favor of the dealership, the covered manufacturer had to provide the dealer "a customary and usual letter of intent to enter into a sales and service agreement" within seven days of the decision.

Costs and Fees

When implementing this program, the AAA was particularly mindful of costs to the parties and sought to minimize them as much as possible. Congress and the AAA created a program that required no direct taxpayer money or Congressional appropriations because all parties were responsible for their own expenses, and the necessary administrative costs and arbitrator compensation were to be split equally between both parties. To provide consistency, streamline the filing process, and limit costs, the AAA applied its fixed filing fee for non-monetary claims to all cases under this program.

In a further effort to minimize expenses to affected parties, the AAA offered parties the option of using its Flexible Fee Payment Schedule (FFPS), a pilot program which allowed parties the opportunity to file for arbitration with the AAA at reduced initial fees and with potentially lower total costs. The FFPS provides more steps in the fee schedule, allowing parties to pay in more increments, thereby saving money if a case does not advance along the ADR continuum, as occurred with many cases that settled in the program.

> **THE EFFICIENCIES...** of this technology benefited parties, counsel, arbitrators, and case managers and were widely utilized by parties. For example, 75% of arbitrators were selected electronically by the parties.

Perhaps due to the accessible and relatively streamlined nature of the program, a notable proportion of parties chose to represent themselves. Of the 1,575 initial case filings, 18% of dealerships were self-represented while 82% were represented by attorneys. To facilitate hearings and reduce total costs of final resolution of cases, where a party owned multiple dealerships represented by the same counsel, the AAA scheduled consecutive final hearings, and combined correspondence and preliminary orders (for example, related to scheduling) to encompass all of those cases. This allowed for greater efficiency for counsel, witnesses, and the parties.

Flexible Fee Payment Schedule Encouraged

In June 2009, the AAA launched a one-year pilot program to potentially reduce the costs of alternative dispute resolution. The Flexible Fee Payment Schedule pilot initiative was designed to alleviate some of the immediate financial strain of resolving a dispute, in part through a "pay as you go" fee schedule. With the FFPS there are three stages at which parties make payments to advance the case through to final arbitration. In implementing the Auto Program, the AAA decided to allow the application of FFPS and encouraged parties to exercise the option.

In June 2010, the AAA ended the pilot period and implemented the FFPS as a regular, permanent fee payment option.

Program Execution

Having prepared to meet the mandates of Congress with the technological and human resources and infrastructure to carry out the Automobile Industry Special Binding Arbitration Program, the Association launched the program. To facilitate and expedite the filing of cases, the AAA created abridged forms customized for the program and accepted claims through email, fax, delivery, and regular mail.

Of the 2,789 covered dealerships that were eligible to appeal their closure under the standards set forth by Congress, over half of them (1,575) elected to file for binding arbitration (1,180 from GM's dealership network and 395 from Chrysler's). Although these dealerships were spread across 48 states, some of the states most affected by dealership closings saw the largest number of case filings: Ohio, Illinois, and Pennsylvania each had over one hundred filings.

OF THE 2,789 COVERED DEALERSHIPS...

that were eligible to appeal their closure under the standards set forth by Congress, over half of them (1,575) elected to file for binding arbitration

FILINGS BY STATE

State	Filings
WA	30
OR	24
MT	16
ND	4
MN	36
ME	12
VT	5
NH	14
NY	58
MA	30
RI	3
CT	16
ID	5
SD	14
WI	51
MI	79
PA	101
NJ	40
WY	7
NE	23
IW	53
IL	111
IN	44
OH	113
WV	23
DE	3
MD	23
NV	7
UT	24
CO	26
KS	36
MO	45
KY	30
VA	32
CA	68
NC	49
AZ	8
NM	10
OK	27
AR	19
TN	30
SC	21
MS	11
AL	27
GA	31
TX	69
LA	19
FL	48

AMERICAN ARBITRATION ASSOCIATION

Consistent with the statute and legislative history clearly encouraging settlement and voluntary resolutions by giving voluntary agreements the full force of a legally binding agreement, the AAA sought to facilitate such settlements prior to the final, binding arbitration phase. The benefit of such resolution is clear: With voluntary settlements, time and money are saved. Moreover, with settlement, parties frequently are more satisfied with the result as they create their own solution. In fact, once the Auto Program was launched, a significant number of dealerships and their respective manufacturers began to enter into settlement negotiations and agreements. In total, over half (803) of all cases filed under the program were settled mutually and voluntarily early in the ADR process, rather than going through full arbitration proceedings.

FINAL CASE DISPOSITIONS

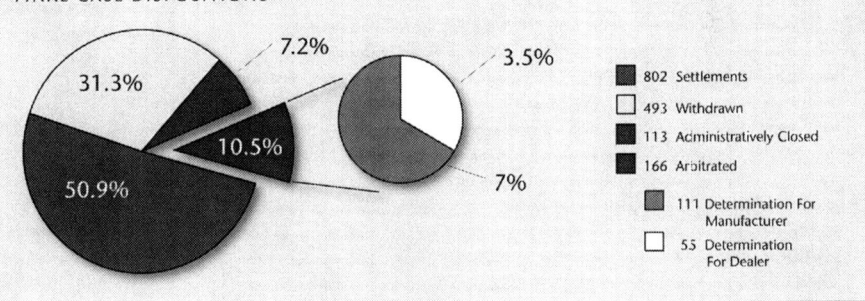

- 50.9% / 802 Settlements
- 31.3% / 493 Withdrawn
- 7.2% / 113 Administratively Closed
- 10.5% / 166 Arbitrated
- 3.5% / 111 Determination For Manufacturer
- 7% / 55 Determination For Dealer

THE CREATION OF A MECHANISM

for appeal through binding arbitration for these disputes facilitated a meaningful dialogue between dealerships and manufacturers that would not have occurred otherwise and which resulted in a remarkable number of voluntary settlements.

At one point in the Auto Program, a large number of hearings were scheduled over a limited number days, including weekends and holidays. It is important to note that although cases that settled did not go through the full ADR process to arbitration, the availability of the binding final arbitration element and the prompt forward momentum of the process enabled and encouraged settlement.

In short, the creation of a mechanism for appeal through binding arbitration for these disputes facilitated a meaningful dialogue between dealerships and manufacturers that would not have occurred otherwise and which resulted in a significant number of voluntary settlements.

Throughout this process, a number of dealerships also chose to withdraw their cases. Ultimately, 494 dealerships unilaterally decided to withdraw from the arbitration process. Because parties are not required to inform the AAA of their reasons for withdrawing a case, the Association is unable to provide data or analyze withdrawals in any detail. Anecdotal

16 AUTOMOBILE INDUSTRY SPECIAL BINDING ARBITRATION PROGRAM

information indicated that some decided they no longer wanted to seek reinstatement, some became concerned about the strength of their cases and arguments, and others had moved on to other business ventures. One-hundred thirteen other cases were administratively closed or dismissed for a variety of reasons, including failure to meet deadlines, comply with program or statutory requirements, or pay necessary fees. Other reasons for cases being administratively closed included three in which the filing party was determined by the arbitrator not to be a dealership, and one case in which the arbitrator determined that the filing party was not the owner of a dealership.

Ultimately, 166 cases — those that were not settled voluntarily by the parties, withdrawn, or closed/dismissed — went through the full arbitration process to a binding decision by the arbitrator.

In the interest of efficiency and transparency for the parties, the AAA developed a comprehensive model Preliminary Hearing Order, which provided a roadmap for the arbitration process and hearings, aligned with the statutory timeframes, for reference by the arbitrator, counsel, and parties. Another widely utilized mechanism that enhanced the efficiency of the process was the pre-hearing briefing process, which was utilized in nearly all cases. After the arbitrator was either chosen or appointed, the American Arbitration Association scheduled preliminary conference calls with parties and the arbitrator in order to set the schedule for the duration of the case and to enhance organization of the parties. While parties and arbitrators were free to adopt their own case structuring plans, most chose to adopt the roadmap for future proceedings developed by the AAA. Hearings were then scheduled accordingly, and documents were forwarded to the arbitrators with exchange between the parties. Arbitrators also resolved a number of on-going case-related issues, such as discovery disputes, witness testimony matters, and burden of proof issues. Throughout the process, many parties elected to place their cases on hold while they conducted independent negotiations and conversations regarding possible settlement agreements, which as the final results indicate, were often successful.

For those cases that went through the full ADR process to final, binding arbitration, hearings were held, typically lasting one to four days. Both parties were given appropriate time to present their case before the arbitrator. Parties were also generally permitted to submit post-hearing briefs. Arbitrators were required by Section 747 to issue their decisions within seven days after the close of the hearing, the first ones being rendered in mid-April, just four months after Congress authorized the creation of the program.

Of the 166 cases that were resolved by binding arbitral decision, the arbitrators found in favor of the dealerships in 55 cases (34% of determinations) and in favor of the manufacturers in 111 cases (66% of determinations). A number of factors may have contributed to these figures, including the parties' approaches to settlement decisions. *See Appendix II for further information on case outcomes.*

ARBITRATORS WERE REQUIRED

by Section 747 to issue their decisions within seven days after the close of the case, the first ones being rendered in mid-April, just four months after Congress authorized the creation of the Program.

THE AAA DEVELOPED...

a comprehensive model Preliminary Hearing Order, which provided a roadmap for the arbitration process and hearings, aligned with the statutory timeframes.

> **BY JULY 23, 2010,** only seven months after the President signed the legislation, all 1,575 cases were successfully completed.

> **IN THE END,** 2,789 dealerships, with no recourse prior to Congressional action, were given an opportunity to seek reinstatement, and 1,575 of those availed themselves of that opportunity.

The Association is unable to quantify exactly how many dealerships were reinstated as a result of all phases of the program. While the AAA does have access to the arbitral decisions, it did not have authority to require parties to disclose the details of any settlements. A comprehensive look at the results of settlements, withdrawals, and arbitral awards would be necessary to give an accurate picture of final overall outcomes.

By July 23, 2010, only seven months after the President signed the legislation, all 1,575 cases filed under this program were successfully completed. The AAA, its arbitrators, and the parties met the statutory deadline, providing a forum for resolution of these disputes through a program that required no appropriated funds.

Throughout the development and implementation of the program, the AAA's senior staff also worked with and briefed Congressional leadership, other members of the House and Senate, and committee staff on the status of the program, issues, and other matters, to maximize compliance with Congressional intent and to keep Congress informed.

EVALUATION AND CONCLUSIONS

Program Evaluation

Although the American Arbitration Association has extensive experience administering programs on behalf of government agencies, the Automobile Industry Special Binding Arbitration Program was singular in its nature, scope, and time constraints. The AAA was able to prepare for, process, and administer 1,575 cases within seven months, while adhering to the direction and will of Congress. The AAA created an easily-accessible and clear-cut program for the efficient, transparent, and fair resolution of disputes through binding arbitration, a mechanism through which dealerships were offered an avenue to appeal the manufacturers' decisions and were given an opportunity to be heard in an independent and impartial venue. In the end, 2,789 dealerships, with no recourse prior to Congressional action, were given an opportunity to seek reinstatement, and 1,575 of those availed themselves of that opportunity. Because of the precise mandates Congress included in Section 747, the legislative history, and the AAA's preparation and execution of the program, there were many expressions of satisfaction with both the structure and implementation of the program by the parties involved, despite the contentious nature of these disputes.

In addition, the program required no direct taxpayer funds or appropriations. Parties split the relatively low administrative costs and arbitrator compensation, and each paid for their respective expenses, as directed by Section 747.

The dispute resolution process was also fast. Many cases were resolved in the early phases of the program because a forum was available and settlements were encouraged. Those that went through the full arbitration process were resolved within the time limits set forth by Congress. After enactment, the AAA had 180 days and a discretionary thirty-day extension to resolve the 1,575 cases filed under the program.

By establishing tailored, expeditious, yet fair rules in a special ADR process, Congress was able to ensure that these matters would be addressed and resolved without subjecting parties to all the costs, complexities, and potential for appeals of traditional litigation.

Although a process in which one party prevails and another does not (such as final binding arbitration) generally results in disappointment by one party, even some parties that did not prevail in this program expressed appreciation for the opportunity to have their case heard in a neutral and fair venue. At the conclusion of the program, the American Arbitration Association solicited feedback through a survey from parties involved in the program.

According to AAA customer survey responses, overall party satisfaction with the process was very positive. Over two-thirds (67%) of the parties responding to the survey were likely, very likely, or extremely likely to recommend the AAA for arbitration in the future. It is worth noting that the survey sampling included parties with all case resolution outcomes (settlement, arbitral determination, withdrawn, etc.). Survey respondents rated the overall case management of the program a 3.76 (on a scale of 1 to 5).

NOTED

"I believe all parties will agree that we [the arbitrators and AAA] completed our Congressional mandate to give fair, expeditious, and economical hearings on extremely complicated issues. Some parties may have not liked the result, but no one faulted the process."

– One of the Program's arbitrators, a former Ohio state judge of over 30 years.

According to AAA customer survey responses, overall party satisfaction with the process was very positive. Over two-thirds (67%) of the parties responding to the survey were likely, very likely, or extremely likely to recommend the AAA for arbitration in the future.

LIKELIHOOD OF RECOMMENDING AAA FOR ARBITRATION IN THE FUTURE

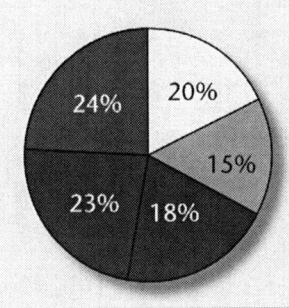

- Very Likely: 20%
- Extremely Likely: 24%
- Likely: 15%
- Not Too Likely: 18%
- Not Likely at All: 23%

THIS PROGRAM

highlights the flexibility ADR can provide in developing a mechanism for fast, efficient, and effective dispute resolution.

Lessons Learned

Standard commercial arbitration has well-established practices and legal foundations, but an entirely new and innovative program such as this one required ongoing monitoring, evaluation, analysis, and response throughout development and implementation. To the extent it was able to do so within the legislative framework mandated by Congress, the AAA continually sought to make improvements and refinements to ensure the efficacy and efficiency of the program. The lessons learned from this program, which could be applicable to future government programs, include:

- The Congressional articulation of specific legal standards created a coherent and fair process outside of litigation. Having specific statutory guidelines enabled the AAA, arbitrators, and the parties to have a clear mandate and direction, in addition to ensuring an equitable process.

- Mandating a relatively short time frame ensured fast resolutions. Additionally, the time constraints provided the parties with an incentive to negotiate and, in many cases, resolve their disputes through voluntary settlement. In large measure, a significant portion, of the cases, over half, were resolved through settlements, a primary goal of Congress and the AAA.

- Requiring manufacturers, as a preliminary step, to provide information upon which termination decisions had been based provided dealerships with useful data and criteria, and may have allowed dealerships to make better-informed decisions on whether they wanted to appeal by participating in the program.

A Model for Future Program Development

Because of its cost-effectiveness, efficiency, and fairness, the AAA's Automobile Industry Special Binding Arbitration Program may serve as a model for other government programs. Although the AAA already had significant experience working with government in resolving tens of thousands of disputes, the Automobile Industry Special Binding Arbitration Program incorporated some original elements potentially adaptable to other areas, disputes, and administrative backlogs. While future programs may not require similar timeframes, parameters, or procedural limitations, this program highlights the flexibility ADR can provide in developing a mechanism for fast, efficient, and effective dispute resolution.

For the purpose of developing similar programs in the future, the Association has evaluated various elements of the Automobile Industry Special Binding Arbitration Program, including those that facilitated the program and those that may have impeded it. In designing ADR systems under statutory or regulatory authority in the future, the inclusion of the following should be considered:

- Authority to appoint interim arbitrators to issue rulings in the early stages of the program, as issues arise.
- Clear guidance regarding the privacy and confidentiality of the proceedings, filings, hearings, and arbitral determinations.
- Possible inclusion of an internal procedural mechanism, such as through a special three-arbitrator panel, where issues such as discovery could be addressed and resolved.
- Unequivocal administrative authority of the administering organization (AAA) to ensure timeliness and balance.
- Requiring parties to report outcomes of settlements.

The AAA stands ready to continue working with legislators, regulators, and policy makers to apply the benefits of ADR to issues facing government at the federal, state, and local levels as an extension of its public service mission.

APPENDIX I

TIMELINE AND KEY DATES

2009

April 30	Chrysler files for bankruptcy protection.
May 14	Chrysler indicates it wants to eliminate 789 of its 3,200 dealerships in a motion filed with the U.S. Bankruptcy Court in New York.
May 15	As it heads toward bankruptcy protection, GM notifies 1,100 of its 6,150 dealers that it will not renew their franchises in the fall of 2010.
June 1	GM enters bankruptcy protection.
June 9	Chrysler exits bankruptcy protection.
July 10	GM exits bankruptcy protection.
December 3	GM and Chrysler announce they will reconsider dealership closures as part of an effort to stave off federal legislation requiring them to keep dealerships.
December 10	A binding arbitration appeal process, administered by the AAA, available to the 2,789 GM and Chrysler dealers designated for closure, is included as part of a $1.1 trillion spending bill.
December 16	President Obama signs a spending bill, the Consolidated Appropriations Act of 2010, which becomes Public Law 111-117.

2010

January 25	Statutory deadline for filing – 1,575 GM and Chrysler dealers file for binding arbitration to appeal their closures.
Late February	Arbitrators appointed, settlement/mediation continue to be encouraged through AAA program, preliminary hearings/conferences begin.
March 5	GM announces it will reinstate 661 dealers with pending arbitration cases.
March 26	Chrysler announces it will reinstate 80 dealers with pending arbitration cases.
June 14	Original statutory deadline for hearings to end. A number of hearings are extended for another month, pursuant to authority granted in the federal statute.
July 14	Extended arbitration hearings are scheduled to end.
July 23	Final due date for arbitrator determinations (7 business days).

Adapted from the Associated Press and other sources.

APPENDIX II
ADDITIONAL STATISTICAL DATA

End-Of-Month And Final Program Totals *By Case Disposition*

Status	January	February	March	April	May	June	July	Final Program Totals
Withdrawn	2	40	179	163	67	29	14	493
Settled		1	66	254	263	163	55	803
Administratively Closed			2	45	6	35	25	113
Arbitral Determination				1	30	81	54	166
• *Dealer*					*9*	*24*	*22*	*55*
• *Manufacturer*				*1*	*21*	*57*	*32*	*111*
Monthly Closure Total	2	41	247	463	366	308	148	1,575
Cumulative Closed	2	43	290	753	1,119	1,427	1,575	1,575
Total Active Cases	1,573	1,532	1,285	822	456	148	0	0

AMERICAN ARBITRATION ASSOCIATION 23

AMERICAN ARBITRATION ASSOCIATION

APPENDIX II (CONTINUED)
ADDITIONAL STATISTICAL DATA

Final Case Numbers *By State*

State	Total Cases Filed	Cases Withdrawn	Cases Settled	Cases Closed, Dismissed or Other	Determinations For Dealership	Determinations For Manufacturer
Alabama	27	6	17	2	1	1
Alaska	0	0	0	0	0	0
Arizona	8	2	5	1	0	0
Arkansas	19	5	8	1	1	4
California	68	29	27	2	4	6
Colorado	26	9	11	1	2	3
Connecticut	16	8	5	0	0	3
Delaware	3	0	2	1	0	0
District of Columbia	0	0	0	0	0	0
Florida	48	18	18	5	3	4
Georgia	31	4	24	3	0	0
Hawaii	0	0	0	0	0	0
Idaho	5	2	2	0	1	0
Illinois	111	29	61	7	4	10
Indiana	44	22	16	1	0	5
Iowa	53	9	36	4	0	4
Kansas	36	4	30	2	0	0
Kentucky	30	14	13	2	1	0
Louisiana	19	1	16	0	1	1
Maine	12	7	3	0	0	2
Maryland	23	14	3	1	0	5
Massachusetts	30	5	14	6	1	4
Michigan	79	17	43	8	7	4
Minnesota	36	6	28	0	2	0
Mississippi	11	2	9	0	0	0
Missouri	45	15	21	4	3	2
Montana	16	3	10	2	1	0
Nebraska	23	9	14	0	0	0
Nevada	7	0	6	0	1	0
New Hampshire	14	4	6	2	0	2
New Jersey	40	10	19	3	3	5
New Mexico	10	2	7	0	1	0
New York	58	23	21	9	2	3
North Carolina	49	21	25	3	0	0
North Dakota	4	0	3	1	0	0
Ohio	113	54	39	8	3	9
Oklahoma	27	9	16	2	0	0
Oregon	24	6	17	1	0	0
Pennsylvania	101	31	45	19	0	6
Rhode Island	3	2	1	0	0	0

24 AUTOMOBILE INDUSTRY SPECIAL BINDING ARBITRATION PROGRAM

APPENDIX II (CONTINUED)
ADDITIONAL STATISTICAL DATA

Final Case Numbers By State Continued

State	Total Cases Filed	Cases Withdrawn	Cases Settled	Cases Closed, Dismissed or Other	Determinations For Dealership	Determinations For Manufacturer
South Carolina	21	7	11	2	0	1
South Dakota	14	4	10	0	0	0
Tennessee	30	6	20	1	1	2
Texas	69	16	38	2	3	10
Utah	24	1	19	0	1	3
Vermont	5	2	2	0	0	1
Virginia	32	15	13	1	1	2
Washington	30	11	14	2	0	3
West Virginia	23	10	5	4	1	3
Wisconsin	51	18	25	0	5	3
Wyoming	7	2	4	0	1	0
TOTALS	1575	494	802	113	55	111

AMERICAN ARBITRATION ASSOCIATION

APPENDIX II (CONTINUED)
ADDITIONAL STATISTICAL DATA

Final Case Numbers By *Initial Filings*

State	Total Cases Filed	Cases Withdrawn	Cases Settled	Cases Closed, Dismissed or Other	Determinations For Dealership	Determinations For Manufacturer
Ohio	113	54	39	8	3	9
Illinois	111	29	61	7	4	10
Pennsylvania	101	31	45	19	0	6
Michigan	79	17	43	8	7	4
Texas	69	16	38	2	3	10
California	68	29	27	2	4	6
New York	58	23	21	9	2	3
Iowa	53	9	36	4	0	4
Wisconsin	51	18	25	0	5	3
North Carolina	49	21	25	3	0	0
Florida	48	18	18	5	3	4
Missouri	45	15	21	4	3	2
Indiana	44	22	16	1	0	5
New Jersey	40	10	19	3	3	5
Kansas	36	4	30	2	0	0
Minnesota	36	6	28	0	2	0
Virginia	32	15	13	1	1	2
Georgia	31	4	24	3	0	0
Kentucky	30	14	13	2	1	0
Massachusetts	30	5	14	6	1	4
Tennessee	30	6	20	1	1	2
Washington	30	11	14	2	0	3
Alabama	27	6	17	2	1	1
Oklahoma	27	9	16	2	0	0
Colorado	26	9	11	1	2	3
Oregon	24	6	17	1	0	0
Utah	24	1	19	0	1	3
Maryland	23	14	3	1	0	5
Nebraska	23	9	14	0	0	0
West Virginia	23	10	5	4	1	3
South Carolina	21	7	11	2	0	1
Arkansas	19	5	8	1	1	4
Louisiana	19	1	16	0	1	1
Connecticut	16	8	5	0	0	3
Montana	16	3	10	2	1	0
New Hampshire	14	4	6	2	0	2
South Dakota	14	4	10	0	0	0
Maine	12	7	3	0	0	2

26 AUTOMOBILE INDUSTRY SPECIAL BINDING ARBITRATION PROGRAM

APPENDIX II (CONTINUED)
ADDITIONAL STATISTICAL DATA

Final Case Numbers By *Initial Filings* Continued

State	Total Cases Filed	Cases Withdrawn	Cases Settled	Cases Closed, Dismissed or Other	Determinations For Dealership	Determinations For Manufacturer
Mississippi	11	2	9	0	0	0
New Mexico	10	2	7	0	1	0
Arizona	8	2	5	1	0	0
Nevada	7	0	6	0	1	0
Wyoming	7	2	4	0	1	0
Idaho	5	2	2	0	1	0
Vermont	5	2	2	0	0	1
North Dakota	4	0	3	1	0	0
Delaware	3	0	2	1	0	0
Rhode Island	3	2	1	0	0	0
Alaska	0	0	0	0	0	0
District of Columbia	0	0	0	0	0	0
Hawaii	0	0	0	0	0	0
TOTALS	1575	494	802	113	55	111

Appendix 13

2011 AUTOMOBILE DEALERSHIP CENSUS

January 1, 2011

Car and light-truck franchises in the U.S.

	Jan. 1, 2011	Jan. 1, 2010	Unit change
Aston Martin*	30	31	(1)
BMW division	338	338	—
Mini	104	90	14
Rolls-Royce	32	31	1
BMW Group	**474**	**459**	**15**
Chrysler Division	2,175	2,052	123
Dodge/Ram	2,171	2,101	70
Jeep	2,144	2,066	78
Chrysler Group	**6,490**	**6,219**	**271**
Maybach	31	32	(1)
Mercedes-Benz	353	352	1
Smart	76	78	(2)
Daimler AG	**460**	**462**	**(2)**
Ferrari	35	35	—
Ford division	3,193	3,261	(68)
Lincoln	1,126	1,221	(95)
Mercury	—	1,645	(1,645)
Ford Motor Co.	**4,319**	**6,127**	**(1,808)**
Buick	2,124	2,369	(245)
Cadillac	950	1,316	(366)
Chevrolet	3,091	3,463	(372)
GMC	1,770	1,949	(179)
Continued brands	7,935	9,097	(1,162)
Hummer	—	154	(154)
Pontiac	—	2,225	(2,225)
Saturn	—	282	(282)
Dropped brands	—	2,661	(2,661)
General Motors	**7,935**	**11,758**	**(3,823)**
Acura	270	271	(1)
Honda Division	1,034	1,033	1
American Honda	**1,304**	**1,304**	**—**
Hyundai	803	790	13
Kia	730	691	39
Hyundai-Kia	**1,533**	**1,481**	**52**
Jaguar	166	169	(3)
Land Rover	167	169	(2)
Jaguar Land Rover	**333**	**338**	**(5)**
Lamborghini	29	29	—
Lotus	39	52	(13)
Maserati	52	51	1
Mazda	640	634	6
Mitsubishi	**399**	**401**	**(2)**
Infiniti	189	182	7
Nissan Division	1,057	1,059	(2)
Nissan Motor	**1,246**	**1,241**	**5**
Porsche	**196**	**200**	**(4)**
Saab	**203**	**218**	**(15)**
Subaru	**622**	**612**	**10**
Suzuki	**278**	**360**	**(82)**
Lexus	231	230	1
Toyota Division	1,240	1,239	1
Scion†	994	997	(3)
Toyota Motor	**1,471**	**1,469**	**2**
Audi	277	270	7
Bentley	40	40	—
VW division	588	580	8
VW Group	**905**	**890**	**15**
Volvo	**316**	**322**	**(6)**
U.S.-badged	**18,744**	**24,104**	**(5,360)**
Import-badged	**10,565**	**10,589**	**(24)**
TOTAL	**29,309**	**34,693**	**(5,384)**

*Estimate
†Included in Toyota Division
Source: Automotive News and company sources

Exclusive outlets

Dealerships handling only the designated brand on Jan. 1, 2011

Detroit 3-badged

Brand	Exclusives within parent corp.	Total franchises
Chevrolet	1,506	3,091
Cadillac	144	950
GMC	79	1,770
Buick	37	2,124
General Motors	**1,766**	**7,935**
Ford division	2,298	3,193
Lincoln	231	1,126
Ford Motor Co.	**2,529**	**4,319**
Dodge/Ram	100	2,171
Jeep	27	2,144
Chrysler Division	2	2,175
Chrysler Group	**129**	**6,490**
Total Detroit 3	**4,424**	**18,744**
Year-ago total	4,561	24,104

Import-badged

Brand	Exclusives	Total franchises
Toyota	995	1,240
Honda	912	1,034
Nissan	855	1,057
Hyundai	529	803
Kia	452	730
Mazda	321	640
Subaru	321	622
Volkswagen	277	588
Mercedes-Benz	241	353
Acura	240	270
Suzuki	234	278
Lexus	211	231
BMW division	201	338
Volvo	174	316
Mitsubishi	168	399
Infiniti	159	189
Audi	145	277
Porsche	87	196
Land Rover	74	167
Saab	51	203
Mini	43	104
Jaguar	29	166
Smart	13	76
Lotus	5	39
Aston Martin*	4	30
Lamborghini	4	29
Bentley	3	40
Maserati	—	52
Ferrari	—	35
Maybach	—	31
Rolls-Royce	—	32
Total import-badged	**6,748**	**10,565**
Year-ago total	6,510	10,589

*Estimate
Source: Automotive News and company sources

Car and light-truck dealerships in the U.S.

	Jan. 1, 2011	Jan. 1, 2010
General Motors	4,458	5,500
Ford Motor Co.	3,424	3,553
Chrysler Group	2,311	2,352
Total Detroit 3-badged	**10,193**	**11,405**
Minus intercorporate duals	30	60
Net Detroit 3-badged	**10,163**	**11,345**
Import-badged exclusives	6,748	6,510
Import-only duals	**742**	**752**
Total new light-vehicle dealerships	17,653	18,607

Source: Automotive News and company sources

A decade of dealerships

Jan. 1	Total light-vehicle dealerships	Numerical change from previous year	Year-to-year percent change
2011	17,653	−954	−5%
2010	18,607	−1,846	−9%
2009	20,453	−1,008	−5%
2008	21,461	−300	−1%
2007	21,761	−328	−2%
2006	22,089	−111	−1%
2005	22,200	23	0%
2004	22,177	−156	−1%
2003	22,333	187	1%
2002	22,146	139	1%

Source: Automotive News and company sources

INDEX

10 Step Sales Procedure, 12
$2 billion lie, 95

AIFP, 29, 38, 43 *see also* Automotive Industry Financing Program
　review of plans, 39
　throughput concept, 43
AIG, *see* American International Group
American International Group, 24, 25
Appleton, Jim, 132
arbitration, filing for, 178
arbitrator bias, 171
Arent Fox LLP, 52, 77, 80, 89, 90, 103
Arnold & Porter, 70
ATAE, 122, 133, *see also* Automotive Trade Association Executives
Auto Nation, 7
automotive firsts, 18
Automotive Industry Financing Program, 29
Automotive News, 95, 139
Automotive Task Force, 3, 29, 81, 134, *see also* White House Auto Team
Automotive Trade Association Executives, 107, 119

Bachrodt, Rachel, 167, 168, 178
Balzekas Jr., Stanley, 49
bankruptcy
　as tool to eliminate dealers, 46
　vs. franchise agreements, 50
　vs. state laws, 47
Bartlett, Rep. Roscoe, 86

Bastille Day, 112
Beans, Fred, 89
Benz, Karl, 18
Big Three Automakers, 16, 19, 27
　non-automotive investments, 21
　survival of, ix
binding arbitration, 123
binding arbitration offer, 158
Blankenbeckler III, Frank, 92, 93
Bloom, Ron, 30, 39, 46, 115, 117, 118
Bozzella, John, 73, 132, 137, 138
Brown, Rep. Corrine, 132, 139
Brown, Sen. Sherrod, 99, 100
Bullard, Todd, 132
Burke, Bill, 162
Bush, Pres. George W., 141

C-SPAN coverage, 92, 95, 102, 114
Callaremi, Lelica, 111
Cardin, Sen. Ben, 86
Carr, Jeff, 74, 75
Chrysler
　bankruptcy, 46
　Great Lakes Business Center, 1
　Minimum Sales Responsibility, 35
　Project Genesis, 7, 74, 75, 97, 152, 166
　Push Production Model, 27
　Rejected Dealers, 4, 5
　sales bank, 27, 28
　service training expense, 65
　specialty tools expense, 64, 65
　termination criteria, 35, 36
　unwise acquisitions, 21
　valued dealer list, 4
Chrysler-Plymouth store (Akron, OH), 13
Chrysler, Walter P., 17
Clinton, Hillary, 133

Cole, David E., 40
Cole, Ken, 132, 137, 138, 143, 154
Commerce Committee, 77
Commerce Committee Hearing, 80
Committee to Restore Dealer Rights (CRDR), 89, 187
Commodity Futures Modernization Act of 2000, 24
Consumer Reports, 21, 125
consumer spending, drop in, ix
Cordray, Richard, 50
CRDR, 101, 122, 133, 134, 167, *see also* Committee to Restore Dealer Rights
  website, 178
CRDRForum.com, 178
credit default swaps, 25
crisis of 2007–2009, ix
crisis, never waste a, 45
Cugnot, Nicolas-Joseph, 18
Cuomo, Andrew, 182

Daimler, Gottlieb, 18
DARCARS 66, 186, *see also* Darcars
Darcars, 67, 68
Darvish, John, 66
Darvish, Tamara, 99, 160 *see also* Darvish, Tammy
Darvish, Tammy, v, 67, 68, 82–84, 86, 87, 112, 117, 124, 134, 139, 140, 163, 186
DaVinci, Leonardo, 17
dealer vs. dealer strategy, 103
dealers
  as customers, 3
  as independent firms, 41
  closures deemed necessary, 3
  elimination of, 3
dealerships reassigned, 42
Deese, Brian, 39, 40, 42, 115, 132, 166
Deming, W. Edwards, 20
Dodd, Sen. Chris, 25
Doran, Tim, 50, 109, 119, 123, 125–128, 132, 137, 142, 154, 159, 167, 187
Dowd, Mary Jo, 52, 77, 132, 163
Durant, William C. "Billy", 19
Durbin, Sen. Richard J. "Dick", 167
Duryea, Frank & Charles, 18

Edwards, Rep. Donna, 132, 139
Ellis-Ruskin, Dina, 73
Elyria, OH (Spitzer HQ), 2, 5, 12, 87, 114
Emanuel, Rahm, 45

Fairlawn Meeting, 54
Fiat S.p.A., 63
Fitzgerald, Jack, v, 7, 8, 51, 52, 57, 59, 66, 67, 77, 78, 80, 81, 86, 99, 113, 124, 134, 139–141, 160, 179, 186
FitzMall dealership chain, 51
Ford
  as lone automaker, x
  borrows billons, 26
  Model T, 17, 19
  mystery shoppers, 12
  training film, 12
Ford, Henry, 17, 19
foreign competition, 187
franchises, theft of, x
Frank, Rep. Barney, 113
fuel prices surge, 23

Gannon, Jack, 1, 2
Geithner, Timothy, 29
General Motors, x
Gettelfinger, Ron, 25
Ghosn, Carlos, 26
Giardini, Tony, 5, 50, 53, 55, 57, 66, 68–72, 78, 80, 83, 85, 87, 90, 92, 95, 99, 100, 102, 108, 110, 168

Index

GM, *see also* General Motors
  appeals process, 33
  birth of, 19
  Channel strategy, 166
  Dealer Performance Summary, 36, 37
  incorrect charges, 147
  open point manipulations, 148
  single store policy, 22
  special tools, Wind Down dealer charged for, 147
  Wind Down Agreement, 32
GM-Chrysler collusion, 141, 154
Golick, Jim, 92
Gore, Al, 141
Gonzalez, Judge Arthur, 63, 64, 66, 68, 71–73, 75, 77
government bailout of GM & Chrysler, 2, 29
Grady, Pete, 149, 150
Grassley, Sen. Chuck, 114

Hedgpeth, Dana, 81
Henderson, Fritz, 80, 92, 94
Homestead Store, 6, 7
Hoppe, David, 141, 142
House-Senate Conference Committee, 168
housing crisis, 24
Hoyer, Rep. Steny, 52–57, 85, 86, 101, 110, 111, 131, 133
Hughes, John, 57, 122, 137, 162
Hutchinson, Sen. Kay Bailey, 81

Iacocca, Lee A., 115

Jackson-Lee, Rep. Sheila, 111, 132
Johnson, Rep. Hank, 132, 133, 139
Jones, Jeff, 71

Kennedy, Sen. Edward M. (Ted), 115
Kiekenapp, Daniel, 92
Kitzmiller, Pete, 123
Kratovil, Rep. Frank, 85, 86, 132, 139

labor costs, 14, 15
Landry, Steve, 28
LaTourette, Rep. Steve, 86, 103–105, 108, 110–114, 131, 139, 162, 163, 167, 168
Lattig, Larry, 68
Lee, Charles, 72
Lehman Brothers, 24
legislation
  Deese amendment, 167
  first draft, 78–80
  H.R. 2743, 85, 95, 96, 99, 105, 108, 112, 113, 139, 167
  H.R. 2750, 105
  H.R. 2796, 87, 105
  H.R. 3288, 171
  Hughes amendment, 165
  LaTourette amendment, 106
  S. 1304, 108, 115, 139, 164, 167
  Sec. 747, 172–176
legislative alternative, 51
Lester, Damon, 132, 137, 142
Lines, Joe, 132, 144
Lopez, Pete, 80

Maffei, Rep. Dan, 85, 86, 112, 132, 139
Mansfield store, 2, 6
market share loss, 2008, 24
mass production model, 17
Masters, Blythe, 25
Mauro, Greg, 49
McEleney, John, 80, 90, 92, 132
Montoya, Jessica, 73
Mulally, Alan, 25, 26, 64
Murphy, Gerry, 123

NADA, 70, 80, 81, 89, 90, 92, 105, 109, 111, 121–128, 132, 133, 137, 139, 142, 159, 160, 168, 187
Nader, Ralph, 20
Nardelli, Robert, 25, 64
Newton, Sir Isaac, 17
North American Minority Auto Dealers (NAMAD), 122, 133, 137

Obama, Pres. Barack, 29, 56, 57, 78, 133, 171, 183
   Spitzer letter to, 58
   Congress letter to, 61
Obey, Rep. Dave, 106
Ostrander, Kate, 87, 103

Paddock, Duane, 92, 94
Paine, Thomas, ix
Palmer, Eldon, 49
Pappert, E. T. (Tom), 115, 117, 118
Pelosi, Rep. Nancy, 140
Perot, H. Ross, 21, 22
Perry, Chip, v
Press, Jim (James), 28, 43, 46, 80, 92
Primm, Michelle, 111

Quinn Gillespie and Associates, 141
Quinn, Jack, 141

Rattner, Steven, 30, 39, 181, 182
Regan, David, 109, 127, 132, 142
Reid, Sen. Harry, 99, 100
rejected dealers *see* Chrysler
   Spitzer reaction to, 4
Renberg, Dan, 90, 103, 106–108, 110, 123, 125, 132, 133, 142, 150, 159, 162, 163, 168
Reuss, Mark, 178

Reynolds, Nichole Francis, 52–54, 57
Roberts, Desmond, 132
Robke, Bud, 102
Rockefeller, Sen. Jay, 69, 80, 81
Roland, Neil, 139
Rules Committee, 108, 113

Sander, Pete, 167, 168
Sanders, Albert, 122, 167
Schuster, Cathy, 101
Senate Hearings, 29
settlements, Spitzer organization, 185
"shared sacrifice", x
Shepardson, Dave, 140
Sherman Anti-Trust Act of 1890, 131
SIGTARP investigation, 180
Sims, Kathleen, 111
Sloan, Alfred P., Jr., 17
Smith, Rob, 89, 109, 132, 186
Smith, Roger, 22
Spitzer family
   history with Chrysler, 10
Spitzer Ford Supermarket (Cleveland OH), 12
Spitzer, AJ, 111
Spitzer, Alan, v, xi, 53, 55, 60, 67, 78, 82–84, 86–88, 93, 96, 104, 110, 126, 127, 134, 139, 140, 145, 154, 160, 163, 179, 182
   education of, 13
   House subcommittee testimony of, 96-99
Spitzer, Alana, 101
Spitzer, Alison, v, xi, 67, 68, 89, 101, 102, 107, 108, 110, 119, 123, 127, 132, 133, 138, 140–142, 144, 165, 185, 186
Spitzer, Amelia, 1, 54
Spitzer, Andrew, 101
Spitzer, Ashley, 91, 92, 101

INDEX

Spitzer, Del, 12, 13
Spitzer, Donn, 13
Spitzer, George G., 10
Spitzer, John A., 10, 12
Spitzer, Kevin, 13
Spitzer, Pat, 50
Spitzer, Sean, 101
Squires, Sanders & Dempsey, 69, 70
Starbucks franchising model, 42
State franchise laws, 44
Studer, Matt, 6
Stupak, Bart, 90
Summers, Larry, 29
Sutton, Rep. Betty, 52, 56, 90, 111
Swartz, Jeremy, 101, 119, 186

Tarbox, Jim, 72, 73
TARP, 26, *see also* Troubled Assets Relief Program
Taylor, Bob, 72
television marketing, 13
Thomas, Robert, 92
threepack strategy, 7
Tonkin, Ed, 109
Toyota Dealership Model, 40, 60
transplant producers, 15
Treasury Auto Team, 30
Troubled Asset Relief Program (TARP), 25

UAW jobs bank, 27
UPS letters, 3, 4, 6, 8

Van Hollen, Rep. Chris, 85, 86, 110, 111, 132, 139, 160
Van Susteren, Greta, 51
Vella, Jackie, 101
Vella, Jim, 5, 55, 114
Verbiest, Ferdinand, 18
Vitantonio, Lou, 54, 55

Wagoner, Rick, 25, 45, 46, 64
Wallin, Courtney, 68, 108
Waters, Rep. Maxine, 132, 139
Weaver, David, 122
Welch, Jack, 64
Wernle, Bradford, 4, 43
Wetjen, Mark, 101, 110
Whatley III, Russell Aubrey, 80
White House Auto Team, x
Wierda, Craig, 126
Wolters, Bill, 132

Young, Gwen, 142

Zetsch, Dieter, 26
Zimmer, John, 102